CRITICS TOAST ALEXIS BESPALOFF'S NEW SIGNET BOOK OF WINE:

" . . . it is as good an introduction to the subject as any book available today. . . . Mr. Bespaloff's book is certainly a good reference work, but it is a good book to read, too."

—Frank J. Prial
The New York Times

" This is the best all-around introduction to wine in print. . . . An easy and enjoyable read."

The Washington Post

" the most useful and reliable single volume on wine . . . Bespaloff writes with remarkable clarity and simplicity."

The Philadelphia Inquirer

" . . . there is perhaps no book that makes the subject of wine so accessible, in such clear, concise, and readable terms."

The New York Daily News

ALEXIS BESPALOFF is the author of *Alexis Bespaloff's Guide to Inexpensive Wines*, editor of *The Fireside Book of Wine*, and wine columnist for *New York* magazine. He recently revised and expanded *The New Frank Schoonmaker Encyclopedia of Wine*.

FOOD FOR THOUGHT

ALEXIS BESPALOFF'S
NEW
SIGNET BOOK
OF
WINE

A COMPLETE
INTRODUCTION

REVISED AND EXPANDED

Ⓢ
A SIGNET BOOK

NEW AMERICAN LIBRARY

A DIVISION OF PENGUIN BOOKS USA INC., NEW YORK
PUBLISHED IN CANADA BY
PENGUIN BOOKS CANADA LIMITED, MARKHAM, ONTARIO

Copyright © 1971, 1980, 1985 by Alexis Bespaloff

Maps of Italy and California drawn by Betsy Welsh;
other maps drawn by Elizabeth van Itallie

Alexis Bespaloff's New Signet Book of Wine is also available
in a Plume edition.

SIGNET, SIGNET CLASSIC, MENTOR, ONYX, PLUME, MERIDIAN and NAL BOOKS
are published by New American Library, a division of
Penguin Books USA Inc., 1633 Broadway, New York, New York 10019

First Printing, April, 1971
First Printing, Revised Edition, February, 1980
First Printing, Revised and Expanded Edition, July, 1986

2   3   4   5   6   7   8   9   10

PRINTED IN CANADA

PREFACE TO THE REVISED AND EXPANDED EDITION

The changes that have occurred in the world of wine since 1980, when this book—originally published in 1971—was last revised, have made it necessary to revise and expand this guide once again. The biggest changes have occurred in California, where dozens of new viticultural areas and hundreds of new wineries have been established in the past few years. Many changes, some of them dramatic, have also occurred in Italy, and a much greater variety of its wines are now shipped here than in the past. The chapters on these wines have been completely rewritten and expanded, as have many other parts of this edition, and there are few pages that have not required at least some updating.

I would like to thank those who were generous enough to read certain parts of the revised manuscript: Burton Anderson, Paul Draper, Matt Kramer, Richard G. Peterson, Alistair Robertson, Bob Thompson, James Trezise, and Manfred Völpel.

CONTENTS

MAPS

ILLUSTRATIONS

ALEXIS BESPALOFF'S
NEW
SIGNET BOOK
OF
WINE

INTRODUCTION

Even the most casual observer must be aware of the increased interest in wine that has taken place in America in recent years. Consumption has nearly doubled in a decade, and perhaps more significantly, only a few years ago the sale of wines in this country exceeded that of spirits for the first time in this century. Despite the greater number of people who now enjoy wine with their meals or as an alternative to cocktails, however, wine is not yet an everyday pleasure for most Americans. The most popular beverage in this country is soda, followed by coffee, beer, and milk. The annual consumption of wine in France and Italy is more than one hundred bottles per person; in Portugal and Argentina it is about eighty bottles, and in Spain, Chile, and Switzerland it is more than sixty bottles. The average American drinks ten bottles of table wine a year.

We simply lack a tradition that encourages people to take for granted a bottle of wine on the dinner table, and to regard wine drinking as one of life's most accessible casual pleasures. Americans had a comparatively late start in the production and consumption of wine, and our momentum was cut short by Prohibition. We made a second start about fifty years ago, both as wine producers and as consumers, and we have gone about it with great enthusiasm. Although many Americans still think of wine as something special and out of the ordinary, there is now a greater variety of the world's fine wines to be found in almost any large American city than in Paris, London, or Rome. Wines of all kinds are readily available in nearly every state, and because an interested American's approach to wine is much more adventurous than the average European's, we tend to be more receptive to a variety of wines and more willing to experiment than the people who produced them.

Although wine is now beginning to be treated casually in this country, there are still those who go to the other extreme and create a mystique out of drinking a glass of wine. Such people tend to discourage those who come into contact with them, and many people who would enjoy wine have been led to believe that you must know a great deal both about wine and about its proper presentation even before you begin. The fear of doing something incorrect has surely kept many people from taking their first steps in wine. In Europe there is no fuss made about drinking wines, just as no one here makes a fuss about drinking coffee. A few Europeans may look into wine more deeply as a hobby, just as there are some Americans who buy fresh coffee beans and grind them to their own specifications. That's no reason for the rest of us to hesitate before drinking a cup of coffee. The only equipment you need to drink wine is a corkscrew and a glass. Two glasses are better, as one of the most agreeable aspects of wine is that it seems to taste better when shared.

There are people who will tell you that good wines don't travel, or that the best wines can be found only where they are made. It may be true that a wine that tasted superb when drunk on a terrace in a seacoast village in the south of France will not taste as good over here, but in this case it's probably the view that doesn't travel. If a wine cannot travel, it is because it doesn't have quite enough alcohol to stabilize it for a long journey, but this applies almost invariably to the pleasant wines that are served in carafes at holiday resorts. To vinify them so as to increase their alcoholic content by the necessary degree or two would be to deprive them of their charm, and in any case these wines are usually undistinguished in the first place. Someone on holiday is not the most critical and objective of tasters, especially if he or she does not normally drink wine at home. There are, it is true, some delightful country wines that are not often seen here, but they are rarely produced in sufficient quantity to make it commercially worthwhile to export them, and they are usually consumed in their entirety within the region where they are made.

The fact is that all good, soundly made wines can travel, and they do. The best wines in the world can be found here, and they will taste every bit as good as on their home ground. As a matter of fact, it is often easier to obtain wines produced in remote areas of the world than to find certain widely acclaimed wines from California that are made in very limited quantities.

Wine can be broadly classified into three main groups: table wines, fortified wines, and sparkling wines. *Sparkling wines* obviously include champagne and various other champagne-style wines made in most wine-producing countries.

Fortified wines are those to which alcohol has been added at some point in their production, and they generally contain between 17 and 21 percent alcohol by volume. Wines thus fortified include sherry, port, Madeira, and Marsala. Vermouth and various aperitif wines are both fortified and flavored. Fortified wines, which range in taste from dry to very sweet, are served before or after a meal and can be enjoyed any time during the day. They are not usually served with a meal.

The term *table wines* includes every kind of natural (unfortified), still (not sparkling) wine that might be served with meals. Most table wines contain 10 to 14 percent alcohol. People sometimes dismiss an inexpensive wine as "just a table wine," but both a three-dollar bottle and a Château Mouton-Rothschild 1970 are, properly speaking, table wines. It is with table wines that this book is primarily concerned, although chapters on both fortified and sparkling wines are included. A few pages are also devoted to brandies, most of which are distilled from wine.

The only way to learn about wines is to taste them, and there is no substitute for pulling a cork. Go into any store that seems to have a reasonably large selection of wines, buy a few different bottles, and then try them one after the other. Even if you come across a wine you don't care for, you will have added to your knowledge without having spent much money. A bottle of wine costs less than a ticket to a new movie these days, and you don't have to stand in line to enjoy it.

Never buy the cheapest wine in any category, as its taste may discourage you from going on. The glass, corks, cartons, and labor are about the same for any wine, as are the ocean freight and taxes for imported wines (which are based on total gallonage, not on value).* Consequently, if you spend a little more, you are likely to get a better wine, because the other costs remain fixed. Cheap wine will always be too expensive.

Learn to trust your own palate and to determine your own preferences by tasting, not by responding to a label. The other side of this rule is not to assume that what you like, at first, is either very good or, more important, very good value. Only as you taste different wines will you begin to understand what you like and why. You will also recognize what makes one wine better than another, and you will appreciate the distinctive taste and complexity of flavor that characterize the finest wines.

To learn even a minimum amount about wine you must do two simple things: take a moment to really taste the wine in front of you, and look carefully at the label to determine just what it is you are tasting. Tasting is discussed in another chapter, but here are some general guidelines to reading wine labels.

READING WINE LABELS

Labels for most of the world's wines, and certainly the best of them, indicate either the wine's place of origin or, in some cases, the name of the grape variety from which it is made. Most European wine names are place-names, so you are being told, most of the time, just where the wine comes from. Chablis, Sauternes, Saint-Emilion, Pommard, Vouvray, and Tavel are villages in France; Soave, Bardolino, Barolo, Orvieto, and Frascati are in Italy; German villages include Bernkastel, Piesport, Johannisberg, and Nierstein; other wine villages include Tokay in Hungary, Neuchâtel in Switzerland, and Valdepeñas in Spain. Wines whose names are those of their district of origin include Beaujolais, Anjou, Côtes du Rhône, Médoc, Chianti, and Rioja. Geography is the key to understanding wines so labeled. If you can focus on the wine's place of origin, rather than on the appearance of the label as a whole, and gradually build up a mental wine map for each

*Federal taxes on table wine are low, only 40¢ per case of twelve bottles; U.S. customs duties on imported wines add another 90¢ per case. State taxes vary considerably, however: 2¢ per case in California, 29¢ in New York, 71¢ in Connecticut and New Jersey, and $5.40 in Florida.

country as you taste its wines, you will more easily recall the wines you enjoy.

The wine laws now in effect in many European countries not only define the geographical limits of specific appellations of origin, but also take into account the grape varieties that are permitted, the maximum quantity produced per acre, the wine's minimum alcoholic content, and other elements of winemaking that affect its quality. The laws simply reflect certain observations about quality based on long periods of trial and error. For example, in many wine regions, specific grape varieties are best suited to certain soils, and these are the ones that produce the finest wines. Some classic combinations of grape and soil include Pinot Noir and Chardonnay in Burgundy, Nebbiolo in northern Italy, and Riesling along the Rhine and Moselle. Elsewhere, the finest wines are produced from a combination of several grape varieties, but the specific varieties, and sometimes the proportions of each, are strictly defined. Chianti, Rioja, and Châteauneuf-du-Pape are three familiar examples, as is Bordeaux, where Merlot and Cabernet Franc are planted along with the classic Cabernet Sauvignon grape. (In California, a number of different red and white grapes are often cultivated side by side, but many winemakers now believe that specific sites are likely to be more suited to one variety than to another.)

Wine laws limit the quantity of wine that can be produced from an acre of vines because quantity and quality have traditionally been mutually exclusive, and the most fertile soils, producing the most grapes, are rarely noted for the quality of their wines. A vineyard in Bordeaux, Burgundy, or the Napa Valley may produce less than two hundred cases of fine wine per acre; fertile districts in the south of France or in central California are capable of producing a thousand cases of undistinguished wine per acre.

A label that reflects the geographical origin of a wine may indicate not only a region, an inner district within that region, or an individual village, but also the ultimate geographical entity, the name of a specific vineyard. Every wine comes from a vineyard, of course, but most of the world's wines are blended together from many plots within a village or from several villages within a district. There are vineyards throughout the world, however, whose wines are vinified, aged, and bottled separately from those of adjoining plots of land. The most famous individually named vineyards are in Bordeaux, Burgundy, and along the Rhine and Moselle; some are less than five acres in size, others extend for 150 to 200 acres. Although it is standard wine humor to satirize the taster who tries to guess whether a wine comes from the right slope or the left slope, the fact is that the exact position of a plot of vines will have a recognizable effect on the quality of its wines year after year. A vineyard's exposure to the sun, its ability to absorb heavy rains without flooding or to retain moisture during a dry spell, the elements in its subsoil that nourish its vines—all these factors and more account for the astonishing fact that the wines of one vineyard plot will consistently sell for two or three times as much as those of an adjoining plot.

Although labeling wines with their place of origin is the most traditional approach, and is used throughout most of Europe, there is another approach that has become increasingly familiar to wine drinkers. That is the use of varietal names, in which wines are labeled with the name of the grape variety from which they are primarily, or entirely, made. This method is used in Alsace, in parts of Italy, and most notably in California, because the grape variety is a more useful indication of the style of a wine than is the name of the village or region from which the wine comes. Cabernet Sauvignon, Pinot Noir, Chardonnay, Zinfandel, and Grenache Rosé are among the best-known varietal wines of California. Other varietal wines include Seyval, Concord, and Catawba in New York State; Riesling and Gewürztraminer in Alsace; Lambrusco, Barbera, and Verdicchio in Italy; and Fendant in Switzerland. Sometimes a label will indicate both the variety and the place of origin: Bernkastel Riesling, Cabernet of Istria, Debröi Hárslevelü, and Sonoma Zinfandel are examples from Germany, Yugoslavia, Hungary, and California, respectively.

The names by which most of the inexpensive wines produced in this country are sold are, unfortunately, the least useful to the consumer. These are generic names—that is, specific place-names, usually European, that are so well known to the public that they have been adopted to market wines from somewhere else. California and New York State Chablis, Burgundy, Rhine Wine, and Sauterne (usually spelled without the final *s*) are the best-known examples of wines whose names have no relation to their origin, and whose characteristics may be similar only in the vaguest way to the wines whose names are being usurped. Chilean Rhine Wine, Argentine Burgundy, and Australian Moselle are other examples of generic labeling. In recent years, a number of producers have turned away from generic labeling to the use of such terms as Red Table Wine, Premium Red, Vintage White, or Mountain White Wine. The better wines produced in all these countries, however, bear the name of the grape variety from which they are made or the district from which they come, which gives the consumer a much more accurate idea of what the wine tastes like.

Another approach to labeling wines is the use of proprietary brand names created by individual producers for their own wines. A proprietary name is likely to be better known to consumers than that of the producer or the wine's place of origin. Emerald Dry, Chateau La Salle, Lake Country Red, Blue Nun, Mouton-Cadet, Nectarose, Partager, and Black Tower are some proprietary brands.

HOW WINE IS MADE

Wine is commonly defined as the fermented juice of fresh grapes. This obviously leaves out such specialty products as cherry wine, dandelion wine, or a beverage made from dehydrated grapes to which water has been added.

Grape juice is transformed into wine by the process of fermentation, in which the natural sugar present in grapes is converted into almost equal parts of alcohol and carbon dioxide gas. The normal sequence in the making of red wines is for the grapes to be brought to the vinification shed or winery, stripped of their stems, and lightly crushed to release their juice. The time-honored process of treading on the grapes by foot (which is pretty rare these days) was carried out not to press the grapes but to crush them so that the released juice could begin to ferment. Effective presses have been in existence since primitive times, and stamping on grapes would be a pretty ineffective way of getting all the juice out of them.

The crushed red grapes are transferred to fermentation tanks. These may be open wooden vats, large cement tanks, or stainless-steel cylinders. In recent years, many wine producers throughout the world have been replacing the traditional wooden vats with large plastic-lined, fiberglass, or stainless-steel tanks. They are much easier to keep clean, and the stainless-steel tanks in particular permit the temperature of the fermenting juice to be more carefully controlled.

The juice now begins to ferment as a result of various chemical transformations effected by yeast cells that were already present on the grape skins. (In some regions where modern techniques are used, the natural yeasts are inhibited, and special strains of cultured yeasts are added to the juice.) As the sugar/water solution becomes an alcohol/water solution (with carbon dioxide gas escaping into the atmosphere), coloring matter and tannin are extracted from the skins. The amount of color and tannin that is desired determines the length of time that the juice is left in contact with the skins, and this vatting, or *cuvaison*, may vary from two or three days to two or three weeks. Short vatting is traditional for wines whose principal attraction is their fruit and charm, longer vatting for wines noted for their depth of flavor and longevity. With very few exceptions, grape juice is clear and untinted. When a white wine is made from black grapes, as for champagne, the grapes are pressed immediately, before the skins can impart excessive color to the juice. Rosés are traditionally made by keeping the juice and skins together just long enough to impart the desired amount of color to the evolving wine, although cheap rosés are sometimes made by mixing red and white wines.

Fermentation normally continues until all of the sugar is converted into alcohol. The resulting wine generally varies in alcoholic content from as low as 7 or 8 percent to as high as 15 to 16 percent, depending on the wine region and the nature of the vintage. Even if the juice is especially rich in sugar, an alcoholic content of 15 to 16 percent kills the yeast cells that produced it, thus stopping fermentation. Almost all the table wines we drink, however, contain 10 to 14 percent alcohol, and in this country a natural table wine is legally defined as one that has less than 14 percent alcohol. Some, such as the white wines of Germany, may contain only 8 or 9 percent.

The alcohol content listed on a wine label, incidentally, is not necessarily an accurate indication of what is in the bottle. Federal law permits a leeway of 1.5 percent, so that a wine labeled as 12 percent alcohol may in fact contain anywhere from 10.5 to 13.5 percent. Labels with precise indications, such as 12.8 percent or 13.6 percent, are more likely to be accurate.

With very few exceptions, red table wines are fermented until they are completely dry: the minute trace of sugar that may be left in the wine cannot be perceived by the taste buds. Consequently, what sometimes makes one red wine taste "drier" than another is the amount of tannin or acids present. Some well-known red wines are slightly sweet, however: *sangría* from Spain and Lambrusco from Italy are the best-known examples. Also, a number of inexpensive California red wines are slightly sweetened before bottling, which rounds out their taste and makes them more appealing to many consumers.

After fermentation is complete, the wine is transferred to small barrels, large casks, or even larger tanks to age and to rid itself of its natural impurities. Depending on local custom, aging can take anywhere from a few weeks to three years or more.

The wine that drains freely from the fermentation tank is called free-run; that which is recovered from the remaining solids by pressing is classified as press wine. Generally speaking, press wine tends to have more color and body than free-run wine, and is harsher and more tannic as well. Sometimes a wine producer will sell off the press wine, sometimes it is blended with the free-run juice to intensify its flavor and add to its longevity.

Because the ferments are naturally present on grape skins at harvest time, winemaking is a natural process, but it must nevertheless be controlled very carefully at every step. If the fermenting juice, called must, gets too cold (an early frost in Germany) or too hot (a late summer in Spain), fermentation will stop and is extremely difficult to start again. What's more, if the new wine were just left exposed to air in its fermentation vat, another natural process would soon take place—through the presence of the vinegar bacteria—that would transform the wine into an acetic acid solution, i.e., into *vin aigre*, or sour wine.

There is another fermentation technique, called carbonic maceration, that is used to some extent in the Beaujolais and Rhône regions of France, and by some California wineries, to produce fruity, light-bodied red wines that can be consumed within months of the vintage. In conventional red-wine fermentation the grapes are in the presence of air. When carbonic maceration is practiced, the grapes, which are not crushed at all, are loaded into a closed container that is filled with carbon dioxide gas. Fermentation occurs within each grape in the absence of air, and color, but not much tannin, is extracted from the skins. Eventually, the grapes are removed from the closed container and pressed, and the must continues its fermentation in the normal way. In California, carbonic maceration is sometimes referred to as whole-berry fermentation.

White wines are made by a somewhat different method. Because they do not need to pick up color from their skins, the grapes are pressed immediately, and the juice ferments away from the skins. As a result, white wines have less tannin than reds, as tannin is derived primarily from the skins. Tannin is an important constituent of fine red wines and gives young red wines an astringent, puckerish taste. Its comparative absence from white wines constitutes one of the principal taste differences between red and white wines.

Perhaps the most significant technological achievement of the past twenty years in the production of white wines in California and throughout the world has been the increasing use of temperature-controlled fermentation tanks, which permits white wines to be fermented slowly at relatively low temperatures. Slow, cool fermentation retains the fruit and freshness that are the principal attributes of most white wines. If such simple, uncomplicated wines are bottled within a few months instead of being aged in wood for a year or more, as was traditional in many wine regions, they will display a youthful appeal rather than the dull, woody, and even oxidized tastes so prevalent in the past.

There are certain naturally sweet white wines, notably Sauternes and Barsac from Bordeaux, Auslese and Beerenauslese wines of Germany, and certain late-harvest wines from California, which are produced by stopping the fermentation while residual sugar remains in the wine.

Besides normal alcoholic fermentation, many wines also undergo malolactic fermentation, by which malic acid is converted into lactic acid with carbon dioxide gas as a by-product. This process is of interest to many winemakers because it decreases the acidity in a wine, and is therefore desirable in cool regions where grapes are usually harvested with a relatively high acid content. It is also of interest to the consumer because if malolactic fermentation takes place after the wine is bottled, the carbon dioxide gas will be trapped in the wine. The resulting delicate sparkle, more noticeable to the tongue than to the eye, may be delightful in certain white wines consumed locally if the microorganisms that cause malolactic fermentation have not also produced off flavors. Such fermentation is undesirable if it occurs in bottles of wine meant for export, which should be biologically stable.

One element of winemaking that is sometimes referred to,

and that can affect the quality of wines, is chaptalization. The process is named after Chaptal, one of Napoleon's ministers, who encouraged the idea of adding sugar to the must during fermentation. After a cold or rainy summer, when grapes have not ripened sufficiently, their lack of natural sugar would result in a wine without enough alcohol to make it healthy and stable. Chaptalization is permitted in several countries, notably France and Germany, in order to raise the alcohol content of a wine to its normal level as determined by good vintages. Chaptalization can be overdone, producing unbalanced wines that are too high in alcohol, but without it many famous wine districts would be unable to produce much drinkable wine in certain years.

The wine laws of Italy and California do not permit chaptalization, but they do permit the use of concentrated grape juice. The effect is basically the same—the concentrate contains a high proportion of sugar, which is converted into alcohol—but other elements present in the juice, notably acid, are also concentrated. Consequently, many winemakers believe that chaptalization is a more effective way to compensate for a lack of natural sugar than is the use of concentrate. In some regions whose wines are particularly high in acid, notably in New York State, it is permitted to add both sugar and water to the must, the water having the effect of reducing high acidity by diluting it. Of course, the water dilutes the wine as well and permits the winemaker to produce more wine from a given amount of grapes.

At some point before a wine is bottled it is fined, or clarified, to remove any impurities that may be suspended in it. A primitive form of fining is used by campers when they throw crushed eggshells into coffee that has been made by boiling water and coffee together in a pot. Suspended coffee grounds will cling to the egg whites on the shells as they fall to the bottom of the pot; as a matter of fact, a traditional fining method that is still used is to mix beaten egg whites into red wine. Gelatin is more widely used today for red wines, and certain clays for white wines.

Just before bottling, wines are filtered to remove any remaining impurities. Because American consumers have traditionally rejected wines that are not completely bright and clear in appearance, many American wineries favor rather severe fining and filtering, which may also diminish a wine's character and depth of flavor. Today, a number of smaller wineries bottle their wines without fining or filtering, or with very little, because they believe the wines will retain more character and develop greater complexity.

Historically, many inexpensive wines were pasteurized to kill any microorganisms that may spoil the wine after it is bottled. Unfortunately, pasteurization may effectively stop a wine from developing in the bottle, and the exposure to heat may also give the wine a slightly cooked taste. An alternative to pasteurization that has been adopted by many California wineries and a number of European firms is microfiltration—the use of an extremely fine membrane filter that removes most of the microorganisms that pasteurization would have killed.

Wine continues to change after it has been bottled, as the various pigments, acids, tannins, alcohols, and other elements present in minute quantities combine and alter the characteristics of the wine. Age alone is no guarantee of quality, however, and it is only the best wines that are sturdy and complex enough to improve for several years. The life cycle of each wine is different, and some wines are at their best when they are bottled, or within six months. All rosés and most white wines are best consumed within a year or two of the vintage, as are many light red wines. Some dry white wines, such as the best Burgundies and California Chardonnays, achieve additional richness and complexity with bottle age, as do the finest sweet white wines from Sauternes, Germany, and California. The best reds from Bordeaux, Burgundy, northern Italy, Rioja, and California will begin to reveal their qualities only after four or five years, and it is by no means unusual to discover that a red wine from a top vineyard is coming into its own only after ten or fifteen years in the bottle.

A note about bottle sizes: fine wines develop more slowly and sometimes more completely in larger bottles. For that reason connoisseurs ideally prefer an old red wine that has been matured in a magnum, which holds two bottles. Although half-bottles provide the opportunity of experimenting at less expense, remember that wine ages more quickly in a half-bottle and that a fine red wine may never fully develop its qualities in such a small container.

As to the contents of wine bottles, both American and imported bottles now conform to metric sizes and contain the same amount of wine, which was not previously the case. The standard bottle of 750 milliliters is equivalent to 25.4 ounces; the half-bottle contains 375 milliliters, or 12.7 ounces; a 1-liter bottle contains 33.8 ounces; the metric magnum holds 1.5 liters, or 50.7 ounces; and the 3-liter jeroboam is equivalent to 101.4 ounces. The gallon and half-gallon sizes in which inexpensive jug wines were once marketed are no longer permitted, and have been replaced by the metric magnum and jeroboam. The bottles for such traditional wines as red Bordeaux, however, are named somewhat differently: magnum (two bottles), double magnum (four bottles), jeroboam (six bottles), and imperial (eight bottles). Champagne bottle sizes are described elsewhere.

WINE
TASTING

For a professional wine buyer, wine tasting is a skill requiring a long apprenticeship and rather delicate judgment. For the person who enjoys wine with his or her meals, tasting is a most agreeable pastime. Unfortunately, many people imagine wine tasting to be a complex and mysterious art, dominated by snobs and dilettantes using a stylized and farfetched vocabulary.

On the simplest level, tasting wines is an inescapable part of drinking them, and there are many people who are content merely to determine whether a wine is "good" or "not good." Sooner or later the casual wine drinker will experiment with new wines, and at that point he or she begins to taste wine. Unlike other pursuits, such as golf or playing the piano, tasting wines is enjoyable from the very start and becomes increasingly fascinating and rewarding with experience.

The principal difference between the professional taster and everyone else is that he (and, increasingly, she) has a greater opportunity to taste many different wines, and thus his perspective is wider and his palate more developed. Furthermore, because a buyer tastes wine soon after the vintage, and months or years before the wine is even bottled, he has the additional opportunity of following the development of various wines from the cradle, so to speak. This is especially important as it is his role to judge young wines long before they are ready to be consumed, and he can do this precisely because he has tasted wines of previous vintages at a similar stage of their evolution.

However, there is another aspect of wine tasting that is most important, and that is concentration. We can't all spend days on end going in and out of wine cellars in Burgundy, the Rheingau, or the Napa Valley, but we can at least devote ten seconds or so to a wine when we first taste it with dinner. Different wines and different occasions call for a flexible approach. A bottle of Château Lafite-Rothschild 1961 served at a formal dinner demands more attention (and appreciative remarks) than does a Valpolicella served with pasta. But in each case a few moments' attention to the wine before you is the only way to build your knowledge and increase your pleasure. Look at the label and note where the wine comes from in general terms, and if it's a special wine, note the specific district or vineyard that produced it, or the grape variety from which it is made, as well as the vintage. As you sip the wine, try to place it geographically in your mind, and compare it to other wines you've tasted from the same place or the same grape. Only in this way will you develop your palate; otherwise you will simply have tasted, in time, a blur of individual bottles that you can neither recall nor repurchase.

It's often assumed, by the way, that wine experts are people who can taste wines whose labels have been covered up and then name the vineyard and vintage. Although some members of the wine trade amuse themselves by putting their colleagues through such blind tastings, the real skill of a wine buyer is demonstrated in exactly the opposite manner. He stands in a particular cellar, tasting a specific wine, and has even noted the barrel from which it was drawn. He must now determine how good it is, how good it will be six months or six years later, and what it is worth. It is precisely this ability to concentrate on the wine at hand—in order to judge its value, not guess its origin—that is the primary attribute of his expertise.

When professional tasters are at work, they always spit out the wines they are judging—either onto the floor of a cellar or into a special receptacle in a tasting room. For one thing, it's not a pleasant experience to swallow very young red wines starting at eight or nine in the morning. For another, a taster in the vineyard region may sample fifty or seventy-five wines in a day, and if he swallowed each wine, his judgment would soon become impaired, to say the least.

Whatever our specific knowledge about wine, each of us prefers to drink what he or she likes. As you taste different wines, it's interesting to try to determine why one wine is more pleasant than another, what attributes make one cost three times as much as another, and why one wine might suit a particular dish more than another at the same price: in short, to taste a wine critically and to sort out your impressions. Wine tasters generally approach a wine in three successive steps—color, bouquet (or smell), and taste. These will be examined in some detail, but remember that when a specific wine is tested, all of these considerations can be reviewed mentally in just a few seconds of concentration.

The first attribute of a wine is its color. Just as we anticipate a dish even more when it's attractively presented on the serving plate, so our enjoyment of a fine wine can be heightened by a look at its color. For this reason, wine is served in clear, uncut glasses. There are two aspects of a wine's color that deserve attention. The first is its appearance in the glass. Whether red or white, a healthy wine should be bright—that is, free of any cloudiness or suspension. If a wine appears dull or hazy, it may be unsound in some way, and its unattractive appearance is your first warning signal. This cloudiness is not to be confused with sediment, which is harmless and will fall to the bottom of the glass. Sediment is a natural by-product of age in older red wines, and such wines should be decanted whenever possible (as described elsewhere). Very occasionally you will come across crystals in a white wine; these are harmless (although admittedly unattractive) tartrates that have been precipitated by excessive cold. Sometimes small crystals are found stuck to the bottom of a cork, even in red wines. Again, these are tartrates, not, as some people imagine, sugar crystals.

The second aspect of color is the actual hue of the wine. The intensity of a wine's color can convey some idea of its character. A pale, watery white wine is likely to be lighter-bodied than a rich, gold one; a pale red wine will probably have less flavor than one that is dark, almost inky. This immediate judgment is really not much different from the one you automatically make about a cup of coffee—is it pale and therefore weak, or dark and strong?

As they age, red wines get lighter and white wines get darker. Young red wines have a purple-red color that soon turns to red, then to a bricklike orange-red before finally acquiring brown hues. This natural evolution reveals how far along the wine has come, irrespective of the vintage on the label. A six-month-old Beaujolais, for example, should still show hints of purple; if the wine in your glass displays faded red or red-orange hues, it's almost certainly too old. That same color would be acceptable, however, in a ten-year-old Bordeaux or California Cabernet Sauvignon.

A white wine, whether it's a pale straw-yellow or medium-gold color when young, will eventually darken with age. Just as a freshly cut apple begins to brown in a few minutes, so a white wine slowly browns over the years. Consequently, a young white wine that already shows signs of browning should be approached with some suspicion.

To judge the hue of a wine, don't look into the glass, as the depth of wine in the glass will affect its color. Tip the glass away from you and look at the outer edge of the wine against a white cloth or backdrop. An indication of just how important color is in judging wines is evidenced by the design of the traditional Burgundian *tastevin*, used to taste new wines still in barrels. It is a shallow silver cup—often used as a decorative ashtray here—with dimpled sides. Those dimples are there specifically to refract light through the wine, so that its color and appearance can be closely examined, even in a dimly lit cellar.

The second step in judging wine is to smell it, and wineglasses are curved in at the top to focus and retain a wine's bouquet. You may ask, Why bother to smell a wine when I'm about to taste it? About 80 percent of what we imagine to be taste is actually based on our sense of smell. When we taste roast beef or a peach, it is in fact the olfactory nerves that are doing most of the work. You know that food loses much of its flavor when you have a head cold, and yet it's your nose, not your palate, that is affected by the cold. The reason that wineglasses should be big (at least eight ounces) is that they are meant to be filled only halfway, so that a wine can easily be swirled in the glass. It is this gentle swirling that releases the wine's bouquet through evaporation.

A wine's bouquet gives you a strong first impression of the wine itself: if a wine has any serious faults, they can be discerned by smell, and you can avoid tasting bad wine. Occasionally, a wine may be corky, which is revealed by a moldy smell, rather than a clean, vinous one. This occurs much less frequently than many people suppose.

Not every wine has a distinctive bouquet. Some are fairly neutral and exude very little smell. This may be because they are simple wines that haven't much to offer, or because they are fine young wines that are still "closed in," requiring more bottle age to develop their bouquet. Some wines are immediately marked by off-odors. One of the most common is an excess of sulfur dioxide, the smell of a burning match. Sulfur dioxide is commonly used as a preservative, particularly for inexpensive whites, but an excessive amount is unpleasant when inhaled (when you taste such a wine, the sulfur dioxide leaves an acrid bite in the back of your throat). From time to time you may come across a white wine that has a suspiciously brown color and a bouquet reminiscent of Madeira or dry sherry without any of the fruit of a good wine. Such a wine is described as maderized (*maderisé*). Maderization is the result of excessive oxidation, and it may have been caused by overlong aging in wood or by a faulty cork that let air into the bottle, or it may be the natural evolution and decay of a white wine that is just too old. Another warning signal is a sour, vinegary smell, which indicates that the wine contains an excess of acetic acid, the vinegar acid. If you leave out a glass of wine overnight, what you smell and taste the next day is just such an excess of acetic acid.

Many off-odors are distinctive, but fortunately, they are not frequently encountered. More often you will be able to detect and recognize agreeable odors. Some of the easiest to identify are the aromas associated with specific grape varieties—the spiciness of Gewürztraminer, the fragrance and floweriness of German Rieslings, the berrylike aromas of California Zinfandel. The bouquet of Cabernet Sauvignon, the classic grape of red Bordeaux, is often compared to green peppers, a cigar box, black currants, even pencil shavings. The aroma of Sauvignon Blanc, the grape of Sancerre and Pouilly-Fumé, is often described as herbaceous, weedy, or grassy.

The bouquet of some wines is the result of the way they are made. Sauternes and sweet, late-harvest Rieslings from Germany and California have a honeyed, concentrated smell that comes from the overripe, slightly shriveled grapes from which they are made. Other smells may be the result of the way the wine was treated: wines aged in new oak barrels have nuances of wood and vanillin, a component of new oak. In general, young wines have more fruit in their bouquet (more of the smell of the grape), whereas older wines exhibit a more refined and subtle character. The sense of smell is probably the most evocative of all the senses (as the perfume manufacturers discovered long ago), and many of us have a greater sense memory for smells than for tastes, so make the most of it.

Finally, you taste the wine. (Remember that judging a wine takes less time than reading about it. Your impressions of color and bouquet should have taken you only a few moments.) The tongue is covered with taste buds that can distinguish only salt, sour, bitter, and sweet, and they are located on different parts of the tongue. You must let the wine rest on your tongue for a few moments, so that you can separate the different taste sensations. At this point some professional tasters chew the wine to make sure that it comes into contact with all their taste buds. Others will "whistle in," drawing air into their mouths and through the wine, to help release its flavor. The slurping sound is an accepted part of serious tastings, but it can be dispensed with at dinner parties.

Although there are certain chemical salts in wine, picked up from the soil in which the vines are planted, they are rarely discernible to the taste. Sweetness will, of course, be more easily discernible, and is found in many white wines and rosés, and a few red wines as well. Most red wines are vinified so as to retain no sugar, and if a Beaujolais or dry red wine seems slightly sweet, it may simply denote the presence of glycerin or other elements that round out a wine and give it a certain richness. It's worth noting that not everyone's palate reacts the same way to sweetness: someone who drinks coffee with three spoonfuls of sugar may describe a dry red wine as "sour," and a medium-sweet white wine or rosé as "dry." Incidentally, cold diminishes the perception of sweetness, so if you've bought a wine that you find too sweet, serve it cooler than you would normally.

Acidity is essential to wine, especially to white wines. Just as a squeeze of lemon on fish, or lemon zest in a drink, perks up its taste, so a certain amount of acidity is always necessary to give a white wine liveliness. Acidity not only gives more character to dry white wines, but also balances sweetness in wines that are not dry, as lemon juice does in lemonade. Moselles, for example, may contain quite a bit of sugar, but they have a lively, piquant taste, rather than a simple, one-dimensional sweet taste, because of the balancing acidity.

Acidity also enables white wines to age. White wines from some so-called great years are often short-lived because they are not acid enough; the heat and sun that produce extra sugar in the grapes (and therefore more alcohol in the wine) also burn away some of the acidity. This often results in big, powerful, but flabby white wines that are too low in acid and that therefore should not be put away for years of bottle aging. Too little sun produces grapes that are not fully ripe and contain too much acidity. The resulting wines are likely to be tart and unpleasant.

Bitterness usually indicates the presence of tannin in wine. Tannin—an important component of fine red wines—gives wine an astringent, puckerish taste that you will also find, for example, in very strong tea. Tannin acts as the spine or skeleton of a wine, and because tannin is an antioxidant that combines with the oxygen in wine, thereby slowing down the aging process, its presence enables a wine to evolve and mature in the bottle for many years. Tannin comes from grape skins and from the new oak barrels in which many red—and some white—wines are aged, and its presence is therefore the result of the vinification and aging methods used. In Beaujolais, where wines are to be drunk early while they retain their freshness, a short vatting (the time the skins are in contact with the juice) is the rule so that relatively little of the astringent tannin enters the wine. In Bordeaux, where red wines of good vintages are expected to last for ten years or more, vatting may take as long as three weeks, followed by up to two years of barrel aging, and the resulting wine will be harsh and bitter at first, and unpleasant to drink before it is at least five years old. An important change in vinification around the world during the past twenty years is a trend toward shorter vatting, so that red wines can be consumed more quickly by a public that no longer cellars wine away for years of maturation.

The tannic bitterness in red wine is softened by foods that contain protein. For example, if you eat cheese while tasting red wines, the protein in the cheese combines with the tannin in the wine and reduces its bitter taste. It's the same effect that occurs when you add milk to strong tea: the protein in the milk combines with and diminishes the tannin in the tea. For this reason, young red wines are usually more appealing when drunk with food than when they are tasted on their own.

As a wine ages in bottle, the tannin combines chemically with the coloring matter to form a harmless deposit. That is why older red wines are both paler in color and less harsh to the palate. (When buying young red wines to mature in your cellar, it is important to distinguish between tannin and acid, because one diminishes with age, the other doesn't.) The amount of tannin you detect in a long-lived red wine tells you whether or not it is ready to drink, or rather, whether or not the wine has evolved sufficiently to make it attractive to you. Unfortunately, many consumers make the mistake of assuming that there is a particular point at which each bottle of fine wine is at its best. In fact, it is difficult to project the evolution of the wines of a region in any given vintage, even more so to determine when a specific wine from a particular vineyard or winery will be fully developed. Furthermore, different people enjoy wines at different stages of development. Some enjoy the vigor and intensity of young wines, others prefer a red wine that has lost virtually all its tannin and displays softness and harmony at the expense of a more positive character.

If you concentrate on a wine for the few moments that it's in your mouth, you should be able to isolate the elements that make up its taste, since it is not difficult to be aware of two or three taste sensations simultaneously. For example, lemonade is a simple combination of sweetness and acidity that most people have no trouble adjusting to suit their own preferences. Red vermouth is quite sweet, but it also contains bitter extracts, so that the initial impression of sweetness, which would be too cloying by itself, is balanced by a bitter aftertaste. Strong tea is a bitter solution dominated by tannin; if you put in a slice of lemon, you add acidity, and if you then add sugar to mask the first two elements, you have created a simple combination of bitter, sour, and sweet.

In addition to tastes, certain tactile sensations can be felt on the palate. Temperature is one; carbon dioxide gas, as in champagne, is another. An excess of alcohol is often perceived as a hot or burning sensation. Although alcohol has little flavor, it can be felt, and it gives some wines an unwanted bite. One sensation that is especially important in evaluating a wine is its weight. Some wines are light and delicate, others are rather big and full, and this aspect of a wine's overall character is particularly relevant when you try to match a specific dish with an appropriate wine.

Finally, a wine should display harmony and balance, whatever its price. An inexpensive wine with no faults and a pleasant taste may be very good value. An expensive wine from a famous vineyard may be bigger and richer and, in many ways, more interesting, but may nevertheless lack the harmony that would make it a pleasure to drink.

Let me state again that the only way to learn about wines is to try different bottles and to be aware of what you are drinking. A good way to define your impressions more accurately is to compare two or three wines at a time: have two half-bottles for dinner, or invite like-minded friends over for an informal tasting. If you compare a Bordeaux to a Rioja, or a Beaujolais to a California Gamay, or a Moselle to an Alsatian Riesling—the possibilities are endless—you will soon learn to distinguish between the major wine-producing regions of the world. More important still, you will discover new wines to enjoy, and good values from each region.

You will soon realize that one of the great pleasures of drinking wines is to talk about them and to compare impressions. Trying to describe the color, bouquet, and taste of a wine is much less difficult when you are talking to someone who is drinking the same wine. The vocabulary of wine tasting may seem vague or precious, at first, but you will discover that its terms are fairly specific and easily understood by anyone who has tasted a number of wines. Although professionals may use technical terms to pinpoint certain impressions, a tasting vocabulary need not be complex. A good wine may be described as delicate, subtle, fresh, lively, mature, positive, spicy, deep, robust, complex, balanced, sturdy, clean, rounded, or crisp. An unattractive wine may be astringent, dull, heavy, harsh, small, thin, hard, ordinary, bland, musty, cloying, or coarse. It's fascinating to realize that although a wine chemist can easily spot a defective wine, he cannot distinguish by chemical analysis between, say, an inexpensive but soundly made red Bordeaux and a considerably more expensive wine from one of the great châteaux of the Médoc. He must eventually taste each wine to determine its character, intensity of flavor, complexity, subtlety, and true value.

One habit that will help to clarify your own taste, and will also help your wine buying considerably, is to keep some sort of record of the wines you drink both at your own table and away from home. Some hobbyists use a specially printed cellar book that has room for various entries. Many people simply use a pocket notebook, others prefer individual index cards. Whatever method you decide on, write down the name of the wine, who made it, and the vintage; when and where you bought it and the price; when you drank the bottle; and, of course, what you thought of it. If you look back at this record every few months you'll be amazed at the number of wines listed that you might otherwise have forgotten. You may also detect a change in your wine preferences and the evolution of a more precise tasting vocabulary.

Another way to keep track of what you drink is to soak off the label and record your comments on the back. The simplest method is to get an itemized bill from the store and to jot down your reactions to each wine as you drink it, if only to separate the wines you enjoyed most from those you found less to your taste.

As to smoking, a great many wine buyers and winemakers are smokers, and experiments indicate that people who smoke can taste as well as those who don't. Anyone who doesn't smoke, however, is quickly thrown off by smoke in the air, and for that reason it is common courtesy not to smoke during a tasting or when fine wines are served.

THE WINES
OF FRANCE

France is traditionally considered the greatest wine-producing country in the world, and its annual output—the equivalent of 800 million cases or so—accounts for about one-fifth of the world's wines. Although France does not make the most wine (in most years Italy's total production is greater), it probably produces a greater variety of fine wines than any other country. The red wines of Bordeaux, the red and white wines of Burgundy, the sweet wines of Sauternes and Barsac, and the sparkling wines of Champagne attest to the quality and diversity of French wines, and the wines of the Charente region are distilled to make cognac, the most famous of all brandies.

The first French vineyards were planted about twenty-five hundred years ago near what is now Marseilles, and viticulture soon spread to the north and the west. There are nearly three million acres of vines in France, and of course, the great bulk of the wine produced is undistinguished. This is the *vin ordinaire* that the French drink every day, which is available in every grocery store, just as milk and soda are here. Only the top 20 percent or so of French wines are bound by the *Appellation Contrôlée* laws, but most of the wines shipped here come from this strictly defined category.

The *Appellation Contrôlée* laws, established in the 1930s, are the key to understanding most French wine labels. The words mean "controlled place-name," and they constitute a

FRANCE

guarantee by the government that the place-name on the label is in fact just where the wine comes from. There are now about 250 individually defined *Appellation Contrôlée* wines, of which perhaps two hundred can be found here. When you have a bottle of French wine in front of you, look for the word directly above *Appellation Contrôlée* or actually between *Appellation* and *Contrôlée*. This will indicate the origin of the wine. It may be a region (Bordeaux, Côtes du Rhône), a district (Graves, Anjou), a village (Saint-Julien, Pommard), or even an individual vineyard, as in Burgundy (Chambertin, Montrachet). As the place-name becomes increasingly specific, the *Appellation Contrôlée* laws become increasingly strict, for they legislate not only the actual geographical limits of a particular place-name, but several other quality-control factors as well. Because certain soils are best suited to certain grape varieties, the law specifies which varieties are permitted. Minimum alcoholic content is another factor, not because the best wines have the most alcohol, but because too little alcohol in a wine will render it unstable. This prevents the use of an established place-name for certain wines produced there in a very poor year, when the worst of them will be too thin and washed-out to be typical. Perhaps the most important control of all, however, is that of quantity. It's been observed that most of the world's best wine regions do not, in fact, contain the best or most fertile soil: the vine seems to thrive in difficult terrain. In Bordeaux, for example, the richest soil, known as *palus*, lies along the riverbanks; wines produced there cannot be sold as Bordeaux, only as *vin ordinaire*. Furthermore, the best grape varieties rarely give a high yield, and should not be permitted to overproduce. An individual vine nourishes its fruit by sending roots down into the soil, as does any plant. If the vine is not pruned back in the winter to limit the number of bunches it can produce, the same root will have to nourish a lot more bunches, and the resulting wine will lack intensity of flavor and a clearly defined character.

Since the *Appellation Contrôlée* laws were first established, however, modern viticultural practices have enabled vineyard owners to produce somewhat more wine per acre while still maintaining the style and quality for which each appellation is noted. Although very abundant vintages generally produce lighter and less-intense wines, there have also been some recent vintages in which excellent wines were produced in relatively large quantities. The *Appellation Contrôlée* laws are now flexible enough to permit some variation from year to year concerning maximum permissible yields. Nevertheless, in any given region the limits set for village appellations are always stricter than for a regional one, and those for individual vineyards strictest of all.

The *Appellation Contrôlée* laws were based on earlier attempts to control the authenticity and quality of French wines, which were in turn made necessary by the confusion resulting from the complete replanting of the French vineyards after their destruction by phylloxera toward the end of the nineteenth century. Phylloxera, a plant louse, was unwittingly brought over from the United States on American rootstocks, and began to infest the European vineyards about one hundred years ago. Various methods were proposed to combat the phylloxera epidemic, which was devastating the vineyards of one country after another, but the technique that finally worked was to graft European *Vitis vinifera* vines to native American rootstocks from the eastern United States that were resistant to this insect. Eventually just about every single vine in

Europe (and many of those in California) was grafted onto an American rootstock.

There is another category of French wines, created in 1949, known as V.D.Q.S.—*Vins Delimités de Qualité Supérieure*, or Delimited Wines of Superior Quality. These wines rank below those of *Appellation Contrôlée* status because their quality is not quite as good or as consistent, and in a few instances, because the quantities produced are rather limited. There are about fifty V.D.Q.S. wines, and their total production is about 15 percent that of the *Appellation Contrôlée* category. A few V.D.Q.S. wines have been elevated to *Appellation Contrôlée* status in the past few years, notably Cahors, Côtes de Provence, Côtes du Ventoux, Côteaux du Languedoc, Côteaux d'Aix-en-Provence, and Minervois, and it is likely that others will be as well. The labels of V.D.Q.S. wines, which include Corbières, Sauvignon de Saint-Bris, Côtes du Lubéron, and Gros Plant du Pays Nantais, are imprinted with an emblem that resembles a small postage stamp; it contains the appropriate words and an illustration of a hand holding a wineglass.

For many years a number of French wines were entitled to label themselves *Appellation d'Origine Simple*. The phrase misled some consumers into thinking that these wines, which rank somewhere between *vin ordinaire* and V.D.Q.S., were somehow associated with *Appellation Contrôlée* wines. In 1973, the name of this category of wines was changed to *Vins de Pays*, and there are now nearly a hundred defined areas whose wines are entitled to use this phrase on their labels. Three-quarters of the *Vins de Pays* come from the Midi region, and 98 percent of the total are reds and rosés. It is likely that as quality improves, some *Vins de Pays* will become V.D.Q.S., just as several V.D.Q.S. wines have been raised to *Appellation Contrôlée* status. *Vin de Pays* now has a specific meaning, but the phrase *vin du pays* is still used informally to refer to the wine of the region—that is, to whatever local wine is being discussed.

In addition to the various appellation wines described above, there are an increasing number of red, white, and rosé wines being shipped here that are simply blends of wines produced anywhere in France. Sold in magnums and labeled with proprietary names, they are meant to provide an inexpensive alternative to jug wines from California and Italy. Some may confuse consumers as to what they really are, because they are marketed by well-known firms in Bordeaux, Burgundy, the Rhône, and elsewhere whose names are traditionally associated with *Appellation Contrôlée* wines. Although these wines were created as a less expensive alternative to *Appellation Contrôlée* wines, consumers who recognize the shipper's name may imagine that they are buying wines of a higher class than is actually the case. In fact, these nonappellation wines, which fall into the Common Market category *Vin de Table*, are usually no better than an anonymous *vin ordinaire*, despite the prices at which some of them are sold. The labels of such wines obviously do not show the words *Appellation Contrôlée*, and that is the simplest way to determine what they are, but at one time the shipper's name could be followed by the place in which the firm was located, such as Bordeaux, Beaune, Nuits-Saint-Georges, and so on, and the wines could be vintage-dated. New regulations forbid the use, on a label of nonappellation wine, of a city or village whose name is associated with an *Appellation Contrôlée* wine, such as Bordeaux or Beaune, nor can such blends show a vintage date. The shipper's name can now be followed only by the French equivalent of a zip code, to avoid misleading the consumer as to the origin of the wine in the bottle. Actually, if a wine is produced or bottled in a town not associated with an *Appellation Contrôlée*, such as Blanquefort or Sète, its name may appear on the label of a *Vin de Table*, but these wines are nevertheless often referred to as "zip code wines." As recently as 1970, more than 90 percent of French wines shipped to this country were of *Appellation Contrôlée* status. By the mid-1980s, the *Vin de Table* category, which includes such brands as Partager, Moreau Blanc, Valbon, Chantefleur, Boucheron, Sommelière, Piat d'Or, Père Patriarche, and Canteval, accounted for more than half of French wine imports.

BORDEAUX

Bordeaux has long been considered one of the centers of the world's finest wines, and is unmatched within France for both quantity and variety. Red, white, and some rosé is produced, and the whites include both dry and sweet wines. Although the thirty to fifty million cases produced annually in Bordeaux amount to less than 5 percent of the wines of France, in many years they account for 20 to 25 percent of all wines entitled to *Appellation Contrôlée* status.

Bordeaux was shipping its wines to England as early as the

BORDEAUX

twelfth century, when Henry II married Eleanor of Aquitaine and thus annexed the region of Bordeaux as part of his empire. At that time, thousands of barrels were shipped annually of a pale red wine called *clairet*. The word evolved into "claret," and properly refers only to red wine from Bordeaux, although it is often used to describe any dry red wine. It's only since the early nineteenth century, when the use of corks and cylindrical bottles became more common, making it possible for bottled wines to be stored on their sides for additional maturation, that claret as we know it today began to be produced: a deep-colored red wine that improves with age and that, in fact, needs years in barrel and in bottle to develop its best qualities.

The Bordeaux wine region lies within the *département* of the Gironde, and its principal city is, of course, Bordeaux itself, with a population of about 225,000. Two rivers, the Garonne and the Dordogne, meet just north of Bordeaux and form the Gironde estuary, which flows into the sea. It is in and around this triangle that the vineyards of Bordeaux are situated.

There are more than thirty-five wine districts in Bordeaux, each one entitled to its own *Appellation Contrôlée*, but there are only five that stand out as producing the very greatest wines. They are the Médoc, Saint-Emilion, and Pomerol, whose names are used only for red wines; Graves, which produces both red and white wines; and Sauternes, containing the inner district of Barsac, whose sweet and luscious white wines are world-famous.

In addition to these five main districts, there are four communes, or parishes, in the Médoc district whose names are important: Margaux, Saint-Julien, Pauillac, and Saint-Estèphe. These are inner appellations of the Médoc, and a wine from one of these communes is generally of a higher class and has more individuality than one labeled simply Médoc. Although Bordeaux is a vast area, if you can remember these ten place-names (including Barsac), you will be well on your way to having a good idea of what you are drinking. For example, a red or white wine with the *Appellation Contrôlée* Bordeaux can come from anywhere within the entire region and will certainly not be from one of the better districts. A wine labeled Médoc, Saint-Emilion, Pomerol, or Graves will naturally come from vineyards within those respective districts, and you know you are getting a wine several steps up in quality from just a plain Bordeaux. If the label bears the name of one of the four communes in the Médoc, you are at a very high level within the hierarchy of Bordeaux appellations. This doesn't mean that a commune wine will always be better than a Médoc, but at least this provides a useful and fairly consistent ranking of relative quality.

Knowing these few names is also useful in reverse: that is, if a bottle of Bordeaux bears an unfamiliar *Appellation Contrôlée*, you know by the process of elimination that it must come from one of the many lesser districts. You may see names such as Côtes de Fronsac, Entre-Deux-Mers, Côtes de Bourg, Premières Côtes de Bordeaux, and the like, and while such wines can be very agreeable indeed, they should cost less than wines from the major appellations.

When you are confronted with the label of an individual vineyard, traditionally called a château in Bordeaux, looking for its *Appellation Contrôlée* is the simplest way to place it geographically. Let's say you are served a bottle of Château Trotanoy, and having enjoyed it, decide to buy a bottle for yourself. You may discover that the wine from this particular vineyard is not so easy to find, but if you noted its *Appellation Contrôlée*, you would have seen that it's a Pomerol. The chances are, then, that another Pomerol will have more of the general characteristics of Château Trotanoy than, say, a Médoc or a plain Bordeaux. If you try to memorize a vineyard name or the general appearance of a label, you will just be searching for one label among hundreds. Instead, you should place each wine you drink in its proper geographical context by noting its appellation of origin. Individual vineyard wines from Bordeaux are available in a wide range of prices. By paying attention to the *Appellation Contrôlée* of each wine you drink, you will not only be able to determine its relative rank among the appellations of Bordeaux, but you will also learn to distinguish the overall styles of wines from each major district. With the major appellations in mind, it becomes much easier to compare wines of different prices within an appellation, or to contrast wines of similar price from different appellations.

Although an individual vineyard in Bordeaux is called a château, there are very few homes that actually merit this description. Most properties consist of just a country house, some have more elaborate buildings dating from the late eighteenth or the early nineteenth century, and a few properties have no more than a large *chai*, or ground-level storage area, where the wines are made and stored. Nevertheless, labels for individual Bordeaux vineyards almost all contain the word *château* (a very few describe themselves as *domaine* or *clos*), and while there are a few properties elsewhere in France that also call themselves by a château name, when you see this word on a label, you can be pretty sure that the wine is from Bordeaux.

One way to approach the wines of Bordeaux is to divide them into two main categories: château wines, which are the product of an individual vineyard; and regional wines, which are marketed by their appellation of origin—Médoc, Saint-Emilion, Sauternes, and so on—rather than with the name of a specific property. The *négociants*, or shippers, of Bordeaux buy wines from a great many properties within a particular appellation of origin, as well as from the many cooperative cellars in the region, and blend them together to produce a wine of consistent quality and style. Most of the region's wines are shipped under two basic appellations, Bordeaux Rouge and Bordeaux Blanc, but the wines most frequently seen here are Médoc, Saint-Emilion, Graves, Sauternes, and Barsac. Margaux and Saint-Julien are occasionally available, but it is rare to find regional wines from Pauillac, Saint-Estèphe, or Pomerol, as almost all the wines from these appellations are bottled and sold by the vineyard proprietors as château wines. Since regional wines are blended, they do not express the characteristics of a particular vintage as clearly as do the wines of a single property. Nevertheless, there are vintage variations among regional wines, and it's always worth looking for the best recent vintages. Regional wines are meant to be consumed without much additional aging, and the best of them are consistent and dependable wines, although many lack the distinction and individuality of château wines selling for the same price. Some of the Bordeaux shippers whose names are featured on labels of regional wines are Barton & Guestier, Calvet, Cordier, Cruse, Eschenauer, De Luze, Sichel, and Yvon Mau.

In recent years, the traditional range of regional wines has been largely replaced, in this country, by proprietary wines, whose names are created and owned by individual shippers and promoted as brands. Mouton-Cadet, Maître d'Estournel, Chevalier Védrines, and La Cour Pavillon are some examples. These, too, are regional blends, almost always Bordeaux Rouge or Bordeaux Blanc, but their labels emphasize the brand name rather than the appellation of origin or the name of the shipper.

Although regional and branded wines make up the most important part of the Bordeaux market, it is the great château wines of Bordeaux that have established the reputation of this region among connoisseurs. Of the more than two thousand individually named properties in Bordeaux, there are approximately a hundred châteaux whose wines are considered the finest of all, and which most fully display the characteristics that have made the wines of Bordeaux famous. Most of these wines have been officially classified at one time or another—the vineyards of Pomerol are a notable exception—and are, therefore, referred to as *crus classés*, or classed growths (*cru* is synonymous with "vineyard"). Not all of these châteaux are readily available here, but there are probably fifty or sixty red wines and perhaps fifteen dry and sweet white wines whose names continually reappear in retail catalogs and on the wine lists of fine restaurants. Although the *crus classés* represent perhaps 3 percent of the wines of Bordeaux, this amounts to more than a million cases of very fine wine, and any discussion of Bordeaux wines will almost invariably turn to the classed growths. The classifications are explained and the wines listed district by district further on.

The great châteaux of Bordeaux are comparatively easy to learn about because the properties are fairly large—150 acres is not uncommon—and they are traditionally under a single ownership. All of the wines from a specific vineyard that are to be sold under the château name are blended together before bottling; as a result, each property markets only one wine bearing the château label in any vintage. In contrast, most Burgundy vineyards are much smaller and almost all have several owners, each of whom makes a slightly different wine according to his skills and intentions. In Germany, also, the vineyards are small and under multiple ownership. In addition, each grower produces several different wines from the same vineyard in a good vintage, and these vary considerably in quality, taste, and price. By comparison with these other two great European wine regions, Bordeaux is relatively easy to understand, and the wines of the top châteaux are produced in sufficient quantities so that they are not difficult to acquire and compare. Many connoisseurs can discuss Bordeaux châteaux with great knowledge and enthusiasm, while remaining mystified about the wines of Burgundy or the Rhine.

It is possible to make comparisons among the wines of the many famous châteaux of Bordeaux because each of them has its own distinct characteristics. It may seem hard to believe, but each parcel of soil will produce a wine that is not only different from parcels nearby, but also consistently better or less good than those of its neighbors. A case in point is Château Latour and Château Léoville-Las-Cases: these two vineyards are contiguous, and it is impossible for a visitor to determine, unaided, where one vineyard ends and the other begins. Yet the first is a Pauillac, the second a Saint-Julien, and a bottle of Latour costs two or three times as much as a bottle of the (nevertheless excellent) Léoville-Las-Cases.

Although the potential quality of a vineyard is determined by its soil and subsoil and its exposure to the elements and to the sun, there are other factors that enter into the quality and personality of the wine of a particular château, not least of them the proportion of different grape varieties planted. The varieties permitted for red Bordeaux are Cabernet Sauvignon, Cabernet Franc, Merlot, Petit Verdot, and Malbec, although the last two are present in rather limited quantities. Cabernet Sauvignon brings finesse, depth of flavor, tannic backbone, and longevity to a wine, the classic qualities of a claret; Cabernet Franc is similar, with perhaps more fruit and acidity and less depth; Merlot is prized for its suppleness and charm. Unlike California winemakers, who can buy the grapes they need and blend the resulting wine in whatever proportion they think most successful, a Bordeaux châteaux owner may only bottle the wine produced from his own vineyard. And the proportion of permitted varieties in a given property depends more on its soil than on the whim of the proprietor. The gravelly soil of the Médoc is particularly suitable for Cabernet Sauvignon, for example, but those sections of a vineyard that consist of clay and limestone are likely to be planted with Merlot, because Cabernet Sauvignon will not ripen as well there. Nor does it ripen well in the soils of Saint-Emilion and Pomerol—Merlot and Cabernet Franc are much more widely planted there. In any case, the proportion of different grape varieties in the wine of a given year may not conform to that in the vineyard, because growing conditions may be more favorable for Merlot in one year, Cabernet Sauvignon the next.

Although Cabernet Sauvignon is considered the classic red-wine grape of Bordeaux, Merlot now accounts for about half the total acreage, Cabernet Sauvignon for only a quarter. Cabernet Sauvignon is the principal variety in the Médoc and Graves, however, as Merlot is in Saint-Emilion and Pomerol. Sémillon is the most widely planted white grape of Bordeaux; Sauvignon Blanc accounts for less than 10 percent of the total, as does Muscadelle, although there is a higher proportion of Sauvignon Blanc in the Graves and Sauternes districts.

Another factor that affects quality is the way the wines are vinified. Since many consumers are now drinking even the finest red Bordeaux within a few years of the vintage, before the wines have fully achieved their potential, some proprietors may decide on a shorter vatting—the time during which the grapes are in contact with the fermenting must—and thus produce a somewhat lighter and quicker-maturing wine. At some châteaux the new wine is always put into new barrels, which gives the wines greater tannic complexity, but which also represents a considerable investment if, say, eight hundred barrels have to be purchased every year. A proprietor who decides not to prune back his vines severely will produce a large crop of somewhat light wines; his neighbor may deliber-

ately make less wine per acre, but that wine will be more
intense and concentrated in flavor.

One of a proprietor's most important decisions occurs within
a few months of the harvest, when all the lots in the cellar are
tasted to determine which ones will be set aside and which
will be assembled to produce the wine eventually bottled with
the château name. Since all the wine produced on the property can legally be sold with that name, this is the most
expensive decision of all, but the one that is the most significant to the quality and reputation of the wine. The lots that
are set aside usually consist of wines made from younger
vines that are less than seven or eight years old or from parts
of the vineyard that did not mature as well in that vintage. For
this reason, the top châteaux generally pick and vinify young
and old vines of each variety separately, and also try to vinify
apart specific parcels of vines within the property, to permit a
greater selection of lots for the final *assemblage*. The wines
that are considered of lesser quality are sold to the trade in
bulk without the château name or bottled by the château and
marketed under a second label.

These are just some of the factors that can affect the
personality, quality, and, eventually, reputation of a wine,
and comparing different châteaux in various vintages provides
an endless source of pleasure to drinkers of Bordeaux.

Some years ago the best châteaux of Bordeaux began to
bottle their wines themselves in their own cellars—rather than
shipping them in barrels—as insurance that the wines bearing
their labels are in no way tampered with; today, all *crus
classés* must be château-bottled. A branded cork bearing the
name of the château and the vintage is used as well. The
labels of such wines bear the words *mis en bouteille au
château*, that is, bottled at the château. Just about every
important château wine imported into this country is now
château-bottled. In recent years, as Americans have learned to
look for *mis en bouteille au château* on a Bordeaux label, a
number of smaller properties have taken to château-bottling
their wines as well. Wines of these *petits châteaux*, as they
are called, have become very popular here, and are now an
important part of the Bordeaux trade; in fact, they have to a
large extent replaced the regional wines of the leading shippers that dominated the Bordeaux market not so many years
ago. Their quality will vary considerably, and it is well to
remember that if a wine is château-bottled you are guaranteed
of its authenticity, but not necessarily of its quality. It's

perfectly possible to bottle a second-rate wine at the property, and this is being done to take advantage of the momentum for château-bottled wines. It is also permissible for a coopérative cellar to market certain of its wines with a château name, although in that case the phrase will read *mis en bouteille à la proprieté*. There are, of course, a number of large, carefully tended properties in various districts that consistently produce good wines, and it's worth experimenting with the selection of *petits châteaux* available in local shops.

In the châteaux of Bordeaux, wines are stored in *barriques*, small oak barrels that hold about sixty gallons, or twenty-five cases, of wine. At the best properties, the red wines mature in barrel for eighteen to twenty-four months, and this aging contributes greatly to their complexity, depth of flavor, and distinctive character. The traditional measure of trade in Bordeaux when new wines are being bought is the *tonneau*, an imaginary measure equivalent to four *barriques*, or a hundred cases.

The word *supérieur*, as in Bordeaux Supérieur, only means that wines so labeled contain 1 percent more alcohol than those labeled simply Bordeaux. It is by no means an indication of superior quality, and in fact, many châteaux that could legally add *supérieur* to their appellations don't bother to do so. The word *monopole* on a shipper's label simply indicates that the firm has a monopoly, or exclusivity, on the particular brand name being used. *Grand vin* doesn't have any meaning, although *grand cru* does.

The Médoc

The Médoc district contains some of the most famous vineyards in the world, and most of its wines are on a very high level indeed. The wines of the Médoc have become well known only in the last two hundred years or so. The wines shipped to England in the Middle Ages, for example, were mostly from Graves. The Médoc, which begins a few miles from the city of Bordeaux and extends for sixty miles, remained a dangerous and unprotected place in which to travel, and it was not until the seventeenth century that important vineyards began to be established there.

The Médoc is actually divided into two parts, originally known as the Haut-Médoc and the Bas-Médoc. These references to high and low are based simply on the position of each district relative to the Gironde, but the proprietors in the

Bas-Médoc, which is the part farthest from Bordeaux, objected to its possible connotations on a label, and their appellation is now simply Médoc. The famous communes of Saint-Estèphe, Pauillac, Saint-Julien, and Margaux are all situated in the Haut-Médoc, but this district is usually referred to simply as the Médoc. Some lesser châteaux do use the appellation Haut-Médoc on their labels, however.

Perhaps the best way to approach the wines of the Médoc is from the top, which is to say, with the Classification of 1855. In conjunction with the Paris Exhibition of that year, representatives of the Bordeaux wine trade were asked to draw up a list of the best vineyards of the Médoc and of Sauternes, which will be discussed separately. By this time the Médoc had become considerably more famous than Graves, and Saint-Emilion and Pomerol were not yet widely known. The resulting classification grouped the wines on five levels of excellence, from *premiers crus* to *cinquièmes crus*. (Although Château Haut-Brion is located in the Graves district, it was already too important to leave out.) A fifth growth was by no means only one-fifth as good as a first growth—the ranking was gradual—and in any case all the classed growths represented the very best that Bordeaux had to offer.

THE CLASSIFICATION OF 1855
FOR THE MÉDOC

VINEYARD	COMMUNE
Premiers Crus—First Growths	
Château Lafite-Rothschild	Pauillac
Château Margaux	Margaux
Château Latour	Pauillac
Château Haut-Brion	Pessac
Deuxièmes Crus—Second Growths	
Château Mouton-Rothschild*	Pauillac
Château Rausan-Ségla	Margaux
Château Rauzan-Gassies	Margaux
Château Léoville-Las-Cases	Saint-Julien
Château Léoville-Poyferré	Saint-Julien

*Reclassified as a *premier cru* in 1973.

Château Léoville-Barton	Saint-Julien
Château Durfort-Vivens	Margaux
Château Lascombes	Margaux
Château Gruaud-Larose	Saint-Julien
Château Brane-Cantenac	Cantenac-Margaux
Château Pichon-Longueville	Pauillac
Château Pichon-Longueville-Comtesse de Lalande	Pauillac
Château Ducru-Beaucaillou	Saint-Julien
Château Cos d'Estournel	Saint-Estèphe
Château Montrose	Saint-Estèphe

Troisièmes Crus—Third Growths

Château Kirwan	Cantenac-Margaux
Château d'Issan	Cantenac-Margaux
Château Lagrange	Saint-Julien
Château Langoa-Barton	Saint-Julien
Château Giscours	Labarde-Margaux
Château Malescot-Saint-Exupéry	Margaux
Château Cantenac-Brown	Cantenac-Margaux
Château Palmer	Cantenac-Margaux
Château La Lagune	Ludon
Château Desmirail	Margaux
Château Calon-Ségur	Saint-Estèphe
Château Ferrière	Margaux
Château Marquis-d'Alesme-Becker	Margaux
Château Boyd-Cantenac	Cantenac-Margaux

Quatrièmes Crus—Fourth Growths

Château Saint-Pierre	Saint-Julien
Château Branaire-Ducru	Saint-Julien
Château Talbot	Saint-Julien
Château Duhart-Milon	Pauillac
Château Pouget	Cantenac-Margaux
Château La Tour-Carnet	Saint-Laurent
Château Lafon-Rochet	Saint-Estèphe
Château Beychevelle	Saint-Julien
Château Prieuré-Lichine	Cantenac-Margaux
Château Marquis-de-Terme	Margaux

Cinquièmes Crus—Fifth Growths

Château Pontet-Canet	Pauillac
Château Batailley	Pauillac
Château Haut-Batailley	Pauillac
Château Grand-Puy-Lacoste	Pauillac
Château Grand-Puy-Ducasse	Pauillac
Château Lynch-Bages	Pauillac
Château Lynch-Moussas	Pauillac
Château Dauzac	Labarde
Château Mouton-Baron-Philippe*	Pauillac
Château du Tertre	Arsac
Château Haut-Bages-Libéral	Pauillac
Château Pédesclaux	Pauillac
Château Belgrave	Saint-Laurent
Château Camensac	Saint-Laurent
Château Cos Labory	Saint-Estèphe
Château Clerc-Milon	Pauillac
Château Croizet-Bages	Pauillac
Château Cantemerle	Macau

More than 130 years have gone by, but this classification remains virtually unchanged to this day, and the names and ratings are more or less familiar to all lovers of claret. Most of the châteaux on the list continue to indicate on their labels that they are a *cru classé* or *grand cru classé,* and any discussion of the vineyards of the Médoc will always revolve around these wines. The classification remains valid in many ways, and many of these wines are still among the best produced in Bordeaux, but this listing must be approached with a certain perspective. Some châteaux have become run-down and produce only small quantities of undistinguished wine; others have been purchased by proprietors determined to increase the quality of a château's wines and to expand its production as well. Since the classification was drawn up, many of the *crus classés* no longer have the same boundaries as they did in 1855. A proprietor is legally permitted to buy vineyards anywhere within the appellation of his property—Margaux, Saint-Julien, Pauillac, or Saint-Estèphe—and sell that wine under the château label. Certain properties have, in fact, doubled or tripled their production in the past twenty years by acquiring land from their neighbors.

*Formerly Château Mouton d'Armailhacq, now Château Mouton-Baronne-Philippe.

The classification gave such prominence to the châteaux of the Médoc that the excellent vineyards of Graves, Saint-Emilion, and Pomerol were neglected until fairly recently. It must be added, however, that the vineyards of the Médoc are much bigger, on the average, than those of the other districts. A château producing twenty or thirty thousand cases is not unusual in the Médoc, whereas there are few châteaux producing even ten thousand cases in Saint-Emilion, Pomerol, and Graves.

Perhaps the most interesting development within the classification itself is that there has been so much attention focused on the four first growths, Lafite-Rothschild, Latour, Margaux, and Haut-Brion, that their prices are now two or three times that of almost any other classified wine. At the time of the classification, a second growth sold for only 10 or 15 percent less than a first, and a fifth growth cost about half as much as a first. To the four first growths of 1855 must be added Mouton-Rothschild, which never accepted its status as "first of the seconds." In recent years its wines have always been as expensive as those of the first growths, and in 1973 it was officially reclassified as a first growth.

This leads to the important point that the classification was, in fact, based on the prices that each wine had sold for in a number of previous vintages. This pragmatic approach to the value of a property is the one still in use today among the brokers and shippers of Bordeaux. In the Bordeaux wine trade, the wines of the classification are referred to simply as the first growths and the classed growths, the latter category including all but the eight most expensive wines. (In practice, Châteaux Ausone and Cheval Blanc in Saint-Emilion and Pétrus in Pomerol are now included in the phrase "the first growths.") Among the classed growths are a number of wines officially rated as third, fourth, or fifth growths, such as Palmer, Talbot, Beychevelle, and Lynch-Bages, that consistently achieve the same prices as the classified seconds, and in some cases, a bit more. To use the classification effectively, look over the list from time to time so that you will know when you are drinking the wine of one of the more famous châteaux of Bordeaux. What you should not do is to pay undue attention to the exact rating of every wine, because a wine's relative price on an extensive retail listing of Bordeaux châteaux will give you a better indication of the way the Bordeaux wine merchants themselves rate the wine today.

There were also a number of other châteaux rated just

below the *grands crus classés* as *crus exceptionnels* and *crus bourgeois*. Although the term *cru bourgeois* is often used informally to describe a property that sets high standards for itself, there is now an association of *crus bourgeois* organized by a number of proprietors in the Médoc. Their most recent listing, published in 1978, includes more than 120 châteaux whose combined production now accounts for about 40 percent of the wines of the Médoc. The properties are located throughout this district, but quite a few are grouped in the northern Médoc, in the villages of Saint-Estèphe, Saint-Seurin de Cadourne, and Bégadan. Some of the best known *crus bourgeois* are listed below.

Château d'Agassac
Château Beau-Site
Château Bel-Air-Marquis-
  d'Aligre
Château Bel-Orme
Château Capbern
Château Castera
Château Chasse-Spleen
Château Citran
Château Coufran
Château Dutruch Grand
  Poujeaux
Château Fourcas-Dupré
Château Fourcas Hosten
Château du Glana
Château Gressier Grand
  Poujeaux
Château Greysac
Château Haut Marbuzet
Château La Bécade
Château Labégorce
Château La Cardonne
Château Lamarque
Château Lanessan
Château Larose Trintaudon

Château La Tour de By
Château La Tour-de-Mons
Château La Tour St.-Bonnet
Château Lestage
Château Liversan
Château Livran
Château Loudenne
Château Malleret
Château Marbuzet
Château Maucaillou
Château Meyney
Château Les Ormes de Pez
Château Patache D'Aux
Château Paveil de Luze
Château Peyrabon
Château Phélan Ségur
Château Potensac
Château Poujeaux-Theil
Château Ramage La Batisse
Château Siran
Château Sociando-Mallet
Château du Taillan
Château Tronquoy-Lalande
Château Verdignan
Château Vieux Robin

  The wines of the Médoc are known especially for their breed and finesse, and are the most elegant of all Bordeaux. In good vintages, the best châteaux need several years of bottle age to reveal their distinctive qualities, and a wine that is still improving after twenty or thirty years in the bottle is not exceptional, although finding such a wine may be.

One way to tour the Médoc is to drive straight out to Saint-Estèphe, the village farthest from Bordeaux, and then to visit the principal properties in turn. Although Saint-Estèphe is the biggest wine-producing commune in the Médoc, it doesn't have as many famous châteaux as do Pauillac, Saint-Julien, and Margaux. The best-known properties are Cos d'Estournel, Montrose, Calon-Ségur, and Lafon-Rochet. Cos d'Estournel, in particular, under the direction of Bruno Prats, has produced excellent wines in recent vintages; its second label is Château de Marbuzet. Château Lafon-Rochet has been revitalized by the Tesseron family, who also own Château Pontet-Canet in Pauillac and Château Malescasse. The less familiar Château de Pez, owned by Robert Dousson, is another fine property. Saint-Estèphe wines are quite firm and tannic when young, and develop slowly: they are among the least supple of all clarets.

Pauillac probably has the highest average quality of wine of any village in France. Three *premier cru* châteaux are located there—Lafite-Rothschild, Latour, and Mouton-Rothschild—as well as a number of other vineyards whose wines are justifiably admired. Château Lafite-Rothschild is one of the few properties whose house actually resembles a château, and few sights are more impressive than the first view of its *chai* for the new wine. In a spacious and high-ceilinged ground-level warehouse, more than a thousand barrels of the most recent vintage are lined up in several long rows, representing perhaps five or six million dollars' worth of maturing wine. Until 1967 a second wine was also made at the property, Carruades de Château Lafite-Rothschild, which came entirely from the Lafite vineyard, but was made up primarily of lighter and quicker-maturing wines from young vines. In 1974, Lafite began once again to market a second wine as Moulin des Carruades. In 1962, the proprietors of Lafite purchased Duhart-Milon, another Pauillac vineyard, and have since renamed it Duhart-Milon-Rothschild; in 1984 they purchased a majority interest in Château Rieussec, in Sauternes.

Château Mouton-Rothschild has been in the hands of Baron Philippe de Rothschild since the 1920s, and he gradually transformed the château into one of the showplaces of the Médoc. Apart from the dramatically lit cellars and the beautifully furnished main house, there is also a fascinating wine museum on the property that attracts a great many visitors every year. Since 1945, the labels of Château Mouton-Rothschild have incorporated a design by a different artist nearly every year. These have included Jean Cocteau (1947), Salvador Dali (1958), Henry Moore (1964), Joan Miró (1969), Marc Chagall (1970), Pablo Picasso (1973); Robert Motherwell (1974), and Andy Warhol (1975). In 1933, Baron Philippe acquired Château Mouton d'Armailhacq, which he renamed Mouton-Baron-Philippe in 1956. Beginning with the 1975 vintage, the label was changed to Mouton-Baronne-Philippe, in honor of the baron's late wife. Baron Philippe also purchased Château Clerc-Milon in 1970. The firm that sells the wines of Mouton-Rothschild also markets a very successful red, white, and rosé regional Bordeaux called Mouton-Cadet.

Château Latour encompasses little more than modest living quarters, apart from its wine *chais*, although the ancient tower that gives the property its name and appears on its label still stands. Stainless-steel fermentation *cuves* were installed in time for the 1964 vintage (Château Haut-Brion had already been using similar *cuves*), and these innovations by first growths have encouraged other châteaux to adopt more modern methods of winemaking. Since the 1966 vintage, Château Latour has been bottling a second wine, which comes entirely from the Latour vineyards, as Les Forts de Latour. In some abundant years the château markets a third wine, also bottled at the château, labeled simply Pauillac. There are many Bordeaux vineyards that have incorporated the name Latour on their labels, but the one great château of this name is this one, in Pauillac.

Château Pichon-Longueville, a second growth of Pauillac, has long been divided into two parts, one labeled Baron de Pichon-Longueville, the other Comtesse de Lalande. Château Lynch-Bages, another deservedly popular Pauillac, is the property of the Cazes family, who also own Château Les Ormes de Pez in Saint-Estèphe; Château Haut-Bages Averous is the second wine of Lynch-Bages.

Saint-Julien does not have any first growths, but it does have eleven classified châteaux within its borders. Just about all of them are available here, and they are excellent wines. Saint-Julien wines are somewhat softer and more supple than those of Saint-Estèphe and Pauillac, and mature more quickly. The three Léovilles are well-known—Châteaux Léoville Las-Cases, Léoville-Poyferré, and Léoville-Barton. The last, now owned by Anthony Barton, is actually vinified, aged, and bottled in the cellars of his other property, Château Langoa-

Barton, yet the two are always different in style, an example of the role that soil and microclimate play in the taste and quality of neighboring vineyards. Château Beychevelle, whose seventeenth-century manor house is one of the sights of the Médoc, is another famous Saint-Julien. Châteaux Talbot and Gruaud-Larose, owned by Jean Cordier, are both popular with American consumers. The Cordier firm owns Château Meyney in Saint-Estèphe and Château Lafaurie-Peyraguey in Sauternes, and markets the wines of another Médoc property, Château Cantemerle. Many connoisseurs agree that Château Ducru-Beaucaillou, home of Jean-Eugène Borie, produces wines that are consistently among the finest of the Médoc. Chateau Haut-Batailley, in Pauillac, also belongs to the Borie family, who purchased Château Grand-Puy-Lacoste, another Pauillac, in 1978. The popular Château Gloria is the creation of Henri Martin, the long-time mayor of Saint-Julien, who gradually expanded a few acres into an important property. More recently, he reunited the château and vineyards of Château Saint-Pierre, whose first vintage under his direction was in 1982. Château Lagrange was acquired by Suntory of Japan in 1983.

Margaux produces wines noted for their elegance and rich texture: they are often described as suave. Château Margaux, a first growth, is its most famous vineyard, and the fact that it bears the same name as the commune itself has often led to confusion. A blend of wines from various properties within the village can be labeled Margaux. But there is only one Château Margaux, and there could be only a general family resemblance between a regional Margaux and the wine of this outstanding property. At the end of 1976, the Ginestet family sold Château Margaux to André Mentzelopoulos for about sixteen million dollars. (Château Latour was bought by an English group in 1962 for about a million pounds, and in the 1930s another first growth, Château Haut-Brion, was acquired by an American, Clarence Dillon.) After Mentzelopoulos' untimely death in 1980, his widow, Laura Mentzelopoulos, and their daughter, Corinne, took over the management of the property and completely renovated both the handsome nineteenth-century château and the cellars. Guided by Bordeaux enologist Emile Peynaud, the château, whose wines had been disappointing for some years, regained its former status with the 1978 and 1979 vintages. A second label, Pavillon Rouge du Château Margaux, is now used again for those lots that do not merit being bottled as Château Margaux. The estate also produces a distinctive white wine, Pavillon Blanc du Château

Margaux, from twenty-five acres of Sauvignon Blanc. As the Médoc appellation may be used only for red wines, any white wines produced in this region—Caillou Blanc of Château Talbot is another example—must be labeled as Bordeaux Blanc.

There are, in addition to Château Margaux, a number of excellent classed growths in Margaux and in the nearby communes of Cantenac, Labarde, Arsac, and Soussans, whose wines are entitled to be sold as Margaux. Château Palmer, classified as a third growth, now sells for more than any second growth; it is under the direction of Peter Alan Sichel, who lives nearby at Château d'Angludet. Château Prieuré-Lichine, another familiar property, has been expanded, and its wines greatly improved, by its dynamic proprietor, Alexis Lichine, who also revitalized Château Lascombes; the latter was bought by a British firm, Bass-Charrington, in 1971. Château Giscours, purchased in 1952 by the Tari family—who have since acquired Château Branaire-Ducru in Saint Julien—has considerably improved its reputation in recent years. Château Brane Cantenac is the home of Lucien Lurton, who also owns Château Durfort-Vivens. Part of the vineyards of Château Desmirail also belonged to Lurton, and in 1980 he bought the rest of the property and the name from Château Palmer. Lurton is also the proprietor of Château Climens in Sauternes and Château Bouscaut in Graves.

Two classified growths that are not situated within the four main communes of the Médoc are Châteaux La Lagune and Cantemerle. There are also two other Médoc communes, Listrac and Moulis, whose appellations are sometimes seen on château-bottled wines. It was in Listrac that Edmond de Rothschild, the principal shareholder of Lafite-Rothschild, decided to expand his vineyard holdings by buying an abandoned property, Château Clarke, in 1973. More than 350 acres were planted beginning in 1974, and the château produced its first wine in 1978.

Graves

The Graves district (whose name is derived from its gravelly soil) begins just at the city limits of Bordeaux, and its most famous vineyard, Château Haut-Brion, can be reached by a local bus. As a matter of fact, land developers in Bordeaux have already bought up parcels of all but the best vineyards nearest the city and are turning them into housing projects. At one time the red wines of Graves were the most famous of all Bordeaux, but today the district is known mainly for its inexpensive white wines. A regional wine labeled simply Graves or Graves Supérieures will invariably be white, and it's often assumed that Graves makes only white wines; actually, half of its production is red. The red wines are usually sold under their individual château names, and are generally of a much higher class than the whites.

White Graves is usually a dry wine, but some regional bottlings are semidry or even noticeably sweet. Until recently, the relative sweetness of a Graves was rarely indicated on its label, but today dry wines are marketed as Graves, those with some sweetness as Graves Supérieures. In addition, producers throughout Bordeaux have been encouraged to use the traditional clear-glass bottle for slightly sweet white wines, and to use a dark green bottle for dry white Bordeaux. The slightly earthy quality of Graves—and of white Bordeaux in general—plus the mellowness that one frequently encounters have probably prevented the wine from being as popular as, say, Chablis or Pouilly-Fuissé. Furthermore, although it is accepted winemaking practice to stabilize white wines with a bit of sulfur dioxide, nowhere is this more evident than in the bouquet and taste of the cheapest Graves. The château wines are certainly more carefully made, and a number of them are distinctive.

It is the red wines from individual châteaux, however, that are of the most interest, and some of them are among the best wines of France. If they lack the finesse of the best Médocs, they have instead a richer texture and are tremendously appealing clarets. Not only is Château Haut-Brion officially rated on a par with the first growths of the Médoc, but two other red Graves, Château La Mission-Haut-Brion and Domaine de Chevalier, consistently sell for more than any second growth of the Médoc. These three properties are also known for their exceptional white wines, produced in very limited quantities.

Château La Mission-Haut-Brion, situated across the road from Château Haut-Brion, produces a second wine labeled Château La Tour-Haut-Brion. The latter was originally a separate vineyard, but for many years the wines of the two adjoining properties have been vinified together and a selection made after the harvest. Part of the original La Tour-Haut-Brion vineyard was replanted with Sémillon and Sauvignon Blanc, and the white wine is marketed as Château Laville-

Haut-Brion. In November, 1983 the 72-acre domain was acquired by the Dillon family. who have owned the 106-acre Château Haut-Brion since 1935. Both properties are now under the direction of enologist Jean Delmas.

The wines of Graves were classified in 1953 and again in 1959. Different levels of quality were not established, as in the Médoc and Saint-Emilion, and all of these wines are ranked equally as *crus classés*, although Château Haut-Brion is understood to be first among equals. The northern part of Graves is thought to produce the best wines of the district, and, in fact, all of the classed growths are situated there, in and around the communes of Pessac and Léognan. A decree passed in 1984 permits any château situated in this part of Graves to add the term Graves Pessac or Graves Léognan to its label.

Graves is the only important district in Bordeaux where many classified properties make both red and white wines.

GRAVES

Crus Classés—Classified Growths

Red Wines

Château Bouscaut	Château La Tour-Haut-Brion
Château Carbonnieux	Château La Tour-Martillac
Domaine de Chevalier	Château Malartic-Lagravière
Château de Fieuzal	
Château Haut-Bailly	Château Olivier
Château Haut-Brion	Château Pape Clément
Château La Mission-Haut-Brion	Château Smith-Haut-Lafitte

White Wines

Château Bouscaut	Château La Tour-Martillac
Château Carbonnieux	Château Laville-Haut-Brion
Domaine de Chevalier	Château Malartic-Lagravière
Château Couhins	
Château Haut-Brion	Château Olivier

Other good red and white wines from Graves include:

Château Ferrande
Château Larrivet Haut-
   Brion
Château La Garde

Château La Louvière
Château Magence
Château Pontac-Monplaisir
Château Rahoul

Saint-Emilion

The picturesque village of Saint-Emilion is about twenty miles northeast of Bordeaux, and to drive there one must cross both the Dordogne and the Garonne rivers. Saint-Emilion is a medieval village whose winding streets are paved with cobblestones, and one of its main tourist attractions is a monolithic church whose chapel was carved out of a granite hillside a thousand years ago, arches, pillars, and all. The local restaurants feature a dish that visitors are always encouraged to try without necessarily being told what it contains: it is *lamproie,* the local eel, cooked in red wine and one of the few fish dishes that is traditionally served with a red wine. The worldwide fame of Saint-Emilion, however, is its wine. Vineyards begin at the very edge of town and, unlike those of the Médoc and Graves, are to a large extent planted on slopes rather than flatlands. Saint-Emilion produces about two-thirds as much wine as the entire Médoc, but as its vineyards are not subdivided into inner appellations, the name Saint-Emilion is perhaps best-known of all the Bordeaux appellations.

The wines of Saint-Emilion are generally fuller and rounder than those of the Médoc—the result of somewhat richer soil and a greater proportion of Merlot grapes. Merlot produces a wine that is relatively charming and supple compared with those made from Cabernet Sauvignon, the principal grape of the Médoc. The Cabernet Franc, also widely planted in Saint-Emilion (where it is known as the Bouchet), gives structure to the Merlot. It's not that the growers of Saint-Emilion prefer Merlot or deliberately want to produce more supple wines; it's simply that Cabernet Sauvignon is unsuited to most of the soils there—it doesn't ripen well, and often produces wines that are comparatively hard and aggressive. Although Saint-Emilions tend to mature more quickly than the wines of the Médoc and Graves, they very much exhibit the classic qualities of Bordeaux.

The vineyards of Saint-Emilion were classified in 1954, and the rankings were formalized the following year, perhaps to coincide with the centenary of the famous 1855 classification of the Médoc. Twelve châteaux were ranked as *premiers grands crus classés*, with Châteaux Ausone and Cheval Blanc in a category apart. These châteaux account for about 3 percent of all the wines made in Saint-Emilion. Another sixty châteaux were ranked as *grands crus classés*, and in 1969 a dozen more were added to this already generous category. Despite their classed status, very few of these seventy-two châteaux are at the level of the *grands crus classés* of the Médoc and Graves, and fewer than twenty are easily found here.

The classification of Saint-Emilion wines differs from the one for the Médoc in that the former is incorporated into the *Appellation Contrôlée* laws, whereas the 1855 ranking exists apart from the Médoc appellations. The 1855 classification is unlikely ever to change, but the one for Saint-Emilion is supposed to be reviewed every ten years. The list of classed growths was expanded in 1969, as noted, and then in 1985 a new classification was published which reduced the total number of classed growths from eighty-four to seventy-four. Château Beau-Séjour-Bécot (formerly Beauséjour-Fagouët) was demoted from *premier grand cru classé* to *grand cru classé*, and several *grands crus classés* lost their ranking.

There is, in addition, a third category of wines entitled to add *grand cru* to their labels. These châteaux are not permanently classified, but must submit their wines to a tasting panel on an annual basis to qualify for *grand cru* status. Nearly two hundred châteaux earn this distinction in a good vintage, and they account for about a third of the region's production. (There is an important cooperative cellar in Saint-Emilion that produces about 20 percent of the region's wines; some of the cooperative's wines may be labeled with a château name and the *grand cru* designation.)

The two best-known and most expensive châteaux of Saint-Emilion are Ausone and Cheval-Blanc, which are ranked with the first growths of the Médoc. (Despite the official classification, the nine other *premiers grands crus classés* of Saint-Emilion are considered on a par with the second and third growths of the Médoc.) Ausone had suffered a decline in quality for some years, but with the arrival of enologist Pascal Delbeck in 1975, the property—which produces only two thousand cases a year—has regained its former status, as has the adjoining Château Belair, which is owned by the same family.

The vineyards of Saint-Emilion are sometimes divided into two main areas, the Côtes and the Graves. The Côtes, or slopes, area surrounds the town of Saint-Emilion, and includes nine of the twelve *premiers grands crus classés*. The other two châteaux, Cheval-Blanc and Figeac, are situated in the Graves, a gravelly plateau that adjoins Pomerol.

Adjoining Saint-Emilion proper are four small *Appellation Contrôlée* communes to whose names Saint-Emilion has been affixed. They are Montagne-Saint-Emilion, Saint-Georges-Saint-Emilion, Lussac-Saint-Emilion, and Puisseguin-Saint-Emillion, and each contains some châteaux whose wines can equal those of Saint-Emilion.

All of the *premiers grands crus classés* in the revised 1985 classification are listed here, as well as the better-known *grands cru classés*.

SAINT-EMILION

Premiers Grands Crus—First Great Growths

Château Ausone	Clos Fourtet
Château Cheval Blanc	Château Figeac
Château Beauséjour (Duffau-Lagarrosse)	Château La Gaffelière*
	Château Magdelaine
Château Belair	Château Pavie
Château Canon	Château Trottevieille

Grands Crus Classés—Great Classified Growths

Château L'Angélus	Château Grand Barrail Lamarzelle Figeac
Château Balestard-la-Tonnelle	Château Grand-Corbin
Château Beau-Séjour-Bécot	Château Grand Mayne
Château Berliquet	Château Grand-Pontet
Château Cadet-Piola	Clos des Jacobins
Château Canon-La-Gaffelière	Château La Clotte
Château Cap de Mourlin	Château La Dominique
Château Corbin	Château La Marzelle
Château Corbin-Michotte	Château Larcis-Ducasse
Château Couvent des Jacobins	Château Larmande
Château Curé-Bon	Château La Tour Figeac
Château Dassault	Château Pavie-Decesse
Château Fonplégade	
Château Fonroque	

*Formerly Château La Gaffelière-Naudes

Château Pavie-Macquin	Château Trimoulet
Château Ripeau	Château Troplong Mondot
Château Soutard	Château Villemaurine
Château Tertre Daugey	Château Yon-Figeac

Other Saint-Emilion châteaux include the increasingly popular Château Monbousquet, now under the direction of Alain Querre; Château Simard, found on many restaurant wine lists; and:

Château Ferrande	Château Lapelletrie
Château Fombrauge	Château Puy-Blanquet
Château La Grace Dieu	

Pomerol

Pomerol is the smallest of the top wine districts of Bordeaux, and produces only 15 percent as much wine as Saint-Emilion. Pomerol adjoins the Saint-Emilion district, and for many years its wines were grouped with those of its better-known neighbor. About sixty years ago Pomerol was accorded a standing of its own, and its wines now have achieved the reputation they merit. As a matter of fact, a number of Pomerol vineyards consistently sell their wines for more than the second growths of the Médoc.

The vineyards of Pomerol are fairly small, as are those of Saint-Emilion, which partly accounts for their late-flowering reputations both in France and abroad. Vineyards were originally established in these two districts by members of the middle class. In contrast, the great vineyards of the Médoc were established in the early eighteenth century by an aristocratic class that was able to carve out much bigger estates in that undeveloped area. The greater production of the Médoc châteaux and the higher social standing of its owners gave this district a momentum from the very beginning. The Classification of 1855 did not even consider the vineyards of Saint-Emilion and Pomerol, and to this day, their limited production has prevented most of them from being as familiar to claret drinkers as the châteaux of the Médoc.

There is very little regional Pomerol available, as its wines are mostly sold under the names of individual châteaux. Merlot is the principal variety planted in Pomerol, whose wines are rich and full-flavored, with a distinctive earthy or trufflelike quality. The ripe, generous taste of Pomerols often makes them more accessible when young than the firmer, more austere wines of the Médoc, but the finest examples are as long-lived as other top clarets.

The most famous Pomerol vineyard is Château Pétrus, which has become the most expensive red wine of Bordeaux. Its production is relatively small—about four thousand cases a year—and the vineyard is planted almost entirely in Merlot, with only 5 percent of Cabernet Franc. In 1969 the property was enlarged to its present size of twenty-eight acres by the acquisition of ten adjoining acres that belonged to Château Gazin. Jean-Pierre Moueix, the leading *négociant* of Saint-Emilion and Pomerol, has been a co-owner of Pétrus since 1964, and his son Christian has been in charge of making the wines since the early 1970s. Jean-Pierre Moueix also owns Châteaux Trotanoy, La Fleur Pétrus, and Lagrange in Pomerol, and Magdelaine and Fonroque in Saint-Emilion.

No classification has ever been established for Pomerol, but the following list indicates the best, and best-known, of its vineyards. Château Pétrus stands apart, on a level with the first growths of the Médoc. Other highly regarded Pomerol châteaux include Trotanoy, Vieux-Château-Certan, Latour à-Pomerol, La Fleur Pétrus, and La Conseillante.

POMEROL

Château Pétrus

Château Beauregard	Clos L'Eglise
Château Certan-de-May	Domaine de L'Eglise
Château Certan-Giraud	Château L'Eglise-Clinet
Château Clinet	Château L'Enclos
Château Gazin	Château L'Evangile
Château La Conseillante	Château Nénin
Château La Croix	Château Petit-Village
Château La Croix-de-Gay	Clos René
Château Lafleur	Château Rouget
Château La Fleur Pétrus	Château de Sales
Château Lagrange	Château Taillefer
Château La Pointe	Château Trotanoy
Château Latour-Pomerol	Vieux-Château-Certan

Sauternes

The luscious, sweet wines of Sauternes are among the most unusual in the world, and they are produced by a unique and expensive process that can take place only in certain years. The Sauternes district, which is about thirty miles from Bordeaux, is geographically contained within the southern part of Graves. Wines produced in the commune of Barsac are, technically speaking, Sauternes as well, but these wines are entitled to be marketed under their own *Appellation Contrôlée*. Some vineyards use the appellation Barsac, others use Sauternes, and a few use both names on their labels to make the most of the situation.

Although the name Sauternes is used (often without the final *s*) to label inexpensive white wines from other countries that range in taste from mellow to dry, they bear no resemblance to the sweet wines made in Sauternes itself, in a rather special way. When the owners of vineyards producing red wines or dry white wines are already picking their grapes, the critical time has just begun for those who make Sauternes and Barsac, as those proprietors wait for their grapes to be affected by a beneficial mold called *pourriture noble*, or noble rot. (Sémillon is the principal grape variety planted in the Sauternes region; many châteaux also have 10 to 30 percent of Sauvignon Blanc, and a few have a little Muscadelle as well. Sauvignon Blanc, which contributes aroma and finesse, is usually harvested before it is affected by the noble rot.) The morning fog that rises from the Ciron River provides the moisture necessary for the noble rot to appear. As the grapes become covered with the unattractive white mold *Botrytis cinerea*, they gradually shrivel up. And as water evaporates from the grape pulp, there is an increased concentration of sugar and flavor elements in the remaining juice. When the grapes are pressed and the rich juice is fermented, not all of the sugar is transformed into alcohol. The resulting wine is rich and sweet.

Sauternes must contain a minimum of 13 percent alcohol, although 14 or 14.5 percent is not uncommon. The residual sugar often amounts to 7 or 8 percent in a good year, and may be as much as 10 percent in the finest years. But Sauternes is not simply a sweet wine: the noble rot not only increases the proportion of sugar in the grapes, it transforms the flavor of the juice as well. The resulting wine has a more intense aroma, a richer, more complex taste, and a more viscous texture than one that is merely sweet.

Although Sauternes can be made only when the right combination occurs—ripe grapes, alternating humidity and sunshine, and the absence of rain or frost in the fall—the finest Sauternes require even more care and risk. The vineyards must be harvested carefully so that only the fully botrytised, or "rotted," grapes are picked, and the rest are left to continue their transformation by the noble rot. This means not just one picking but several. It also means leaving part of the crop on the vines until late October or mid-November, in the hope that all the grapes will by then have been fully affected by the noble rot. Waiting those extra weeks involves risk, and sending harvesters through a vineyard six or eight times is expensive. In practice, much of the Sauternes region is harvested in only two or three pickings during late September or early October. As a result many wines produced in Sauternes are not much more than agreeable, sweet white wines that lack the intensity and concentration of the best Sauternes. Most important, they lack the distinctive botrytised taste, complex and honeyed, that distinguishes the finest wines, made from shriveled and rotted grapes, from those that are made primarily from ripe grapes only partly affected by *Botrytis cinerea*. Most of the wines from this region are blended and bottled by Bordeaux firms and sold as Sauternes or Barsac (or as Haut-Sauternes or Haut-Barsac, meaningless terms with no legal definition whatsoever). These regional bottlings almost invariably lack the character for which these wines are famous. Many are comparatively thin and weak sweet wines, and are likely to disappoint those who try them hoping to discover the qualities that make Sauternes unique. The finest Sauternes and Barsacs available here are château-bottled wines from about a dozen properties.

Sauternes is not as popular as it was in the last century, and although prices of château-bottled wines have increased in the past few years, these unique wines are still comparatively undervalued. Furthermore, some good château-bottled examples are not much more expensive than regional blends, most of which are lighter-bodied and less intense. At one time it was appropriate to serve a Sauternes or Barsac with a first course of fish, and this practice still exists today in Bordeaux to a limited extent. Although Sauternes is usually served with dessert, some connoisseurs feel that a sweet dessert tends to overwhelm the wine. Many who enjoy the distinctive taste of

Sauternes have discovered that Roquefort cheese is one of the best accompaniments to this wine, since it provides an excellent contrast to the richness of the wine and brings out its qualities, instead of smothering them. Sauternes is not to everyone's taste, but you must not deny yourself the experience of tasting a bottle of this unique wine.

There is one vineyard in Sauternes that is considerably more famous than all of the others, and that is Château d'Yquem. Its wines cost three or four times as much as those of the other châteaux, and its 250 acres constitute one of the most famous vineyards in the world. Yquem first produced a dry wine, labeled Y (and pronounced *ee-grec*), in 1959, and continues to do so in certain years; it is made primarily from Sauvignon Blanc.

Because producing Sauternes is a risky endeavor, a number of other properties now make a dry white wine as well. Château Guiraud produces a dry wine labeled G, Château Rieussec makes R, Château de Malle makes Chevalier de Malle, and Château Coutet produces Vin Sec du Château Coutet, to cite a few examples. Some are made entirely, or primarily, from Sauvignon Blanc; others contain more Sémillon. (Château Doisy-Védrines produced a dry white from Sauvignon Blanc that became so popular that its name, Chevalier Védrines, is now a trademark for both red and white regional wines.) The dry wines are harvested first; thus, if a Sauternes vintage is spoiled, or considerably reduced, by rain in October or November, the proprietors still have wine to sell. Because Sauternes must be sweet, the dry wines made in the region may be labeled only as Bordeaux Blanc.

The wines of Sauternes were classified in 1855 along with those of the Médoc, and many of these château-bottled wines are imported into this country.

THE CLASSIFICATION OF 1855 FOR
SAUTERNES AND BARSAC

Grand Premier Cru—First Great Growth

Château d'Yquem

Premiers Crus—First Growths

Château La Tour-Blanche	Château Coutet
Clos Haut-Peyraguey	Château Climens
Château Lafaurie- Peyraguey	Château Guiraud
	Château Rieussec

| Château de Rayne-Vigneau | Château Rabaud-Promis |
| Château de Suduiraut | Château Sigalas-Rabaud |

Deuxièmes Crus—Second Growths

Château Myrat	Château Nairac
Château Doisy-Daëne	Château Caillou
Château Doisy-Védrines	Château Suau
Château D'Arche	Château de Malle
Château Filhot	Château Romer
Château Broustet	Château Lamothe

BURGUNDY

Burgundy, perhaps the most evocative of all wine names, conveys different impressions to different people. The historian knows Burgundy as an independent duchy that was annexed to France in the late fifteenth century. The decorator associates the name with a deep red color, although Burgundy produces white wines that are among the finest in the world. Many consumers recognize Burgundy as a name used in several countries other than France to label inexpensive red wines, although the province of Burgundy, situated in east-central France, is strictly delimited. And to many wine drinkers Burgundy means wines that are rich and heavy, although many of the finest Burgundies are noted for their delicacy, finesse, and refinement.

All of Burgundy produces about half as much wine as Bordeaux, but most of this comes from Beaujolais and the Mâconnais. Perhaps a more relevant comparison might be between Bordeaux and the heart of Burgundy—the Côte d'Or—which contains such famous wine villages as Gevrey-Chambertin, Nuits-Saint-Georges, Pommard, Beaune, and Puligny-Montrachet. There are less than twenty thousand acres of vines in the Côte d'Or, compared to 190,000 acres in Bordeaux, and the total amount of wine produced in the Côte d'Or is appreciably less than is made in the Médoc district of Bordeaux alone. This is another way of saying that the best wines of Burgundy will always be scarce and expensive.

The vineyards of Burgundy are divided into several main districts: Chablis, to the north; the Côte d'Or, which consists of the Côte de Nuits and the Côte de Beaune; and to the south, the Chalonnais, the Mâconnais (including Pouilly-Fuissé), and the vast Beaujolais district.

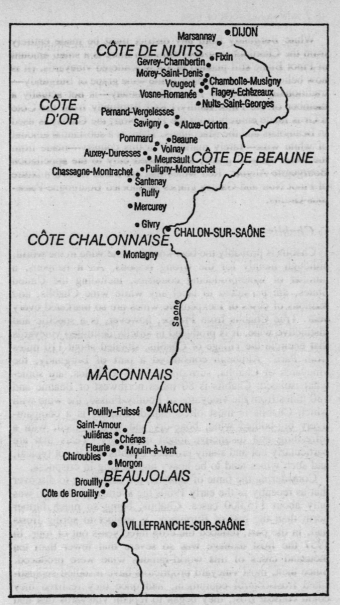

Marsannay • DIJON

CÔTE DE NUITS

Gevrey-Chambertin • Fixin
Morey-Saint-Denis
Vougeot • Chambolle-Musigny
Vosne-Romanée • Flagey-Echèzeaux
• Nuits-Saint-Georges

CÔTE
D'OR

Pernand-Vergelesses
Savigny • Aloxe-Corton

Pommard • Beaune
Volnay
Auxey-Duresses • • CÔTE DE BEAUNE
Meursault
Chassagne-Montrachet • Puligny-Montrachet
• Santenay
• Rully
• Mercurey
• Givry • CHALON-SUR-SAÔNE

CÔTE CHALONNAISE

• Montagny

Saône

MÂCONNAIS

Pouilly-Fuissé • • MÂCON
Saint-Amour
Juliénas • • Chénas
Fleurie • • Moulin-à-Vent
Chiroubles •
• Morgon
Brouilly • BEAUJOLAIS
Côte de Brouilly •

• VILLEFRANCHE-SUR-SAÔNE

BURGUNDY

White Burgundy from any district must be made entirely from the Chardonnay grape, although there is a small amount of Pinot Blanc still planted in a few scattered vineyards. (It is now believed that the famous white wine grape of Burgundy—traditionally called the Pinot Chardonnay—is not actually a member of the Pinot family.) Red Burgundy from the Côte d'Or is made entirely from the Pinot Noir; the Gamay is used in Beaujolais and the Mâconnais. There is a substantial amount of white wine—rarely marketed in this country—made from the lesser Aligoté grape, and entitled only to the appellation Bourgogne Aligoté. Red wines that are made from a mixture of Pinot Noir and Gamay grapes are labeled Bourgogne-Passe-tous-Grains.

Chablis

Chablis is probably the best-known white wine in the world, although mainly for the wrong reasons. As it happens, a number of wine-producing countries, including the United States, are permitted to label any white wine Chablis, and millions of cases of inexpensive wines are so marketed every year. True Chablis from France, however, is a specific and distinctive wine. It is produced in strictly delimited vineyards that encircle the village of Chablis, situated about 110 miles from Paris. Although considered a part of Burgundy, the vineyards of Chablis, surrounded by wheatfields, are somewhat isolated: Chablis is 80 miles northwest of Beaune and 130 miles from the vineyards of Pouilly-Fuissé, the wine with which Chablis is most often linked. Chablis is a comparatively big-bodied wine, bone-dry and well defined, with a refreshing and distinctive touch of acidity. Years that are particularly hot and sunny produce Chablis that is not typical, and such wines tend to be heavy and lacking in crispness.

Considering the fame of Chablis, it's surprising to discover that as recently as the early 1960s the average production was only about 115,000 cases. Chablis, being so much farther north than the rest of Burgundy, is subject to spring frosts that, in the past, reduced the crop three years out of four. In 1957 the frost damage was so severe that fewer than ten thousand cases of this world-famous wine were produced. Since then, most vineyard proprietors have installed sophisticated frost-control equipment, and once they realized they could combat frost, they began to replant vineyards that had been abandoned since the nineteenth century. In 1957 there were fifteen hundred acres of vineyards in Chablis; today more than four thousand acres are planted in vines. The average production now exceeds 900,000 cases, and in an abundant vintage Chablis can produce well over a million cases of wine.

The vineyards of Chablis, which are planted entirely in the Chardonnay grape, produce wines with four different appellations. The principal appellation seen on labels is, of course, Chablis, which accounts for more than half the production. The highest appellation, Chablis *grand cru*, is limited to only seven vineyards: Les Clos, Valmur, Grenouille, Vaudésir, Les Preuses, Bougros, and Blanchot. *Grand cru* Chablis is always expensive, partly because the wine is produced in favored sites, but also because it is scarce. There are only 250 acres of *grand cru* vineyards, and no more can be planted. About thirty individual vineyards are entitled to the appellation Chablis *premier cru*, of which the ones most often seen here are Montée de Tonnerre, Fourchaume, Vaillons, La Forêt, Mont de Milieu, and Vaulorent. It's not necessary for the consumer to remember individual vineyard names, since the words *grand cru* and *premier cru* are always prominently displayed on the label. Petit Chablis is the least interesting of the Chablis appellations, as the wines come from vineyards on the outskirts of the district. These lighter-bodied wines are attractive when young, but few examples retain their appeal much beyond a year. What's more, the price of Petit Chablis in recent years has been almost as high as that of Chablis, so it is not often imported into this country.

Côte d'Or

The Côte d'Or, or Golden Slope, gets its name from the appearance of these hillside vineyards when they have taken on their autumn foliage. The vineyards of the Côte d'Or begin just below Dijon and continue, with a break midway, for about thirty miles down to Chagny. This strip of soil, never more than half a mile wide, produces less than 15 percent of all the wines made in Burgundy, but it is here that are situated the famous villages and vineyards that most people associate with the name Burgundy. The northern half is the Côte de Nuits, and known primarily for its red wines. The Côte de Beaune, to the south, produces more red wine than white but is famous for its superb white wines.

Red Burgundies, which account for about 80 percent of the

wines of the Côte d'Or, are considered easier to enjoy than Bordeaux, as they are softer, fuller, rounder wines. They have a more beguiling bouquet, generally described as more perfumed, and they seem to taste less austerely dry than claret. Unfortunately, many consumers think of red Burgundies as heavy, almost sweet wines, because of the many poor examples that are produced: such wines do not display the elegance and balance of the finest examples. The best white Burgundies have a richness and depth of flavor that justifies their reputation as one of the finest dry white wines in the world.

While good Burgundies may be very appealing to many wine drinkers, they are also considerably more difficult to understand than are the wines of Bordeaux. In the first place, there are more village names to remember in the Côte d'Or than in Bordeaux: fourteen or so that are important, several others that are less frequently encountered and that therefore provide some good values. Apart from these village names and several regional appellations, there are now twenty-nine individual vineyards, officially rated as *grands crus*, which are legally entitled to their own *Appellation Contrôlée*. That is, the name of the vineyard—Chambertin, Montrachet, Musigny—may appear by itself on a label, without the name of the village in which it is situated. In Bordeaux, of course, even the best vineyards bear a commune or district appellation, which makes it considerably easier to place them geographically. Thus, Château Lafite-Rothschild has the *Appellation Contrôlée* Pauillac on its label, and Château Haut-Brion is identified as a Graves.

Not only is it necessary for the intelligent buyer of good Burgundy to know the wine villages and to have some familiarity with the *grands crus*, but one other important factor further complicates the choice of wine. Almost all of the vineyards in Burgundy, which are fairly small to begin with, are owned by several different growers. For example, Montrachet, only nineteen acres in size, has over a dozen owners. The twenty-three acres of Grands-Echézeaux are divided among ten owners; and Clos de Vougeot, whose 125 acres make it the biggest vineyard in Burgundy, has more than eighty owners today. This multiple ownership can be traced back to the French Revolution, when large domains owned by the Church and by members of the nobility were confiscated and sold in small parcels to the local farmers. The laws of inheritance in Burgundy have made these holdings even smaller, whereas in Bordeaux the large châteaux are maintained as corporate entities and have continued intact. Since each grower decides for himself when to replant old vines, how severely to limit his yield per acre, when to harvest, and exactly how to vinify his wines, the result is a number of different wines of different quality from the same vineyard. Two people can discuss the merits of Château Latour 1970, which they enjoyed separately, and be certain they are talking about the same wine. Two people comparing notes on previously consumed bottles of Chambertin 1969 or Volnay Caillerets 1971 must first establish who produced each wine.

There are three important levels of quality in the Côte d'Or: village wines, *premiers crus*, and *grands crus*. This rating system is incorporated into the official *Appellation Contrôlée* laws for Burgundy and was based on historical precedent and careful analysis of each vineyard. There has never been an official classification of the Côte d'Or vineyards similar in status to the 1855 classification for the Médoc, but an attempt was made in 1861. Each of the best vineyards was named a *Tête de Cuvée*, and this traditional distinction is still found on some labels, particularly for those vineyards that did not merit *grand cru* status under the *Appellation Contrôlée* laws. One indication of how difficult it must have been to rate each one of the small Burgundian vineyards is the fact that they are traditionally referred to as *climats*. In other words, it is understood that rain, for example, will affect each plot of land in a different way, depending on the ability of the subsoil to absorb water, that its exact position on a hillside will determine its exposure to the sun, and so forth. Perhaps a modern way of translating *climat* would be "microclimate."

The principal wine villages are shown on the map, and will be discussed in detail. One confusing aspect of some of these villages' names came about in the late nineteenth century when a number of villages appended to their names that of their most famous individual vineyard. Thus Gevrey became Gevrey-Chambertin, Chambolle became Chambolle-Musigny, Nuits changed to Nuits-Saint-Georges, and so on. As the great vineyard of Montrachet is partly situated in both Chassagne and Puligny, both of these villages added its name to their own. Consumers sometimes believe that they have drunk the wine of a specific great vineyard when in fact they have been served a village wine, which can come from vineyards anywhere in the named village. It must be remembered, however, that none of these villages produce a great deal of wine and their names on a label should by no means be thought of as a regional appellation. For example, Saint-Emilion produces twenty times as much wine as does Pommard, and there is a hundred times as much wine made in Beaujolais as in Vosne-Romanée.

The *premier cru* vineyards of the Côte d'Or are not difficult to spot because their names always follow those of their respective villages. Thus, some *premier cru* wines from Volnay are Volnay Caillerets, Volnay Champans, Volnay Clos des Ducs, and so forth. Some *premier cru* wines from other villages include Gevrey-Chambertin, Clos Saint-Jacques; Pommard, Les Rugiens; Chassagne-Montrachet, Clos de la Boudriotte; and so on. Not infrequently you will see the words *premier cru* after a village name, without the name of a specific vineyard, such as Chassagne-Montrachet Premier Cru. This usually indicates that the wine comes from more than one *premier cru* vineyard or that the producer felt that the phrase by itself would make his wine more salable than the name of a specific, but unfamiliar, vineyard.

The highest rating in the Côte d'Or is that of *grand cru*, and the twenty-nine vineyards so classed are listed further on, village by village, along with some of the better-known *premiers crus*. If you recognize the village names, certain *grand cru* vineyards are easy to locate: Chambertin, Musigny, Montrachet, Romanée-Saint-Vivant, for example. Other *grand cru* names, however, bear no relation to that of their village of origin, and only homework will lead to familiarity: for example, Clos de la Roche, Richebourg, Bonnes Mares. *Grand cru* wines account for perhaps 5 percent of all the wines of the Côte de Nuits and Côte de Beaune, and they are always expensive. They are also among the greatest red and white wines in the world, and their study will be repaid by their excellence.

A grower in Burgundy does not produce a single wine, as does a Bordeaux château. He deliberately has vines in several vineyards, and often in two or three adjoining villages, so that he is protected to some extent from the hailstorms and frosts that occasionally occur and that often affect only a very small area at a time. Of course, another factor leading to scattered holdings is that domains in Burgundy are built up slowly as money is accumulated and vines become availabe for sale.

A visitor to a Bordeaux château will be taken on a tour of the *chai*, see hundreds of barrels of new wine aging in spacious surroundings, and then be offered a glass of one or perhaps two vintages currently in wood. Visiting a cellar in Burgundy means crowding in among barrels, called *pièces*, piled two or three high, and tasting will include as many as a dozen different wines from different villages and vineyards. A famous Bordeaux château may produce fifteen thousand to thirty thousand cases of a single wine in a year. A Burgundian grower whose domain is big enough to justify bottling his own wines at the property may produce only five hundred to one thousand cases each of several different wines. His share of a *grand cru* vineyard may only be big enough to produce four barrels, or one hundred cases, a year. A domain that produces four or five thousand cases is considered quite large in the Côte d'Or.

It is evident, then, that whereas in Bordeaux a knowledge of the main districts and of a few major châteaux will get you off to a good start, knowing Burgundy is a bit more time-consuming. You must know the villages and at least a few *grand cru* vineyards, and then pay strict attention to the name of the shipper or grower whose wine you are drinking.

The relative merits of wines blended and bottled by shippers and those estate-bottled by individual growers is a subject that often provokes discussion among Burgundy drinkers. Most growers in Burgundy sell their wines in barrel to the big shipping firms, who blend together wines from each appellation to make what they hope will be a consistently dependable Beaune, Pommard, Nuits-Saint-Georges, and so on. A number of growers have traditionally preferred to bottle their wines themselves, as do the châteaux of Bordeaux. Such wines bear the words *mis en bouteille au domaine, mis au domaine*, or *mis en bouteille à la propriété*, and these estate-bottled wines are the Burgundian equivalent of the château-bottled wines of Bordeaux. The phrase *mis en bouteille dans nos caves*, ''bottled in our cellars,'' is often used by shippers and does not signify estate-bottling.

Those who prefer estate-bottled Burgundies suggest that the wines of each shipper tend to have a family resemblance that cuts across the individual appellations. Each shipper has certain ideas about what a good Burgundy should taste like and tries to maintain his standards and his style, sometimes at the expense of the particular characteristics of a village or vineyard. By comparison, the best of the growers produce wines that have more individuality and that define more clearly the style of each appellation. In reply, a shipper might point out that he is a specialist in the aging and bottling of fine wines, and that his judgment and experience in these matters are more reliable than that of many growers, especially those who have only recently decided to estate-bottle their wines. Furthermore, a shipper who buys from a great many growers is likely to have more perspective on the style of each appellation and greater flexibility in blending wines to a consistent style than a grower whose production and concerns are limited to wines from his own vineyards. Unfortunately, many estate-bottled wines today are of inferior quality, just as many shippers' wines are undistinguished and lack definition. Perhaps the most important element in this controversy is the reputation of the firm or person whose name is on the label. There are several dozen individual growers whose wines are recognized as outstanding examples of Burgundy, and a number of serious shippers who produce a wide range of excellent Burgundies. The controversy is somewhat complicated by the fact that a number of Burgundy shippers are themselves owners of substantial domains—sixty to two hundred acres—along the Côte d'Or, among them Bouchard Père & Fils, Chanson, Joseph Drouhin, Louis Jadot, and Louis Latour.

There is another controversial issue concerning the style and quality of fine Burgundy. Many people who enjoy red Burgundies feel that the overall style of these wines has been gradually transformed over the past twenty years or so by what is often referred to as the new vinification. According to this view, the longer vatting practiced years ago to produce deep-colored, tannic, and long-lived red Burgundies has given way to shorter vatting and lighter wines that are sooner ready to drink, but often lack intensity and flavor. It is undoubtedly true that some Burgundian winemakers have responded to the demand from many wine drinkers for red wines that can be consumed within a few years of the vintage, but it is also true that many shippers and growers continue to make long-lived wines in more traditional ways. As it happens, a number of Burgundian producers believe that the most significant factor affecting the quality of Burgundy has been that of overproduction, not vinification. As the demand for red and white Burgundies has intensified, many growers have increased their production per acre, which usually results in weak, light wines without much character or depth. Although *Appellation Contrôlée* laws for Burgundy limit the amount of wine that can be produced for each appellation, the old system of declassification permitted growers to market their excess production easily. For example, a grower who owned vines in the *grand cru* vineyard of Chambertin was not permitted to produce more than thirty hectoliters per hectare, which is about 133 cases per acre. (A hectoliter equals about eleven cases of wine, a hectare 2.47 acres.) However, if his production in a given vintage was greater than thirty hectoliters, he could simply declassify the excess and sell it with the village appellation Gevrey-Chambertin, whose limits were fixed at thirty-five hectoliters per hectare. Any excess beyond that could be further declassified and sold as Bourgogne Rouge, as the limits for that regional appellation were fifty hectoliters. In other words, a proprietor who owned a hectare in Chambertin could produce as much as fifty hectoliters and expect to sell all of it with one appellation or another. The *cascade des appellations*, as the declassification system was often referred to, meant that, in this example, the same barrel of wine was entitled to be sold under any one of three different appellations. Although growers who bottled their own wines may have had the incentive to produce a smaller quantity of finer wine, those who sold off their wine in barrel to local shippers had little reason to deprive themselves of additional income.

New legislation adopted in 1974 did away with the concept of declassification. Before each harvest, a committee of growers and legislators estimates the production for each village and *grand cru* vineyard appellation based on that year's growing conditions. After the harvest the estimates are confirmed and a maximum yield limit is established that also takes into account the quality of the vintage. The wine from each plot is then entitled to only one appellation. That is, a grower in Chambertin can declare his wine as Chambertin or Gevrey-Chambertin, but not as both; a grower in Gevrey-Chambertin can declare his wine as such or as Bourgogne Rouge, but not as both. A grower is permitted a leeway of 20 percent above the base limits established for that year, but the additional 20 percent is entitled to the appellation only if a sample of the wine is approved by a tasting panel. If a grower exceeds even the 20-percent allowance, then none of his wine is entitled to the appellation. Many observers feel that this new law, which effectively ended the *cascade des appellations*, has encouraged growers in the Côte d'Or to limit their production. Winemakers can still choose to vinify their red wines in a lighter style rather than a tannic one, but the washed-out and insipid red and white wines that resulted from overproduction in recent years may eventually be replaced by wines with more flavor and complexity. The new law also means that the practice of declassification no longer exists. In the past, it was a common practice for a retailer to advertise that a particular Bourgogne Blanc, for example, was really a declassified Meursault from a grower who overproduced, or that a Gevrey-Chambertin was really a declassified Chambertin. Anyone who makes such a claim today about a Burgundy is, at the very least, misinformed.

What follows is a closer look at the individual wine villages of the Côte d'Or, starting with the Côte de Nuits. With a few exceptions, all the wines of the Côte de Nuits are red; the limited amount of white wine produced in Chambolle-Musigny, Morey-Saint-Denis, Nuits-Saint-Georges, and Vougeot rarely exceeds fifteen hundred cases altogether.

Just below Dijon is the little village of Marsannay, whose wines are sometimes seen over here, especially the delightful Bourgogne Rosé de Marsannay (from the Pinot Noir grape) and the Pinot Noir de Marsannay.

Fixin, pronounced by its inhabitants as *fee-san*, produces less than a tenth as much wine as Nuits-Saint-Georges or Pommard, but good wines from its best vineyards can occasionally be found here.

The next village is world-famous: Gevrey-Chambertin. Its two principal vineyards, Chambertin and Chambertin-Clos de Bèze, sit side by side and extend for about seventy acres. Vines were planted in Gevrey by the abbey of Bèze as early as the seventh century, and its wines soon achieved a high reputation. In the thirteenth century, the story goes, a farmer named Bertin planted vines in the adjacent field, which was known as *champ de Bertin*, or Bertin's field. Although these two vineyards are now known for their outstanding red wines, it's interesting to note that at one time there was also a white Chambertin, an early example of trial and error. Most of the proprietors of one vineyard own vines in the other, so it's hard to distinguish between the two plots. Moreover, whereas Chambertin can only be labeled as such, wines from Chambertin-Clos de Bèze can also be sold as Chambertin.

There are, in addition to these two vineyards, seven other vineyards of *grand cru* stature bearing the name Chambertin, including Chapelle-Chambertin, Charmes-Chambertin, Latricières-Chambertin, Ruchottes-Chambertin, Mazys-Chambertin, Mazoyères-Chambertin, and Griotte-Chambertin. Mazoyères-Chambertin is no longer seen on labels because its wines may be sold as Charmes-Chambertin. The two great vineyards produce about ten thousand cases a year, the other seven together about twenty thousand cases. Gevrey-Chambertin produces more wine than any other village in the Côte d'Or, and the best of them are the biggest-bodied of all Burgundies.

The village of Morey-Saint-Denis lies between the considerably more famous ones of Gevrey-Chambertin and Chambolle-Musigny. Its name is not often seen on wine labels here partly because many of its growers, who own vines in the adjoining towns, market their wines under the name of those better-known villages; and also because a quarter of the wine produced in Morey comes from *grand cru* vineyards and is sold without reference to the village. These vineyards are Clos de la Roche, Clos Saint-Denis, Clos de Tart, and a small part of Bonnes Mares; the twenty-one acre Clos des Lambrays has been entitled to *grand cru* status since 1981; Clos de la Roche is by far the biggest vineyard; Clos de Tart and Clos des Lambrays are among the few top vineyards in Burgundy under single ownership.

Chambolle-Musigny is known for its elegant and distinguished wines, and its two *grand cru* vineyards, Musigny and most of Bonnes Mares, are in the top rank of all Burgundies. A very small amount of white wine, Musigny Blanc, is also produced in that vineyard by the Comte de Vogüé.

The little hamlet of Vougeot produces some attractive red wines sold as such, but its fame is derived from its single great vineyard, Clos de Vougeot. First planted in vines by the Cistercian monks in the twelfth century, its 125 acres have been maintained as a single vineyard throughout the centuries. The vineyard is so extensive, however, that some parcels are much better situated than others. Moreover, there are so many proprietors who own vines in this vineyard—some of them producing only one or two barrels a year—that quality varies considerably from bottle to bottle. The Clos de Vougeot itself is now the headquarters of the Chevaliers du Tastevin, an organization founded in the 1930s to promote the wines of Burgundy, and the large hall is frequently the scene of convivial dinners. A white wine from Vougeot, Clos Blanc de Vougeot, is produced in limited quantities.

Flagey-Echézeaux does not have its own village appellation because its wines can be sold as Vosne-Romanée, but it does contain two *grand cru* vineyards. Grands-Echézeaux, which adjoins Clos de Vougeot, is divided among several proprietors. Wines from the eleven vineyards entitled to the Echézeaux appellation can also be sold as Vosne-Romanée Premier Cru. The production of Echézeaux is about four times that of Grands-Echézeaux.

Vosne-Romanée produces village wines of a very high level, and its best vineyards are among the most famous and most expensive in the world. The village includes the four-and-a-half-acre vineyard of Romanée-Conti, the most expensive of all Burgundies, whose total production never exceeds eight hundred cases. The property is owned by the Domaine de la Romanée-Conti, which also owns all fifteen acres of La Tâche and parts of Richebourg, Grands-Echézeaux, Echézeaux, and Montrachet—fifty acres in all. The Domaine also makes and markets the wine from that part of the Romanée-Saint-Vivant vineyard originally owned by General Marey-Monge. A three-acre vineyard that does not have official *grand cru* status but that is on a par with the best of Burgundy is La Grande Rue, situated between Romanée-Conti and La Tâche. The *grand cru* wines of Vosne-Romanée are all expensive, but a number of *premiers crus* produce excellent wines as well.

Nuits-Saints-Georges, with its five thousand inhabitants, is the biggest village in the Côte de Nuits, and its wines are among the best-known of all Burgundies. Nuits-Saint-Georges and Gevrey-Chambertin produce between them about half the wines of the Côte de Nuits sold with village appellations, but this is not nearly enough to satisfy world demand. The wines of Prémeaux, which adjoins Nuits-Saint-Georges, can be marketed as Nuits-Saint-Georges. Its best-known vineyard is Clos de la Maréchale.

The appellation Côte de Nuits-Villages is a regional one for the whole district, and such wines come from the less important towns of the Côte de Nuits, such as Corgoloin, Comblanchien, and Brochon, not from Nuits-Saint-Georges itself. The lesser appellation Bourgogne-Hautes Côtes de Nuits applies to wines produced in the hills behind the Côtes de Nuits.

At this point, the Golden Slope disappears for a few miles, and when it reappears it becomes the Côte de Beaune. The first important village is Aloxe-Corton, dominated by the impressive hill of Corton, on whose slopes lie the best vineyards. Aloxe-Corton (locally pronounced *ah-loss*) makes some very agreeable red wines, but the best of its wines are labeled Corton, often with a supplementary plot name. In other words, Aloxe-Corton is a village appellation, and its *grand cru*, logically enough, is Corton, but there are several vineyards on the hill of Corton, such as Corton Clos du Roi, Corton Bressandes, Corton Renardes, and Corton Maréchaudes, whose *grand cru* wines can be sold either with the specific vineyard designation or simply as Corton.

Until now, all of the wines discussed have been red, but in Aloxe-Corton we encounter the first of the important white-wine vineyards, Corton-Charlemagne. In the Côte de Beaune the only *grand cru* vineyard producing red wines is Corton; all the others produce white wines. Corton-Charlemagne bears testimony to the influence of the Emperor Charlemagne, who owned vineyards in Burgundy in the eighth century. At its best, it is a superlative wine of great power and breed. The vineyard actually produces more wine than any other *grand cru* except Clos de Vougeot and Corton. The best-known of Corton-Charlemagne's several owners is the firm of Louis Latour, which also markets red wines from their holdings in Corton under the proprietary name Château Corton Grancey. The wines from most of the Corton-Charlemagne vineyards can also be sold simply as Charlemagne, but this *grand cru* appellation is very rarely used.

Pernand-Vergelesses lies behind Aloxe-Corton, and adjoins it: Île-des-Vergelesses is its best vineyard. Savigny-les-Beaune is one of the biggest wine-producing villages of the entire slope, and almost all of its wines are red. Being less familiar, this excellent wine is usually less expensive than those of its more illustrious neighbors.

Beaune is not only the center of the Côte de Beaune, but of Burgundy itself. It is the biggest town of all, and most of the shippers have their offices here. Beaune is also the scene of one of the world's most famous wine events. Every year, on the third Sunday in November, the wines of the Hospices de Beaune are auctioned off, and buyers from several countries arrive to participate in the auction and in the general festivity that prevails for three days.

The Hospices de Beaune is a charitable hospital built in the fifteenth century by Nicolas Rolin and his wife, Guigone de Salins. Over the years vineyard parcels have been bequeathed to the Hospices, and the money obtained from the sale by auction of their wine is used to support the institution. The wines are generally considered to be overpriced, but the sums they fetch often affect the general price levels of the year's crop throughout the Côte d'Or.

The Hospices de Beaune now owns about 135 acres in several villages, and produces about fifteen thousand cases a year. The wines are auctioned in lots identified for the most part by the name of a benefactor (who is not necessarily the donor of the particular parcel named in his honor) rather than that of an individual vineyard. One cannot simply refer to a bottle of Hospices de Beaune wine, but must properly identify it with the village and the specific parcel, or *cuvée* among the thirty-odd that make up the Hospices' holdings. What's more, the wines are aged and bottled by the buyer, not by the Hospices, so that if the many barrels that make up a particular *cuvée* are auctioned off to several buyers, as is usually the case, there will be variations among the different bottlings of that *cuvée*. Among the most famous red ones are Beaune, *Cuvée* Nicolas Rolin; Beaune, *Cuvée* Guigone de Salins; Corton, *Cuvée* Docteur Peste; and Pommard, *Cuvée* Dames de la Charité. The Hospices' white wines are almost all from Meursault and include Meursault-Charmes, *Cuvée* Albert Grivault, and Meursault Genevrières, *Cuvée* Baudot.

Beaune is one of the three or four largest wine-producing villages along the Côte d'Or, and virtually all of its wines are red. Perhaps the best-known of its white wines is Beaune Clos des Mouches of Joseph Drouhin. A wine labeled Côte de Beaune-Villages, often a good value, does not come from Beaune, but from any one of sixteen other villages, including such unfamiliar ones as Saint-Aubin, Saint-Romain, and Chorey-les-Beaune. Bourgogne-Hautes Côtes de Beaune is an appellation used for wines produced in the hills behind the Côte de Beaune.

Pommard is probably the most famous name in Burgundy, and there can be no doubt, unfortunately, that some of the red wine sold as Pommard doesn't even bear a nodding acquaintance with the village itself. Good examples display a distinctive *terroir*, or undertaste, that characterizes the wines from this village. Although there are no *grands crus* in Pommard, most experts agree that the *têtes de cuvées* of the 1861 classification, Rugiens and Epenots, deserve the same status today.

Volnay, despite its simple name, has not achieved the same popularity in this country as Pommard and Nuits-Saints-Georges. Its elegant red wines, at best, display a delicacy and finesse that belie the popular misconception of Burgundy as a heavy wine.

Meursault is the first of the white-wine villages. Its vineyards along with those of Chassagne-Montrachet and Puligny-Montrachet, produce almost all of the greatest white wines of Burgundy. Meursault actually produces as much white wine as the other two villages combined, and its wines are characterized by a certain texture and tangy dryness that set them apart. Although there are no *grand cru* vineyards in this village, Perrières, Charmes, and Genevrières are considered its best sites. Some red wine is produced in Meursault, notably Meursault-Blagny. Part of the Santenots vineyard is also planted in Pinot Noir: the whites are sold as Meursault-Santenots, the reds as Volnay-Santenots.

Set back from the main highway are the two villages of Monthélie and Auxey-Duresses. Monthélie produces red wines with the lightness of its neighbor, Volnay. Auxey-Duresses makes both red and white wines, and both are very agreeable. Wines from less-commercialized villages such as these are worth looking for.

Chassagne-Montrachet is famous for its white wines, but in fact more than half of its production is red. The white wines of Chassagne are, of course, outstanding, and within the village are parts of two great vineyards, Montrachet and Bâtard-Montrachet, as well as all four acres of Criots-Bâtard-Montrachet.

Puligny-Montrachet makes white wines only and of a very high quality. The rest of Montrachet and Bâtard-Montrachet are situated within its borders, as well as all of Chevalier-Montrachet and Bienvenue-Bâtard-Montrachet.

Montrachet, whose production usually varies between three and four thousand cases a year, is considered to be the best vineyard in the world for dry white wines, and it can indeed produce superlative wines. It's also true that not all of its several owners are equally conscientious, and the high price that Montrachet commands is often due as much to its fame and scarcity as to the quality of its wine. The adjoining *grand cru* vineyards should not be overlooked, nor should the many excellent village and *premier cru* wines of Chassagne-Montrachet and Puligny-Montrachet from good sources.

Santenay is the southernmost village of note in the Côte de Beaune, and its agreeable wines, almost all red, are well worth trying.

Village	Grands Crus	Premiers Crus
	CÔTE DE NUITS: *Red Wines*	
Fixin		Clos de la Perrière
		Clos du Chapitre
		Les Hervelets
		Les Arvelets

Village	Grands Crus	Premiers Crus
Gevrey-Chambertin	Chambertin	Clos Saint-Jacques
	Chambertin-Clos de Bèze	Varoilles
		Les Cazetiers
	Latricières-Chambertin	Combe-au-Moine
	Mazys-Chambertin	
	Ruchottes-Chambertin	
	Chapelle-Chambertin	
	Charmes-Chambertin	
	Griotte-Chambertin	
Morey-Saint-Denis	Clos de Tart	Clos Bussière
	Clos Saint-Denis	
	Clos de la Roche	
	Clos des Lambrays	
	Bonnes Mares (part)	
Chambolle-Musigny	Musigny	Les Amoureuses
	Bonnes Mares (part)	Les Charmes
Vougeot	Clos de Vougeot	
Flagey-Echézeaux	Grands-Echézeaux	
	Echézeaux	
Vosne-Romanée	Romanée-Conti	La Grande Rue
	La Romanée	Les Gaudichots
	La Tâche	Les Beaumonts
	Richebourg	Les Malconsorts
	Romanée-Saint-Vivant	Les Suchots
		Clos des Réas
Nuits-Saint-Georges (including Prémeaux)		Les Saint-Georges
		Les Vaucrains
		Les Cailles
		Les Pruliers
		Les Porrets
		Aux Boudots
		La Richemone
		Clos de la Maréchale
		Clos des Corvées
		Aux Perdrix

CÔTE DE BEAUNE: *Red Wines*

Village	Grands Crus	Premiers Crus
Aloxe-Corton	Le Corton (includes Clos du Roi, Bressandes, Renardes, etc.)	Les Chaillots Les Meix
Pernand-Vergelesses		Ile des Vergelesses
Savigny-les-Beaune		Les Vergelesses Les Marconnets La Dominode Les Jarrons Les Lavières
Beaune		Les Grèves Les Fèves Les Marconnets Les Bressandes Les Clos des Mouches Les Cent Vignes Clos du Roi Les Avaux
Pommard		Les Epenots Les Rugiens Le Clos Blanc La Platière Les Pézerolles Les Chaponnières
Volnay		Clos des Ducs Les Caillerets Les Champans Les Fremiets Santenots Le Clos des Chênes
Monthélie		Les Champs Fuillots
Auxey-Duresses		Les Duresses Clos du Val

Chassagne-Montrachet	Clos Saint-Jean
	Clos de la Boudriotte
	Morgeot
	La Maltroie
	Les Caillerets
Santenay	Gravières
	Clos Tavannes

CÔTE DE BEAUNE: *White Wines*

Village	*Grands Crus*	*Premiers Crus*
Aloxe-Corton	Corton-Charlemagne	
Beaune		Les Clos des Mouches
Meursault		Les Perrières
		Les Genevrières
		La Goutte d'Or
		Charmes
		Santenots
		Blagny
		Poruzot
Puligny-Montrachet	Montrachet (part)	Les Combettes
	Bâtard-Montrachet (part)	Le Champ Canet
		Les Caillerets
	Chevalier-Montrachet	Les Pucelles
	Bienvenue-Bâtard-Montrachet	Les Chalumeaux
		Les Folatières
		Clavoillon
		Les Referts
Chassagne-Montrachet	Montrachet (part)	Les Ruchottes
	Bâtard-Montrachet (part)	Morgeot
		Les Caillerets
	Criots-Bâtard-Montrachet	Les Chenevottes

Southern Burgundy

Southern Burgundy is made up of three districts, the Chalonnais, the Mâconnais, and Beaujolais. Beaujolais is well known for its red wines, and the Mâconnais contains the inner appellation of Pouilly-Fuissé, but the Chalonnais wines are not established in world markets, despite their resemblance and proximity to the famous wines of Burgundy. The two most interesting villages in the Chalonnais, which takes its name from the city of Chalon-sur-Saône, are Givry and Mercurey, noted primarily for their red wines, although both produce some white wines as well. Made from the Pinot Noir, and governed by *Appellation Contrôlée* laws very similar to those in effect in the Côte d'Or, the red wines are, not surprisingly, quite similar to those of the Côte de Beaune. The best examples are good, well balanced, and often as attractive as wines from better-known villages of the Côte d'Or. The best-known proprietors in Mercurey are the Burgundy shipping firm of Bouchard Aîné & Fils and Faiveley, who owns Clos des Myglands. Givry doesn't produce very much wine, but Mercurey makes more red wine than does Gevrey-Chambertin or Pommard. The village of Montagny produces only white wine; Rully produces red and white wine in about equal quantities.

The Mâcon district produces red and white wine as well as some rosé, and the wines have long been available here. The red, made from the Gamay, lacks the style of the best wines of Beaujolais. The whites, from the Chardonnay, are generally better wines, and have become a popular alternative to the more expensive white Burgundies of the Côte de Beaune. In recent years some shippers have been marketing the white wines of Mâcon by its varietal name—Chardonnay—in imitation of the approach used by California wineries. Most of the wines of Mâcon are produced by cooperative cellars, the best-known of which are Lugny, Viré, and Prissé.

The most famous wine of the Mâconnais is Pouilly-Fuissé. The appellation is limited to wines coming from the four hamlets of Solutré-Pouilly, Fuissé, Chaintré, and Vergisson. Although this wine is extremely popular and often found on restaurant wine lists, there is actually not much of it made. An abundant year will produce perhaps 400,000 cases, and many vintages produce considerably less. As a result of continually increasing demand, especially from consumers in the United States, this wine, which is really not much more than a good Mâcon Blanc, now costs almost as much as wines from the villages of Meursault, Chassagne-Montrachet.

Close to the four communes of Pouilly-Fuissé are those of Loché and Vinzelles, which produce about one-tenth as much wine. They are marketed as Pouilly-Loché and Pouilly-Vinzelles, and are similar in style to those of Pouilly-Fuissé.

Saint-Véran, a new appellation that went into effect with the 1971 vintage, comes from several communes that were formerly entitled to the appellation Beaujolais Blanc and Mâcon Blanc. Production is about half that of Pouilly-Fuissé.

BEAUJOLAIS

Beaujolais is one of the best-known of all red wines, and deservedly so, as the best of them are among the most enjoyable wines produced anywhere. Many people think that all Beaujolais is alike and are willing to settle for the cheapest example when they are looking for a pleasant red wine. Compared to the best wines of Bordeaux and the Côte d'Or, those of Beaujolais are not as exciting, as scarce, or as difficult to understand, but there is actually quite a variation in price, quality, and taste available from this extensive district in southern Burgundy. Poor examples lack the charm and distinctive flavor that makes Beaujolais almost unique among red wines, and bottles of this popular wine should be chosen with some attention.

The Beaujolais district begins near Mâcon (about sixty miles south of Beaune) and stretches down to the outskirts of Lyons, forty-five miles farther south. The vineyard district stretches about ten miles across, along the western bank of the Saône River. The region takes its name from the village of Beaujeu, originally a barony established more than a thousand years ago. Beaujeau is no longer an important town, and the center of the Beaujolais wine trade now is Villefranche, which lies about halfway between Mâcon and Lyons. The hills and valleys of Beaujolais make up one of the most picturesque and agreeable vineyard districts in France, and the landscape has charmed many tourists who have come to the area in search of Roman ruins or to visit the remains of the monastery of Cluny with its gigantic twelfth-century church.

In an abundant vintage, the Beaujolais district produces more than twelve million cases of wine. (A certain amount of agreeable white and rosé wines are also produced, but 99 percent of Beaujolais is red.) Beaujolais is made from the Gamay grape. Although this variety is scorned in the vineyards of the Côte d'Or, the Gamay comes into its own in the granitic soil of southern Burgundy and produces wines much more charming and agreeable than would be produced from the Pinot Noir. The wines of Beaujolais are at their best when consumed young, before they are two years old, and the wines are vinified with this in mind. Vatting is limited to three days or less so that a minimum of tannin is imparted to the wine. The wines are then bottled—and often consumed— within six months of the vintage, so that they retain the freshness and fruit that make Beaujolais so agreeable.

For many years bistros in Paris and Lyons have featured Beaujolais *nouveau* or *primeur* (the names are interchangeable), which are specially selected light and delicate wines that can be released for sale as early as mid-November, just weeks after the harvest. In the past ten years or so, these fresh and charming wines have become popular in England and the United States as well, and it is no longer unusual to find new Beaujolais on sale here in late November. In fact, the popularity of this wine is such that in some years as much as one third of the entire crop is sold as *nouveau* or *primeur*. These wines are not meant to last, and are best consumed before Christmas. (*Beaujolais de l'année* is used informally to refer to wine from the most recent vintage.) New Beaujolais accounts for a limited proportion of the wines shipped here, which are rarely quite as delicate, since light-bodied wines don't keep very well. Wines chosen to be bottled for export are generally fuller-flavored and sturdier, although the best examples will naturally display the grace and charm typical of Beaujolais.

The Beaujolais district can be divided into three parts: Beaujolais, Beaujolais-Villages, and the nine *crus* of Beaujolais. The southern portion produces somewhat lighter wines entitled to call themselves simply Beaujolais. The appellation Beaujolais Supérieur differs from Beaujolais only in that this wine requires an extra degree of alcohol and production per acre is slightly less. Actually, most of the wine sold by its producers as Beaujolais could equally well be sold as Beaujolais Supérieur, yet very little is so declared, because it is really the same sort of wine. What this means to the consumer is that there is essentially no difference in quality between wines labeled Beaujolais and Beaujolais Supérieur.

The next step up the ladder of *Appellation Contrôlée* laws for the Beaujolais district is Beaujolais-Villages. Wines so labeled come from about thirty-five towns in the center of the region, whose vineyards consistently produce better wines than those farther south. Occasionally, the actual village name will appear on the label, but as these are not at all known here, the wines are usually labeled simply Beaujolais-Villages.

About 25 percent of all Beaujolais is entitled to be called Beaujolais-Villages.

The finest of all Beaujolais comes from nine communes, or crus, in the northernmost part of the region: Moulin-à-Vent, Fleurie, Brouilly, Côte de Brouilly, Morgon, Saint-Amour, Chénas, Juliénas, and Chiroubles. These communes produce the wines with the most distinction, they are longer-lived, and the price is somewhat higher than for a simple Beaujolais. As these wines are often labeled with only the name of the cru, without the word Beaujolais, it pays to remember their names if you are looking for something special from the district. Each wine has its special characteristics and its devotees, and these crus are among the most agreeable wines found anywhere.

The Beaujolais crus account for about one-quarter of all Beaujolais in an average year, and of the nine crus, Brouilly, Morgon, Moulin-à-Vent, and Fleurie alone produce about two-thirds of the total. Moulin-à-Vent is usually the most expensive, as its wines are considered the sturdiest and longest-lived. Although Moulin-à-Vent doesn't have the power or depth of a wine from the Côte de Nuits, it does have considerably more character than the typical Beaujolais and can be served with more robust foods.

Fleurie and Brouilly produce lighter and more elegant wines, with an enchanting perfumed bouquet. Although it might be imagined that Côte de Brouilly is a lesser appellation than Brouilly (as is the case with Beaune and Côte de Beaune), the opposite is in fact the case. Côte de Brouilly is an inner appellation reserved for vineyards on the slopes of Mont Brouilly. Morgon produces a very sturdy wine that needs some bottle age before it's ready to drink. Although the crop is comparatively large, the wine is not often seen in this country.

Juliénas and Chénas both have a rather distinctive goût de terroir, or taste of the soil, that sets them apart from their neighbors. Juliénas can be found here, but most of the production of Chénas is legally sold as Moulin-à-Vent. The wines of Saint-Amour, despite its romantic name, are not often exported to the United States, but those of Chiroubles, which are generally more attractive and distinctive, are becoming popular here.

Beaujolais is made by thousands of small producers, most of whom sell their wine to local shippers. About one-third of all the Beaujolais produced, from the simplest wines to the best crus, come from the eighteen cooperative cellars in the region. Occasionally, the name of a particular vineyard appears on a Beaujolais label—and some of these are quite good—but Beaujolais is a region where individual vineyards are not nearly as important a guide to quality as in Bordeaux or Burgundy, for example. Georges Duboeuf is the leading shipper of the region; good examples are also produced by Paul Beaudet and Mommessin, and by such Burgundy shippers as Louis Jadot, Louis Latour, and Joseph Drouhin.

In sum, the wines of Beaujolais vary from rather light and fragile wines to the richer and fuller wines of some of the *crus*. There is naturally a tremendous choice, but it is a sad fact that there is much more Beaujolais drunk than is produced in the vineyards themselves. A cheap Beaujolais will rarely have the delightful characteristics of a true Beaujolais, and a Beaujolais or Beaujolais-Villages that is much more than a year old will almost always have lost most of its fruit and charm. As it happens, if you shop around you can often find a wine from one of the *crus* for only a little more money than one labeled simply Beaujolais or Beaujolais-Villages, and the differences in quality can be considerable. Beaujolais tastes best at cellar temperature (55° to 60° F), and you might try putting a bottle in the refrigerator for thirty or forty minutes to cool it down. The wine tastes all the fresher and seems more delightful.

THE RHÔNE VALLEY

The Rhône River joins the Saône at Lyons and continues south, reaching the sea near Marseilles. The wines of the Côtes du Rhône come from vineyards planted on both banks of the Rhône, starting about twenty miles south of Lyons at Vienne and continuing 120 miles to Avignon. About 95 percent of Rhône wines are red, but the region includes a famous rosé—Tavel—and some unusual white wines.

The hot and sunny climate typical of the Rhône Valley produces red wines that are generally more robust and fuller-flavored than those of Burgundy. The growing conditions along this part of the Rhône are more dependable than in most parts of France, and consequently, the best vintages for Rhône wines do not always correspond, for example, to those for Bordeaux and Burgundy. The intense heat here produces wines that contain more alcohol—and hence more body—than in more northerly vineyards, and this is reflected in the minimums set by the *Appellation Contrôlée* laws. Whereas 9 percent is required for Beaujolais and only 10 percent for a Beaujolais *cru* such as Moulin-à-Vent, the minimum for Côtes du Rhône is 10.5 percent and for Châteauneuf-du-Pape 12.5 percent.

Although Rhône wines are usually all grouped together, there are actually two distinct districts within this region: the southern Rhône, near Avignon, whose best-known wines are Châteauneuf-du-Pape, Tavel, and the the regional Côtes du Rhône; and the northern Rhône, between Vienne and Valance, which includes Côte Rotie, Hermitage, and Crozes-Hermitage.

Châteauneuf-du-Pape, a village located about ten miles from Avignon, produces about a million cases a year of what is surely the most famous of all Rhône wines. Although thirty thousand cases a year of white Châteauneuf-du-Pape are produced—the wine is distinctive and full-flavored—it is for its red wines that the village is world-famous. The name comes from a now-ruined castle, built in the fourteenth century as a summer house for Pope Clement V. During most of the fourteenth century the popes were French, and Avignon replaced Rome as the papal seat. The summer residence was called Châteauneuf, or new castle, to distinguish it from the existing papal fortress in Avignon. It was at this time that vines were first planted in the district. When the castle was destroyed two centuries later, the vineyards went untended until the nineteenth century. At that time the wines of Châteauneuf-du-Pape were reintroduced to Parisian society, and the wine has now established itself as one of the best-known red wines in the world.

Winemakers have discovered over the years that the intense heat of the Rhône Valley does not favor the growth of any of the finest grape varieties. Instead, a number of different varieties are used, each one contributing a particular characteristic to the finished wine. In Châteauneuf-du-Pape, thirteen grape varieties are permitted, but five are white-wine grapes used only in very small amounts in the production of red wines. And of the remaining varieties, only four are widely planted—Grenache, Syrah, Mourvèdre, and Cinsault. Grenache, which accounts for about three-quarters of the total acreage, contributes color and alcohol; Syrah and Mourvèdre are more tannic and enable a wine to age longer; and Cinsault adds fruit and aroma. Each grower plants his vineyards in somewhat different proportions, so that the wines of Châteauneuf-du-Pape vary from domain to domain. This variation in wine is further affected by the different vinification methods used in the district. Châteauneuf-du-Pape has long been known as a wine that needs several years of bottle age to reach maturity, and a number of growers continue to employ the long vatting and long maturation in barrel that produce long-lived wines. At the same time, the increasing demand for well-known wines throughout the world and the eagerness of the consumer to drink good vintages as soon as they are available have caused a number of domains to vinify their Châteauneuf-du-Pape to produce a full-bodied but relatively supple, fast-maturing wine that will be ready to drink sooner. You should, therefore, be prepared to experiment among the different shippers and domains to find the style you prefer. Although Châteauneuf-du-Pape is rarely an exceptional wine, it is usually dependable and widely available. Leading estates include Château de Beaucastel, Château Fortia, Château de la Gardine, Château Rayas, Château de Vaudieu, Domaine de Mont-Redon, Domaine du Nalys, Domaine de la Nerte, Domaine du Vieux Télégraphe, and Clos des Papes, as well as Les Cèdres of Paul Jaboulet Aîné and La Bernadine of Chapoutier.

About eight miles on the other side of Avignon is Tavel, which produces what many people consider the finest rosé of France. Made primarily from the Grenache grape, the wine is dry, has a most attractive and distinctive pink-orange hue, and is certainly the rosé with the most character and balance. About 400,000 cases are made annually, and a great deal of that comes from the Cooperative of Tavel, although it goes to market under various names. There are, as well, a number of large domains producing estate-bottled Tavel.

Close to Tavel is the village of Lirac, which produces red and rosé wines. The rosé is similar in style to that of Tavel, but less well known.

Most of the wines of the southern Rhône are sold simply as Côtes du Rhône. Production is abundant—fifteen to twenty million cases are produced, virtually all of it red. Côtes du Rhône is made from a number of different grape varieties, primarily Grenache and Carignan. Although many examples of Côtes du Rhône lack character or distinction, there are an increasing number of well-made, fuller-flavored wines to be found as well. More than a dozen villages within the region are entitled to label their wines Côtes du Rhône-Villages, and this appellation is generally of a higher quality: Cairanne, Chusclan, and Vacqueyras are perhaps the best known. The village of Gigondas, which was granted its own *Appellation*

Contrôlée in 1971, produces wines that are bigger and more distinguished than regional Côtes du Rhône, and more expensive.

Côtes du Ventoux and Côteaux du Tricastin, both situated just east of the Côtes du Rhône region, achieved *Appellation Contrôlée* status in 1973. They produce large quantities of relatively inexpensive wines, primarily red, which are similar in taste to a lighter Côtes du Rhône. A small amount of sweet, intensely flavored Muscat wine is made in the Rhône village of Beaumes-de-Venise, and marketed as Muscat de Beaumes-de-Venise. The wine, whose fermentation is stopped by the addition of spirits, must contain a minimum of 11 percent sugar and 15 percent alcohol.

Although Châteauneuf-du-Pape, Tavel, and the regional appellation Côtes du Rhône account for almost all the shipments to this country of Rhône Valley wines, most connoisseurs agree that the finest wines of the Rhône come from the northern part of the region. Côte Rotie and Hermitage are both powerful, deeply flavored red wines made from a single grape variety, the Syrah. (The vineyards of Côte Rotie also produce a very limited amount of white Viognier grapes that are traditionally vinified along with the Syrah.) These two appellations produce about eighty thousand cases of distinguished, long-lasting red wine. Hermitage is usually described as richer and more solid, Côte Rotie as having perhaps more finesse. Crozes-Hermitage comes from vineyards that encircle those of Hermitage and that produce nearly ten times as much wine. The soil and exposure are different, production per acre is bigger, and the wines are generally lighter-bodied as well as less expensive. The villages of Cornas and Saint-Joseph, on opposite banks of the Rhône, produce good red wines in limited quantities, with those of Cornas generally longer-lived.

A soft and flowery white wine, with a ripe, fruity bouquet, is made at Condrieu from the Viognier grape. More famous is the little vineyard of Château Grillet, which produces less than a thousand cases a year of an expensive wine similar to Condrieu. Much more readily available here are the flavorful dry white wines of Hermitage and Crozes-Hermitage made primarily from the Marsanne grape.

Well-known producers of northern Rhône wines include Paul Jaboulet Aîné, Chapoutier, and Délas Frères, as well as Guigal (which recently acquired the Vidal-Fleury firm) and Chave.

THE LOIRE VALLEY

The Loire is famous to tourists for its historic châteaux and for a variety of agreeable wines produced along its banks. But although the châteaux of the Loire are centered around Tours, the wines of the Loire Valley are produced along most of its 650-mile course. About two-thirds of the wines produced along the Loire are white, and a certain amount of agreeable and popular rosé is made. A limited amount of red wine is also produced, although the red wines are not so easily found in this country. If the Loire Valley produces no great wines (with the possible exception of some sweet wines that are rarely exported), it does produce quite a variety of delightful wines that can be—and should be—consumed young.

Starting at Nantes at the mouth of the Loire, the first wine district is Muscadet. This appellation is atypical of French wine names as it is not the name of a place, but the grape variety used to make the dry white wines of the region. The Muscadet grape, originally known as the Melon de Bourgogne, was brought from Burgundy in the sixteenth century and ultimately gave its name to the vineyard region around Nantes. American wine drinkers may have been put off at first by its name, similar to that of the sweet Muscatel wines produced from the Muscat grape, to which Muscadet bears no relationship whatsoever. In the past a good deal of Muscadet was sold as Chablis, which gives some indication of its taste, although this refreshing wine is usually lighter-bodied and somewhat more acid. Nantes is the capital of Brittany, a region famous for its shellfish, and Muscadet is a perfect accompaniment to seafood, a first course, or lighter foods in general. It is the only *Appellation Contrôlée* wine of France with a maximum alcoholic content—12 percent.

The best examples of Muscadet come from the Sèvre-et-Maine district, and these words will be found on the label. Rather than being an inner appellation, however, Sèvre-et-Maine actually produces about 85 percent of all Muscadet, so most of the wines imported here come from this district. You will also find bottles labeled Muscadet *sur lie*, or on the lees. Theoretically, this indicates that the wine was bottled directly from the barrel or vat while still resting on its lees, or natural deposits, without first being transferred to another container. Current regulations, however, specify only that the wine must be bottled no later than June following the vintage, and many wines labeled *sur lie* lack the distinctive crispness and yeasty freshness that make these wines special. Well-known producers of Muscadet include Marquis de Goulaine, Barré Frères, Domaine de l'Hyvernière, Jean Sauvion & Fils (which owns Château de Cléray), Donatien-Bahuaud (which owns Château de la Cassemichère), and Louis Metaireau.

Another light, dry white wine produced in this region is Gros Plant du Pays Nantais. Gros Plant is the local name for Folle Blanche, and this V.D.Q.S. wine, occasionally shipped here, is at its best within a year or so of the harvest.

The next wine city up the Loire is Angers, which has given its name to the district of Anjou. The best-known of the Anjou wines is, of course, Rosé d'Anjou. This light, mellow, and agreeable wine is made primarily from the Groslot grape, plus Gamay and Cabernet Franc. The relative sweetness of the wine depends on the shipper's specifications, although none of the Anjou rosés on the market is dry. Another rosé, labeled Cabernet d'Anjou, is made from the Cabernet Franc grape of Bordeaux. This wine is generally less sweet and has somewhat more character than does Rosé d'Anjou.

The Anjou district also produces white wines ranging in character from fairly dry to quite sweet and rich. The wines are made from the Chenin Blanc grape, known locally along the Loire as the Pineau de la Loire, although it is not related to the Pinot Blanc of Burgundy. The three main producing areas are the Côteaux de la Loire, the Côteaux de l'Aubance, and the Côteaux du Layon, the Aubance and the Layon being tributaries of the Loire. The Côteaux du Layon produces by far the most wine—mellow and rounded in character—but it is hard to find here. The wines produced in Quarts de Chaume and Bonnezeaux from grapes affected by *Botrytis cinerea*, as in Sauternes, can be especially rich and luscious.

The village of Saumur produces white wines from the Chenin Blanc and rosés and reds from the Cabernet Franc. The reds are attractive, especially those from the village of Champigny, which are labeled Saumur-Champigny. Most of the white wines of Saumur are transformed into *mousseux*, or sparkling wines.

The city of Tours is the one most familiar to tourists, as it is here that most of the historic châteaux are found. Chambord, Azay-le-Rideau, Chenonceaux, and Amboise (where Leonardo da Vinci is buried) are among the most famous. Unfortunately, most of the Touraine wines are of minor interest and consumed locally. The most-famous exception is the wine of

Vouvray, a village ten miles from Tours. The town is noted for its chalk hills, and its inhabitants have dug caves into the slopes that are used both as wine cellars and as homes. A number of the houses built along the slopes are mere facades with the greater part of these homes situated within the hillsides themselves.

We know Vouvray in the United States as a pleasant and fairly dry white wine, but if you visit the local cellars, you'll discover that Vouvray can be very dry, mellow, or quite sweet, and that it can be still, *pétillant*—slightly sparkling—or fully sparkling like Champagne. The Chenin Blanc grape is used to make Vouvray and in sunny years it produces a most attractive mellow wine; when there is less sunshine, the wine will be drier in taste. In recent years, however, the trend here and elsewhere toward drier wines has encouraged the Vouvray winemakers to alter their vinification so that their wines are often fairly dry; in fact, much of it is made into *mousseux*. As for the rich dessert wines, they are carefully produced in exceptionally sunny vintages, and, like Sauternes, are capable of aging for ten or twenty years. Vouvray producers include Monmousseau, Rémy-Pannier, Marc Bredif, Château Moncontour, and Prince Poniatowsky.

Across the river from Vouvray is Mountlouis, whose wines are similar to those of Vouvray, though perhaps not quite as good.

The Touraine also produces red wines in the villages of Chinon, Bourgueil, and Saint-Nicolas-de-Bourgueil. Rabelais was born in Chinon, and he often sang the praises of wine in general and of his local wine in particular. Made from the Cabernet Franc grape, these wines combine the tannic character of a light Bordeaux with an appealing fruitiness.

Up the Loire past Orléans and just before Nevers are two villages that produce the best dry white wines of the Loire Valley—Sancerre and Pouilly-sur-Loire. Although we know the hamlet of Sancerre for its wines, it is as famous to the French for its goat cheese. Many of the winegrowers also maintain a herd of goats, and they serve their homemade cheeses with as much pride as their wines. The wines of Sancerre have a distinctive character that has established their reputation in Paris and, now, in this country. The wine is made from the Sauvignon Blanc grape that is used to make the dry white wines of Bordeaux, but it takes on a completely different character in Sancerre—very dry, full-flavored, and with an attractive tang. For this reason Sancerre is a good wine to serve wih full-flavored dishes that call for a white wine.

The growers of Sancerre have also planted part of their vineyards with the Pinot Noir grape, and they make very agreeable rosé and red wines as well. Some of the Sancerre labels found here are Clos la Perrière of Archambault, Domaine La Moussière of Alphonse Mellot, Clos de La Poussie of Cordier, Comte Lafond, and Michel Redde.

The village of Pouilly-sur-Loire produces two wines. The Chasselas grape (well-known in Switzerland as the Fendant) produces a wine labeled appropriately enough, Pouilly-sur-Loire. This is an agreeable country wine that is not often seen here and that is at its best within a year of the vintage. The village also produces in greater quantity a wine from the Sauvignon Blanc grape, locally known as the Blanc Fumé, or Smoky White (there are various explanations, none of them definitive). The correct name of this wine is Blanc Fumé de Pouilly-sur-Loire, to distinguish it from a Pouilly-sur-Loire. As it happens, a number of potential customers here and elsewhere, seeing the words Pouilly-sur-Loire on the label, incorrectly assumed that the lesser wine was being palmed off on them. The name was thus shortened to Pouilly-Fumé, an unusual appellation for France, as the village and grape name are combined. This, in turn, has led many people to confuse Pouilly-Fumé from the Loire with Pouilly-Fuissé from southern Burgundy, made from the Chardonnay grape. In any event, Pouilly-Fumé is readily found here, and its rich flavor makes it a good all-purpose accompaniment to food. The best-known label is de Ladoucette, produced at Château du Nozet.

The white wines of Quincy and Reuilly are also considered Loire wines, although these towns are actually situated along the Cher, a tributary of the Loire. The wines, made from Sauvignon Blanc, have a crisp, dry taste similar to those of Sancerre and Pouilly-Fumé, as do those of Ménétou-Salon, a village situated halfway between Sancerre and Quincy.

ALSACE, PROVENCE, AND OTHER WINES

Alsace

The hillside vineyards of Alsace are among the most beautiful in all of France, and the area is dotted with delightful little villages of the kind that are used as illustrations in children's storybooks. France is separated from Germany here by the Rhine, but the vineyards of Alsace are set back from the river's edge and extend for about seventy miles along the slopes of the Vosges Mountains. Alsace often produces ten or eleven million cases of white wine a year, which makes it the biggest producer of *Appellation Contrôlée* white wines after Bordeaux and Champagne. Their flavorful and refreshing qualities complement perfectly the rich cuisine of the region, with its *foie gras*, sauerkraut dishes, and sausages.

Between 1870 and 1918 Alsace and the neighboring province of Lorraine were part of Germany. At the time, Germany did not want Alsatian wines to compete with her own Rhine and Moselle wines and encouraged the production of cheap, inferior wines, much of which was used for blending or in the manufacture of Sekt, German sparkling wine. After World War I, the growers of Alsace realized that their best chance for commercial success would be with finer wines, and they set about replanting their vineyards with better grape varieties. Today, about 75 percent of the vineyards of Alsace are planted in four varieties—Riesling, Gewürztraminer, Sylvaner, and Pinot Blanc (also known as Klevner). The rest is made up of Pinot Gris (marketed in the past as Tokay d'Alsace, although it bears no relation to the Tokay of Hungary), Muscat, Chasselas, and Pinot Noir. The last is used to make a small quantity of light red and rosé—95 percent of Alsatian wines are white.

The wines of Alsace were finally granted the *Appellation Contrôlée* Vin d'Alsace in 1962, but the wines themselves are traditionally labeled and marketed with the name of a specific grape variety. Riesling, Gewürztraminer, and Sylvaner are the best-known, and each is made entirely from the named grape. The *Appellation Contrôlée* laws also permit a blend of different grapes—in practice, usually the Chasselas, Sylvaner, and Pinot Blanc—to be sold as *Edelzwicker*, or noble blend, but this name is rarely seen here. Crémant d'Alsace is a relatively new appellation that was created for sparkling wines.

The wines of Alsace are fermented until they are dry, and this is what distinguishes them from German wines, with which they are sometimes confused. Whereas German Rieslings, Sylvaners, and Gewürztraminers are fragrant and sweet, those made in Alsace are fuller-flavored, with more body and alcohol, and austerely dry. The Sylvaner produces comparatively light, agreeable wines without much distinction. The Alsatians consider the Riesling to be their finest wine, and many customers agree that the dry Rieslings of Alsace are more appropriate with food than the sweeter wines produced in Germany. It is the Gewürztraminer, however, that most people associate with Alsace. The wine has an intense, spicy bouquet and a unique, pungent taste that makes it one of the most unusual and readily identifiable white wines in the world. The wine was originally made from the Traminer grape. *Gewürz* means "spicy," and Alsatian shippers used to select the most intensely flavored lots of Traminer and market them as Gewürztraminer. As a result, one shipper's Traminer might turn out to be spicier than another one's Gewürztraminer. To simplify matters, a new wine law that went into effect at the beginning of 1973 prohibited the use of Traminer on an Alsatian label—all the wines made from this variety must now be sold as Gewürztraminer. Actually, some Alsatian shippers believe that a natural clonal selection has occurred over the years so that there is now a Gewürztraminer grape that has replaced the Traminer originally planted in the vineyards.

Some wines shipped from Alsace are labeled *grand cru*. Only wines made from Riesling, Gewürztraminer, Pinot Gris, and Muscat may be so designated, and the regulations concerning production per acre and minimum alcohol content are stricter than for the rest of the crop. In addition, a number of specific vineyard sites have now been classified as *grands crus*, and their names may appear on a label. Words such as *Réserve* or *Réserve Personnelle* are not legally defined and their significance depends on the standards of the individual shipper.

In especially sunny years some producers—notably Hugel—make wines labeled *Vendange Tardive*, or late harvest, from Riesling, Gewürztraminer, or Pinot Gris. To qualify for this designation, which was made official in 1984, the juice must contain a minimum sugar content about equal to that of a German Auslese; the wines, however, are dry. Even rarer are sweet wines labeled *Sélection de Grains Nobles*, the equivalent of a German Beerenauslese.

Alsatian shipping firms—Hugel, Trimbach, and Dopff & Irion are the best-known here—market almost half of the wines of the region, a third are produced by the many cooperative wine cellars, and the rest is estate-bottled and sold by individual growers. Unlike their counterparts in Bordeaux and Burgundy, who buy only wine, many Alsatian shippers also buy grapes and make the wines in their own cellars. This gives the shippers greater control over the style and quality of wines they market. The wines are generally bottled within six months or a year of the harvest, and since 1972, all Alsatian wines must be bottled within the region—none are permitted to be shipped in bulk and bottled elsewhere.

Provence

The region of Provence extends along the Mediterranean coast from Marseilles east to Nice. This 120-mile stretch is dotted with fishing villages and with such famous resorts as Saint-Tropez, Cannes, Antibes, and Juan-les-Pins. A holiday mood and a *salade niçoise* on a terrace overlooking the water can add a great deal of enchantment to the agreeable rosés of Provence, and it is disappointing to discover that these wines rarely taste quite the same when consumed at home. It's true that many of these delicate and charming wines served in carafes do not travel well, but then neither does the mood in which they were first enjoyed. Of the vast amount of wine produced in this part of France, mostly for local consumption, there is a certain amount that stands out from the rest. The best-known wines are labeled Côtes de Provence, and they were elevated from V.D.Q.S. status to *Appellation Contrôlée* with the 1977 vintage. About eight million cases are produced within the appellation, two-thirds of it rosé. An increasing amount of red wine is also made, as well as a certain amount of white wine. Château de Selle, owned by the Domaines Ott, is one of the region's most familiar wines.

Côteaux d'Aix en Provence, which was made an *Appellation Contrôlée* in 1984, includes reds, whites, and rosés produced near the town of Aix-en-Provence. Château Vignelaure, planted primarily with Cabernet Sauvignon, and Château de Fonscolombe are both situated in this region.

The seacoast villages of Bandol and Cassis each produce red, white, and rosé wines that are entitled to *Appellation Contrôlée* status. Bandol produces mostly reds and rosés—they are dry wines with a fairly well-defined character. Domaine Tempier is perhaps the best-known Bandol estate. Cassis is known primarily for its white wine, full-flavored and a favorite accompaniment to the local *bouillabaisse*. The wines of Cassis bear no relation to the *crème de cassis* made in Dijon. The latter is a black-currant syrup used on desserts and to flavor certain drinks, notably Kir, a popular aperitif that is a mixture of white wine and *crème de cassis.*

Other Wines

Near the Swiss border, not far from Geneva, two white wines are produced that are occasionally seen in this country. Crépy, made a few miles from the lake of Geneva, is a light, dry wine made from the Chasselas grape. Being a wine made in the mountains near Switzerland and from a grape widely grown there, it's no surprise that Crépy resembles Swiss white wines. Seyssel is a dry white wine from the Haute-Savoie, and much of its production is transformed into a sparkling wine. Seyssel *mousseux* is well known to skiers at nearby Mégève and Chamonix, and is shipped to this country as well.

The vast area of the south of France, commonly known as the Midi, produces tremendous amounts of ordinary wine and is by far the largest viticultural area in the country, accounting for 40 percent of all its vineyards. The Languedoc-Roussillon, as this region is more properly called, extends west of the Rhône River along the Mediterranean to the Spanish border. Cooperative cellars produce about two-thirds of the region's wines, which are almost all red. Most of this wine is totally anonymous and is used to make the commercial blends sold within France and exported as *Vins de Table.* A few districts, however, produce *Appellation Contrôlée* wines, including Fitou, Minervois, and Côteaux du Languedoc; Corbières, Costières du Gard, and Faugères are entitled to the V.D.Q.S. appellation. In 1973 a program of replanting was begun in the Languedoc-Roussillon, and to such traditional varieties as Carignan, Cinsault, Grenache, and Alicante Bouschet were added Syrah, Merlot, and Cabernet Sauvignon.

In the Dordogne region just east of Bordeaux, a number of relatively unfamiliar *Appellation Contrôlée* wines are produced from the same grape varieties as in Bordeaux. Among the wines that occasionally find their way here are the red and white wines of Bergerac, and the white wines of Montravel and Monbazillac.

The vineyards around Cahors, a city about 120 miles east of Bordeaux, produce deep-colored, full-bodied red wines made primarily from the Malbec grape (known locally as the Auxerrois). For many years this wine, greatly admired by those who were able to find it, was produced in limited quantities. In 1971, Cahors was elevated from V.D.Q.S. to *Appellation Contrôlée* rank; production was increased to well over a million cases, and many examples today are no longer as dark, tannic, and intense as in the past. Much of the production comes from a cooperative cellar at Parnac.

The Jura district, east of Burgundy, produces a limited amount of red, white, and rosé wines, of which Arbois rosé is the most often seen in Paris. There are also several thousand cases a year produced of a very special white wine, Château-Chalon, made in a rather unusual way. After fermentation, the wine is aged for at least six years in small barrels that are not completely filled, thus exposing the wine to air. The resulting oxidation causes a yeast film to form, similar to that produced in certain sherries by a similar process, and the finished wine is known as a *vin jaune*, or yellow wine. Château-Chalon (which is the name of a village, not a vineyard) is a most curious white wine; although not fortified, it is similar to a dry sherry, but perhaps less complex.

THE WINES
OF GERMANY

Germany produces only 2 or 3 percent of the world's wines, and its vineyards—situated within a relatively small area in the southwestern part of the country—amount to less than a tenth those of France or Italy. Nor is wine the national beverage, as it is in those two countries; beer is the German's daily drink. Nevertheless, Germany makes what are acknowledged to be among the very greatest white wines in the world. The classic Riesling grape, when planted in the best sites along the Rhine and Moselle, produces a truly superb wine with an incomparable bouquet and with extraordinary elegance and breed.

Until the eighteenth century most German wines were red, but today about 90 percent of Germany's vineyards produce white wine. Red wines are still made—primarily from Blauer Spätburgunder (Pinot Noir), Portugieser, and Trollinger grapes—in Baden and Württemberg, in the Rheinpfalz, along the Ahr, and in the villages of Assmannshausen in the Rheingau and Ingelheim in the Rheinhessen, but they are almost always too light to compare favorably with red wines available from other countries. All of Germany's white wines, with the possible exception of those from Franconia, bear a family resemblance: a distinctive, flowery bouquet, and a taste characterized by a harmonious balance of sweetness and acidity that gives them a distinctive piquancy. There are many con-

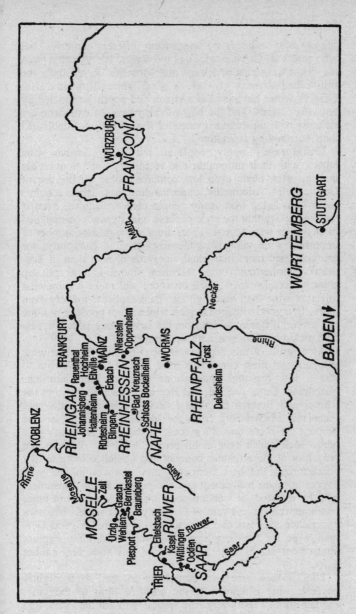

GERMANY

sumers who willingly try wines from different countries, but who reject all German wines as too sweet. It's true that even the driest examples of Rhines and Moselles do not have the full-bodied dryness of, say, a good white Burgundy. But German wines have instead a charm and appeal unequaled by any other wines, and the best of them have an extraordinary richness of bouquet and ripeness of flavor that has established their outstanding reputation.

Unfortunately, many people are put off by German wine labels, with their unfamiliar and seemingly unpronounceable names, often made even less comprehensible by the use of Gothic script. Admittedly, understanding these labels requires more knowledge than many people care to acquire, even if they recognize that the style of these wines cannot be matched in any other wine region. There are a much greater number of important wine villages in Germany than in Burgundy, for example, and more individual vineyards of note than in Bordeaux. Furthermore, most German vineyards are split up among several owners, each of whom will make a somewhat different wine than his neighbor. To complicate matters even more, in a good vintage German winemakers produce not one but several different wines from the same vineyard by successive pickings of increasingly ripe grapes.

As a result of this discouraging complexity, German wine shippers and most consumers have limited their attention to just a few regional appellations such as Liebfraumilch, Niersteiner Gutes Domtal, and Bereich Johannisberg from the Rhine, and Bereich Bernkastel, Zeller Schwarze Katz, and Piesporter Michelsberg from the Moselle; wines so labeled account for more than 80 percent of the German wines sold here. Such wines exist at all prices, and most of them can only hint at the aromatic bouquet and opulence of taste that characterizes the best German wines, without in any way suggesting their refinement and complexity. Many consumers who have tasted, at least on occasion, fine wines from other countries remain unaware of Germany's best wines. My own experience suggests that anyone who is offered a good German wine for the first time will almost invariably express amazement and delight that wines of this style and caliber exist.

The German vineyards extend up to, and even slightly beyond, what is known as the northern limit of the vine. Farther north, excessively cold winters will kill the vines, and summers lacking in adequate sunshine would prevent grapes from properly ripening. The best wines are made on slopes and steep hillsides facing south, where their height and direction enable the grapes to catch the maximum amount of sunshine. The poor soil that characterizes these vineyards is unsuitable for any other crop, and the steep incline of many vineyards makes it impossible to use modern machinery. It is by the hand labor of thousands of growers that these vines are tended, and it's only because the wines produced can be so remarkable—and expensive—that it is still commercially worthwhile for these vineyards to be cultivated. There are about ninety thousand growers tending their own vines in Germany, and 85 percent of them own less than five acres. Only five hundred or so estates consist of more than twenty-five acres, but it is among these larger domains that most of the famous wine-producing names are found.

The Rhine is the informing river of German viticulture, and all German wines are produced either along the Rhine or along the banks of its many tributaries. The principal wine regions along the Rhine itself are the Rheinpfalz, or Palatinate, known for its soft, full, rounded wines; the Rheinhessen, which produces a tremendous quantity of agreeable wines; and the Rheingau, a comparatively small district that produces the very finest of the Rhine wines—elegant, rich, and well balanced. The Nahe joins the Rhine at Bingen, and despite its geographical position halfway between the Rhine and Moselle, its wines have the richness and style of Rhine wines. The Moselle (spelled Mosel in German) joins the Rhine at Koblenz. Its wines, and those of its two tributaries, the Saar and the Ruwer, are light-bodied and fragrant and possess a refreshing crispness derived from their acidity.

The vineyards of Franken, or Franconia, along the Main, produce wines quite different from those of the Rhine and Moselle, and less often seen here. These drier wines have less bouquet and more body, and a distinctive earthy taste. Franconia wines, once referred to generically as Steinweins after its most famous single vineyard, are easy to spot because they are always shipped in the distinctive *Bocksbeutel*, a squat, flat-sided, gourdlike bottle.

The two regions of Baden and Württemberg produce about 25 percent of Germany's wines, and a third of that is red. Stuttgart is the principal city of Württemberg, whose wine villages are spread out on both sides of the Neckar River. Baden is the southernmost of the German wine regions, and part of its vineyards extend between the Black Forest and the Rhine, opposite the Alsace region of France.

Except for the wines of Franconia, just about all German wines are sold in slender tapering bottles—Rhine wines in brown bottles, Moselles in pale green. This distinction can be of help in remembering their general characteristics: the rich, full, deep flavor of the Rhines, and the pale, fresh, delicate, and graceful wines of the Moselle.

Virtually all of Germany's fine wines are made from the Riesling, and it is along the Rhine and Moselle that this grape has most successfully demonstrated why it is considered one of the world's half-dozen classic varieties. The Riesling needs a long growing season, however, and does not ripen fully every year, so that despite the quality of its wines, it accounts for only 20 percent of the acreage in Germany. It is the principal variety in the Mosel-Saar-Ruwer and the Rheingau, but is planted in less than 15 percent of the Rheinpfalz vineyards, and only 5 percent of those in the Rheinhessen. Until quite recently it could be assumed that the finest wines of the Rheingau and the Mosel-Saar-Ruwer—those from individual vineyards and top estates—were made from the Riesling, whether or not the variety was named on the label. Because of increased plantings of other varieties in recent years that assumption can no longer be made, and with few exceptions producers whose wines are made from the Riesling now indicate that on their labels.

The Riesling is widely planted throughout the world, and although it sometimes retains its name, as in France's Alsace region, the true Riesling of Germany is often identified by a somewhat different name in other countries—Johannisberg Riesling or White Riesling in California, Rheinriesling in Austria, Riesling Renano in Italy, Rjanski Rizling in Yugoslavia, Rhine Riesling in Australia, and so on. More often than not, wines from other European countries that are simply labeled Riesling are made from a variety known as the Welsch Riesling or Italian Riesling, and are rather neutral in taste. A California wine labeled Riesling is actually made from the Sylvaner, and wines marketed as Riesling from South America, where very little Riesling is planted, are more likely to be made from Sauvignon Blanc or Sémillon. It would therefore be a mistake to expect any of the so-called Rieslings produced around the world to have any similarity whatsoever to those of Germany. With few exceptions, even wines made from the true Riesling in other countries lack the elegance, distinctive aroma, and particular combination of fruit and acidity of German Rieslings.

The Sylvaner (spelled Silvaner in German) was once the most widely cultivated variety, and accounted for almost a third of all plantings as recently as 1960. Today, it covers less than 10 percent of the vineyards, but is still widely found in the Rheinhessen, Rheinpfalz, and Franconia, where it is sometimes called the Franken Riesling. The Sylvaner produces wines without much finesse or distinction, neutral and low in acid, which makes them useful for blending. Nevertheless, the best examples from good vintages, especially from vineyards in the Rheinhessen, can be very good.

The Müller-Thurgau, now the most extensively planted variety in Germany, was developed about a hundred years ago by Professor Müller, who came from Thurgau in Switzerland. It was long assumed to have been a cross of Riesling and Sylvaner, but some ampelographers now believe that it was produced from two clones of Riesling. It has the advantage of being adaptable to a wide variety of soils and ripening early, making it a good all-purpose variety. It produces wines that have an aromatic bouquet when young, and that are mild and low in acid, which makes them useful in blending, although when bottled on their own they age rather quickly.

The Traminer, famous in Alsace for its spicy, aromatic wines, is not widely planted in Germany. The Ruländer, known as the Pinot Gris in France, the Gutedel, known as the Chasselas in Switzerland, and the Weisser Burgunder, or Pinot Blanc, are cultivated to some extent, primarily in Baden. The most significant recent development has been the increased plantings of new varieties. Some, such as the Morio-Muskat and the Scheurebe, have been known for some time. Others, including the Kerner, Bacchus, Faberrebe, Huxelrebe, Ortega, Optima, and Ehrenfelser, have been registered only in the past fifteen or twenty years, and these new varieties are now found in some of the best-known estates along the Rhine and, to a lesser extent, the Moselle. Each has particular attributes that make it worth cultivating—resistance to frost, early ripening, higher sugar contents, low acidity— and they are useful for blending with Riesling in lesser years. Some of them are also bottled individually, and marketed with their own names, especially Kerner and Scheurebe.

In most of the world's vineyard districts, a good vintage is one in which the grapes ripen fully and the resulting wine is dry, balanced, and complete, with a proper degree of alcohol.

In Germany, the best vintages are those in which the grapes are not only ripe, but overripe, so that the grape sugar and natural flavor extracts present in the grapes will produce wines that are sweet, intense, and complex. These considerations are the basis of the new German wine regulations that went into effect in 1971. The new laws established three basic categories for German wines based not simply on geographical origin, but also on the ripeness of the grapes at the time of picking as expressed by their natural sugar content.

The lowest category of wine is *Deutscher Tafelwein*, German table wine. These wines, which rarely account for more than 10 percent of Germany's total production, can be labeled with only the broadest regional appellations of origin—Rhein-Mosel (which includes the subregions Rhein, Mosel, and Saar), Bayern, Neckar, and Oberrhein—and only if at least 85 percent of the wine was produced in the named region. A wine labeled simply *Tafelwein* can be blended from wines produced outside Germany. Relatively little *Deutscher Tafelwein* is shipped to this country, even though the category includes the once popular regional wine Moselblümchen. (In 1982 the subcategory *Landwein* was established as the equivalent of the French *vin de pays* for better wines within the *Deutscher Tafelwein* category. A *Landwein* must come from one of fifteen specified regions; its minimum natural alcohol content is slightly higher than for a *Tafelwein*; and it may contain no more than 1.8 percent sugar.)

The most important category of German wines, in terms of volume, is *Qualitätswein bestimmter Anbaugebiete*, quality wines from specified regions, also known as *Q.b.A.* or simply as *Qualitätswein*. There are eleven delimited regions within the *Qualitätswein* category—Mosel-Saar-Ruwer, Rheingau, Rheinhessen, Rheinpfalz, Nahe, Franken, Württemberg, Baden, Ahr, Hessische Bergstrasse, and Mittelrhein. Wines from the last three regions listed, which produce about 1 percent of Germany's wines, are almost never seen here. The name of one or another of these regions must appear on the label of every *Qualitätswein*, which gives the consumer at least a general idea of where the wine comes from, no matter how puzzling or unfamiliar the rest of the label may be.

The third and highest category of German wines is *Qualitätswein mit Prädikat*, or quality wine with a special attribute. The special attribute—designated on the label by the word *Kabinett*, *Spätlese*, *Auslese*, *Beerenauslese*, *Trockenbeerenauslese*, or *Eiswein*—does not reflect the origin of the wine but the ripeness of the grapes when they were picked. Chaptalization, adding sugar to the must, is permitted for *Tafelwein* and *Qualitätswein*, but is prohibited for *Prädikat* wines. Before 1971, the word *Kabinett*—or *Cabinet*, as it could then be spelled—was used at a grower's discretion to indicate a wine of special quality. Kabinett is now clearly defined as the first level among *Prädikat* wines. *Spätlese* means late-picked, and now refers to wines made from fully ripe grapes that have been left on the vines at least a week after the harvest has begun so that they will ripen even further. Such wines are somewhat sweeter and richer than a Kabinett wine from the same vineyard. A wine labeled *Auslese*, selected picking, is made from especially ripe bunches of grapes that are fermented separately. Auslese wines are even sweeter and richer in taste than those labeled Spätlese, and have a more concentrated flavor. *Beerenauslese*, selected berry picking, is several steps higher in quality and scarcity: grapes that are unusually ripe are picked individually and set aside to make a particularly sweet and intense wine. The very scarcest and most highly prized wines of all are called *Trockenbeerenauslese*, which means selected picking of naturally dried berries. They are made from overripe grapes that have been attacked by *Botrytis cinerea*, the noble rot called *pourriture noble* in Sauternes and *Edelfäule* in Germany. The juice that remains in these shriveled grapes has a very high proportion of natural sugar, and its flavor is intensified to a remarkable degree. The resulting wine, which ferments very slowly and with great difficulty, is the rarest and most extraordinary wine that a German vineyard can produce. It is very sweet, of course, but has a balancing acidity that makes it harmonious rather than cloying.

Beerenauslese and Trockenbeerenauslese wines are made only in exceptionally fine years, and then only in minute quantities. A large estate that produces, say 500,000 bottles of wine altogether might harvest a thousand bottles of Trockenbeerenauslese and perhaps three times that amount of Beerenauslese. The prices for these rare wines are correspondingly high—$50 to $100 a bottle is not unusual.

There is one other designation that occasionally appears on a label of *Prädikat* wine—*Eiswein*, or ice wine. An Eiswein is made late in the year from fully ripe grapes that have frozen on the vine when the temperature has dropped to 20°F or less. The frozen grapes are gathered in the early-morning hours, before the sun appears, and are carefully crushed to obtain only the rich unfrozen juice. Because the juice from which this rare wine is made concentrates not only the sugar in the grapes but also the acid, Eiswein is characterized by a relatively high acidity that gives it a distinctive elegance and finesse, as well as exceptional longevity. Until 1982 the Eiswein designation appeared on a label only in conjunction with one of the special attributes, such as Auslese or Beerenauslese. Today, Eiswein has been established as a *Prädikat* on its own, and the minimum sugar requirements are the same as for a Beerenauslese.

Before the new wine laws went into effect, each producer was allowed a certain amount of leeway in determining which of the special designations to put on his labels. Now the minimum requirements for a *Prädikat* wine, and for each additional level of ripeness up to Trockenbeerenauslese, are determined by the wine's Oechsle degree. The Oechsle scale, named after the scientist who invented it in the early nineteenth century, measures the sugar content of unfermented juice. For example, to qualify for the category *Qualitätswein mit Prädikat*, a Rhine wine made from the Riesling must have a minimum natural sugar content of 73° Oechsle; a Moselle, 67° (which is equivalent to about 16 or 17 percent sugar, and to a potential alcohol content of about 9 percent). Such a wine could be labeled Kabinett, the lightest and least-expensive level of *Prädikat* wines. The Oechsle degree required for each of the special attributes varies from region to region and from one grape variety to another; the minimums established for a Riesling from the Rheingau are 85° for a Spätlese, 95° for an Auslese, 125° for a Beerenauslese, and 150° for a Trocken-beerenauslese (which is equivalent to about 33 percent sugar; the bottled wine is likely to contain only 6 or 7 percent alcohol).

Since the quality of German wines is to a large extent determined by the Oechsle scale, it is possible to make some interesting comparison among German vintages since the new laws went into effect. In 1976, considered a remarkable year, no *Tafelwein* was made at all, less than 20 percent of the crop was *Qualitätswein*, and *Prädikat* wines accounted for more than 80 percent of the harvest. More specifically, Spätlese, Auslese, and higher grades accounted for more than 80 percent of the 1976 wines made in the Mosel-Saar-Ruwer, two-thirds of the Rheingau wines. By comparison, in the six vintages 1977 to 1982, *Prädikat* wines accounted for an average of less than 30 percent of the crop, and most of that was Kabinett, with only some Spätlese, very little Auslese, and virtually no Beerenauslese and Trockenbeerenauslese. In the excellent 1983 vintage, almost 50 percent of the crop was entitled to *Prädikat* status, and more than half of that was Spätlese, Auslese, and higher categories.

Ripeness plays a role not simply in the quality, but also in the variety of German wines. In most wine regions around the world, a producer makes wine from the same vineyard or group of vineyards every year—the number of wines does not change, only their quality. In Germany, a large estate on the Rheingau may own vines in, say, thirty vineyards in half a dozen villages. In a fine year, when each vineyard yields a wide range of *Prädikat* wines, the estate may bottle more than a hundred different wines. In a lesser year, when few wines exceed the *Qualitätswein* category, the estate may produce only a third as many wines.

Grape juice that contains a high proportion of natural sugar will not be able to complete its fermentation, and it is the residual sugar remaining in the wine that has traditionally given German wines whatever degree of sweetness they possessed. About thirty years ago some German winemakers began to use *Süssreserve*, or sweet reserve, and this technique has now been adopted by most producers. *Süssreserve* is unfermented grape juice, rich in sugar, that is kept aside and then added to a wine just before bottling to increase its sugar content. This permits the winemaker to ferment his wines out until they are dry, since he will have the opportunity of adding sweetness back later on. The winemaker no longer has to arrest the fermentation of a Kabinett, Spätlese, or even Auslese when just the right amount of residual sugar remains in the wine, and he can control the exact degree of sweetness of the bottled wine. About 15 percent of a good crop is set aside as *Süssreserve*, which may be used to sweeten the wines of a poor year as well. Not all producers use *Süssreserve*, and in exceptionally ripe years, when very high Oechsle degrees are achieved, some producers prefer to arrest the fermentation in an Auslese wine while residual sugar remains, although they will probably permit Kabinett and Spätlese wines to ferment until they are dry.

By way of suggesting the relative sweetness of the different *Prädikat* wines, there might be 25 to 30 grams per liter—2.5 to 3 percent—of sugar in a Kabinett wine (compared to 25 grams or so in a typical Liebfraumilch); 35 to 50 grams in a Spätlese, 60 to 80 grams in an Auslese, 100 to 125 grams in a

Beerenauslese, and 150 to 200 grams—15 to 20 percent—in a Trockenbeerenauslese. These are only general figures, however, because there are bound to be variations in the sugar content—and intensity of flavor—of wines labeled Spätlese or Auslese from different regions, different vintages, and different producers. Note that minimum sugar requirements—expressed in Oechsle degrees—apply to the unfermented juice when the grapes are picked, not to the wine when it is bottled.

Although the sweetness of one of these wines is the most obvious aspect of its taste, the winemakers consider that the amount of acidity present is just as important because it determines whether the wine is harmonious and well-balanced or simply sweet and clumsy. In addition, the presence of botrytised grapes, those affected by the noble rot, adds a distinctive, honeyed flavor and complexity of taste that sweetness alone cannot provide. Although the particular taste that comes from botrytised grapes is almost always found in Trockenbeerenauslese and Beerenauslese wines, there are years—such as 1976—in which the noble rot is so prevalent in the vineyards that even Auslese and Spätlese wines display the characteristically honeyed taste. Sometimes *Botrytis cinerea* does not occur even in a good vintage. In 1959 and 1983, for example, grapes dried up on the vines without being affected by the noble rot. Even though Trockenbeerenauslese wines were produced, they lacked a botrytised character.

The presence of the noble rot also affects the sequence in which grapes are harvested in Germany. In a typical good vintage, each level of *Prädikat* wines is harvested in order of increasing ripeness. When there is a great deal of noble rot, however, growers may begin the harvest by picking the grapes for Auslese and Beerenauslese wines, and there are even instances when the first wines to be made were Trockenbeerenauslese. The usual description of the German winemaker consciously deciding whether or not to risk leaving his grapes on the vine for an additional two or three weeks of ripening is not always an accurate one. What the winemaker must decide in an outstanding year is just how much Trockenbeerenauslese and Beerenauslese wines to make, since the grapes he sets aside for these superb wines will, to some extent, diminish the richness and concentration of the rest of his crop. The one wine that is always produced by a conscious decision is Eiswein. Since a grower may have to wait until December or even January for the grapes to freeze on the vines, he can produce an Eiswein only by deliberately leaving a part of the crop unpicked and hoping that the necessary frost occurs before the fully ripe grapes simply spoil.

None of the wines described so far is dry, but there are two new types of wine that are now being made in Germany, Trocken, dry, and Halbtrocken, half-dry. In the past few years a number of producers have begun to market dry wines in an effort to provide the German consumer with a wine he or she could drink with meals, and by the mid-1980s Trocken and Halbtrocken wines accounted for a third of all *Qualitätswein*. The maximum permissible sweetness of these wines is determined by a formula based on both sugar and acid. Basically, a Trocken wine cannot exceed 9 grams of sugar, and most have only 4 or 5 grams; a Halbtrocken cannot contain more than 18 grams of sugar, and most have about 14 grams. In a good vintage, a grower may decide to make Trocken and Halbtrocken wines of Spätlese and even Auslese quality by fermenting them out until they are dry, and such wines have noticeably more body and flavor. Because these wines are so different from traditional German wines and are likely to confuse many consumers, and because most countries have adequate sources of dry white wines, Trocken and Halbtrocken wines are not widely exported. Nevertheless, some of the most important estates along the Rhine and Moselle are now producing these wines, and you may occasionally come across a bottle.

Although the success of a vintage and of individual wines in Germany is to a large extent measured in Oechsle degrees, the origin of each wine is still of prime importance, as it is throughout the world, in determining its particular style and personality. The new wine laws have established three increasingly specific appellations of origin within the eleven *Qualitätswein* regions: *Bereich*, or district; *Grosslage*, or collective vineyard site; and *Einzellage*, or individual vineyard site. There are thirty-four *Bereiche*, most of whose names are those of well-known wine villages. Since the average size of a *Bereich* is about 7,500 acres, these district appellations should not be confused with wines from the village whose name is used. For example, Bereich Johannisberg includes virtually all of the wine-producing villages along the Rheingau. There are only five *Bereiche* for the Mosel-Saar-Ruwer, and the best-known, Bereich Bernkastel, encompasses sixteen thousand acres of vineyards and sixty villages. Bereich Nierstein in the Rheinhessen and Bereich Schloss Böckelheim in the Nahe are other examples of these rather extended regional appellations. It is under such names as these, plus Liebfraumilch, that most branded German wines are sold.

The most specific appellations of origin, as in most wine-producing countries, are those of individual vineyards, now called *Einzellagen.* German labels for individual vineyards almost always indicate the village of origin followed by the vineyard. Thus, a wine labeled Bernkasteler Graben comes from the Graben vineyard in the village of Bernkastel (which takes the possessive *er*, as a person from New York is called a New Yorker). Piesporter Treppchen, Rauenthaler Baiken, and Forster Jesuitengarten are wines that come from individual vineyards, or *Einzellagen*, in the village of Piesport, Rauenthal, and Forst respectively. Exceptions to this rule, vineyards so famous that their names may appear on a label without that of the village in which each is located, include Schloss Johannisberg, Schloss Vollrads, Steinberg, Scharzhofberg, and Maximin Grünhaus.

The new laws reduced the number of individual vineyards in Germany from more than thirty thousand to 2,600, and the minimum size of an *Einzellage* was set at five hectares, or a little more than twelve acres. Many small vineyards were combined, and even sizable vineyards were considerably expanded. Bernkasteler Bratenhöfchen was expanded from six acres to forty-five, Piesporter Goldtröpfchen from eighty-six acres to nearly 260. The average size of the *Einzellagen* created by the new laws is over ninety acress.

Despite the dramatic reduction in the number of individual vineyard names, there are still quite a few for the consumer to keep in mind—118 in the Rheingau, for instance, and over five hundred in the Mosel-Saar-Ruwer. The new laws established an intermediate appellation called a *Grosslage,* which is made up of a number of neighboring *Einzellagen.* A *Grosslage* appellation consists of a village name followed by what seems to be an individual vineyard—Bernkasteler Kurfürstlay, Piesporter Michelsberg, Rauenthaler Steinmächer, Forster Mariengarten. In fact, Bernkasteler Kurfürstlay is a name that can be used for wines made in any one of eleven villages along the Moselle, and six villages along the Rheingau can market their wines as Rauenthaler Steinmächer. There are 152 *Grosslagen* in Germany, including twenty in the Mosel-Saar-Ruwer and ten in the Rheingau. The average size of a *Grosslagen* is fifteen hundred acres. A consumer who does not recognize the names of the principal *Grosslagen* is likely to confuse wines so labeled with those from individual vineyards, especially since many names now used for *Grosslagen*, such as Bernkasteler Badstube and Johannisberger Entebringer, were actually those of individual vineyards before 1971. The names of the most important *Bereiche*, *Grosslagen*, and *Einzellagen* for the major wine regions are listed further on.

With few exceptions, each *Einzellage*, or vineyard site, is divided among several owners. Consequently, the names of individual proprietors and domains, whose holdings may be scattered among a number of vineyards in several villages, must also be taken into consideration when choosing German wines. The label of an estate-bottled wine bears the word *Erzeugerabfüllung*, bottled by the producer, followed by the name of the producer. (Before 1971, *Originalabfüllung* was used to indicate an estate-wine.) As in Burgundy, the consumer must have some familiarity with the names of the best producers as well as those of the best vineyards. Unlike Burgundy, however, where most growers bottle only a few thousand cases, there are quite a few large domains in Germany that produce twenty-five thousand to fifty thousand cases of wine a year, and their names consistently appear on any list of German wines. The owners of these large domains—which will be listed region by region further on—include noble families, orders, and the German state.

Many German winemakers traditionally bottle the contents of each cask separately, rather than blending them together. Before 1971, the number of the actual barrel from which a wine came was sometimes indicated on a label, preceded by *Fass* for Rhine wines, *Fuder* for Moselles. Also, *feine* or *feinste* (as in *feine* Auslese) was an indication by the producer that the wine was especially fine. These designations are no longer permitted, as they are considered too arbitrary. Nevertheless, some estates still bottle the contents of each cask separately, and may, therefore, market several different wines labeled Spätlese, Auslese, and so on from a given vintage. Today, the relative qualities of similarly labeled wines might be indicated by the use of different lot numbers on a producer's price list, or by the use of different colored capsules on the bottles. The consumer who has already made an effort to remember the names of the best vineyards and best estates may be discouraged to learn that two bottles of Auslese from a particular domain may not, in fact, be identical, but the winemaker's insistence on preserving the quality and individuality of each barrel of his wine must at least be recognized.

In addition to the vineyard proprietors who bottle their own wines and those who sell their wines in bulk to the many German wine shippers, nearly two-thirds of all growers are members of cooperative wine cellars. More than three hundred cooperative cellars exist in Germany today, and they account for about a third of all the wines made. Cooperatives produce a relatively small proportion of wines in the Rheingau, but more than a quarter of the wines of the Mosel-Saar-Ruwer come from cooperatives, half the wines of Franconia, and more than three-quarters of those from Baden and Württemberg. *Winzergenossenschaft* or *Winzerverein*, wine grower's cooperative, are the words you are most likely to see on the label of one of these wines.

Other German words that are useful to know are *Kellerei*, cellar; *Weingut*, wine domain; *Erben*, heirs; *Freiherr*, baron; *Graf*, count; and *Fürst*, prince. Weissherbst, not often seen here, is a rosé produced for the most part in Baden and Württemberg from Blauer Spätburgunder grapes. Schillerwein is a rosé made in Württemberg, from red and white grapes pressed and fermented together.

One other indication that must appear on the labels of all *Qualitätswein* and *Prädikat* wines is the *Amtliche Prüfungs-nummer*, or certification number. This is usually shortened to *A.P. Nr.* followed by a numbered code. To obtain a certification number, each lot of wine must undergo laboratory analysis and must be approved at a quality-control tasting.

Despite the exceptional quality of the best German wines, the branded regional wines marketed by a number of German shippers dominate the market here. Most consumers are put off by the diversity of German wine names, and in any case weather conditions do not permit individual producers to make fine wines every year. The simplified labeling and consistent quality of the leading brands, as well as their appealing taste, account for their popularity.

The single best-known wine of Germany is Liebfraumilch, which accounts for half of all the wines exported. The name may have originally referred to the wines produced in the small vineyard belonging to the Liebfrauenkirche in Worms (situated on the border between the Rheinhessen and Rhein-pfalz), but the name has long been used for wines produced throughout the Rheinhessen, Rheinpfalz, Rheingau, and Nahe from Riesling, Sylvaner, or Müller-Thurgau grapes. The laws concerning Liebfraumilch were amended in 1982: it must come exclusively from the Rheinhessen, Rheinpfalz, Rheingau, or Nahe (that is, wines from different regions may no longer be blended together); and the name of the region of origin must now appear on the label. In practice, most Liebfraumilch—which must contain a minimum of 1.8 percent sugar—comes from the Rheinhessen and it is unlikely that much Riesling finds its way into the blend. Among the best-known brands are Sichel Blue Nun, Kendermann Black Tower, Deinhard Hanns Christof, Langenbach Crown of Crowns, Julius Kayser Glockenspiel, Valckenberg Madonna, Goldener Oktober, and Madrigal.

Apart from Liebfraumilch, the most frequently seen regional appellations are Bereich Bernkastel, Bereich Johannisberg, and Bereich Nierstein. A number of *Grosslagen* wines are also readily available from several shippers, including Bernkasteler Kurfürstlay, Piesporter Michelsberg, Zeller Schwarze Katz, Johannisberger Erntebringer, and Niersteiner Gutes Domtal. At least 85 percent of a wine must come from the *Bereich, Grosslage* or *Einzellage* on the label, and at least 85 percent of a vintage-dated wine must come from that vintage. If a label also indicates the name of a specific grape variety, as in Bereich Bernkastel Riesling or Piesporter Michelsberg Riesling, 85 percent of the wine must be made from the named grape. These requirements apply not only to regional wines, but to estate-bottled wines from individual vineyards as well. In the case of *Prädikat* wines from the top estates, however, it is likely that the wine comes entirely from the vineyard, vintage, and variety shown on the label.

One problem that everyone who admires German wines must face is how to match them with food. *Qualitätswein*, which includes branded regional wines and Liebfraumilch, can certainly be drunk with a meal, especially in warm weather, as can many Kabinett wines. The finer *Prädikat* wines, Spätlese and up, are too sweet to accompany most foods, and not sweet enough to stand up to rich desserts, which tend to overwhelm them. The Germans themselves drink these wines on their own, in the afternoon or late in the evening. The delicate flavor and refreshing acidity of many German wines, especially Moselles, make them a delightful wine to serve as an aperitif before dinner. Since German wines are comparatively low in alcohol—few contain more than 10 percent—they can be drunk more casually and copiously than many of the headier white wines produced elsewhere.

Although white wines are usually consumed young, the finest German whites—Auslese, Beerenauslese, Eiswein, and

Trockenbeerenauslese—will improve with a few years of bottle age. The initial sweetness and opulence will give way to a more harmonious and complex taste. Even Spätlese wines, especially those from the Rhine, will acquire added interest with bottle age.

German wine labels are considered the most specific in the world, especially for the finest wines, but a knowledge of German wines is not so easily acquired. There are nearly 1,400 wine villages and 2,600 vineyards whose names may appear on a label. Add to that the various levels of ripeness among *Prädikat* wines and the result is a truly awesome number of possibilities. Nevertheless, a rule of thumb can be formulated when selecting German wines: once you decide whether you want a Rhine or Moselle, if you choose a *Prädikat* wine of Spätlese or Auslese quality made from the Riesling in a good vintage, you will be well on your way toward a good bottle. If you then select a wine from one of the top estates, you will almost inevitably be getting a single vineyard wine as well. In time you can make your own evaluations of wines from different vineyards and from different estates, but by focusing on the vintage, special attribute, and the reputation of a major estate, you can drink fine wines without having to learn the names of villages and vineyards. Anyone who has enjoyed a few bottles of fine German wine, however, will want to know more about just where each wine comes from, and the following pages contain some basic information about the major regions.

THE GERMAN WINE REGIONS

Rheinpfalz

The Rheinpfalz usually produces more wine than any other region in Germany, and enjoys the warmest weather as well. Its wines are generally fuller, softer, and less acid than those of more northerly regions, and Auslese and Beerenauslese wines are not uncommon. The Pfalz vineyards are not actually situated along the Rhine, but extend for about fifty miles along the slopes of the Haardt Mountains, ten or fifteen miles west of the river. The Deutsche Weinstrasse, or German wine road, runs through the entire region almost to the northern end of Alsace. Nearly half the Pfalz wines are made from Müller-Thurgau, Sylvaner, and Kerner, and this region supplies much of Germany's carafe wines. The Riesling predominates in the Middle Haardt, however, the central section that contains the best wine-producing villages: Forst, Deidesheim, Ruppertsberg, Wachenheim, and Bad Dürkheim (whose wines are labeled simply Dürkheimer). When choosing wines from this district, it is helpful to remember that three producers in particular are famous for the high quality of their wines: Bassermann-Jordan, Bürklin-Wolf, and von Buhl.

The two *Bereiche* names of the Pfalz are rarely seen, and of its twenty-six *Grosslagen*, the best-known are Forster Mariengarten and Deidesheimer Hofstück.

VILLAGE	IMPORTANT VINEYARDS
Forst	Kirchenstück, Jesuitengarten, Ungeheuer, Pechstein
Deidesheim	Leinhöhle, Hohenmorgen, Herrgottsacker, Grainhübel, Nonnenstück
Ruppertsberg	Hoheburg, Nussbien, Reiterpfad
Wachenheim	Goldbächel, Rechbächel, Gerümpel
Dürkheim	Speilberg, Herrenmorgen, Steinberg

Rheinhessen

The Rheinhessen begins where the Rheinpfalz ends, at Worms, and these two regions account for almost half the vineyard acreage in Germany. The Rheinhessen is not an elongated region, but triangular, with Worms, Mainz, and Bingen as its three points. Müller-Thurgau and Sylvaner account for a third of the acreage, and a certain amount of full, ripe Spätlese and Auslese wines are made from these grapes. The Rheinhessen is also the area with the most extensive plantings of new varieties, and nearly a third of the vineyards consist of Scheurebe, Bacchus, Kerner, and Faberrebe. The bulk of Rheinhessen wines are used to make up shippers' regional blends, however, notably Liebfraumilch.

The best wines of the region come from a number of villages situated along the Rhine as it flows north toward Mainz. The Riesling is extensively planted in this section, whose best-known villages are Nierstein, Nackenheim, and Oppenheim. To this group must be added the village of Bingen, situated some miles away opposite the Rheingau village of Rüdesheim; Scharlachberg is Bingen's best-known vineyard. The estates of Franz Karl Schmitt and Anton Balbach, both located in Nierstein, produce some of the region's best wines.

Bereich Nierstein is the best-known of the region's three *Bereiche*. Of the twenty-four *Grosslagen*, the ones most frequently seen are Niersteiner Spiegelberg, Niersteiner Gutes Domtal, and Oppenheimer Krötenbrunnen.

VILLAGE	IMPORTANT VINEYARDS
Nierstein	Hipping, Orbel, Pettenthal, Hölle, Olberg
Oppenheim	Sackträger, Herrenberg, Daubhaus

Rheingau

The Rheingau accounts for only 3 percent of Germany's vineyards, but it has a higher proportion of Riesling—about 80 percent—than any other region. Its best wines are, with the very best of the Moselle, the finest wines of Germany. Rheingau wines have more body and depth, and perhaps more character, than those of the Moselle, which impress more with their grace and delicacy. Spätlese and Auslese wines from the Rheingau are richer and more opulent than those of the Moselle, and generally longer-lived as well.

The Rheingau extends along the Rhine for about twenty-five miles as it flows from east to west. The vineyards face south, which enables them to obtain the maximum amount of sunshine, and they are protected from cold winds by the Taunus Mountains to the north. There are two villages that are situated along this stretch of the Rhine, but that are considered as part of the Rheingau: Hochheim, which is actually on the Main River just before it joins the Rhine; and Assmannshausen, known primarily for its red wines. The English traditionally refer to all Rhine wines as Hocks, derived from the village of Hochheim, from which the wines of this region were originally shipped to England. To this day, many English wine lists divide German wines into Hocks and Moselles.

There are many outstanding vineyards in the Rheingau, but three of them are so famous that each of their names may appear alone on a label without being preceded by that of a village: Schloss Johannisberg, Schloss Vollrads, and Steinberg. These vineyards are unusual because they are quite large, eighty acres or more, and because each has a single owner. Steinberg is owned by the Hessian state, and at one time its wines were made at Kloster Eberbach, a twelfth-century monastery located in Hattenheim. The Hessian state is actually the largest single owner of vineyards along the Rheingau with nearly five hundred acres in several villages. Its simple label, with a stylized black-and-gold eagle and the identification *Staatsweingüter* is a familiar one.

Schloss Vollrads belongs to the Matuschka-Greiffenclau family, who built the imposing castle in the fourteenth century. A distinctive feature in the presentation of the wines of Schloss Vollrads is that a different-colored capsule is used for each category—green for *Qualitätswein*, blue for Kabinett wines, pink for Spätlese, white for Auslese, and gold for Beerenauslese and Torckenbeerenauslese. In addition, specially selected lots within each of the first four categories are indicated by adding gold bands to the capsules. The present Graf Matuschka-Greif-fenclau has taken a particular interest in Trocken and Halbtrocken wines, and such wines are identified by silver bands on the capsules.

Schloss Johannisberg is probably the single most famous vineyard in Germany, and its renown is such that the Riesling grape is known as the Johannisberger in Switzerland, and as the Johannisberg Riesling in California. The vineyard was given to the von Metternich family by the emperor of Austria more than 150 years ago, but it was famous long before that. The wines of Schloss Johannisberg were traditionally marketed with two different labels—one showed the family crest, the other a drawing of the castle. In the early 1980s, these were replaced by a gold label that depicts the castle and is used only for *Prädikat* wines; *Qualitätswein* are now marketed under the Domäne Clemens label. Here again, different colored capsules are used for the various quality categories, but they simply conform to the label designation and have no special significance.

The interested consumer will enjoy comparing wines from each of the Rheingau villages and from the different estates, many of which are quite extensive. Langwerth von Simmern, Schloss Reinhartshausen, Schloss Groenesteyn, and Schloss

Schönborn are some of the most respected names. The largest privately owned domain is that of Graf von Schönborn, whose 150 acres includes holdings in forty-five individual vineyard sites located in thirteen different villages. The wines are labeled Schloss Schönborn, with the village and vineyard designation appearing in smaller type. In fact, a number of estates have adopted this Schloss method of labeling, in which the estate name is more prominently displayed than that of each vineyard. Only the names Schloss Vollrads and Schloss Johannisberg, however, actually refer to a single vineyard. Another large estate is that of Wegeler Erben, in Oestrich, whose 140 acres, almost all Riesling, are cultivated in seven villages. The estate is owned by the Deinhard firm, which also owns one hundred acres of vineyards along the Moselle and the Ruwer and in the Rheinpfalz. The famous Schloss Eltz vineyards are now owned by the state—the castle is still the property of Graf Eltz—and have been leased to a group that includes the von Schönborn domain, which has marketed the wines under its own label since 1981.

Only one *Bereich* has been established for the Rheingau— Bereich Johannisberg. There are ten *Grosslagen*, the most familiar of which are Hochheimer Daubhaus, Rauenthaler Steinmächer, Eltviller Steinmächer, Hattenheimer Deutelsberg, Johannisberger Erntebringer, and Rüdesheimer Burgweg.

VILLAGE	IMPORTANT VINEYARDS
Hochheim	Domdechaney, Kirchenstück, Königin Victoria Berg
Rauenthal	Baiken, Gehrn, Wülfen
Eltville	Taubenberg, Sonnenberg, Sandgrub
Kiedrich	Wasseros, Sandgrub
Erbach	Marcobrunn, Steinmorgen
Hattenheim	Steinberg, Nussbrunnen, Wisselbrunnen, Mannberg
Hallgarten	Schönhell, Hendelberg
Oestrich	Lenchen, Doosberg
Winkel	Schloss Vollrads, Hasensprung
Johannisberg	Schloss Johannisberg, Klaus, Hölle

Geisenheim	Rothenberg, Kläuserweg
Rüdesheim	Bischofsberg, Berg Rottland, Berg Schlossberg

Nahe

The wines of the Nahe are not very well known in this country, and even German consumers are relatively unfamiliar with its best sites. The best of the Nahe wines are very good indeed, and although they are said to combine the best characteristics of the two districts that adjoin it—the Rheingau and the Moselle—they are much closer in style to the best Rheingaus. The best wine-producing villages are Bad Kreuznach (which shortens its name on a label to Kreuznacher), Niederhausen, and Schlossböckelheim. Although *Schloss*, or castle, is associated with two famous Rheingau vineyards— Schloss Johannisberg and Schloss Vollrads—Schlossböckelheim is the name of a village, not a specific vineyard.

There are two *Bereiche*, Bereich Kreuznach and Bereich Schloss Böckelheim, and seven *Grosslagen*, including Schlossböckelheimer Burgweg and Rüdesheimer Rosengarten (not to be confused with Rüdesheimer Rosengarten in the Rheingau).

VILLAGE	IMPORTANT VINEYARDS
Schlossböckelheim	Kupfergrube, Felsenberg, Königsfels
Niederhausen	Hermannshöhle, Hermannsberg
Kreuznach	Hinkelstein, Krotenpfuhl, Narrenkappe

Moselle

Compared to the majestic flow of the Rhine, the erratic path of the Moselle seems frivolous and nowhere more so than in the section known as the Middle Moselle. Yet it is along these steep banks that are found the world-famous wine villages of Piesport, Bernkastel, Wehlen, Zeltingen, Urzig, Graach, and a few others whose names, coupled with that of their best vineyards, identify some of the finest wines to be found anywhere. The Moselle zigzags here to such an extent that the greatest vineyards, always planted so as to face toward the south, are located first on one bank, then on the other. In some cases, the village itself is on the opposite bank, so that these choice slopes can be used entirely for the production of wine. During the vintage, the growers must keep crossing the river to bring the grapes back to their press houses.

Fifteen years ago, the Riesling accounted for 80 percent of the acreage along the Moselle; today, that figure has dropped to less than 60 percent. Furthermore, because the Riesling yields less wine per acre than do other varieties, it now accounts for less than half the wine produced along the Moselle. The finest wines still come from the Riesling, but the consumer can no longer assume that a Moselle has been made from that grape unless its name appears on the label. The wines of the Moselle are noted for their flowery and fragrant bouquet, for their delicacy and elegance, and for a fruity acidity that gives them a lively and refreshing taste. They are light-bodied wines that are comparatively low in alcohol—8 or 9 percent is not uncommon—which makes them very appealing with many foods and also by themselves as an aperitif.

The most famous vineyard along the Moselle is Bernkasteler Doctor, which was expanded in 1971 from three to twelve acres by incorporating parts of the Badstube and Graben vineyards. In 1984 the size of the vineyard was reduced to eight acres, which includes the original site and the best parts of the adjoining Graben vineyard. The principal owners are Dr. Thanisch and Deinhard; Lauerburg owns one-third of an acre, and the two-thirds of an acre acquired by Heilig-Geist-Armen-Spende are leased to Deinhard. The Sonnenuhr, or sundial, vineyard of Wehlen, about one hundred acres in size, is also famous. The Joh. Jos. Prüm estate has the biggest share of this vineyard, and other branches of this family have holdings as well.

Some of the proprietors whose names are often found on the best bottles include Bergweiler, Berres, and von Kesselstatt, proprietor of the Josephshof vineyard. The von Schorlemer name is now used by a cooperative cellar. There are also several hospitals, schools, and religious orders with extensive holdings along the Moselle (and the Saar and Ruwer as well): Vereinigte Hospitien, St. Nikolaus Hospital, Friedrich-Wilhelm-Gymnasium, Bischöfliches Konvikt, and Bischöfliches Priesterseminar. The last two estates were combined with that of the Hohe Domkirche in 1966 to form the Bischöfliche Weingüter, but the wines are still labeled with the name of each estate.

The villages of Zell and Kröv have given their names to two popular wines, Zeller Schwarze Katz, or Black Cat, and Kröver Nacktarsch, or Bare Bottom, whose labels usually illustrate their names. Both these names are now *Grosslagen*, but the new boundaries for Kröver Nacktarsch are so limited that this wine is not often seen anymore.

Along the Moselle, Bereich Bernkastel is by far the best known, as it encompasses virtually the entire Middle Moselle. Bernkasteler Kurfürstlay and Piesporter Michelsberg are the most popular *Grosslagen*, and widely used by shippers as regional wine appellations. Ürziger Schwarzlay, Graacher Münzlay, and Bernkasteler Badstube are other *Grosslagen*, as are Zeller Schwarze Katz and Kröver Nacktarsch, already referred to.

VILLAGE	IMPORTANT VINEYARDS
Trittenheim	Apotheke, Altärchen
Piesport	Goldtröpfchen, Günterslay, Falkenberg
Brauneberg	Juffer
Bernkastel	Doctor, Lay, Graben
Graach	Josephshöfer, Himmelreich, Domprobst
Wehlen	Sonnenuhr
Zeltingen	Sonnenuhr, Himmelreich
Ürzig	Würzgarten, Goldwingert
Erden	Treppchen

Saar

The Saar joins the Moselle just below Trier, the Ruwer just above that historic city. Wines from these two districts are labeled, as are those of the Moselle, with the overall regional appellation Mosel-Saar-Ruwer. In fine years, Saar and Ruwer wines are even more delicate and elegant than those of the Moselle, and some connoisseurs prefer the particular finesse of these wines to the softer and rounder flavor of Moselles. In lesser years, however, Saar and Ruwer wines are disappointingly thin and acid.

The most famous vineyard of the Saar is Scharzhofberg, whose name may appear by itself on a label, without that of Wiltingen, the village in which it is located. In 1971, the vineyard was expanded from forty-five acres to sixty-seven acres, and is now split up among ten owners, the most respected of which is Egon Müller. Scharzberg, which was the name of an individual vineyard prior to the new laws, has now been transformed into the *Grosslage* name Wiltinger Scharzberg, which can be used to label wines produced anywhere in the entire Saar region. Bereich Saar-Ruwer encompasses both regions. Dr. Fischer, Rheinart, and the State Domain are vineyard proprietors along the Saar.

VILLAGE	IMPORTANT VINEYARDS
Serrig	Kupp, Würzberg
Ayl	Herrenberg, Kupp
Ockfen	Bockstein, Geisberg, Herrenberg
Wiltingen	Scharzhofberg, Kupp
Oberemmel	Altenberg, Rosenberg
Kanzem	Altenberg, Sonnenberg

Ruwer

There are two particularly famous vineyards along the Ruwer, each with a single proprietor. Maximin Grünhaus, owned by von Schubert, is in Mertesdorf, but since 1971 its name has been treated as if it were that of a village, and may appear by itself on a label. The vineyard name is followed by that of a specific section of the property: Abtsberg is considered the best, followed by Herrenberg and Bruderberg. In Eitelsbach, the Karthäuserhofberg vineyard is divided into five sections, the biggest of which are Kronenberg, Sang, and Burgberg. Perhaps with a sense of irony, the proprietors have devised one of the smallest of all German wine labels to bear so many long names. The *Grosslage* Kaseler Römerlay is used for the entire Ruwer.

VILLAGE	IMPORTANT VINEYARDS
Avelsbach	Herrenberg, Altenberg
Waldrach	Laurentiusberg, Krone

Kasel	Nieschen, Kehrnagel, Hitzlay
Maximin Grünhaus	Abtsberg, Herrenberg, Bruderberg
Eitelsbach	Karthäuserhofberg

Franconia

The wines of Franconia, shipped in the distinctive *Bocksbeutel*, are comparatively dry, less typically German in flavor, and characterized by a *Bodengeschmak*, or taste of the earth, that sets them apart from the more fragrant wines of the Rhine and Moselle. In the past, the Sylvaner was the variety most typically associated with the wines of this region, but the Müller-Thurgau now accounts for half the plantings. Although Franconia is not a major wine district in terms of volume, its vineyards are rather extensively spread out along the Main River and its tributaries. Frankenwein and Steinwein have often been used as regional names for these wines, but the latter may be used only for the wines from the Stein vineyard in Würzburg. The Staatliche Hofkellerei, Juliusspital, and Bürgerspital have extensive holdings in this region.

Franconia is divided into Bereich Mainviereck, Bereich Maindreieck, and Bereich Steigerwald, and two of its *Grosslagen* are Würzburger Himmelspforte and Randersacker Ewig Leben.

VILLAGE	IMPORTANT VINEYARDS
Würzburg	Stein, Innere Leiste, Schlossberg
Escherndorf	Lump, Berg
Randersacker	Teufelskeller, Sonnenstuhl
Iphofen	Julius-Echter-Berg, Kronsberg

THE WINES
OF ITALY

Italy can claim to be the most completely vinous nation of all: vines are planted in every one of its twenty regions, from Piedmont to Sicily; in most years it produces more wine than any other country; and its wines offer a greater diversity of names and styles than are found anywhere else. Although Italy's annual production is the equivalent of 800 to 900 million cases—Italy and France together account for about 40 percent of all the world's wines—the American consumer was for many years confined to a few well-known labels from a limited number of producers. Today, an adventurous wine drinker can find a much more varied selection of attractive and moderately priced wines from Italy, as well as an increasing number of that country's finest wines.

The range of white wines has expanded from the popular Soave, Frascati, Orvieto, and Verdicchio to include distinctive bottlings from such classic grape varieties as Chardonnay, Pinot Grigio, Pinot Bianco, Sauvignon, and Traminer, as well as from such local varieties as Tocai Fruilano, Cortese, and Vernaccia. In addition to the familiar Chianti, Valpolicella, and Bardolino, the selection of red wines varies from the light, brisk Merlots and Cabernets produced in the northeast to such rich, complex, wood-aged wines as Barolo, Barbaresco, and Brunello di Montalcino. Even as the best Italian wines have become more widely available here, however, many consumers have been slow to recognize their merits. One reason may be that the wines of each region are not structured into a clear upward progression from district to village to vineyard, as is the case in France and Germany. In fact, in Italy, as in California, there are relatively few single-vineyard wines; consequently there exists no ranking of classified vineyards, as in Bordeaux, or listing of *grands crus* and *premiers crus*, as in Burgundy, that make it easier for an informed consumer to identify the finest wines and determine their relative standing.

The consumer who wants to venture beyond the half-dozen best-known Italian wines faces a confusing array of names that do not seem to follow any specific pattern. Some wines are known by the grape variety from which each of them is made, some by their village or district of origin, others by a combination of both, and a few are still marketed with such colorful names as Lacryma Christi or Est! Est!! Est!!! Since the names of many Italian wine villages are not yet as familiar to consumers as are those of France and Germany, and since the grape varieties grown in Italy include many that are not readily found elsewhere, it's not always easy to recognize one or the other. Barolo and Barbaresco are villages, Barbera and Bonarda are grapes. Albana and Cortese are grapes, Lugana and Carema are villages. Verdicchio, Verduzzo, and Lambrusco are grapes. What's more, it's not unusual for the same name to be used for a wine that can be made either dry or sweet, still or sparkling.

Italy has been producing wine for more than three thousand years, and even twenty centuries ago wine was the daily drink of the people. Italians have always taken wine for granted, and this casual attitude is reflected in the easygoing way in which some of Italy's vineyards are cultivated to this day. Rows of vines are interspersed between plantings of wheat, corn, and olive trees, and this system of mixed cultivation, called *coltura promiscua*, goes back to a time when wine was only one of the products of a particular property. Twenty-five years ago *coltura promiscua* accounted for 70 percent of Italy's vineyards. Nowadays, most of these vineyards have been uprooted, and extensive new plantings make better use of available land as well as permitting the use of tractors and other mechanical aids. *Coltura promiscua* now accounts for less than 25 percent of all vineyards, and in some areas— Soave, for example—less than 5 percent of the land is in mixed cultivation.

Another significant change that has affected most Italian wines is the adoption of modern winemaking techniques. Many of the dull, poorly vinified white wines of Italy, often aged in wood until they were oxidized, have been transformed into clean, crisp wines that are bottled early to retain their fruit and freshness. Regions whose wines had been accepted by local consumers but were previously unsuitable for the international export market have achieved great success in recent years as a result of new equipment and modern vinification methods. Many red wines, too, have been made more appealing by altering the winemaking and aging methods used previously.

Much of the improved quality of Italian wines, especially the less expensive whites, is due to the growth of cooperative cellars, which enable growers of limited means to have their grapes made into sound wines by the use of modern equipment and techniques that they would be unable to employ in their own small cellars. There are now nearly eight hundred cooperative cellars in Italy, with about 300,000 members, and they account for nearly half of the country's wine production.

In the past, the Italians' informal approach to winemaking, combined with their traditionally individualistic attitude, made it difficult to establish quality controls similar to those enforced in many other countries. In a number of wine districts, growers and shippers banded together to form a *consorzio*, or association, to establish certain minimum standards. This self-discipline varied in intensity from one *consorzio* to another. The most famous *consorzio* was established by the producers in Chianti Classico. In 1963 the Italian government—spurred on by Italy's entry into the Common Market—took an active role in establishing wine laws for the most important districts. These laws, which are in some ways more complete than the *Appellation Contrôlée* laws of France, are known as *Denominazione di Origine Controllata*, or DOC. The first decrees were issued in 1966, and the DOC laws went into effect in 1967, when fourteen DOC wines accounted for about eleven million cases of wine. There are now about 220 DOC zones, all of whose wines display the words *Denominazione di Origine Controllata* on their labels, and they account for 80 to 100 million cases of wine a year, which usually amounts to 10 to 12 percent of Italy's total production. (By comparison, the production of French *Appellation Contrôlée* wines amounts to between 140 and 200 million cases a year.)

The DOC laws specify the geographical limits of each

appellation, the grape varieties that may be used, the maximum amount of wine that can be produced per acre, and the minimum alcohol content of the wine, among other details. Reflecting the generally favorable climate that prevails throughout much of Italy, the DOC laws are more generous with regard to maximum production per acre than are the *Appellation Contrôlée* laws of France. For example, the production permitted in Soave and Valpolicella is almost twice as much as in Saint-Emilion or Pommard, and more wine per acre can be made in Barolo than in Beaujolais. These limits are not often achieved, of course; on the other hand, the addition of up to 15 percent of wine from outside the named district of origin is permitted for certain DOCs, which enables their producers to improve the light, weak reds of lesser vintages with the deeper-colored, fuller-bodied wines from warmer regions.

Although many Italian wines are labeled with the name of the grape variety from which each is made, every DOC wine must be produced within a specific region or district whose boundaries are strictly defined. Thus, the varietal name is combined with an appellation of origin—Barbera d'Asti, Nebbiolo d'Alba, Sangiovese di Romagna, Lambrusco di Sorbara, Cabernet del Trentino, or Pinot Grigio del Piave. Previously, non-DOC varietal wines could be labeled with only the name of the grape; now all varietal names must be accompanied by an appropriate geographical designation, as Barbera del Piemonte, Merlot delle Venezie, Pinot Grigio del Veneto, Sangiovese di Toscana, or Chardonnay dell'Umbria.

The DOC laws for many districts also specify that if a wine is made from grapes grown within an inner zone, it may be labeled *classico*. In some districts, such as Chianti and Soave, the *classico* zone may account for less than a third of the wines produced; in others, such as Valpolicella, as much as 60 percent of the wines can be marketed as *classico*. Most wines labeled *superiore* must have a slightly higher minimum alcohol content and must be aged somewhat longer before being sold, a few months for some white wines, perhaps a year for certain reds.

Of the 220 or so DOC wines, only four account for about a third of the total production—Chianti, Soave, Valpolicella, and Bardolino. In fact, three-quarters of all the DOC wines produced come from about twenty appellations, among them Moscato d'Asti, Caldaro, Montepulciano d'Abruzzo, Valdadige, Oltrepò Pavese, Piave, Grave del Friuli, Frascati, and Barbera d'Asti. The success in America of Lambrusco and of moderately priced magnums of inexpensive red and white wines is such that DOC wines account for less than 25 percent of the Italian wines shipped here, but nearly a hundred different DOCs can be found.

Although the DOC laws have now been in effect for many years, many of the *consorzi* are still functioning, and, in fact, a number of new ones were created after the advent of DOC. Their purpose is to provide an even stricter measure of self-regulation than the DOC laws, to encourage the production of wines of a higher quality within each district. Each *consorzio* has its own seal—the best-known is the black rooster used for Chianti Classico—and it appears on a strip attached to the neck of each bottle. A producer in any region who chooses not to join the local *consorzio* can nevertheless continue to sell his wine with the appropriate DOC name, of course, but without the *consorzio* seal.

A few years ago a higher and even more select category of wines was created, *Denominazione di Origine Controllata e Garantita*, or DOCG. The principal differences between the DOC and DOCG laws for a given wine are that the latter reduce the maximum production per acre and also specify that every wine must be approved by a tasting commission before it can be sold with the DOCG seal. Four wines were granted DOCG status in 1980 and 1981: Brunello di Montalcino, Barolo, Barbaresco, and Vino Nobile di Montepulciano. Because of the minimum aging requirements established for each of these wines, the first DOCGs did not appear on the market until the mid-1980s. In 1984, Chianti became the fifth DOCG wine.

Unlike the wine laws of France and Germany, the DOC and DOCG laws of Italy specify a minimum amount of wood-aging for many red wines, which may be as much as three or four years. The laws simply reflect the traditions of each region, but in recent years the long aging in large casks that has always been considered integral to the taste of such wines as Barolo, Barbaresco, and Brunello di Montalcino has led to controversy among winemakers and consumers, some of whom feel that the resulting wines are often faded and dried-out. No barrel-aging requirements exist for even the finest red wines of Bordeaux and Burgundy, for example, nor for those of California. By codifying existing attitudes toward aging in order to protect the quality of certain wines, the Italian laws impose a wood-aging minimum that a number of producers now feel diminishes their wines. Some winemakers now prefer to age at least some of their red wines for a limited amount of time in the small oak barrels used in France and California, rather than for several years in the large casks that are more traditional in Italian cellars.

The DOC laws also formalized the specific grape varieties that may be used for each appellation and, where more than one variety is used, the proportions of each. Since the DOC laws were established, however, a number of producers have planted such varieties as Chardonnay and Cabernet Sauvignon in areas where they were not previously cultivated; others have been experimenting with existing varieties, but in proportions different from those specified in the DOC regulations. What happened, in effect, was that wine laws were finally established—in the late 1960s and early 1970s—to protect and maintain traditional approaches to winemaking just as a number of Italian producers, influenced by France and California, began to alter their existing wines and to create new ones. As a result, an increasing number of excellent wines are being produced in Italy that are not entitled to DOC status, but may be sold only as *vino da tavola*, or table wine. These include Sassicaia, Tignanello, Le Pergole Torte, Brusco dei Barbi, Bricco Manzoni, San Giorgio, Vintage Tunina, and a number of wines made from Cabernet Sauvignon and Chardonnay.

Apart from a wine's appellation of origin and such supplementary indications as *classico* and *superiore*, there are a number of other words and phrases that are often encountered on Italian wine labels. These include *rosso* (red), *bianco* (white), *rosato* (rosé), *secco* (dry), *abboccato* or *amabile* (semisweet), *dolce* (sweet), *spumante* (sparkling), *frizzante* (lightly sparkling), *cantina* (cellar), *cantina sociale* (cooperative cellar), *azienda vinicola* (wine company), *casa vinicola* (winery), *tenuta* (estate), *fattoria*, *podere* (farm or estate), *azienda agricola* (estate winery), *vigna* or *vigneto* (vineyard) and *imbottigliato* (bottled).

The Italian Wine Regions

What follows is a description of Italian wines grouped into four sections and arranged in approximate geographical order: Piedmont and the Northwest includes Valle d'Aosta, Lombardy, and Liguria; Veneto and the Northeast includes Trentino-Alto Adige and Friuli-Venezia Giulia; Tuscany and Central

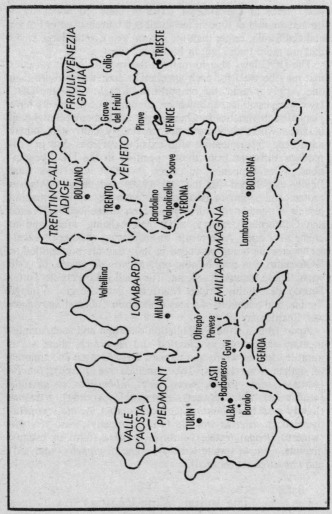

NORTHERN ITALY

Italy includes Umbria, the Marches, and Emilia-Romagna; and from Rome to the South includes the rest of Italy and Sicily.

PIEDMONT AND THE NORTHWEST

The Piedmont region, situated at the foot of the Alps that separate Italy from France and Switzerland, is known for the variety of fine red wines produced from its more than 230,000 acres of vineyards. Turin, the capital of the region, is the center of the vermouth trade; Asti, thirty miles southeast of Turin, is world-famous for its sweet, aromatic, sparkling wines. Asti Spumante and vermouth are discussed elsewhere, however. It is the table wines that concern us here, and Piedmont has a greater number of DOC zones than any other region in Italy—more than three dozen, almost all of them red. The finest Piedmont reds are made from the Nebbiolo grape. *Nebbia* means mist, and the name of the grape apparently derives from the fog that often covers the hillside vineyards of Piedmont in the fall, when the Nebbiolo grapes are harvested.

The most famous Nebbiolo wine is Barolo, produced around the town of that name southwest of Alba. Like most Nebbiolo-based wines, Barolo is full-bodied, sturdy, and long-lived and needs several years to develop its qualities. According to law, Barolo must have a minimum alcoholic strength of 13 percent when bottled (compared, for example, to a minimum requirement of 11.5 percent for the *grands crus* of Burgundy and 12.5 percent for Châteauneuf-du-Pape), and the wine must be aged for at least three years, two of them in cask. A Barolo labeled *Riserva* must be aged at least four years, one labeled *Riserva Speciale* five years. The new DOCG laws for Barolo maintain the minimum three-year aging requirement, specify five years of aging for a DOCG *Riserva*, and discontinue the *Riserva Speciale* category.

Barolo and several other big red wines of Piedmont are often compared to the Burgundies and Rhône wines of France, but the comparison can be misleading. Barolo is a rich, full-flavored wine, but it has its own distinctively earthy bouquet, often compared to tar, truffles, mushrooms, and faded roses, that sets it apart from French wines. In addition, the extended time that traditional Barolo spends in large casks—five or six years is not uncommon—results in a more evolved and mature taste than is found in, say, a Burgundy of equal age. Today, a number of Barolo producers are bottling their wines after only two years of barrel age, and others are starting to use the small oak barrels preferred in Bordeaux and California. What this means to the consumer is that Barolo is now available in a number of styles, from the subdued and comparatively faded taste that was prevalent only a few years ago to wines with more color, fruit, and vigor.

Another significant change that has occurred in the Barolo district is the increasing use of specific vineyard names. A number of producers have begun to vinify and bottle wines from different sites separately, and such names as Brunate, Rocche, Rocchette, and Cannubi now appear on labels with growing frequency, sometimes preceded by *bricco* (hilltop) or *sorí* (denoting a site with a favorable southern exposure). The production of Barolo amounts to more than 500,000 cases a year, and there are more than two dozen firms whose labels can be found here, some in very limited quantities. Among the best-known Barolo producers (most of whom also make other Piedmont wines) are Bersano, Borgogno, Luigi Calissano, Ceretto, Pio Cesare, Aldo Conterno, Giacomo Conterno, Contratto, Duca d'Asti (Granduca), Luigi Einaudi, Fontana-fredda, Franco Fiorina, Bruno Giacosa, Marchesi di Barolo, Prunotto, Renato Ratti, Vietti, and Valentino Migliorini, who also produces a proprietary wine labeled Bricco Manzoni from a combination of Nebbiolo and Barbera grapes.

The village of Barbaresco, a dozen miles northeast of Barolo, gives its name to another famous wine made entirely from Nebbiolo. Two years of age are required by law, of which one must be in wood. Barbaresco, too, has been granted DOCG status, and a Barbaresco *Riserva* must now be aged for at least four years. In general, the wine is somewhat lighter than Barolo, and it matures in less time, although fine examples may display more elegance and refinement. Most of the firms that make Barolo also produce Barbaresco, and it's not unusual to find a Barbaresco from one firm that is more tannic and richly textured than a Barolo from another. Producers that specialize in Barbaresco include Castello di Neive, de Forville, Marchesi di Gresy, and Parroco di Neive. Ceretto, which uses the Bricco Rocche label for its best Barolo, markets its finest Barbaresco as Bricco Asili. Perhaps the most famous winemaker in Barbaresco is Angelo Gaja, who has adopted the vinification and aging techniques of Bordeaux to produce long-lived wines that combine tannin, fruit, and finesse. Gaja makes single-vineyard Barbarescos from his 140-acre estate—Sorì Tildin, Sorì San Lorenzo, and Costa Russi—as well as several other wines, including Vinòt, a *nouveau* wine made from Nebbiolo by carbonic maceration, and barrel-aged Cabernet Sauvignon and Chardonnay.

The third famous Nebbiolo wine of Piedmont comes from vineyards around Gattinara, situated in the Novara-Vercelli hills, about seventy-five miles north of Barolo. Up to 10 percent Bonarda grapes is permitted in Gattinara, and the wine must age for at least four years, two of them in wood. Gattinara is the smallest of the three appellations, producing only fifty or sixty thousand cases of wine, compared to 250,000 or so for Barbaresco. Only wines from delimited hillside vineyards can be labeled Gattinara, and some producers market wines from adjoining vineyards as Spanna, which is the local name for Nebbiolo. Spanna is not a DOC wine, and the quality is variable, although some examples, such as those of Vallana, are on a par with the wines of Gattinara. Producers of Gattinara include Antoniolo, Dessilani, Ferrando, and Travaglini; Monsecco is a proprietary wine created by Count Ravizza and now produced by Le Colline.

Five other villages around Gattinara produce DOC wines— Ghemme, Boca, Fara, Sizzano, and Lessona. Although all these wines are made primarily from the Nebbiolo grape, each appellation has different minimum requirements, and as much as 50 or 60 percent of other varieties, primarily Vespolian and Bonarda, can be used as well. These wines must undergo two or three years of aging in cask, and their flavor is, unsurprisingly, similar to that of Gattinara. Ghemme is the best-known, but none of the wines are widely available here, as all five appellations together rarely produce more than forty thousand cases a year.

Two other Nebbiolo wines that get their names from the villages near which they are made are Carema and Donnaz. Both come from grapes grown at fairly high altitudes: Donnaz from the Val d'Aosta, in the northwest corner of Italy, Carema from the border between Val d'Aosta and Piedmont. These attractive reds, produced in limited quantities, tend to be lighter and fruitier than other Nebbiolo wines.

A certain amount of Nebbiolo is also marketed as a varietal wine, either as Nebbiolo d'Alba, which is a DOC, or simply as Nebbiolo del Piemonte. But although Nebbiolo produces the region's most famous wines, this grape is planted in less than 3 percent of the vineyards of Piedmont. The most widely cultivated grape is Barbera, which accounts for more than half the total acreage in Piedmont, and for about twenty-five million cases of wine a year, almost as much red wine as is produced in Bordeaux. There are five DOC wines in Piedmont produced from Barbera, the best-known of which are Barbera d'Asti and Barbera d'Alba; two others are Barbera del Monferrato and Barbera dei Colli Tortonesi—all four together account for only a small part of the total Barbera crop, most of which is marketed simply as Barbera or Barbera del Piemonte. The village of Gabiano has given its name to a fifth DOC for Barbera produced in the Monferrato hills.

The other principal red-wine grape varieties of Piedmont are Dolcetto, Freisa, and Grignolino. All these names may appear on labels, but the varietal wines that are entitled to DOC status are also associated with a specific region of origin, for example Dolcetto d'Alba, Freisa di Chieri, and Grignolino d'Asti. What makes the different DOC names confusing at first is that different varieties may be planted in a given region—Barbera d'Asti, Dolcetto d'Asti, Freisa d'Asti, Grignolino d'Asti—and a given variety may be planted in more than one region, as in the case of the Barbera DOCs cited above. What's more, a number of these red wines may be dry or semisweet, still or sparkling. The examples shipped here are almost always dry, but, of course, their individual characteristics vary depending on the grape variety and the zone of origin. In general, Grignolino produces the lightest wines, and since both its quality and quantity are uneven, it is now less widely planted than in the past. Freisa is relatively light and fruity, and is the variety most likely to be made into an *amabile* or sparkling wine. Despite its name (*dolce* means sweet), Dolcetto is almost always dry and full-flavored; Dolcetto d'Alba, the most frequently encountered DOC, can be an excellent wine, combining ripe fruit with tannic structure.

The best-known white-wine grape of Piedmont, of course, is Moscato Canelli, used to make Asti Spumante. The grape is also used to make a *frizzante*, or lightly sparkling, wine with the DOC Moscato Naturale d'Asti. Although dry white wine accounts for a very small part of Piedmont's total production, that made from the Cortese grape at Gavi has achieved an excellent reputation in a relatively short time; the DOC Gavi or Cortese di Gavi was established only in 1974. Among the labels associated with this wine are the Gavi dei Gavi of La Scolca, Principessa Gavia of Villa Banfi, La Battistina, and La Giustiniana.

Lombardy and Liguria

The Valtellina vineyards, situated northeast of Milan, are in the Lombardy region, but as they are planted primarily with Nebbiolo, whose local name is Chiavennasca, the wines bear some similarities to those of Piedmont. The steeply terraced vineyards, situated on either side of the city of Sondrio, extend along the north bank of the Adda River, which flows from east to west at this point on its course to Lake Como. Although some white wines are made there, the DOC Valtellina applies only to red wines, and these must contain at least 70 percent Chiavennasca. Wines entitled to the higher appellation Valtellina Superiore, which account for about half of the region's production, must be made at least 95 percent from the Chiavennasca; their labels almost always feature the name of one of the district's inner zones—Valgella, Sassella, Grumello, and Inferno. In addition, an unusual dry red wine, similar to an Amarone from Valpolicella, is made from slightly dried grapes and labeled Sfursat or Sforzato; it has a minimum alcohol content of 14.5 percent and is likely to have more body than other Valtellina wines. Producers include Nino Negri (which markets the proprietary wines Fracia and Castel Chiuro), Rainoldi, and Enologica Valtellinese.

Another important DOC wine district in Lombardy is Oltrepò Pavese, situated about thirty miles south of Milan, beyond the city of Pavia and the Po River. Red wines labeled simply Oltrepò Pavese are made primarily from Barbera and Croatina grapes, but within the DOC Oltrepò Pavese are a number of wines labeled with such varietal names as Barbera, Bonarda, Riesling, and Pinot, as well as three unusual reds—Barbacarlo, Buttafuoco, and Sangue di Giuda. The Oltrepò Pavese contains Italy's most extensive plantings of Pinot Nero, most of which is used, as is the district's excellent Pinot Bianco and Pinot Grigio, for sparkling wines. Frecciarossa (red arrow) is the name of an estate in the Oltrepò Pavese that produces red, white, and rosé wines.

Franciacorta is a DOC district situated east of Milan, between Bergamo and Brescia. The reds are made from Cabernet Franc, Barbera, Nebbiolo, and Merlot, the whites from Pinot Bianco. Much of the white-wine production is made into sparkling wines by such firms as Guido Berlucchi and Ca' del Bosco.

The Liguria region, which adjoins Piedmont to the south, extends along the Ligurian Sea, with Genoa at its center.

Liguria's two best-known DOC districts are Cinqueterre, near
La Spezia, long famous for its white wines; and Dolceacqua,
near San Remo, achieving a reputation for its reds, produced
from the Rossese grape, and also labeled Rossese di Dolceacqua. Vermentino and Pigato are the principal white-wine
grapes of Liguria.

VENETO AND THE NORTHEAST

The overall quality of the wines produced in the three northeastern provinces of Italy collectively referred to as the Tre
Venezie—the Veneto, Friuli-Venezia Giulia, and Trentino-
Alto Adige—is such that the area accounts for about a third of
the country's total crop of DOC wines. The most famous
wines of the Tre Venezie are Soave, Valpolicella, and Bardolino, but this part of Italy is becoming widely known for its
extensive range of varietal wines. These include such well-
known French and German varieties as Merlot, Cabernet
Franc, Cabernet Sauvignon, Pinot Nero (Pinot Noir), Chardonnay, Pinot Bianco (Pinot Blanc), Pinot Grigio (Pinot Gris),
Riesling Renano (Rhine Riesling), Sauvignon, Sylvaner,
Traminer, and Müller-Thurgau. There are also a number of
less familiar native varieties that include, among the reds,
Lagrein, Marzemino, Raboso, Schiava, Teroldego, and
Refosco, known in France as Mondeuse; the whites include
Picolit, Prosecco, Verduzzo, and Tocai Friulano, not to be
confused with the Tokay of Hungary, which is made primar-
ily from the Furmint grape.

Merlot, Cabernet Franc, and Cabernet Sauvignon produce
light, pleasing and distinctive red wines which are, for the
most part, not barrel-aged. Cabernet Franc is more widely
planted than Cabernet Sauvignon in northern Italy, and a wine
labeled simply Cabernet is likely to be made primarily or
entirely from the former. Excellent wines are also produced
from Chardonnay, which is, in a way, a relatively new variety in Italy. In the late 1970s a number of northern Italian
winemakers realized that much of what they had always
assumed was Pinot Bianco, and sold as such, was actually
Chardonnay. As Chardonnay was much better known as a
varietal wine than Pinot Bianco, especially in the United
States, many producers began to vinify and bottle Chardonnay
separately, and to label it as such. Chardonnays produced in
certain specific zones were first granted DOC status in 1984.

The Veneto

The Veneto region, whose capital is Venice, produces three of Italy's best-known wines—Soave, Valpolicella, and Bardolino. This trio from Verona, whose combined production is ten to twelve million cases a year, accounts for about two-thirds of all the DOC wines shipped to America, with Soave leading the way by a wide margin.

The vineyards around the village of Soave produce a pale, dry white wine with a great deal of charm if it is cleanly made and bottled young. Not so long ago it was still common to bottle Soave two or three years after the vintage, which gave the best of them more character but less delicacy and fruit. Soave is made primarily from the Garganega grape, with some Trebbiano. The two red wines, Valpolicella and Bardolino, can be among the most most enjoyable of Italy—fresh and light-bodied, with a characteristic dry aftertaste. Valpolicella is the sturdier of the two, Bardolino somewhat paler in color and lighter in body. The wines are made from Corvina Veronese, with varying proportions of Rondinella, Molinara, and other varieties. The picturesque town of Bardolino is situated on the eastern shore of Lake Garda, and many of its hillside vineyards are exposed to extra sunshine reflected off the surface of the lake. Valpolicella is a valley north of Verona whose hillsides are covered with vines. The inner zone of Valpantena, just above Verona, produces wines marketed as Valpolicella-Valpantena.

An unusual red wine, Recioto della Valpolicella, is made in limited quantities from selected bunches of grapes that are spread out on trays or hung on hooks and left to dry, thus increasing the proportion of sugar in the juice. (*Recioto* is derived from *recie*, or ears, and refers to the top of the bunch, which has had the most exposure to sun and is likely to have the ripest grapes.) The wine made from these specially dried grapes has more alcohol and more flavor than a Valpolicella, and may be matured in large casks for several years. A wine labeled simply Recioto della Valpolicella is likely to be semi-sweet and often has a slight sparkle as well. If such a wine is left to ferment until it is dry, it is labeled Amarone. Recioto della Valpolicella Amarone is a particularly sturdy, long-lived, and heady wine—14 or 15 percent alcohol is not uncommon—and very different in style from a Valpolicella. Recioto di Soave, made in the same way from white grapes, is a semisweet wine.

The best-known shipper of Veronese wines is Bolla; other producers include Allegrini, Bertani, Folonari, Lamberti, Masi,

Santa Sofia, Tedeschi, and the Cantina Sociale di Soave, one of Europe's biggest cooperative cellars. Pieropan is a firm noted for its Soave, Le Ragose for its Valpolicella. Campo Fiorin is a proprietary name used by Masi for a rich red from the Valpolicella zone.

Although Soave, Valpolicella, and Bardolino dominate the wine scene in the Veneto, a wide variety of other wines are produced throughout the region. Bianco di Custoza is a light, dry white wine made primarily from Trebbiano in vineyards situated in the southern part of the Bardolino district, southeast of Lake Garda. Several appealing wines produced on the Lombardy side of Lake Garda are usually associated with those of Verona: Lugana is another Trebbiano-based white wine; Groppello is a red-wine grape whose name is occasionally seen on labels. Wines produced on the western shore of Lake Garda, near Brescia, are entitled to the DOC Riviera del Garda Bresciano; the appellation includes a red wine and Chiaretto, a dark rosé.

The Gambellara district, just east of Soave, produces a white wine made primarily from Garganega. Just south of Vicenza is the extensive Colli Berici district, whose vineyards are planted with such varieties as Cabernet, Merlot, Pinot Bianco, Sauvignon, and Tocai. North of Vicenza, the Breganze district is best known for its Merlot and Tocai; the Colli Euganei zone near Padua.

The vineyards of the Piave district, which extend on either side of the Piave River, are situated just north of Venice, in the province of Treviso. The principal varieties are Merlot, which accounts for more than half the total, Cabernet, Pinot Nero, Pinot Bianco, Pinot Grigio, Tocai Italico, and two local varieties, the white Verduzzo and the red Raboso. Each is entitled to DOC status in conjunction with the district name— Merlot del Piave, Piave Pinot Bianco, and so on.

East of Piave are the districts that produce Tocai di Lison and two red wines, Merlot di Pramaggiore and Cabernet di Pramaggiore. North of Piave is the area that includes the two wine villages of Conegliano and Valdobiaddene, whose vineyards are planted primarily with the Prosecco grape. The resulting wine, which may include a small proportion of Pinot Grigio or Pinot Bianco, may be still, lightly sparkling, or sparkling, and each version may be dry or semisweet. Sparkling wines from an area called Cartizze may be labeled as such or as Superiore di Cartizze. One of the best-known firms producing Prosecco di Conegliano-Valdobiaddene is Carpenè Malvolti. Also in the province of Treviso is the Venegazzù estate founded by Count Loredan-Gasparini, and under new ownership since the mid-1970s, which is known for a range of wines that includes a Bordeaux-style Cabernet-Merlot blend labeled Riserva della Casa and a *méthode champenoise* sparkling wine.

Friuli-Venezia Giulia

The Friuli-Venezia Giulia region is situated in the northeastern corner of Italy, on the border with Austria and Yugoslavia. Part of the region, whose capital is Trieste, once belonged to Yugoslavia, and that influence can be recognized in the local cuisine, the non-Italian names of some of its wine producers, and the extensive cultivation of certain grape varieties more often seen in Yugoslavia and Austria than in other parts of Italy.

Among the varieties found in the vineyards of Friuli-Venezia Giulia are Merlot, Cabernet Franc, Cabernet Sauvignon, Pinot Nero, Chardonnay, Pinot Bianco, Pinot Grigio, Riesling Italico (Wälschriesling), Riesling Renano, Sauvignon, and Traminer, as well as such native varieties as Refosco, Tocai Friulano, Verduzzo, Ribolla, and Picolit. Although Merlot is the most widely planted grape in this region, it is the delicate and elegant white wines that have made the vinous reputation of this part of Italy. New equipment and modern technology, especially temperature-controlled fermentation, have enabled the producers here to achieve excellent results with many varieties.

The wide range of varieties cultivated in Friuli-Venezia Giulia are found in varying proportions in the DOC zones of the region—Grave del Friuli, Collio Goriziano, Colli Orientali del Friuli, Isonzo, Aquileia, and Latisana. As is the case in such viticultural areas of Alsace and California, where a number of different varieties are grown in the same sites, the name of the grape from which each wine is made is more significant than where it comes from. With one exception, all the DOC wines of Friuli-Venezia Giulia consist of a varietal name in conjunction with an appellation of origin.

The biggest DOC district is Grave del Friuli, an extensive plain named, as is the Graves district of Bordeaux, for its gravelly soil. More than half of Grave del Friuli's vineyards are planted with Merlot, which produces a relatively light but distinctive red. Most of the Cabernet wines are made from

Cabernet Franc, as is the case throughout northern Italy, but Cabernet Sauvignon is also planted. Such wines may be labeled Cabernet, with no further qualification. A full selection of white varietal wines are produced in Grave del Friuli, of which Chardonnay and Pinot Grigio are the ones most likely to be found here. Producers include Duca Badoglio, Collavini, Friulvini, and Plozner.

The Collio Goriziano district, whose name usually appears on labels simply as Collio, is the easternmost winegrowing area of northern Italy, and highly acclaimed for its white wines. Tocai Friulano and Merlot account for more than half of Collio's production, but Pinot Bianco, Pinot Grigio, and Sauvignon are among the other varieties cultivated there. A white wine from this district labeled simply Collio—a blend of Ribolla, Malvasia, and Tocai—is the only exception to the rule that every DOC wine of Friulia-Venezia Giulia be made from a specific variety whose name must appear on the label along with that of the district of origin. Another distinctive wine from Collio is a flavorful style of Pinot Grigio, known as *ramato*, whose pale coppery color results from letting the juice stay in contact with the grape skins for a time before fermentation. Among the better-known producers are Livio Felluga, Marco Felluga (which also owns the Russiz Superiore estate), EnoFriulia, Mario Schiopetto, and Jermann. The last produces a special white wine labeled Vintage Tunina, which is a blend of several varieties, including Pinot Bianco, Sauvignon, and Chardonnay.

Colli Orientali del Friuli (the Eastern Hills of Friuli) is a district situated to the north of Collio. Here, too, Merlot and Tocai Friulano account for more than half the total, but a full range of varietal wines are produced, including Verduzzo and Picolit. Verduzzo may be dry or *amabile*, and the most renowned examples of *amabile*, which come from a specific commune, are labeled Verduzzo di Ramandolo. Picolit, whose production rarely exceeds three thousand cases, is a rare sweet white wine with a minimum alcohol content of 15 percent made from especially ripe grapes that are particularly difficult to cultivate.

Merlot is the most widely planted variety in each of the three smallest DOC districts of Friuli-Venezia Giulia: Isonzo, whose second most important variety is Tocai Friulano; Aquileia, where Refosco is second to Merlot; and Latisana, where Cabernet is also important.

Trentino–Alto Adige

The third of the regions grouped together as Tre Venezie is Trentino–Alto Adige, which contains the northernmost of Italy's vineyards. The region consists of two provinces— Trentino, whose principal city is Trento, situated about fifty miles north of Verona; and Alto Adige, whose capital is Bolzano, even farther north, and closer to the Alps that separate that part of Italy from Austria.

The province of Trentino encompasses about twenty-five thousand acres of vineyards, and red wines account for more than 80 percent of its production. Schiava, a local variety, is the most widely planted red-wine grape; other native red varieties include Lagrein, Marzemino, and Teroldego, as well as the more traditional Merlot, Cabernet Franc, Cabernet Sauvignon, and Pinot Nero. White grapes cultivated in Trentino include Pinot Bianco, Chardonnay, Pinot Grigio, Riesling Italico, Riesling Renano, Müller-Thurgau, Sylvaner, Sauvignon, Traminer Aromatico, the local Nosiola, and two types of Muscat, Moscato Giallo and Moscato Rosa. The principal DOC of this district is Trentino in conjunction with a varietal name, as Merlot del Trentino, Pinot Bianco del Trentino, and so on.

A number of other DOCs have been established in Trentino as well. North of Trento is the village of Sorni, which gives its name to a red made primarily from Schiava and a white made primarily from Nosiola. Just above Sorni are vineyards planted with Teroldego on a wide plain known as Campo Rotaliano; the distinctive red wines are labeled Teroldego Rotaliano. Casteller is a light red wine produced from Schiava, Merlot, and Lambrusco in vineyards situated, for the most part, south of Trento. The Valdadige appellation, whose *rosso* and *bianco* are each made from a combination of several varieties, extends south from Trento and into the province of Verona. Wines from Trentino include those of Bollini, Cavit, Pojer & Sandri, Zeni, and the enological institute of San Michele all'Adige. Also, such renowned sparkling-wine firms as Ferrari and Equipe 5 are located in Trentino.

The province of Alto Adige was once part of the Austro-Hungarian Empire, and even today many of its residents are more likely to speak German than Italian, and to refer to the area of Südtirol, or South Tyrol. The varieties cultivated in Alto Adige are virtually the same as in Trentino; Schiava is the dominant red and, now that it has been identified correctly, Chardonnay may be the most widely planted white. As in Trentino and Friuli, the Chardonnay produced in Alto Adige was granted DOC status in 1984. Incidentally, the Traminer grape, which achieved its principal success in Alsace, is thought to have its origins near the Alto Adige village of Termeno (Tramin in German).

Just as the most extensive DOC of Trentino is so named, so Alto Adige is the biggest appellation of the region around Bolzano. There are more than a dozen varieties whose names may be combined with Alto Adige, as Schiava dell'Alto Adige, Pinot Grigio dell'Alto Adige, and so on. Because many of these wines are exported to Germany and Austria, however, the appellation Alto Adige is likely to be replaced on a label with its German equivalent, Südtirol, as in Südtiroler Vernatsch and Pinot Grigio dell'Alto Adige becomes Südtiroler Merlot or Südtiroler Cabernet. And because a number of grape varieties have different names in German than in Italian, a wine such as Schiava dell'Alto Adige becomes Südtiroler Ruländer. Other varieties whose names may vary from one label to another are Pinot Nero and Blauburgunder, Pinot Bianco and Weissburgunder, Traminer Aromatico and Gewürztraminer, and Riesling Renano and Rheinriesling. A further complication occurs in the case of the wines made from the indigenous Lagrein grape—if vinified as a rosé, it is usually labeled Lagrein Kretzer, the red as Lagrein Dunkel; the Italian equivalents are Legrein Rosato and Lagrein Scuro, respectively.

The DOC Terlano (Terlaner in German) is used for white wines made from half a dozen different varieties, and labeled accordingly, as Terlano Sylvaner, for example. A wine labeled simply Terlano (or Terlaner) is a blend of several varieties, with Pinot Bianco making up at least half the total. Valle Isarco is another white-wine appellation whose vineyards, northwest of Bolzano, extend along the Isarco River. Meranese di Collina is a light red wine made from Schiava near the town of Merano.

Perhaps the best-known DOC of Alto Adige is Lago di Caldaro or Caldaro (Kalterersee in German), whose light red wines are made primarily from Schiava. Although most of the vineyards that produce Caldaro are in Alto Adige, the zone extends into Trentino as well. The DOC Santa Maddalena (Sankt Magdalener in German) is situated just north of Bolzano; this light red wine, too, is made from Shiava. Firms that produce Alto Adige wines include Castel Schwanburg,

Hofstätter, Kettmeir, Alois Lageder, and in very limited quantities, Giorgio Gray (under the Kehlburg, Herrnhofer, and Bellendorf labels) and Herbert Tiefenbrunner. Santa Margherita, whose headquarters are in the eastern Veneto, northeast of Venice, is best known for its Pinot Grigio, Chardonnay, and Pinot Bianco, made from grapes grown in the Alto Adige and Trentino. The firm also produces more than a dozen other wines from the Tre Venezie, including Cabernet di Pramaggiore, Tocai di Lison, Prosecco di Conegliano-Valdobbiadene, and two proprietary wines—Ruzante, a light red made primarily from Refosco; and Luna dei Feldi, a white made from Chardonnay, Müller-Thurgau, and Traminer.

TUSCANY AND CENTRAL ITALY

The region of Tuscany, with Florence as its capital, is the home of one of the most famous red wines in the world: Chianti. Fifty to sixty million cases of wine are produced in Tuscany, and Chianti usually accounts for about a quarter of the total. Perhaps no wine was as closely associated with a particular bottle as Chianti was with the straw-covered *fiasco*, or flask. In recent years, the distinctive and picturesque *fiasco* has virtually disappeared from retail shelves here, and is now used primarily for wines sold to tourists in Italy. The expensive hand labor required to weave the straw meant that in many cases the consumer was paying more for the straw than for the wine in the bottle. And because *fiaschi* are difficult to store properly on their sides, they were unsuitable for the region's finest wines, which benefit from bottle age. But the principal reason that Chianti producers were delighted to discontinue the use of *fiaschi* is that they perpetuated the image of Chianti as a cheap and ordinary wine, obscuring the fact that the best examples can be taken seriously and are well worth the higher prices at which they must be sold.

The wines of Chianti are generally divided into two basic categories. One is the young, fresh, light-bodied, and occasionally *frizzante* wine served in the trattorias of Florence as early as March following the vintage; the other is a bigger, more tannic wine that needs time to mature in cask and bottle. Both styles are made from the same four or five grape varieties. According to the DOC law established in 1967, and in effect until 1984, Sangiovese accounted for 50 to 80 percent, blended with 10 to 30 percent of Canaiolo, and 10 to

30 percent of two white grapes, Trebbiano and Malvasia. Up to 5 percent of Colorino or certain other varieties could also be used. The Sangiovese contributes body and character, the Canaiolo delicacy and fruitiness, and the white grapes soften the wine. The original blending formula, established by Barone Bettino Ricasoli in the late nineteenth century, consisted of 85 percent Sangiovese, 10 to 15 percent Canaiolo, and 5 percent Malvasia, the latter to be included only for those wines meant to be consumed young. When the DOC laws were established, they reflected the relatively high proportion of white grapes planted in the Chianti region, and since the name Chianti Bianco was discontinued, producers were permitted to use white grapes in the production of the red wine.

Many producers believed that the use of white grapes in more than minimal amounts resulted in a Chianti that was relatively light-bodied, quick to age, and not typical of the appellation. When Chianti was granted a DOCG, in 1984, these considerations were taken into account. Sangiovese must make up 75 to 90 percent of the total, and the proportions of white grapes now permitted for Chianti may vary from only 5 to 10 percent (and from 2 to 5 percent for Chianti Classico). Also, the proportion of nontraditional grapes that may be used for Chianti—Cabernet Sauvignon, for example—has been increased from 5 to 10 percent. Maximum production per acre has been reduced by about a third as well.

The traditional vinification of Chianti makes use of an unusual technique called *governo alla toscana*. Especially ripe grapes are placed on trays or hung on hooks for several weeks in well-ventilated rooms to dry out, which concentrates their sugar content. The grapes are then crushed, and when they begin to ferment, they are added to the wine already made in the normal way. The *governo* system adds body and alcohol to the new wine, and—because it induces malolactic fermentation—suppleness as well. This technique was traditionally associated with wines meant to be consumed young, but in practice it was also used by some producers for their better wines. Today, what is still referred to as the *governo* system rarely makes use of specially dried grapes, which is an expensive process, but rather of grape concentrate, which is juice whose natural sugar content has been concentrated by sophisticated means. Because chaptalization, the addition of sugar to fermenting must to increase a wine's alcohol content, is illegal in Italy, this adaptation of the *governo* process is now used for almost all Chianti, especially in poor years, when the grapes lack adequate sugar. Until 1984, Chianti could contain up to 15 percent neutral, high-alcohol wines or concentrated must from outside the region; under the DOCG laws, outside wines may no longer be used and the concentrate must be made entirely from grapes grown in Chianti.

The quality of Chianti can vary greatly from one label to another, especially since some wines are bottled within a few months and fade quickly, while others are aged in wood for two or three years and improve in bottle for another five. Whereas each vintage of the famous red wines of Bordeaux and Burgundy, for example, is kept in barrel approximately the same length of time before being bottled, the wines of Chianti are aged depending on their character and quality. It is not unusual for a firm to be bottling the wines of a recent light vintage while the bigger wines of a previous vintage are still maturing in large casks. This leads to another distinction to be made among the wines of Chianti, based on the age of the wines. A Chianti that is at least three years old can be sold as a *Riserva*. The required aging need not take place entirely in wood, but may be a combination of cask and bottle, although the DOCG laws specify that a *Riserva* must be aged a minimum of one year in cask. Most producers bottle *Riservas* only in the best years, and use only the best part of the crop; wines so labeled generally represent the finest Chianti available.

Within the Chianti region is the inner Chianti Classico zone, which lies directly between Florence and Siena. Its boundaries were defined more than 250 years ago, and the producers within the zone claim that theirs is the only true Chianti. The best wines from the Chianti Classico zone are acknowledged to display more body, character, and longevity than most other Chianti, but since wine made in the surrounding area has been sold as Chianti for well over a hundred years, the vineyard proprietors in the original zone formed a Chianti Classico *consorzio* in 1924 to define the limits of the Classico area and to regulate the quality and authenticity of its wines. The seal of the Chianti Classico *consorzio*, which appears on the neck of the bottle, is the *gallo nero*, or black rooster, on a gold ground surrounded by a red circle, which has become one of the best-known quality symbols in the world of wine. When the DOC laws for Chianti went into effect in 1967, they confirmed the geographical limits of the Classico zone as originally defined by the *consorzio*, so a wine may be entitled to the DOC Chianti Classico even if its producer is not a member of the *consorzio*. Consequently, the *consorzio* no longer promotes the *gallo nero* as a guarantee of a wine's appellation of origin, but of its superior quality, and continues to act as a self-regulating body with somewhat stricter standards than those established by the DOC laws. For example, a certain proportion of Chianti Classico wines are rejected each year by a *consorzio* tasting panel as not being up to the standards of the *gallo nero* seal.

In the past fifteen years, the area planted in vines in the Classico zone has increased considerably, and production has more than doubled. Three to four million cases of Chianti Classico are produced today, which accounts for about a quarter of all the wine made in the Chianti region. Most proprietors within the Classico zone belong to the *consorzio*, but some major shippers, including Brolio, Antinori, and Ruffino, prefer to trade on their own reputations without benefit of the *gallo nero*. Melini is now the biggest producer of Chianti Classico within the *consorzio*.

What this means to the consumer is that of the wines labeled with the DOC Chianti Classico (which account for about two-thirds of the Chianti shipped to this country), some also carry the black-rooster neck strip, others do not. Among the dozens of Chianti Classico producers whose wines are found here are Badia a Coltibuono, Bertolli, Brolio, Castello di Fonterutoli, Castello di Gabbiano, Castello dei Rampolla, Castello di Uzzano, Castello di Verrazzano, Castello di Volpaia, Melini, Monsanto, Monte Vertine, Nozzole, Palazzo al Bosco, Ricasoli, Riecine, Ruffino, Santa Cristina, and Villa Antinori.

There are six delimited areas within the Chianti region in addition to the Classico zone—Colli Aretini, Colli Fiorentini, Colli Senesi, Colline Pisane, Montalbano, and Rufina—but their names are not often seen on bottles shipped here. In 1927, producers in the Colli Fiorentini zone formed their own *consorzio*, whose emblem consists of a pink cherub, or *putto*, on a blue ground. In the past few years this *consorzio* has expanded to include producers in the other non-Classico zones, and they, too, may use the *putto* seal.

The best-known firm outside the Classico area is Frescobaldi, whose vineyards are situated east of Florence in the Rufina zone (not to be confused with Ruffino, a well-known firm that produces several Chianti Classicos, including Riserva Ducale). Frescobaldi's best known Chianti comes from their 370-acre Castello di Nipozzano estate; Montesodi, produced only in the best vintages, and in limited quantities, comes from a specific vineyard within that estate. Pomino, a small district within the Chianti Rufina zone whose name has long been used by Frescobaldi for both red and white wines, was granted DOC status in 1983. The white, much better known, is made primarily from Pinot Bianco and Chardonnay.

A number of producers within the Chianti region have experimented with wines made entirely from red grapes, and thus not entitled to the Chianti appellation. One of the best known is Tignanello, first made by the Antinori firm in 1971, again in 1975, and in most vintages since 1979. The wine consists of Sangiovese with 15 or 20 percent of Cabernet Sauvignon, and has inspired other firms to make similar blends. Some producers are making wines entirely from Sangiovese (one example is Le Pergole Torte, from the Monte Vertine estate), and others are experimenting with Cabernet Sauvignon bottled on its own. The most famous such wine is Sassicaia, bottled and distributed by Antinori. The wine is made primarily from Cabernet Sauvignon, with some Cabernet Franc, at the Tenuta San Guido estate, in the hills near Bolgheri, southeast of Livorno.

Although the DOC Chianti applies only to red wines, most firms also produce a white wine. Some are labeled simply as Bianco, others are marketed with proprietary names. Several producers, including Antinori, Brolio, Frescobaldi, and Ruffino, created the name Galestro for a special Tuscan white wine. It must be fermented at a low temperature, to retain its fruit and delicacy, and its alcohol content may not exceed 10.5 percent. Galestro, which is now produced by more than a dozen firms, is made primarily from Trebbiano and Malvasia, along with such varieties as Pinot Bianco, Pinot Grigio, and Sauvignon. (The Chianti Classico *consorzio* also created a white-wine name, Bianco della Lega, in an attempt to market the Trebbiano and Malvasia that can no longer be blended into Chianti.)

Other Tuscan white wines include Bianco di Pitigliano, Bianco Vergine della Valdichiana, and the well-known Vernaccia di San Gimignano, made from that grape variety on hillside vineyards near the picturesque medieval town of San Gimignano, about twenty-five miles southwest of Florence. Producers of this attractive dry wine—the only DOC white in Tuscany not made from Trebbiano and Malvasia—include Riccardo Falchini, Guicciardini Strozzi, and Teruzzi & Puthod, whose wine is labeled Ponte a Rondolino.

Vin Santo is an unusual white wine produced throughout Tuscany, usually from Trebbiano and Malvasia. The grapes are dried to concentrate their natural sugar, crushed and fermented in small barrels, where they are left for a minimum of three years. The resulting wine, which is likely to have 15 or 16 percent of alcohol, may be dry or sweet, and good examples are characterized by an intense, complex, and somewhat oxidized taste reminiscent of sherry.

Carmignano, a small district fifteen miles west of Florence, is actually contained within the Chianti Montalbano zone. Its wines traditionally contain a small proportion of Cabernet Sauvignon, and are usually firmer and longer-lived than the Chianti produced from adjoining vineyards. The best-known producer is Contini Bonacossi, whose wines are labeled Villa di Capezzana and Villa di Trefiano.

The village of Montalcino, about twenty miles southeast of Siena, gives its name to one of Italy's most famous red wines—Brunello di Montalcino. Brunello is the local name for a variant of Sangiovese known as Sangiovese Grosso. The wine in its present form—rich, wood-aged, long-lived, and from the Brunello grape alone—was first made in the late nineteenth century by Ferruccio Biondi-Santi, whose estate, Il Greppo, continues to produce the best-known and most expensive examples. The increasing fame of this wine has resulted in extensive new plantings, and annual production, which was around twenty-five thousand cases in the late 1960s, now exceeds 300,000 cases. Brunello di Montalcino, which has been elevated to DOCG status, may not be sold until the fifth year after the harvest and must age for a minimum of three and a half years in cask, four and a half for a *Riserva*. The best of them are among the finest and longest-lived of all Italian red wines, but there are those who feel that the mandatory three and a half years in cask can result in wines that are too tannic, woody, and somewhat dried-out, especially in lesser vintages. As a result, many firms also produce a second wine from Brunello grapes that is not aged as long in wood and is more accessible when young. In 1984, the DOC Rosso di Montalcino was established for such wines, which may be sold a year after the vintage. Besides Biondi-Santi, leading producers include Altesino, Case Basse, Castelgiocondo, Emilio Costanti, Tenuta Caparzo, Tenuta Col d'Orcia, Fattoria dei Barbi, Mastrojanni, Poggio Antico, Il Poggione, and Villa Banfi. Fattoria dei Barbi also makes a proprietary red wine called Brusco dei Barbi using the traditional *governo alla toscana* discussed elsewhere.

In the early 1980s, Villa Banfi, the American firm that

imports Riunite Lambrusco, created extensive new vineyards and a large modern winery in the Montalcino area. Under the direction of enologist Ezio Rivella, more than two thousand acres have been planted on a seven-thousand acre property. About half the vineyards produce Moscadello di Montalcino, a sweet, low-alcohol, lightly sparkling white wine; the remaining acreage is planted with Brunello, for Brunello di Montalcino; Cabernet Sauvignon, marketed with the name Tavernelle; Chardonnay, labeled Fontanelle; and Pino Gris, labeled San Angelo.

From Montepulciano, situated fifteen miles east of Montalcino, comes a red wine called Vino Nobile di Montepulciano. The *nobile* does not derive from the character of the wine, but from the fact that it was first produced by the local nobility in the fourteenth century. Vino Nobile di Montepulciano is made primarily from the Sangiovese grape in a district that overlaps part of the Chianti region—both Montepulciano and Montalcino are in the Colli Senesi zone—and many of the producers make both a Chianti and a Vino Nobile from their vineyards. Although Vino Nobile, unlike Chianti, must be aged a minimum of two years in wood, the quality of these wines is uneven—some are distinctive, complex, and long-lived, others are similar to Chianti. Producers include Avignonesi, Fanetti, Fassati, Fattoria del Cerro, Fattoria di Fognano, Poderi Boscarelli, and Poliziano.

Umbria

Adjoining Tuscany to the southeast is the region of Umbria, whose capital is Perugia, and whose best-known wine is Orvieto. The hilltop village of Orvieto, situated about halfway between Florence and Rome, is dominated by its famous cathedral, begun in the late thirteenth century. The white wine of Orvieto has a long history, but its popularity was gradually eclipsed by such wines as Soave and Verdicchio. In the past few years, however, a number of Tuscan firms have taken a greater interest in this wine; well over a million cases a year are produced, and it is now much more widely available here. Orvieto, made primarily from Trebbiano, with lesser amounts of Malvasia, Grechetto, and Verdello, is marketed either as *secco*, dry, or *abboccato* semisweet. It is the *abboccato* version of this wine that established its fame, but today, in response to consumer demand for dry white wines, it is Orvieto *secco* that is most often seen. Castello della Sala of

Antinori is a well-known example; others are Bigi, Cotti, Decugnano dei Barbi, Petrurbani, Ruffino, Le Velette, and Vaselli.

The red and white wines of Torgiano, produced a few miles south of Perugia, have achieved recognition in recent years due to the efforts of its leading producer, Giorgio Lungarotti. The red wine, which the Lungarotti firm markets under the proprietary name Rubesco, is made primarily from Sangiovese, plus some Canaiolo; special lots are given longer wood-aging and bottled as Rubesco Riserva. The white, made from Trebbiano and Grechetto, is labeled Torre di Giano. Lungarotti, whose six hundred acres of vineyards include about sixty acres each of Chardonnay and Cabernet Sauvignon, also produces limited amounts of Cabernet Sauvignon and Chardonnay, and a proprietary red wine, San Giorgio, which is a blend of Sangiovese, Canaiolo, and Cabernet Sauvignon.

The Marches

Verdicchio, one of Italy's most popular white wines, is produced in the region of the Marches, situated east of Umbria, along the Adriatic Sea. Just as Chianti was long associated with the straw-covered *fiasco*, so Verdicchio, named after the grape variety from which it is primarily made, owes some of its success to the distinctive amphora-shaped bottle in which it is sold. The complete name of the DOC is Verdicchio dei Castelli di Jesi—Jesi is a village northwest of the city of Ancona—and most bottles are so labeled. Southwest of Jesi is another, smaller district whose wines are entitled to the DOC Verdicchio di Matelica, but this name is rarely seen here. Fazi-Battaglia is the best-known producer.

The most extensive DOC district in the Marches produces light red wine entitled to the appellation Rosso Piceno; the wine is made from Sangiovese and Montepulciano. Rosso Cònero, another red wine from this region, is made primarily from Montepulciano.

Emilia-Romagna

Emilia-Romagna, the region that adjoins Tuscany to the north, is famous for its hearty cuisine, and its capital, Bologna, is as esteemed by Italian gastronomes as Lyons is by the French. Emilia-Romagna's best-known wine is Lambrusco, which has become the best-selling Italian wine in America. Lambrusco, made by the Charmat process used for many of the world's sparkling wines, is a slightly sweet red wine, relatively low in alcohol, with just enough sparkle so that it sometimes foams up when poured and leaves a prickly sensation on the tongue when drunk. The wine is moderately priced and, served chilled, has become quite popular with people who find most red wines too dry.

Lambrusco is made from the grape of that name near Modena, northwest of Bologna. There are four DOC Lambrusco wines, the best-known of which is Lambrusco di Sorbara. Lambrusco entitled to a DOC accounts for only a small part of the total production, however, and virtually all the wines shipped to this country are non-DOC; furthermore, the wines produced for export are grapier and sweeter than the fresh, light dry wines that are enjoyed in the restaurants of Bologna. The popularity of Lambrusco is such that in some years it has accounted for as much of two-thirds of all the Italian wines sold here. Current figures, however, also include the white and rosé wines shipped by Lambrusco producers, which now amount to more than half the total. Riunite is the leading brand; others are Cella, Giacobazzi, and Zonin.

A great deal of pleasant red and white wine is made in an extensive area that stretches from Bologna southeast to the Adriatic. The DOCs for the white wines are Albana di Romagna and Trebbiano di Romagna; for the red wine, Sangiovese di Romagna.

FROM ROME TO THE SOUTH

Visitors to the restaurants and cafés of Rome will find themselves drinking the attractive white wines of the Castelli Romani, a group of once-fortified hill towns a few miles southeast of the city. Although this district produces red wines as well, the whites are much better known and are entitled to DOC status. The wines are made primarily from Malvasia and Trebbiano grapes, and although they can all be vinified either dry or semisweet, the ones shipped here are almost always dry. Among the various DOCs, the wines of Marino, Colli Albani, and Colli Lanuvini can be found here, but it is the light-bodied dry white wine from the village of Frascati that is the best-known of all; Fontana Candida is the most familiar brand.

Beyond the Castelli Romani is the Aprilia district, whose

CENTRAL AND SOUTHERN ITALY

white wine is labeled Trebbiano di Aprilia, and whose two red wines are Merlot di Aprilia and Sangiovese di Aprilia.

A white wine with the colorful name Est! Est!! Est!!! di Montefiascone comes from vineyards situated about fifty miles north of Rome. The name derives from a story—whose details vary from one version to another—about a German bishop who was journeying to Rome and instructed his servant to travel ahead and chalk *Est!* (it is) on the side of those inns whose wines were worth a stop. The servant was so taken with the wines of Montefiascone that he wrote *Est! Est!! Est!!!* on the wall of a local inn. The bishop stopped and apparently concurred, as the legend states that he settled in Montefiascone and spent the rest of his days enjoying its wine. The story is better than the wine, which is not often seen here.

Two wines from the Abruzzi region that are produced in relatively large quantities are the red Montepulciano d'Abruzzo and the white Trebbiano d'Abruzzo. The red, made primarily from Montepulciano grapes to which a small proportion of Sangiovese may be added, should not be confused with Vino Nobile di Montepulciano, a Tuscan wine made from the Sangiovese grape in the village of Montepulciano. Casal Thaulero is the best-known brand of Montepulciano d'Abruzzo.

The region of Campania, whose capital is Naples, includes such tourist attractions as Amalfi, Pompeii, Mount Vesuvius, and the islands of Capri and Ischia. Perhaps the best-known wine name of this region is Lacryma Christi (Tears of Christ), which was finally incorporated into the DOC Vesuvio in 1983. The appellation includes red, white, and rosé wines produced in vineyards just south of Naples; the better wines are entitled to the name Lacryma Christi del Vesuvio. Red and white wines are made on Capri and Ischia and near the town of Ravello, which is also known for its rosé.

The finest wines of the region, however, are produced in the province of Avellino, about thirty miles east of Naples, by one of Italy's most distinguished winemakers, Antonio Mastroberardino. He makes two distinctive, dry white wines from vineyards in the Irpina Hills, Fiano di Avellino and Greco di Tufo—Fiano and Greco are local grape varieties—and a red wine that takes its name from the village of Taurasi. Made from the Aglianico grape, Taurasi must be aged a minimum of three years. Mastroberardino's Taurasi and Taurasi Riserva, the latter made only in the best vintages, are considered among the finest and longest lived of Italy's red wines.

Apulia, the region that forms the heel of Italy, has gained some unexpected attention because it is the home of Primitivo, a red-wine grape that some ampelographers believe to be identical to the Zinfandel of California. The best known DOC of Apulia is probably Castel del Monte, whose vineyards are on the hills northwest of the city of Bari. The popular rosé, whose production is greater than that of the red and white together, is made primarily from the local Bombino Nero variety; Rivera is the leading producer. The Torre Quarto estate is best known for its red wine made primarily from the Malbec grape. Favonio is the brand name used by Attilio Simonini to market his distinctive varietal wines made from Pinot Bianco, Chardonnay, Cabernet Franc, and Pinot Nero. Agl018ncio del Vulture, from the adjoining region of Basilicata, is a red wine made from the Aglianico grape grown near Mount Vulture. Cirò, whose red, white, and rosé wines come from hillside vineyards, is the best-known DOC of Calabria.

The island of Sicily produces more than 10 percent of Italy's wines, but much of it is used for the production of vermouth, or to add body and alcohol to wines made elsewhere. Sicily is the home of Marsala, a fortified wine described elsewhere, and of a number of appealing red and white wines whose quality has improved dramatically since the 1960s. The principal grape varieties cultivated in Sicily are likely to be unfamiliar even to those who enjoy the island's wines: Catarratto, Inzolia, and Caricante for the whites; Nerello Mascalese, Perricone, Calabrese, and Nero d'Avola for the reds.

The island's best-known red and white wines are probably those sold with the proprietary name Corvo, which are produced by the Duca di Salaparuta firm in Casteldaccia, near Palermo; special lots of the white wine are labeled Colomba Platino. Regaleali, an estate in the mountains southeast of Palermo with more than four hundred acres of vineyards, has been revitalized by its owner, Count Tasca d'Almerita. Wines from the slopes of Mount Etna, on the eastern end of Sicily, are entitled to the DOC Etna. Faro is a red wine made on the northeastern tip of the island; Alcamo is a white produced near the town of that name. Settesoli is a cooperative at Menfi; Segesta is a brand name.

The red and white wines of Sardinia, made from a wide variety of grapes that includes Nuragus, Vermentino, and Cannonau, are occasionally seen here; Sella & Mosca is the best-known firm.

OTHER EUROPEAN WINES

SPAIN

A tremendous amount of wine is made in Spain, which ranks third in production among western European countries, after Italy and France. Most of the wine shipped here from Spain, however, consists of sweet, fruit-flavored *sangría*. What's more, sherry, which accounts for less than 3 percent of the wine made in Spain, also outsells traditional Spanish table wines here. Nevertheless, as any visitor to Spain knows, a wide range of table wines are produced throughout that country including many sound red wines, and these are becoming more widely available here.

The appellation of origin laws of Spain, known as *Denominación de Origen*, now include more than thirty districts, the most important of which are the sherry district, discussed elsewhere, and Rioja. Some of the best wines of Spain, and the ones most often seen here, come from the Rioja district in northeastern Spain, not far from the French border. The vineyards extend for about seventy miles along the Ebro River, from Haro to Logroño and on to Alfaro. The district gets its name from a little river, the Río Oja, that flows toward the Ebro near Haro. Wines have been made in this region for several centuries, and in fact the first attempt to guarantee the authenticity of these wines dates back to 1560.

Rioja is one of the most carefully controlled wine districts in Spain, and since 1926 labels of authentic Rioja are all imprinted with a seal that resembles a small postage stamp.

Although the wines of Rioja have a long history, the character of the wines produced was altered about a hundred years ago, when phylloxera struck the vineyards of Bordeaux. A number of French winemaking families moved across the Pyrenees to the nearby Rioja district and brought with them their vinification techniques. Now history has turned the table and as the Bordeaux growers have adopted more modern winemaking methods, those of many Rioja firms remain in some ways as they were in the nineteenth century. That is, the fermenting must is kept in contact with the grape skins for an extended period, so that the red wines are particularly rich in color and tannin, and the better wines are kept in a barrel a comparatively long time: three or four years is not uncommon. Such wines are not everyone's taste, and consumers used to French and California wines often find older Riojas faded or too woody. As a result, many firms are now altering the way they make their wines, with shorter vatting and less barrel aging, to produce wines that are less tannic and dried out. Nevertheless, red Riojas are often more mature when they are bottled than similarly priced wines from other countries, which makes many of them good values.

A number of the white wines of Rioja also suffer from excessive aging in wood. However, an increasing number of producers are now vinifying their whites at lower temperatures to preserve their freshness and fruit, and bottling them within months of the vintage and without wood aging.

Rioja is a comparatively large viticultural area, producing between ten and fourteen million cases of wine a year. About three-quarters of the total is red, made primarily from the Tempranillo grape, as well as Garnacha and limited amounts of Graciano and Mazuelo. The white wines are made almost entirely from Viura, but that variety is also extensively planted among the red-wine grapes, and because growers traditionally harvest all their grapes together, most red Riojas contain about 10 to 15 percent white wine.

Although a few of the major Rioja shippers own vineyards, just about all of them buy wine or grapes from farmers and wine from cooperative cellars—which now account for over half of the production of Rioja—and blend them in their own cellars to produce a consistent house style. Most shippers also blend together wines from the three inner districts within Rioja—Rioja Alta, Rioja Baja, and Rioja Alavesa—so the relative merits and characteristics of the wines from each district are not of much concern to the consumer.

Rioja is a blended wine, and there are no famous individual vineyards in Rioja, as in France and Germany, so most shippers in this region traditionally market their wines with several different brand names. This can be confusing to the consumer at first, because the names seen on Rioja labels, such as Viña Real, Viña Pomal, Monte Real, Banda Azul, and Brilliante are proprietary names belonging to individual shippers. Thus a firm's dry white wine will have one name, its mellow white wine another; a young red wine and an older red wine will each be marketed with a different name.

In the past, vintage years on Spanish labels have not always been as accurate as they are in other wine producing countries. Many wines sold in Spain are simply labeled as $2°$ *ano* or $3°$ *ano*, meaning the wine was bottled in the second or third year after the vintage; that is, the age of the wine is more important than its vintage year. Since 1980, when new legislation went into effect, the vintage year on a label—sometimes preceded by the word *Cosecha* or *Vendimia* (both mean vintage)—is likely to be accurate.

More important than a vintage date is the word *Reserva*, which indicates that the shipper has specially selected this wine, as it matured in his *bodega*, for further aging in cask and bottle. Some firms market their *Reservas* with an individual proprietary name, others use the same name for a younger wine and a *Reserva*. Because of the trend toward less wood-aging of Riojas, the minimum aging requirements for *Reservas* have recently been reduced. A *Reserva* may not be sold until the fourth year after the harvest, and must be aged in a combination of large vats, small barrels, and bottles. The exact formula may vary, however, so that a producer who prefers less wood-aging may compensate by increasing the time his wines spend in bottle before being released for sale. A wine labeled *Gran Reserva* must be aged in wood and bottle even longer than a *Reserva*. Many *Reservas* represent the best wines that are made in this district, and they can be very good wines indeed; others, unfortunately, will strike many consumers as simply old and withered.

To assure continuity of quality, only those firms that have a minimum storage capacity of seventy-five hundred hectoliters, equivalent to about eighty thousand cases, are permitted to export their wines, and there are less than forty firms that qualify. Some well-known Rioja firms (and their popular brands) include AGE (Siglo), Bodegas Bilbaínas (Viña Pomal, Brillante, Cepa de Oro), Compañía Vinícola del Norte de España, or CUNE (Viña Real, Imperial), Domecq Domain (Privilegio), Bodegas Franco Españolos (Brillante), Bodegas Lan, López de Heredia (Viña Tondonia, Viña Bosconia), Marqués de Cáceres, Marqués de Murrieta, Marqués de Riscal Bodegas Monticello (Cumbrero), Bodegas Bodegas Muerza (Rioja Vega), Bodegas Olarra (Cerro Añon, Reciente), Federico Paternina (Banda Azul, Banda Dorada), and Bodegas Santiago (Gran Condal).

The district of La Mancha in central Spain is the most important one from the standpoint of quantity, and produces about a third of the country's total production, almost all of it white; Valdepeñas is the best-known red.

North of Madrid, near Valladolid, is the Vega Sicilia estate, which produces very limited quantities of red wines from a combination of Bordeaux and native grape varieties. The wines are aged in wood for a minimum of ten years; a second label, Valbuena, is used for wines with less aging.

Along the Mediterranean shore, north and south of Barcelona, are a number of districts producing interesting wines generally grouped together as Catalonian wines. The village of Alella produces a dry red wine and both sweet and dry white wines. Tarragona, once famous for a fortified red wine known as Tarragona Port, now produces inexpensive table wines. The most readily available wines of Catalonia come from the region of Penedès, situated about halfway between Barcelona and Tarragona. The region is famous for its *méthode champenoise* sparkling wines, described elsewhere, and for some excellent red and white table wines. The best-known firm is Torres, in Vilafranca del Penedès, whose one thousand acres of vineyards contain such classic French varieties as Chardonnay, Sauvignon Blanc, Cabernet Sauvignon, and Pinot Noir in addition to the traditional Parellada, Garnacha, Cariñena, Monastrell, and Ull de Llebra (the Tempranillo of Rioja). Torres, which has adopted a number of innovative winemaking techniques, markets its wines with several proprietary names, including Viña Sol, Sangre de Toro, and Coronas. A relative newcomer to the Penedès area is Jean Leon, whose vineyards are planted primarily with Cabernet Sauvignon and Chardonnay.

SPAIN AND PORTUGAL

PORTUGAL

The most famous wine of Portugal is port, but it actually accounts for only 5 percent of the country's wine production and most of it is exported. Table wine, on the other hand, is very much a part of the Portuguese way of life: annual consumption is more than a hundred bottles per person.

The most popular wines of Portugal shipped here are the many pleasant rosés that are to be found in just about every store and restaurant. Often shipped in distinctive bottles and crocks, these agreeable wines have undoubtedly converted many people to the pleasures of wine drinking. The best-known brands are Mateus and Lancers.

Apart from rosé, however, Portugal produces a variety of inexpensive red and white wines that are becoming more widely distributed in this country. The best of these wines are made under the supervision of the Portuguese government, which has established wine laws similar in style and intent to the *Appellation Contrôlée* laws of France. The first six appellations for which controls were established (apart from port) are Vinho Verde, Dão, Colares, Bucelas, Carcavelos, and Moscatel de Setúbal. Bottles of each of these wines are entitled to bear a distinctive neck label as a guarantee of authenticity.

Vinho Verde, very popular in Portugal, is now becoming better known in this country. Its name literally means "green wine," but only in the sense of new wine: it can be red or white. Vinho Verde is produced in the northwest of Portugal, in the Minho province, north of the Douro River. These light-bodied wines are comparatively low in alcohol, and when consumed locally they are noted for their refreshing acidity. Red Vinho Verde—one of the few red wines that is normally served chilled—has a rather harsh taste and is rarely exported. If Vinho Verde is bottled early, within a few months of the vintage, malolactic fermentation takes place in the bottle, giving these wines a slightly sparkling quality that adds to their charm. This natural *pétillance* is usually absent from Vinho Verde that is exported, and some of the white Vinho Verde that is available here is mellow rather than crisply acid.

The Dão wines come from an extensive region in the central part of Portugal. The red wines—more easily found here than the mild, agreeable whites—are generous and full-flavored. Grão Vasco is the best-known label of Dão, as Aveleda is of Vinho Verde.

About twenty miles from Lisbon, along the Atlantic coast, are the vineyards of Colares, which produce a long-lived red wine (and a little bit of undistinguished white wine). Although Colares is rarely seen here, the vineyards themselves are quite unusual and deserve mention. For one thing, the vines grow in sand dunes near the ocean, and planting new vines requires digging special reinforced trenches ten or twenty feet deep in the sand. For another thing, the Ramisco vines of Colares have never been attacked by phylloxera, so this wine is one of the very few wines in Europe still being made from vines that have not been grafted onto native American rootstocks.

Carcavelos and Moscatel de Setúbal are both fortified sweet white wines produced in very limited quantities and not often exported. Bucelas, rarely seen here, is a light, dry white wine from a village of that name about fifteen miles north of Lisbon.

Two relatively new appellations are Bairrada, primarily a red-wine region situated south of the Douro, between Dão and the Atlantic Ocean; and the Algarve, in the southernmost part of Portugal. The village of Pinhel, just south of the

Douro, near the Spanish border, gives its name to a very agreeable red wine produced there. Because appellation laws have not yet been established for many of Portugal's wine-producing regions, some of the most popular wines, and a few of the best, are marketed with such proprietary brand names as Periquita, Barca Velha, and Serradayres.

Colheita, or vintage, *Reserva*, and *Garrafeira* are words sometimes found on Portuguese wine labels. One or another is used by a shipper when he wants to indicate that he has especially selected the wine for additional aging because of its superior quality.

SWITZERLAND

The per capita consumption of Switzerland is more than five times that of the United States, and the thirsty Swiss import about three times as much wine as they make themselves. Most of what they produce is white, and much of it agreeable enough: dry, crisp, refreshing, and uncomplicated.

Some wine is made in the Italian part of the country, notably Merlot del Ticino, but almost all of Switzerland's wines come from the French-speaking region known as La Suisse Romande. The cantons, or districts, that are best known for their wines are those of Neuchâtel, Vaud, and Valais. The most widely planted white-wine grape is the Chasselas, known in the Valais as the Fendant and in the Vaud as the Dorin.

Neuchâtel, the most familiar of Swiss wines, comes from vineyards along the northern shore of the Lake of Neuchâtel. This pleasant white wine sometimes has a *pétillant*, or sprightly, quality, the result of malolactic fermentation, which produces a small amount of carbon dioxide gas often retained in the wine. Cortaillod, a village along the shore of Lake Neuchâtel, gives its name to an attractive red wine made from the Pinot Noir grape. A rosé, Oeil de Perdrix, is also produced in this district.

The canton of Vaud, along the shore of the Lake of Geneva, is divided into two main wine districts: La Côte is the district west of the city of Lausanne, Lavaux is the district to the east. The wine villages of Dézaley and Saint-Saphorin, whose names appear on Swiss wine labels, are in Lavaux. Beyond Lavaux is the Chablais district, which encompasses the village of Aigle and Yvorne. All of these wines are exported to this country, and they may be labeled with the name of the producing village, such as Saint-Saphorin or Yvorne, or with the village and district, as Dézaley de Lavaux or Aigle de Chablais.

The vineyards of the Valais lie along the Rhône River, on either side of the city of Sion. The wines of this district are labeled with the name of the grape from which they are made, sometimes in conjunction with the name of the district or its principal city—Fendant, Johannisberg (actually the Sylvaner), Fendant de Sion, Johannisberg du Valais, and so forth. Dôle is a light red wine made in the Valais from a combination of Pinot Noir and Gamay grapes.

AUSTRIA

Vienna may be famous for its coffee and pastry, but wine is very much a part of the Austrian way of life: the per capita consumption of wine in that country is about forty-five bottles a year. Almost all of the wine made in Austria is white, and the Austrian's casual approach to wine is nowhere more evident that in the *Heurigen*, or wine taverns, that are found throughout each wine region. Everyone who has *Heurige*, or new wine, to sell hangs a bough or wreath outside his establishment to alert passersby, and these refreshing wines are consumed on the premises—by the glass or from open carafes—in a tradition that dates back almost two hundred years. Some *Heurigen* are open all year round, others sell wines for only a few weeks in the spring and summer. The new wine may actually be more than a year old, since a wine can be sold as *Heurige* until November of the year following the vintage.

The most widely planted grape in Austria is Grüner Veltliner, whose mild, agreeable wines account for about a third of the total production. Other white-wine grapes include Müller-Thurgau, Welschriesling, Rheinriesling (which is the true Riesling of Germany), Traminer, Neuburger, and Weissburgunder (Pinot Blanc). The principal red-wine grapes are Portugieser, Blaufränkisch, Saint Laurent, and Zweigeltrebe (a cross of Blaufränkisch with Saint Laurent).

As in Germany, late-picked and overripe grapes are used to make wines labeled Kabinett, Spätlese, Auslese, Beerenauslese, and Trockenbeerenauslese. These words, which were freely used in the past, have now been clearly defined by new

Austrian wine laws and have virtually the same meaning as in Germany. The sugar content of the grapes is expressed in degrees KMW (Klosterneuburger Mostwaage), just as the Oechsle scale is used in Germany, and minimum requirements have been established for each category.

A Viennese who wants to drink local wines does not have far to travel, because wines are made at the edge of Vienna itself, at Nussberg and Grinzing. A dozen miles south of Vienna is the village of Gumpoldskirchen, which produces one of the best-known Austrian white wines. Gumpoldskirchner (the suffix *er* is added to the village or district name when it appears on a label) is usually made from three varieties—Rotgipfler, Zierfandler (also called Spätrot), and Neuburger.

About forty miles west of Vienna, along the Danube, is a region that produces some of Austria's most appealing white wines, primarily from Grüner Veltliner. Dürnstein and Loiben are the best-known wine villages of the Wachau district, and the villages of Krems and Langenlois each gives its name to adjoining districts.

Another important wine region is Burgenland, southeast of Vienna. The region is dominated by the Neusiedlersee, a long shallow lake that tempers the climate of the vineyards that surround it. The picturesque village of Rust is the most famous in Burgenland, and a number of nearby villages are now entitled to use its name for their wines. Apetlon, Mörbisch, Oggau, and Donnerskirchen are other well-known wine villages. Climatic conditions in Burgenland are particularly conducive to the appearance of *Edelfäule*, or noble rot, and in good vintages a surprisingly high proportion of the crop consists of Beerenauslese and Trockenbeerenauslese wines. Most of these botrytised wines are made from Wiessburgunder, Müller-Thurgau, and Neuburger grapes, rather than the Riesling, as in Germany. *Ausbruch*, a word traditionally found on the labels of some sweet wines from Burgenland, has now been legally defined, and may be used only for wines whose quality is between a Beerenauslese and a Trockenbeerenauslese.

Austrian wines may be labeled with the name of a grape variety, with that of the district or village of origin, or with a combination of both, such as Kremser Grüner Veltliner, Langenloiser Rheinriesling, Dürnsteiner Müller-Thurgau, Apetloner Weissburgunder, and Oggauer Blaufränkisch. In addition, a number of Austrian wines are labeled with proprietary brand names. For example, the firm of Lenz Moser markets Schluck (which means "sip") and Alte Knabe; and Kremser Schmidt is a popular wine produced by the cooperative cellar at Krems.

HUNGARY

Although Hungary is not one of Europe's biggest wine-producing countries, it has always maintained a special position among wine lovers as the home of the famous sweet wines of Tokay. At one time these luscious dessert wines were considered an essential part of any complete cellar, and the finest examples were served at royal banquets and state occasions. Tokay was assumed to possess special invigorating qualities that led doctors to prescribe it to dying patients, and bridegrooms would consume a glass to ensure male heirs. No longer as popular as in the past, Tokay is nevertheless an interesting and unusual wine, enhanced by the legends that surround it.

The village of Tokay (spelled Tokaj locally) is situated in the northeast corner of the country, at the foothills of the Carpathian Mountains. A number of neighboring villages are permitted to market their wines as Tokay, and these hillside vineyards are planted, for the most part, with the Furmint grape. The volcanic soil of the district imparts a distinctive *terroir* of Tokay, a tang or undertaste that distinguishes it from the sweet dessert wines of Sauternes and the Auslese and Beerenauslese wines of Germany.

Tokay is made in a very special way. After the normal harvest, grapes are left on the vines to develop the same noble rot that affects the grapes in Sauternes and along the Rhine and Moselle. These shriveled grapes, with their much higher concentration of sugar, are known as *aszu*. The *aszu* grapes are specially picked and put into containers or butts, known as *puttonyos*. A certain number of *puttonyos* are then added to the normally ripe grapes, and the lot fermented together. The more containers of *aszu* berries that are added to a vat, the sweeter and richer the resulting wine will be, and consequently bottles of Tokaji Aszu (as the wines are labeled) indicate the number of *puttonyos* that were added: five *puttonyos* is the highest grade available in this country. Very limited quantities of Tokay were once made entirely from the free-run juice of *aszu* berries, and this essence, Tokaji Eszencia, has achieved legendary fame. Wines labeled Tokaji Eszencia are still produced in good vintages, but rarely exported.

Apart from Tokaji Aszu, there are also other wines made in the Tokay vineyards. Tokaji Furmint is the normal wine of the district, and its label may carry the word *edes*, meaning sweet. Tokaji Szamorodni is made from grapes harvested without special attention to the *aszu* berries among the vines (*szamorodni* means as it is grown), The wine may consequently be dry or sweet, depending on the proportion of shriveled berries that turn up in the vats, and this will be shown on its label.

Famous as it is, Tokay accounts for less than 5 percent of Hungary's wines, which are produced in a number of districts situated throughout the country. For the most part, Hungarian wines are labeled with a combination of the village of origin plus the grape variety used. A notable exception is the most famous red wine of Hungary, Egri Bikavér. The wine comes from vineyards around the village of Eger (just as German wine villages take on the possessive *er* when used on wine labels, so Hungarian towns add *i*), but Bikavér means Bull's Blood. This full-bodied dry red wine is made primarily from the Kadarka grape. There are other variations as well on the village-plus-variety labeling rule among the limited number of wines imported here: Vörös simply means red wine, as in Szekszárdi Vörös; from Villány comes Villányi Burgundi; and Leányka is a white-wine variety whose name may appear alone on a label, without that of a village of origin.

A number of white wines are produced along the shore of Lake Balaton, which is the largest lake in central Europe. Vines are grown along the slopes of Mount Badacsony, on the north shore of the lake, and two of the better-known wines are Badacsonyi Szürkebarát and Badacsonyi Kéknyelü. The latter, the drier of the two, is named after a grape variety, but Szürkebarát is a fanciful name meaning Gray Friar: the wine is made from the Pinot Gris. From the village of Debrö comes a sweetish wine with a peachlike bouquet, Debröi Hárslevelü.

In addition to the many native grape varieties cultivated throughout Hungary, certain amounts of Cabernet Sauvignon, Merlot, and Chardonnay have also been planted, and wines labeled with these varietal names are now being shipped here.

GREECE

The vine may have appeared in Greece as early as 1500 B.C., and wine was certainly a common beverage in Homer's time, twenty-seven hundred years ago. Ancient Greek literature abounds in reference to wine, and it's quite possible that these early Greek wines were of exceptional quality. Greece continues to produce a variety of wines today, and if they are not remarkable, many of them are nevertheless attractive.

To many people, Greek wine means Retsina, and in fact most Greek table wines are in this category. Retsina is a generic name applied to any wine that has been flavored, during fermentation, with a small but unmistakable amount of pine resin. Retsina has an unusual and pungent flavor that is described by those who do not like it as the taste of turpentine. Those who enjoy Retsina find it to be an excellent complement to the oily dishes that abound in Greek cuisine. Retsina is usually a white wine, but it also made as a red wine and a rosé, and is then labeled Kokinelli.

Apart from Retsina, there are a number of enjoyable red, white, and rosé table wines characterized by a distinctive and robust flavor that goes very well with rich foods. The problem for the consumer when buying Greek wines is that some names found on their labels are generic, many are the proprietary brand names of individual firms, and a few refer to a place or to a grape variety. For example, Roditis or Roditys is a name used by many firms for a dry rosé. Castel Danielis is a branded red wine from one firm, Achaia-Clauss, which also markets red and white wines labeled Demestica; and another firm, Cambas, uses the brand name Hymettus for a white wine and Pendeli for a red. Naoussa and Nemea are place-names. In a store, read a Greek wine label carefully. If you're in a Greek restaurant, tell the waiter whether or not you want Retsina, and if not, tell him just how dry you want your wine to be. For example, the most famous red wine of Greece is Mavrodaphne, but it's a sweet dessert wine similar in style to port, and not the best choice to accompany a meal.

YUGOSLAVIA

A number of moderately priced Yugoslavian wines can be found here, from vineyards situated throughout that country.

The best-known wines come from the northern province of Slovenia, part of which once belonged to Austria. It is, therefore, not surprising that extensive plantings now exist of Riesling (actually the lesser Italian or Laski Riesling, also known as the Graševina), Traminer, and Sylvaner, as well as Cabernet and some Merlot for the reds. The villages of Lutomer and Maribor are often seen on Yugoslavian wine labels, coupled with the grape from which the wine is made: Lutomer Riesling, Sylvaner de Maribor, and so forth. Native varieties whose names may appear on labels include such reds as Prokupac, Plavac, and Vranac; Sipon is a white-wine grape.

ROMANIA

Romania produces a variety of red and white wines from such native grape varieties as Grasă and Fetească, as well as Furmint, Kadarka, and, increasingly, such traditional varieties as Cabernet Sauvignon and Pinot Noir. The sweet white from Cotnari, often compared to the Tokay of Hungary, is Romania's most famous wine. Tîrnave and Murfatlar are other traditional white-wine districts. Some of these wines have occasionally been shipped here in very limited quantities. Moderately priced Romanian wines labeled Cabernet Sauvignon, Pinot Noir, Valea Blanc, Sauvignon Blanc, and Tarnave Castle Riesling are now being marketed here under the Premiat label. (Similarly, Bulgaria, whose vineyards are extensively planted with Cabernet Sauvignon and Merlot, ships such varietal wines as Cabernet Sauvignon, Merlot, and Chardonnay to this country under the Trakia label.)

RUSSIA

The vineyards of Russia have been considerably expanded in recent years as part of a government-sponsored program to increase the production both of table grapes and of wines. More than three million acres of vines are planted, and Russia is now the third-largest wine-producing country in the world, after Italy and France. Many different sweet and dry table wines are made, as well as fortified wines and a considerable amount of sparkling wines, but almost none are exported.

THE WINES OF
CALIFORNIA

For the American consumer, California continues to be the most interesting varied, and exciting wine region in the world today. For several decades California has supplied about 70 percent of the wine consumed in this country, and the quality of its moderately priced everyday jug wines has long been acknowledged. It is only in the past fifteen years or so that the excellence and diversity of its best wines have attracted the attention and admiration of wine drinkers here and abroad, and that California has been widely recognized as one of the world's fine wine regions.

One indication of the pace at which changes have occurred is that as recently as the early 1960s, half of the state's wine production consisted of inexpensive fortified wines such as port, sherry, and Muscatel. Dessert wines (as all fortified wines are officially designated in this country, whether they are sweet or dry) have gradually declined in importance to less than 5 percent of the total, but it was not until 1973 that table wines—from the least expensive jug wines to the finest bottles—actually accounted for more than half of California's total production. Today, table wines represent about 80 percent of the wines made in California, and much of the rest consists of sparkling wines. The increased production of table wines, and especially fine table wines, is a reflection of growing consumer interest. Just as the great wine châteaux of

Bordeaux prospered only when, in the nineteenth century, an affluent French middle class was prepared to pay a higher price for wines of better quality, so the increased plantings of the best grape varieties in California became possible only when enough American consumers began to discriminate among wines and were willing to pay a premium for the best of them. In 1969 there were only 110,000 acres of wine grapes in California; five years later that figure had more than doubled, and by the mid-1980s the total plantings of wine grapes approached 375,000 acres. In fifteen years the acreage of such classic varieties as Cabernet Sauvignon Chardonnay, Sauvignon Blanc, Johannisberg Riesling, and Pinot Noir increased from less than ten thousand acres to more than eighty thousand. There is now twice as much Cabernet Sauvignon in California as in the Médoc district of Bordeaux, five times as much Chardonnay as in Burgundy's Côte d'Or.

Just as the interest in fine wines led to more vineyard acreage, so the number of California wineries has doubled in a decade, to more than six hundred. In the past, the commercial distribution pattern for wine in this country was such that large wineries and even medium-sized ones were expected to offer a complete line of wines, including a variety of table wines, dessert wines such as port and sherry, and sparkling wines as well. While a number of wineries successfully continue to produce a range of twenty to fifty different wines, the American consumer's willingness to pay more for fine wines has enabled both new wineries and some established ones to focus their attention on relatively few wines. There are now a great many new wineries whose total production is between fifteen and forty thousand cases, no more than is produced by many châteaux in the Médoc, and many others that produce less than ten thousand cases a year.

The quality of California wines has developed so quickly that several of the wines that are considered among the finest ever produced in the state, and on a par with the best in the world, have come from wineries that did not even exist as recently as 1975. Every year dozens of new wineries introduce their first wines, and some of them are remarkable enough to establish what is virtually an overnight reputation. Whereas almost all of Europe's great vineyards are already well known, California's best wines are still being discovered. Because many of California's vineyards are planted with vines that, although bearing, are not yet mature; because growers are still trying to determine the best sites for specific grape varieties; and because so many of the wines are being made by relatively young winemakers who are still developing their style, it is certain that as good as California wines are today, the state has yet to produce its finest bottles.

Most wine drinkers no longer make the mistake of grouping all California wines together, and have learned to distinguish among, say, an inexpensive jug of Mountain Burgundy, a moderately priced but a distinctive Zinfandel, and a remarkable Cabernet Sauvignon or Chardonnay produced in limited quantities. Many consumers also realize that California table wines cannot be compared as a group to the European wines that are available here. Although the wines that are imported are by no means limited to the cream of the crop, they certainly include the finest examples from the best vineyards of Europe. A tremendous amount of cheap and ordinary wine that we rarely see here is made in France, Germany, Italy, Spain, and other wine-producing nations. What we do see all the time are our own moderately priced, dependable table wines, of which California produces tens of millions of gallons annually. The unflattering connotations of the word "domestic" have probably contributed a great deal to the condescending attitude that many Americans have had about their own wines. Considering that many of the great European wine regions were established five hundred or a thousand years ago, it's remarkable what a long way we've come in such a comparatively short time.

It was only two hundred years ago that the first vines were planted in southern California by Spanish missionaries. These Franciscans established additional missions throughout the state, and they planted vineyards as far up the coast as Sonoma, north of San Francisco. By the 1830s, when these clerical holdings were secularized, European immigrants and farmers from the East had begun to set up commercial vineyards in California.

In the 1850s a Hungarian, Agoston Haraszthy, made a significant contribution to the wine industry by publishing the results of his experiments in grape growing and winemaking. He later brought over about 100,000 vine cuttings from Europe, which greatly increased the number of grape varieties available to California winemakers.

The gradual development of the California wine industry owes a great debt to the many Europeans who established wineries in the second half of the nineteenth century and the early years of this one. They include Italians (Giuseppe and

Pietro Simi, John Foppiano, and Samuele Sebastiani), Frenchmen (Paul Masson, Pierre Mirassou, Georges de Latour at Beaulieu Vineyard, and Etienne Thée and Charles Lefranc at Almadén), Germans (Carl Wente and the Beringer brothers), Czechs (the Korbel brothers), a Finn (Gustave Niebaum at Inglenook), an Irishman (James Concannon), a Prussian (Charles Krug), and a Hungarian (Agoston Haraszthy at Buena Vista). Then, less than a hundred years after it began, this industry was crippled by Prohibition. Many wineries went out of business and only a few were able to survive by producing sacramental wines or by growing grapes for home winemaking, which was still legal. The better wine varieties were uprooted and replaced by high-yield, thick-skinned grapes that could be shipped east without damage. As recently as 1971 two-thirds of the California crush—as the harvest is usually referred to—was made up of table and raisin grapes, primarily Thompson Seedless. Wine grapes accounted for more than half the total crush for the first time in 1974.

After the repeal of Prohibition, commercial winemaking started again almost from scratch, as there was a shortage of vinification equipment, of tanks and barrels to store the wine, of land planted in anything but high-yield varieties, of skilled personnel, and of a public accustomed to drinking table wines. It's not unfair to say that winemaking in California is not much more than fifty years old.

Actually, most of California's current success has been achieved in the relatively short period that began in the late 1960s. Part of that success was the result of adopting new winemaking technology, such as the use of temperature-controlled stainless-steel tanks to ferment white wines slowly at low temperatures, thus retaining the wine's fruit and delicacy while diminishing the possibility of browning and oxidation; controlled fermentors also permit winemakers to use higher temperatures to bring out the flavor of certain red wines. Just as important as technology has been the willingness of Californians to experiment with every aspect of winemaking, and to explore more fully the options that are available to winemakers everywhere. These include such techniques as skin contact—leaving the juice of white grapes in contact with their skins for a few hours before fermentation begins, to extract more flavor and aroma; and barrel fermentation—fermenting selected lots of white wine in small oak barrels rather than large tanks, to add to their richness and complexity.

Perhaps the most significant aspect of California winemaking, and the one that most clearly sets it apart from the traditional European approach, is its flexibility. A European winemaker is to a large extent bound within established norms: the boundaries of a given vineyard or appellation have already been defined; the grape varieties he may use are limited by law; and the winemaking techniques are traditional. In contrast, a California winemaker can choose the site on which to establish his vineyard and plant whichever varieties he cares to. Or he can buy grapes with which to make wines from any region, and is free to add a new variety or discontinue an old one from one vintage to the next. A winemaker from Bordeaux cannot suddenly produce Burgundy or Rhine wine, but a California winemaker who specializes in Cabernet Sauvignon, the classic grape of Bordeaux, can begin to make Chardonnay or Johannisberg Riesling, varieties associated with Burgundy and the Rhine, respectively, just by finding a source for those grapes.

Not only can a winemaker change direction, but a grape-grower, too, can change over his vineyards, either by uprooting his vines and planting new ones, or by cutting an existing vine off above the ground and grafting on a different variety, a technique known as T-budding or budding over. Thus growers can convert from red varieties to more profitable white varieties, or replace varieties unsuitable for a particular region with more appropriate ones.

Winemakers in Europe and California are likely to have different goals, which affects the styles of their wines. The European, producing wines from specific grape varieties in a delimited region, will strive for appellation character, that is, for wines that reflect their place of origin. In California, where appellations of origin are only beginning to be established, and where many different varieties are grown in the same region, the winemaker strives for varietal character, that is, for wines that express the potential of the grape from which each is made. As a result, many of the California wines made in the 1970s from such varieties as Chardonnay and Cabernet Sauvignon emphasized power and intensity of flavor at the expense of subtlety and refinement. By the 1980s, producers and consumers alike had realized that although ripe, full-bodied, heady wines often stand out in a tasting, they are usually difficult to drink with pleasure at the dining table, and the style of California wines began to evolve accordingly.

Many elements contribute to a wine's style, but two that seem to have considerable impact are the degree of ripeness of the grapes at harvest (which affects the wine's alcohol content), and the extent to which the wine is aged in oak barrels. California has more sun during the growing season than do the top wine regions of Europe, so the grapes contain more sugar when they are picked, and do not need to have sugar added, as is usually the case in France and Germany. But the comparatively warm temperatures in many of California's grape-growing regions often result in wines with a relatively high alcohol content—13.5 to 14.5 percent is not uncommon. In the recent past, many winemakers believed that maximum ripeness meant more varietal character; some still do, but others feel they can get the flavor, structure, and weight they want in a wine with less alcohol. They are trying to counteract California's abundant sunshine by picking their grapes earlier, when they contain less sugar and more natural acidity, which results in wines with less power and better balance.

Perhaps the most widely discussed aspect of making California wines is the use of small, sixty-gallon French oak barrels from the forests of Nevers, Limousin, and Tronçais, as well as the use of fifty- and sixty-gallon American oak barrels. Although many delicate, fruity, charming red and white wines are bottled without being aged in wood, most winemakers agree that oak provides additional depth and complexity to such wines as Cabernet Sauvignon and Chardonnay, as well as a tannic structure that enables fine red or white wines to mature more gracefully. Too much oak obscures a wine's taste, instead of enhancing it, however, and as the preference for rich, oaky wines has evolved into a greater appreciation for balanced, elegant ones, winemakers are using oak more judiciously. But just as some producers were striving for restraint and complexity from the start, so others still prefer the big, impressive, powerful style, and make their wines accordingly.

The choices available to California winemakers represent a challenge and an opportunity, but they also pose a problem for the consumer. As winemakers are finding their way with specific varieties and with the overall style of the wines they produce, the wines themselves do not always maintain a continuity of style. Among the established European wines, the primary difference between one year and the next is based on the character of the vintage; in California, the style of a particular wine may change arbitrarily. This provides the interested consumer with an ongoing sense of discovery, but it sometimes makes it difficult to define the style of a winery and of its individual wines, or to choose wines on the basis of past experience.

Reading a California Label

California table wines are often divided into two broad categories based on the way they are marketed: _generic wines_, labeled for the most part with the names of famous European wine regions; and _varietal wines_, labeled with the name of the specific grape variety from which each wine is primarily made. The most familiar generic names for red wines are Burgundy, Claret, and Chianti, and for white wines, Chablis, Sauterne (usually spelled without the final _s_ in California), and Rhine Wine. These names are among the best-known to wine drinkers and have, therefore, been used almost from the beginning of California winemaking to suggest, in a general way, the kind of wine contained in the bottle. Actually, generic wines have more in common with each other than with the European wines whose names are being used. Most California wineries sell generic wines, and their popularity is such that they account for most of the table wine sold in this country. While generic names are here to stay, there is also a trend away from the use of European place-names, and some wineries now label their less expensive wines simply as Red Table Wine, Mountain White Wine, Premium Red, Classic Red, Vintage White, and so on.

This category includes the least-expensive table wines available in this country, and many of them provide excellent value. Most of them are sold in jugs, and now that metric sizes have been adopted, the familiar half-gallons and gallons have been replaced by the 50.7-ounce magnum and the 101.4-ounce jeroboam. If there is a problem with generic wines, however, it is not that they don't taste like the European originals, but that there are no standards to help the consumer find his or her way among different brands. Perhaps the most important variable among generic wines is that some are dry and many are not. While a certain amount of sweetness in both white and red wines appeals to a large segment of the public, those who prefer completely dry table wines cannot simply assume that a Chablis will be drier than a Sauterne or a Rhine wine. For one thing, some wineries market identical wines under different generic lables. For another, many wineries maintain a minimum amount of sweetness in all their wines, others in none of them. The sweetness, which usually comes from grape concentrate added just before bottling, is often 1 percent and not infrequently 2 percent, which is far from dry.

As pleasant as generic wines can be, it is among varietal wines that the finest California wines are to be found. Consumers were not always as familiar with the name of individual grapes as they are today, and as recently as the 1950s many wineries found it easier to sell a wine made primarily from Cabernet Sauvignon as Claret than with its varietal name. Today the situation is completely reversed. As more consumers have discovered that the best varietal wines represent the best that California has to offer, varietal labeling has caught on to such an extent that there are now more than two dozen varietal names in general use (they are described further on). The number of wineries marketing the most popular varietals increases every year: Chardonnay is offered by nearly four hundred wineries, Cabernet Sauvignon by more than three hundred, and more than two hundred firms market Sauvignon Blanc, Zinfandel, and Johannisberg Riesling.

Since 1983 a varietal wine must be made at least 75 percent from the grape named on its label. In practice, the finest wines are made entirely, or almost entirely, from the named grape. There are some notable exceptions, however: many winemakers feel that wines made from certain varieties can be improved by judicious blending with a complementary one. Thus, Merlot and, occasionally, Cabernet Franc may be added to Cabernet Sauvignon, and some producers choose to soften the intense taste of Sauvignon Blanc by adding Sémillon. If more than 25 percent of a complementary variety is added, however, that fact may be shown on the label, but the wine cannot be labeled with a single varietal name. Inexpensive varietal wines, on the other hand, are often stretched by blending in neutral wines. Since it is the character of a specific grape variety that distinguishes varietal wines and gives them their personality, the extent to which they are diluted can have an important effect on their taste.

A third way to label wines is with a proprietary name, which a winery creates to market a particular blend: Emerald Dry, Eshcol, and Spiceling are some examples. Such names are most often used for moderately priced wines, but may appear on the labels of expensive bottles as well—Insignia and Opus One are proprietary wines.

If one factor that affects a wine's quality and taste is the grape variety from which it is made, another that is becoming increasingly important is where the grapes are grown. Although some consumers may still think of California as a single area, the state includes regions as cool as Bordeaux, Burgundy, Champagne, and the Rhine and as warm as the Rhône Valley, central Italy, southern Spain, and North Africa. Certain parts of the state are best suited to high-yield grape varieties that can be distilled into brandy or blended to produce fortified dessert wines, others to ordinary table wine, and certain limited areas to the production of red and white wines with the finesse and individuality of the best European wines.

Perhaps the most basic distinction to be made among California wines—both generic and varietal—is that between the wines produced in the cooler coastal counties that extend north and south of San Francisco and those produced in the San Joaquin Valley. Also known as the Central Valley, the San Joaquin Valley stretches for more than two hundred miles from Lodi (pronounced *low*-die) down to Bakersfield, and it is in this warm interior valley that most of California's wine grapes are grown, as well as almost all of its table and raisin grapes. Despite the tremendous increase in coastal vineyards, more than 80 percent of California wine made from wine grapes (that is, excluding that made from table and raisin grapes) comes from the San Joaquin Valley.

The interior valley has always been a source of generic wines, but as more consumers have associated varietal wines with quality there has been a tendency to label comparatively undistinguished wines with varietal names. Every wine, after all, is made from one or more grape varieties, but in the past, producers of inexpensive generic wines saw no advantage in labeling such wines with the name of the grape from which each was primarily made. The extensive new acreage in the San Joaquin Valley made it possible for varietally labeled wines to be produced in large quantities from such grapes as Barbera, Ruby Cabernet, Zinfandel, Chenin Blanc, and French Colombard. Generally speaking, wines made from grapes grown in the warm interior valley tend to have less varietal character, individuality, and liveliness than those from cooler regions. Consequently, while some varietal wines from the San Joaquin Valley are well made and moderately priced, a number of others are no more distinctive than the generic Burgundy and Chablis they are meant to replace.

Just as European winemakers have established, through trial and error, that specific varieties produce the finest wines only in certain regions, so California growers are gradually determining the best sites for each of the major wine grapes. The traditional technique used in California is that of heat summation, based on the average daily temperature during the six-month growing season from April to October. The coolest areas are designated as Region I, the warmest as Region V, whatever their actual location, and these five designations have been widely used to determine which grape varieties will flourish best in a particular district. In recent years, more exacting and sophisticated techniques are being used to match grape varieties with specific microclimates throughout the state.

The traditional fine-wine area in California has been the North Coast counties that fan out from San Francisco—Napa, Sonoma, Mendocino, Alameda (which contains the Livermore Valley), and Santa Clara. In the last fifteen years, winemakers have discovered that fine wines can also be made in such counties as Monterey, San Luis Obispo, Santa Barbara, and Amador, among others. As new vineyards and new wineries have been created, there has been an increasing use of appellations of origin in California labels. The names most frequently seen are those of counties—Napa, Sonoma, Monterey—and if such a name appears on a label, at least 75 percent of the wine must come from that county. New appellations of origin, known as viticultural areas, were first established in 1983. A viticultural area is a delimited grape-growing region whose geographical features and boundaries have been recognized and defined; it is the growers in an given area who must define its boundaries and then petition the government for the right to use the name of the area on their labels. If a viticultural area appears on a label, at least 85 percent of the wine must come from that area. There are now more than forty viticultural areas, and they vary greatly in size: Cole Ranch in Mendocino consists of only sixty acres of vineyards, the Anderson Valley in Mendocino encompasses about five hundred acres, the Napa Valley appellation includes virtually all of Napa County's thirty thousand acres, and the Salinas Valley takes in almost all of Monterey's thirty-five thousand vineyard acres. Some regions have a number of inner appellations. Sonoma County, for example, includes within its boundaries Sonoma Valley, Alexander

Valley, Dry Creek Valley, Russian River Valley, Sonoma-Green Valley, Chalk Hill, Sonoma Mountain, Knights Valley, and a part of Los Carneros. Some areas are known as one-owner appellations—there is only one producer in Guenoc Valley, only one in McDowell Valley, both of which have been established as viticultural areas.

The idea of appellations of origin is still a relatively new one in California, and the stylistic differences between wines coming from different areas are as likely to reflect the philosophy of a given winemaker as the area in which the grapes were grown. Just because an area can be defined geographically doesn't mean that the wines produced from its vineyards are necessarily special, or even distinctive (it's the area that's defined, not the quality of the fruit grown there), but the increased emphasis on appellations will encourage wineries and the growers from whom they buy their grapes to focus more intently on the particular varieties best suited to a specific combination of soil and microclimate. Even now, many consumers are already aware of such felicitous pairings as Carneros Pinot Noir, Dry Creek Valley Zinfandel, Alexander Valley Chardonnay, Monterey Gewürztraminer, Edna Valley Sauvignon Blanc, and Napa Valley Cabernet Sauvignon.

Wines with the most specific place of origin are those that come from individual vineyards. No less than 95 percent of a vineyard-designated wine must come from the named vineyard. As in Europe, the wine from a particular vineyard may display a distinctive personality, and an increasing number of California wineries are producing single-vineyard wines. Of course, vinifying, aging, and bottling wine from a specific plot of land separately and putting its name on the label may retain's the wine's individuality, but is no guarantee of better quality.

Phrases such as *produced and bottled, estate-bottled, vintner-grown*, and *proprietor-grown* all have specific meanings, but they are less significant than the reputation of the winery. In California many of the finest wines are made from purchased grapes rather than from grapes grown by a producer in his own vineyards, so the concept of estate bottling is less important than in Bordeaux (where the best wines come from individual vineyards) or in Burgundy (where the shipper usually buys wine, not grapes, and therefore has less control over the winemaking process than does a California winery).

One increasingly important category of California wine that is not legally defined is that of reserve wines—that is, wines labeled Reserve, Private Reserve, Special Selection, Proprietor's Selection, Vintage Selection, and so on. A winery's reserve bottling of a given varietal—usually Cabernet Sauvignon or Chardonnay—is often twice the price of its regular bottling, yet the basis of selection varies considerably from one producer to another. A reserve wine may come from one or two specific vineyards whose grapes are vinified apart, it may be selected from the winery's entire inventory, or it may simply be the regular wine aged longer in wood. Whatever criteria are used, a reserve is likely to be more intense and more tannic, and is expected to be longer lived. A reserve wine is one that the winery finds in some way more impressive; whether or not it's worth the higher price depends on the taste of each consumer.

A vintage-dated wine must contain no less than 95 percent of grapes harvested in the vintage indicated. It has often been claimed that there are no bad vintages in California, along with the corollary statement that there are no variations from one California vintage to another. The first claim has some validity. In most of Europe's fine-wine districts grapes don't ripen fully every year, whereas in California it is unusual for grapes to be unripe at the time of the harvest. Nevertheless, there are years when a very cool growing season in parts of California has resulted in grapes that never fully ripened; there have been years when rains during the vintage caused a certain amount of rot to form on the grapes; and years when extensive drought conditions affected the quality of the wines. In some years a heat spell in the fall may cause certain grapes to become overripe, which results in raisiny, unbalanced wines high in alcohol; in other years, several different varieties, which normally ripen one after the other over six to eight weeks, may be ready for picking within two weeks of each other, making timely harvesting and vinification difficult.

As the range of vintage-dated varietal wines has increased, consumers have become much more aware of vintage variations in California, as well as of varietal and regional differences. After all, when grapes as different as Cabernet Sauvignon, Pinot Noir, and Johannisberg Riesling grow side by side, it's inevitable that a particular growing season will favor one variety over another. And just as there are differences to be found in a given vintage between wines produced in the Médoc and in Saint-Emilion, or between Rieslings from the Moselle and the Rheingau, so there are bound to be differences between Cabernet Sauvignon from Napa and

Mendocino, or between Chardonnays produced in Sonoma and Monterey, which are nearly two hundred miles apart. Ironically, just as Bordeaux vintages represent, for many consumers, all of France, so the relative success of Napa Valley Cabernet Sauvignon is often, and erroneously, used as a vintage guide to all California wines.

In addition to the basic information contained on a California wine label, which can be more or less explicit depending on the wine, many wineries volunteer additional details about how each of their wines is made. Special back labels indicate, for example, the sugar content of the grapes when they were picked (expressed in degrees Brix), and the date of picking; the temperature at which the wine was fermented, and for how long; the kind of wood in which the wine was aged; when it was bottled; the amount of alcohol and acid in the finished wine; and the wine's exact varietal content. While this is more information than most consumers need to know when they pull the cork, it does indicate the extent to which California winemakers are prepared to experiment with, and discuss, every aspect of winemaking.

Late-Harvest Wines

One of the most dramatic developments in recent years has been the recognition of *Botrytis cinerea* in California vineyards. This beneficial mold, called *pourriture noble* in Sauternes and *Edelfäule* in Germany (both mean noble rot), shrivels ripe grapes, intensifies their flavor, and increases the sugar content of the juice. It was long believed that climatic conditions in California would not permit *Botrytis cinerea* to develop, but in 1969 Wente Bros. harvested naturally botrytised Johannisberg Riesling grapes in its Arroyo Seco vineyards in Monterey County. In 1973 Wente Bros. made an even sweeter wine, and Freemark Abbey, in the Napa Valley, produced a botrytised Johannisberg Riesling, which it called Edelwein, with 10 percent residual sugar. By the mid-1970s Joseph Phelps Vineyards, Chateau St. Jean, and other wineries were producing remarkable late-harvest Johannisberg Rieslings with an intensity and richness equal to Beerenauslese and Trockenbeerenauslese wines from the Rhine.

The earliest examples of such wines were labeled Spätlese and Auslese to suggest their similarity to German wines, but the use of German words was soon prohibited. Such wines are now labeled Late Harvest, Select Late Harvest, and

Special Select Late Harvest; minimum sugar levels have been established for each of these categories, which correspond to the German categories Auslese, Beerenauslese, and Trockenbeerenauslese. In any case, the label must also indicate the sugar content of the grapes at the time of picking and the wine's residual sugar after fermentation, so that the consumer can determine just how sweet each late harvest wine is. Most California late-harvest wines continue to be made from Johannisberg Riesling, as in Germany, although a few have been made from Sémillon and Sauvignon Blanc, as in Sauternes, and from Chenin Blanc, as in the Loire Valley.

Light Wines

Light wines, which are lower in alcohol than most table wines and contain fewer calories as well, were introduced in 1981. They were aimed at the same calorie-conscious consumers who buy light beer, diet soft drinks, and bottled water. Light wines are lower in calories because they have less alcohol — most contain only 7 to 9 percent — but it was only recently that they could be produced by California wineries. Previously, California law required a minimum alcohol content of 10 percent for white wines and 10.5 percent for reds, even though the federal requirements were only 7 percent. Consequently, wines with 8 or 9 percent alcohol — such as German Moselles and Italian Lambruscos — could be imported, but California winemakers could not produce similar wines.

At the end of 1979 the California law was changed to conform to federal regulations in order to accommodate wineries that wanted to produce "soft" wines, sweet, low-alcohol wines made by stopping fermentation while a substantial amount of residual sugar remained in the wine. As it happens, the change in the California law also permitted producers of late-harvest wines to retain even more residual sugar in their luscious dessert wines; previously, such wines had to be fermented until they contained at least 10 percent of alcohol. The new regulations also enabled California wineries to introduce moderately priced bottles and magnums of low-alcohol "light" wines with one-quarter to one-third fewer calories than their regular wines. A number of firms began to market "light" wines, but these were not successful with consumers.

* * *

In addition to table wines, dessert wines, sparkling wines, and vermouth, there is a category known as special natural wines, which are flavored, usually sweet, and sometimes lightly carbonated, and which include wines made from apples or pears as well as from grapes. Some, such as Thunderbird, contain 20 percent alcohol. Others, which are known as pop or refreshment wines, contain about 10 percent alcohol. Boone's Farm, T J Swann, and Annie Green Springs are among the best-known in this category. In the early 1970s, special natural wines accounted for as much as one out of every six bottles of wine consumed in this country, but the fad for these fruit-flavored wines has peaked.

Wine coolers, which became very popular in the mid-1980s, are an inexpensive mixture of wine, water, citrus flavors, sugar, and carbon dioxide gas; most have an alcohol content of 5 to 7 percent.

THE PRINCIPAL GRAPE VARIETIES

Most European wines are labeled with the name of the district, village, or vineyard from which each comes, as defined by its appellation of origin. In California, a wine's origin has played a less important role than the grape variety from which it is primarily or entirely made. Even among fine varietal wines, the name of the grape is often as much as the consumer is told about the wine in the bottle, and anyone who takes an interest in California wines soon learns to distinguish among the different varietal names with which so many of these wines are labeled today. Just as someone who enjoys European wines tries to recognize and evaluate the particular characteristics of Médoc, Beaujolais, Sancerre, Barolo, Chianti, or Rioja, so he or she looks for certain varietal characteristics in a Cabernet Sauvignon, Chardonnay, Johannisberg Riesling, or Zinfandel.

Most of the acreage devoted to the classic European grape varieties was planted in the early 1970s, and a few figures indicate just how extensive the new plantings have been. The acreage of Cabernet Sauvignon, for example, increased from 4,000 in 1969 to 22,000 fifteen years later, Chardonnay from 1,800 to 26,000, Pinot Noir from 2,000 to 9,000, Johannisberg Riesling from 1,000 to 11,000, Sémillon from 750 to 3,000, Gewürztraminer from 400 to 4,000, and Merlot from 100 to

2,000; and perhaps the most dramatic increase of all, Sauvignon Blanc jumped from 600 acres to 14,000. As impressive as these increases are, these eight classic varietals account for less than 15 percent of California's total production of wine grapes.

Red Wines

Cabernet Sauvignon, the classic red grape of Bordeaux, is responsible for the finest red wines of California. The wines, noted for their tannic, austere qualities when young, have a complexity that comes from the variety and, in some cases, from the small oak barrels in which the wine is often matured. A certain amount of Merlot is used in the Médoc region of Bordeaux to soften the harshness of young Cabernet Sauvignon, and this practice has been adopted in California as well. As more *Merlot* was planted in California, it was inevitable that it would be bottled on its own as a varietal. (After all, the wines of Saint-Emilion and Pomerol are made primarily from Merlot.) A number of wineries now market a Merlot, and some even blend in Cabernet Sauvignon to add backbone to the rich, but somewhat softer wines made from this grape. A very small amount of *Cabernet Franc* is planted in California, and is sometimes blended with Cabernet Sauvignon to add bouquet.

Pinot Noir, from France's Burgundy region, is generally acknowledged to be the least successful of the classic grape varieties in California. California Pinot Noir is often light and indistinct, but even attractive, full-bodied examples often lack the complexity of flavor and elegance of fine red Burgundies. Selected clones, or variants, of Pinot Noir have been planted in cooler districts more suited to this variety, and despite the difficulties posed by this fragile variety, many winemakers continue to experiment with different vinification techniques. Excellent examples of Pinot Noir have been produced, but not as consistently as have other varieties. Much of the Pinot Noir planted in Napa and Sonoma is now used for sparkling wines. *Red Pinot* is not a Pinot at all, and the name is almost never seen anymore, as there are less than two hundred acres planted. *Pinot Saint George* is another name for the Red Pinot.

Gamay Beaujolais is now officially classified as a clone of Pinot Noir, and wines made from this variety may legally be sold under either name. Since the name Gamay Beaujolais has become familiar to consumers, many wineries continue to sell lighter-bodied examples with that name and market fuller ones as Pinot Noir. It is the variety called *Gamay* or *Napa Gamay* that is often thought to be most similar to the one cultivated in the Beaujolais region, although some ampelographers believe that Napa Gamay is really the French variety Valdiguié. In general, Gamay Beaujolais produces lighter, fruitier wines than does Napa Gamay. Both Napa Gamay and Gamay Beaujolais are usually bottled early and meant to be drunk young. Several wineries even produce a Gamay Beaujolais Nouveau, in the style of France's Beaujolais Nouveau, which is bottled and sold within weeks of the harvest.

Zinfandel, although of European origin, is often referred to as an all-American variety, since it makes wines unlike those produced anywhere else. The origin of Zinfandel, long considered a Hungarian variety, remains something of a mystery. It has now been identified as similar if not identical to the Primitivo of southern Italy, but that variety is referred to as foreign by many of its growers, which suggests that it was brought to Italy from another country. Plantings of Zinfandel increased considerably in the early 1970s, and it displaced Carignane as the most widely cultivated red-wine grape in California. When grown in the Central Valley, it usually produces undistinguished wine suitable for blending into generics. In cooler areas, its distinctive spicy or berrylike aroma and taste are evident, and it makes a very individual and appealing wine. Some winemakers make a light, fruity Zinfandel to be consumed young. Others prefer a Zinfandel that is big, tannic, and intense, and that needs some bottle age to develop. There are, in addition, occasional Late Harvest Zinfandels made from especially ripe grapes that produce wines with 15 or 16 percent of alcohol. Some are completely dry; others are vinified to retain some natural sugar. Although several producers continue to market distinctive and widely acclaimed Zinfandels, this variety is less popular than it once was, perhaps because consumers are confused by the many different styles on the market. A number of wineries have discontinued this varietal wine, but many others have achieved success by making Zinfandel as a *blanc de noirs* and marketing it as White Zinfandel.

Petite Sirah produces intensely colored, full-flavored, and tannic wines that were used for many years in generic blends. This variety is widely planted in the coastal counties and in the Central Valley, and many wineries now market the wine as a varietal. It is believed that California Petite Sirah is not the Syrah of France's Rhône region, but the Duriff. About one hundred acres of true *Syrah*, used to make such wines as Hermitage and Côte Rotie, have also been planted in California.

Barbera is widely grown in northern Italy and in California's Central Valley, where it produces an agreeable wine without any distinctive character. A limited amount of Barbera is made in the coastal counties as well, and is characterized by good flavor and lively acidity.

Charbono, another north Italian variety, is similar to Barbera, although softer and fuller-bodied. For many years Inglenook was the only one to market the wine as a varietal, but limited amounts of Charbono are now produced by other wineries as well, from less than one hundred acres.

Carignane, widely planted in southern France (where it is spelled Carignan), is a high-yield variety used almost entirely as a blending wine, although a few wineries market it as a varietal. *Grenache*, another variety from southern France extensively planted in the Central Valley, is best known as a varietal rosé.

Ruby Cabernet, a cross of Cabernet Sauvignon with Carignane, has been widely planted in the Central Valley, where it gives an abundant yield of agreeable wines. In fact, Carignane, Grenache, Barbera, and Ruby Cabernet account for more than half the total red-grape crop in California.

Carnelian, a new cross of Cabernet Sauvignon, Carignane, and Grenache, was developed as a high-yield variety for use in the Central Valley. *Carmine* and *Centurion* are other Cabernet-based crosses.

White Wines

Chardonnay, the classic grape of Burgundy, is considered the most successful white-wine variety in California. At their best, Chardonnays are rich, full-flavored, complex, and elegant, and they are the longest-lived of dry white wines. Most winemakers now age Chardonnay in small oak barrels, so that the bouquet of these wines often combines oak with the natural fruit of the grape.

Pinot Blanc is increasingly cultivated in California, and there is probably more acreage there today than in Burgundy. The wines are similar to Chardonnay, but perhaps a bit lighter and more acid, which makes them particularly suitable for fine sparkling wines.

Sauvignon Blanc is the grape used, in combination with

Sémillon, to make Bordeaux Blanc and Graves, which can be dry or semidry. It is also used by itself along the Loire to make such assertive dry wines as Pouilly-Fumé and Sancerre. Sauvignon Blanc had never been a popular varietal wine until Robert Mondavi introduced a dry, flavorful Sauvignon Blanc labeled Fumé Blanc in the late 1960s. Many wineries now market dry versions of this varietal as Fumé Blanc; others continue to use the name Sauvignon Blanc for a wine that is almost always dry. However it's labeled, Sauvignon Blanc's grassy, herbaceous character makes it one of California's most distinctive white wines.

Sémillon is the grape that gives Sauternes its special character when attacked by noble rot, but few California winemakers have attempted to make a botrytised wine from this variety. Sémillon is not often seen as a varietal on its own, but many winemakers now blend this grape into their Sauvignon Blanc to soften the latter's assertive character. Sémillon may also be labeled Chevrier, which is the historical name for this variety.

The Riesling grape that is grown along Germany's Rhine and Moselle rivers is called *Johannisberg Riesling* or *White Riesling* in California. It produces fragrant and charming wines that usually have more body and alcohol than Rieslings from Germany, and that are, therefore, closer in style to full-flavored Rhine wines than to the delicate and piquant wines of the Moselle. A few wineries make a dry Johannisberg Riesling, as in Alsace, but most retain a certain amount of sugar to produce a semidry wine. In addition to the wide range of medium-dry Johannisberg Rieslings produced in California, winemakers there have also been remarkably successful at making late-harvest wines similar to the Auslese, Beerenauslese, and even Trockenbeerenauslese wines of Germany.

Sylvaner can be sold in California as Riesling, and most of them are, although some wineries label this wine Riesling-Sylvaner or Franken Riesling. The wine does not have the fragrance and elegance of a true Riesling, but good examples have perhaps more distinction in California than in Germany. Some California Rieslings are just off-dry, others are semisweet.

Grey Riesling, which is not a Riesling at all, is capable of producing wines that are dry, crisp, and relatively flavorful, although most examples are semidry and undistinguished.

Emerald Riesling, a cross of Riesling with Muscadelle,

produces pale-colored, light-bodied, rather neutral wines, which are often blended with Muscat to add aroma and flavor.

Chenin Blanc, used to make such Loire Valley wines as Vouvray, Anjou Blanc, and Saumur, produces fruity, appealing wines in California. A few Chenin Blanc wines are completely dry, but most range from semidry to semisweet, the exact degree of sweetness varying from one winery to another. (For that matter, Vouvray, too, is made as a dry, semidry, and sweet wine.) In the past, dry Chenin Blanc was occasionally marketed as White Pinot, which is misleading, since this grape bears no relation to the Pinot Blanc. The name probably derives from the Chenin Blanc's local name along the Loire—Pineau de la Loire.

Wines labeled *Gewürztraminer* have a spicy aroma and a pronounced taste that makes them one of the most distinctive white wines in the world. *Gewürz* means spicy, and even muted versions of this wine still retain its characteristic penetrating bouquet and intense flavor. In France's Alsace region, Gewürztraminer is almost always dry; in California, most examples range from semidry to semisweet.

French Colombard, an anonymous component of many generic blends, is the most widely planted white-wine grape in California. Increasingly bottled as a varietal, it can be made into pleasant off-dry wine with a touch of acidity, especially in the cooler coastal regions. Inexpensive semisweet versions are often bland. French Colombard and Chenin Blanc, most of it cultivated in the Central Valley, account for two-thirds of California's white-wine crop.

Muscat Canelli, an intensely flavored grape widely cultivated in northern Italy to make Asti Spumante, is planted to a limited extent in California, where it produces a distinctive and aromatic wine. Most examples are sweet, a few are semidry. (The Muscat of Alexandria, widely planted in the San Joaquin Valley, is a raisin grape historically used to make cheap Muscatel.)

Green Hungarian is such an appealing name that a few firms market this varietal, although the wine itself is fairly neutral.

Folle Blanche, known in France's Muscadet region as Gros Plant, makes a light-bodied, dry wine.

Flora, a cross of Sémillon and Gewürztraminer, has not been widely planted and is rarely seen as a varietal.

Rosés and Blanc de Noirs

Most California rosés are blended from different varieties and sold as Vin Rosé or with a proprietary brand name. Of the varietal rosés, Grenache Rosé, popularized by Almadén, is the best known. Grenache is grown in southern France, and is one of the varieties used to make Tavel, France's best-known dry rosé; California Grenache Rosé is usually medium-dry. Rosés are also made from Zinfandel, Gamay, Pinot Noir, Petite Sirah, and Cabernet Sauvignon. The best of them, which retain the varietal characteristics of the grape from which each is made, are among the most distinctive and attractive rosés available.

In response to the increased demand for white wines, a number of wineries began to market white wines made from black grapes, which are often referred to as *blanc de noirs*. The color in red wine is extracted from the skins during fermentation, so if black grapes are pressed immediately after picking and the juice fermented away from the skins (as in the Champagne district of France), the result is a white wine. In practice, the California versions are usually pale salmon or pink in color, so the word Blanc or White that almost always appears on the label is not really accurate, although it obviously permits wineries to avoid the less desirable word Rosé. The wines are marketed as if they were white, however, and are meant to be served chilled on occasions when white wines are called for.

At first, Pinot Noir was the variety most often used to make a *blanc de noirs*; the wines are labeled Pinot Noir Blanc or Blanc de Pinot Noir. Then, in the mid-1980s, White Zinfandel became so popular that the *blanc de noirs* category acquired a new, more salable name—blush wines. Gamay and Cabernet Sauvignon are also used to make *blanc de noirs*.

The California Wine Regions

The changes that are continually taking place in California today mean that any description of its wine regions and wineries must necessarily be tentative. New winemaking districts are being created where vines were not previously cultivated, and microclimates particularly suited to one or another variety are being discovered within established vineyard regions. Wineries are in an even greater state of flux. The personality of a winery may change almost overnight because of new ownership or a new winemaker, and other factors play a role as well. A winery that has traditionally produced generic wines may introduce a line of varietal wines; one known for certain varietal wines may decide to market others in even greater quantities; a winery may produce its wines from purchased grapes until its own vineyards are fully bearing, at which time the style of its wines may change. Nor is a winery's history easy to establish: some winemakers made their first wines under someone else's roof while their own wineries were being constructed; others began by making such limited amounts of wine that it was not until the second or third crush, or vintage, that they were able to bottle enough wine to market commercially. The following discussion of the principal wine regions and brief descriptions of more than two hundred wineries is meant to be no more than an introduction to the diversity that characterizes the California wine scene today.

NAPA

Of all the California wine regions, Napa is probably the most famous to consumers and the one with the finest reputation. The reasons for this are not hard to discover: not only does the Napa Valley contain some of California's best-known wineries, but the number of fine wines produced there since Repeal is greater than anywhere else. There are vintage-dated varietal wines, especially Cabernet Sauvignon, from such wineries as Beaulieu Vineyard, Inglenook, Charles Krug, and Louis M. Martini going back to the 1930s and 1940s, while Sonoma and Monterey, for example, began to produce such wines only in the 1960s. Today, outstanding wines are made in other regions as well, and many winemakers would agree that certain varieties grow even more successfully in other counties than in Napa. Nevertheless, Napa retains its reputation, which has been further enhanced by a number of excellent new wineries created in the 1970s and 1980s.

The Napa Valley wineries are particularly accessible to visitors. The city of Napa is fifty miles north of San Francisco, and the distance from Napa to Calistoga, at the northern end of the valley, by way of Yountville, Oakville, Rutherford, and St. Helena is about twenty-five miles. The Silverado

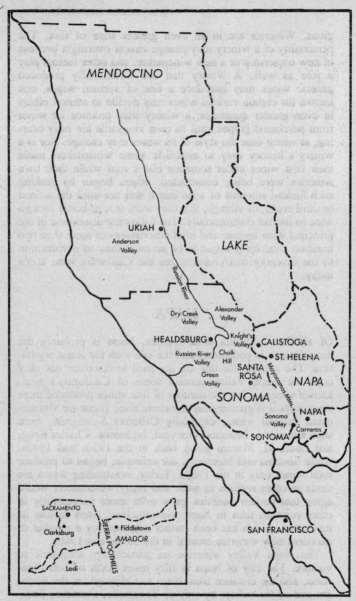

NORTHERN CALIFORNIA

Trail, at the base of the mountains east of the valley floor, parallels the main highway that runs through the Napa Valley; to the west the Mayacamas Mountains separate Napa and Sonoma counties.

There are about thirty thousand acres of vineyards in Napa, of which Cabernet Sauvignon and Chardonnay each account for more than six thousand acres. These two varieties, plus Sauvignon Blanc, Pinot Noir, Johannisberg Riesling, and Merlot, make up two-thirds of Napa's total acreage. The Napa Valley appellation encompasses virtually all of the vineyards in the county, including those in the Chiles, Pope, and Wooden valleys. Established viticultural areas within Napa include the Los Carneros region, Howell Mountain, and the Stag's Leap District. Other areas that may eventually be defined include Mount Veeder, Spring Mountain, and perhaps Oakville and Rutherford. Although there are few official viticultural areas within Napa, growers and winemakers know that the region includes many different microclimates. The region around Calistoga to the north, for example, is actually warmer than the southern part of the Napa Valley; another distinction is made between grapes grown on the valley floor and those from hillside vineyards to the east and west. Probably the best-known area in Napa is Carneros (Spanish for sheep), at the southern end of the Napa Valley, near San Pablo Bay. The Carneros district (part of whose vineyards are in Sonoma County) is known for having a long, cool growing season particularly suited to Chardonnay and Pinot Noir, although a number of other varieties are cultivated there as well. Many Napa wineries have now established vineyards there, as have growers who sell their grapes to different winemakers; the best-known vineyard is René di Rosa's Winery Lake.

This description of Napa Valley wineries begins with several large, well-established ones, all of which are situated along an eight-mile stretch of Highway 29 from Oakville to just past St. Helena. Beaulieu Vineyard, founded by Georges de Latour in 1900, is best known for its Cabernet Sauvignon. The winery, usually referred to as BV, now produces three Cabernets: one is labeled Rutherford; another, Beau Tour, is blended with Merlot; the third, produced in limited quantities, is the famous Georges de Latour Private Reserve, first made in 1936. The Private Reserve, traditionally one of the finest Cabernets made in California, comes from two vineyards near Rutherford, and is the biggest and longest-lived of BV's Cabernets. BV makes several varietal wines, including

Chardonnay, Pinot Noir, Sauvignon Blanc, Gamay Beaujolais, and Johannisberg Riesling. The winery also bottles special lots of Pinot Noir and Chardonnay from grapes grown in the Carneros district, and makes a third Pinot Noir, labeled Beau Velours, from a blend of that variety and Petite Sirah. André Tchelistcheff, a Russian-born enologist, joined BV in 1938 and was responsible for the style and quality of its wines for thirty-five years. He pioneered the use of small oak barrels as an adjunct to large redwood tanks to age wines, and was one of the first to recognize the potential of the Carneros district as a site for Pinot Noir and Chardonnay. After his retirement from BV in 1970, Tchelistcheff became a consultant to BV until 1973, and thereafter to a number of other wineries throughout the state.

Inglenook, founded by Gustave Niebaum in 1879, is less than a mile from Beaulieu Vineyard. In 1964 the winery was sold to United Vintners, which was in turn acquired by Heublein, Inc., in 1968. (Heublein, which also brought Beaulieu Vineyard in 1969, no longer owns United Vintners, but continues to own Inglenook and BV.) In recent years, the Inglenook winery has once again focused its attention on estate-bottled Napa Valley varietal wines, primarily Cabernet Sauvignon, Chardonnay, and Sauvignon Blanc, along with several others, including Charbono, an unusual red. Inglenook continues to market its best lots of Cabernet Sauvignon with the well-known Cask designation, and produces Reserve bottlings of Merlot, Sauvignon Blanc, Chardonnay, and Pinot Noir. Inglenook also offers a less expensive Napa Valley Cabernet Sauvignon and Chardonnay labeled Cabinet Selection. Inglenook Navalle, a very popular line of inexpensive generic and varietal jug wines, is produced in Madera, in the San Joaquin Valley.

Louis M. Martini wines were first made in Napa in 1934. The firm owns more than a thousand acres of vineyards, but because they are located in both Napa and Sonoma, the wines were previously labeled with a California appellation; today, the appellations North Coast, Napa, or Sonoma are used. Martini has achieved a particular reputation for such red wines as Cabernet Sauvignon, Zinfandel, Barbera, Pinot Noir, Petite Sirah, and Merlot, and for such whites as Chardonnay, a Sauvignon Blanc–Sémillon blend, and the unusual Folle Blanche; the winery is among the few whose Chenin Blanc and Gewürz Traminer are dry. In fine vintages, individual lots of Cabernet Sauvignon, Pinot Noir, Merlot, or Zinfandel are vinified and bottled separately and labeled Special Selection. In addition, Martini also produces limited amounts of single-vineyard varietal wines from its several vineyard sites, including Monte Rosso in Sonoma and La Loma and Las Amigas in Napa's Carneros district.

North of St. Helena is the picturesque nineteenth-century Rhine House, which serves as a tasting room for Beringer Vineyards. Beringer was revitalized in 1970, when it was purchased by Nestlé of Switzerland. The late Myron Nightingale, who retired in 1984, was brought in as winemaker, a new winery was built across the road from the Rhine House, and the firm now offers a full range of varietal wines, as well as a Private Reserve Cabernet Sauvignon, Chardonnay, and Fumé Blanc. Beringer, which owns two thousand acres of vineyards in Napa and Sonoma, also produces a Cabernet Sauvignon and Sauvignon Blanc from the Knights Valley area in Sonoma. Nightingale and his wife, Alice, who had experimented with induced-botrytis Sémillon at the Cresta Blanca winery in the 1950s, resumed their work at Beringer in 1980, and this special wine was named Nightingale in their honor. Beringer also markets a successful line of generic and varietal jug wines under the Los Hermanos label, and moderately priced varietal wines under the Napa Ridge label.

The Charles Krug Winery, founded in 1861, was purchased by Cesare Mondavi in 1943, and is now under the direction of his son, Peter Mondavi. Krug, which owns twelve hundred acres in Napa, was the first winery to successfully market Chenin Blanc as a varietal. The firm produces a full range of generic and varietal wines, including a Vintage Selection Cabernet Sauvignon and a Chardonnay made from grapes grown in the Carneros district. Krug also markets a separate line of jug wines under the name CK Mondavi.

The Christian Brothers, a teaching order founded in France in the seventeenth century, first planted vineyards in California in 1882 and moved to the Napa Valley in 1930. They own about fourteen hundred acres in Napa, and most of their table wines bear a Napa appellation; they also own two hundred acres in the San Joaquin Valley, where they make dessert wines and brandy. In addition to the usual range of generic and varietal wines, the Christian Brothers also market a dry Sauvignon Blanc as Napa Fumé Blanc and a sweet Muscat wine as Chateau La Salle. With few exceptions, the Christian Brothers produced only nonvintage wines until 1979, when the winery first introduced a few vintage-dated varietal wines; all of the varietal wines are now vintage-dated.

The Robert Mondavi Winery, which was built near Oakville in 1966, was the first large new winery established in the Napa Valley since Prohibition. When Mondavi left Charles Krug, his intention was to produce only vintage-dated varietal wines, which was a much more unusual concept at the time than it is today. From the beginning, Mondavi experimented with various aspects of winemaking, including fermentation temperatures and the effects of different kinds of oak on the flavor and complexity of each varietal wine. The winery, which now owns more than a thousand acres in Napa, has reduced its original range of varietal wines to Cabernet Sauvignon, Pinot Noir, Chardonnay, Chenin Blanc, Johannisberg Riesling, and Fumé Blanc, which is the name Mondavi originated for a dry Sauvignon Blanc. The winery also makes a sweet white wine called Moscato d'Oro. Specially selected lots of Cabernet Sauvignon, Chardonnay, Fumé Blanc and Pinot Noir are bottled and sold as Reserve wines. Robert Mondavi and Baron Philippe de Rothschild of Château Mouton-Rothschild in Bordeaux created a joint venture to produce a Napa Valley Cabernet Sauvignon which has been given the proprietary name Opus One. The first vintages of Opus One, 1979 and 1980, were released in 1984. Mondavi also owns the Woodbridge winery, near Lodi, where popular vintage-dated red, white, and rosé varietal table wines are made.

When Robert Mondavi established his own firm, there were fewer than twenty wineries in the Napa Valley; today there are more than 140, most of them created in the late 1970s and early 1980s. A number of wineries produced more than twenty-five thousand cases a year, and their wines can be found in most major cities; many others produce only a few thousand cases and sell little wine outside California. About eighty of Napa's wineries are described here in a loose geographical order, starting on the Silverado Trail near the city of Napa, continuing north toward Calistoga, and then doubling back to Napa along the main highway, with occasional detours to the hillsides west of the valley.

Clos Du Val is unusual in that it was originally set up to make only two wines — Cabernet Sauvignon, which still accounts for more than a third of its production, and Zinfandel. The first wines, made in 1972 under the direction of Bernard Portet, a Frenchman who grew up in Bordeaux, established the winery's continuing reputation for elegant and stylish wines. In addition to its 140 acres of Cabernet Sauvignon, Merlot, and Zinfandel near the winery, another 110 acres of Chardonnay and Pinot Noir have been developed in the Carneros district, and Portet has added these two varieties, as well as Merlot, Sauvignon Blanc, and Sémillon, to his range of wines. Gran Val is the winery's second label.

Stag's Leap Wine Cellars, also located along the Silverado Trail, was established in 1972 by Warren and Barbara Winiarski. There are forty-five acres of Cabernet Sauvignon and Merlot planted at the winery, and wines made from this acreage can be recognized by the designation Stag's Leap Vineyards on their labels. In some years, special lots of Cabernet Sauvignon are bottled separately and labeled Cask 23. The winery also produces Petite Sirah, Gamay Beaujolais, Chardonnay, White Riesling, and Sauvignon Blanc; its second label is Hawk Crest. Stags' Leap Vintners, located nearby, was established by the Doumani family, who added Cabernet Sauvignon, Merlot, and Pinot Noir to the original plantings of Chenin Blanc and Petite Syrah (as it is labeled). Richard Steltzner, a grape-grower whose fifty-acre vineyard was planted in the late 1960s, began producing limited amounts of Cabernet Sauvignon in 1977 and established his own winery in 1983. Shafer Vineyards is a family-owned winery with about forty-five acres planted in Cabernet Sauvignon, Chardonnay, and Merlot. In 1973 Stanley and Carol Anderson began to plant Chardonnay in what is now a thirty-six-acre vineyard, and they made their first wines in 1980; the S. Anderson Vineyard produces Chardonnay and *méthode champenoise* sparkling wines.

A number of relatively new wineries are situated on or near the Silverado Trail. The Chimney Rock winery, established in 1986, includes seventy-five acres of Cabernet Sauvignon, Chardonnay, and Sauvignon Blanc planted on land that was previously part of a golf course. The Pine Ridge Winery, established by Gary Andrus, grows Cabernet Sauvignon, Merlot, and Chardonnay on one hundred acres in the Stag's Leap, Rutherford, and Oak Knoll districts; it also produces Chenin Blanc. Members of the Disney family purchased 180 acres of vineyards in the mid-1970s and began producing Cabernet Sauvignon, Chardonnay, and Sauvignon Blanc, under the Silverado Vineyards label, in 1981.

The William Hill Winery has planted Chardonnay and Cabernet Sauvignon in a part of the nine hundred acres of mountain land it owns on Atlas Peak and Mount Veeder, situated on opposite sides of the Napa Valley. This winery's first Cabernet Sauvignon was produced in 1978, its first Chardonnay in 1979.

Donn Chappellet established the Chappellet Vineyard on Pritchard Hill, east of the Napa Valley, and the estate now includes more than a hundred acres of vineyards. The first wines were produced in 1968, and the following year a dramatic new winery was built in the form of a three-sided pyramid. Chappellet, best known for its intense and long-lived Cabernet Sauvignon, also produces Chardonnay, Johannisberg Riesling, a dry Chenin Blanc, and occasionally a Merlot. Long Vineyards, established by Robert and Zelma Long on Pritchard Hill, produces less than two thousand cases a year of highly acclaimed Chardonnay, Johannisberg Riesling, and Cabernet Sauvignon.

The Villa Mt. Eden Winery, set back from the Silverado Trail, dates back to 1881 and was modernized in the 1970s; its eighty-acre vineyard is planted primarily with Cabernet Sauvignon, Chardonnay, and Chenin Blanc. Silver Oak Cellars, situated nearby, produces Cabernet Sauvignon only, virtually all of it from Sonoma's Alexander Valley, plus a limited amount from Bonny's Vineyard, near the winery, and from other Napa sites. The Girard Winery produces Chardonnay, Cabernet Sauvignon, and Chenin Blanc from about forty acres of vineyards. Groth Vineyards, which produced its first wines in 1982 under the direction of winemaker Nils Venge, specializes in Chardonnay, Sauvignon Blanc, and Cabernet Sauvignon. Norma de Leuze and the late Gino Zepponi, founders of the ZD winery, made their first wines in Sonoma in 1969. They moved to their present winery in Napa in 1979; produces ZD's primarily Chardonnay, Cabernet Sauvignon, and Pinot Noir.

Caymus Vineyards was established by Charles Wagner, a grapegrower who, in 1971, began to make wines from his seventy-acre vineyard and from purchased grapes. Caymus was one of the first to make a *blanc de noirs* from Pinot Noir grapes, labeled Oeil de Perdrix, and has achieved particular success with its Cabernet Sauvignon; its second label is Liberty School. Randy Dunn, the winemaker at Caymus, established Dunn Vineyards to produce a limited amount of Cabernet Sauvignon from vineyards planted on Howell Mountain. Conn Creek Vineyards, established by Bill and Kathy Collins in 1974, produces Cabernet Sauvignon, Chardonnay, and Zinfandel, most of which comes from its 120-acre vineyard;

Chateau Maja is a proprietary name used for less-expensive Chardonnay, Cabernet Sauvignon, and a dry Chenin Blanc.

Rutherford Hill Winery, formerly Souverain of Rutherford, was bought from Pillsbury Mills in 1976 by some of the owners of Freemark Abbey, including William Jaeger and Charles Carpy. It produces primarily Chardonnay and Merlot, as well as Cabernet Sauvignon, Sauvignon Blanc, and Gewürztraminer from eight hundred acres of vineyards owned by the winery partners. The Jaeger family also makes limited amounts of Merlot, from its twenty-two-acre vineyard, under the Jaeger Inglewood Vineyard label. Buehler Vineyards, situated in the hills overlooking Lake Hennessey, has more than sixty acres planted, primarily with Cabernet Sauvignon and Zinfandel, with some Pinot Blanc.

Joseph Phelps Vineyards, in the hills east of St. Helena, has more than two hundred acres planted near the winery and elsewhere in Napa and also has an interest in a 150-acre vineyard in Sonoma's Carneros district. The winery produced its first wines in 1973 and, under the direction of its German-born winemaker, Walter Schug, achieved success with such varietals as Chardonnay, Sauvignon Blanc, Gewürztraminer, Cabernet Sauvignon, and Zinfandel, as well as with limited amounts of the true French Syrah and the German Scheurebe. Phelps is also known for its range of Johannisberg Rieslings, which range from a light, crisp Early Harvest to botrytised late-harvest wines equal to the Beerenauslese and Trocken-beerenauslese wines of Germany. Insignia is a proprietary name for a wine made primarily from selected lots of Cabernet Sauvignon and Merlot in proportions that vary from year to year. In 1980, Schug, who continued as Phelps' winemaker until 1983, established his own winery, Schug Cellars, to focus on Pinot Noir from the eight-acre Heinemann Vineyard and Chardonnay from the Carneros district; he shares cellar space north of Calistoga with Storybook Mountain Vineyards, which specializes in Zinfandel. Bruce Neyers, in charge of marketing at Phelps, established the Neyers Winery in 1980 to produce limited amounts of Cabernet Sauvignon and Chardonnay.

Not far from Phelps is Heitz Cellars, created by Joe Heitz, one of the most respected winemakers in California. Heitz produces a range of wines that includes Cabernet Sauvignon, Chardonnay, Zinfandel, and Grignolino. In 1984 Heitz bought a sixty-five-acre vineyard planted primarily with Cabernet Sauvignon to supplement the forty-seven acres of Chardonnay and Grignolino he already owned. Heitz's most famous wine is the Cabernet Sauvignon he produces from Martha's Vineyard, owned by Tom and Martha May. When the wine was first made, in 1966, there were only twelve acres planted with Cabernet Sauvignon; today, all of the vineyard's forty acres are planted with that variety. Since 1976, Heitz has also produced a Cabernet Sauvignon from the eighteen-acre Bella Oaks vineyard owned by Bernard and Belle Rhodes.

North of St. Helena, on Howell Mountain, is Burgess Cellars. Formerly the Souverain winery of Lee Stewart, it was purchased in 1972 by Tom Burgess, who has twenty acres of Cabernet Sauvignon at the winery and fifty acres of Chardonnay near Yountville. Burgess has reduced his original range of wines to three—Chardonnay, Cabernet Sauvignon, and Zinfandel; his second label is Bell Canyon Cellars. Back on the Silverado Trail is Duckhorn Vineyards, which began producing limited quantities of Cabernet Sauvignon and Merlot in 1978; Sauvignon Blanc was first produced in 1982. Rombauer Vineyards, which concentrates on Cabernet Sauvignon and Chardonnay, produced its first wines in 1980. Stratford is known for its Chardonnay, made from grapes grown in several California regions. Farther up the Silverado Trail is Cuvaison, which for many years specialized in Chardonnay, Cabernet Sauvignon and Zinfandel. The Swiss company that bought the winery in 1979 also bought land in the Carneros district, and more than 350 acres have been planted there, primarily in Chardonnay, which now accounts for almost all of the winery's production. Cuvaison also makes a limited amount of Cabernet Sauvignon, and markets additional wines under the Calistoga Vineyards label.

North of Calistoga, at the foot of Mount St. Helena, is Chateau Montelena, a winery founded in 1882 and revitalized by its present owners, whose first wines were produced in 1972. Chateau Montelena's Cabernet Sauvignon and Zinfandel come from its own vineyards, as does its Napa Chardonnay; it also produces Chardonnay from grapes grown in Sonoma's Alexander Valley. The winery, which makes a limited amount of Johannisberg Riesling as well, occasionally markets wines under the Silverado Cellars label. The Robert Pecota Winery, which first produced wines from its forty acres of vineyards in 1978, specializes in Cabernet Sauvignon and Sauvignon Blanc. Farther south, on Diamond Mountain, Al Brounstein established Diamond Creek Vineyards. Twenty acres of Cabernet Sauvignon and small amounts of Merlot, Malbec, and Cabernet Franc were planted in 1968, and the first wines were made in 1972; wines from three plots, Volcanic Hill, Red Rock Terrace, and Gravelly Meadow, are vinified and bottled separately.

One of the most striking wineries in California is that of Sterling Vineyards, modeled on the spare white churches found on some Greek islands. An aerial tramway transports visitors from the base of a hill to the winery above. The first wines Sterling marketed were from the 1969 vintage (including the first vintage-dated Merlot made in California), and its production, which comes entirely from its twelve hundred acres of vineyards, consists of Cabernet Sauvignon (including special lots of Sterling Reserve and a *blanc de noirs* labeled Cabernet-Blanc), Merlot, Sauvignon Blanc, and Chardonnay. Sterling also produces single-vineyard wines, including Cabernet Sauvignon and Chardonnay from Diamond Mountain Ranch, and Chardonnay and Pinot Noir from the Winery Lake vineyard. In 1983, the Seagram company purchased Sterling from the Coca-Cola Company of Atlanta. Close by is the Stonegate Winery, where the Spaulding family began to produce wines in 1973; the winery now concentrates on Chardonnay, Sauvignon Blanc, and Cabernet Sauvignon. In addition to vineyards adjoining the winery, the family owns twenty acres of hillside vineyards in the Mayacamas Mountains; the Chardonnay and Merlot produced there is labeled Spaulding Vineyard. Schramsberg Vineyards and the Hanns Kornell Champagne Cellars, whose sparkling wines are discussed elsewhere, are situated nearby, in the northern part of the Napa Valley.

Stony Hill Vineyard, a famous small winery in the hills west of St. Helena, was founded in the early 1950s by the late Frederick McCrea and his wife, Eleanor. Its thirty-five acres of vineyards are planted primarily with Chardonnay, as well as Gewürztraminer, White Riesling, and Sémillon; in favorable years, the latter is made into Sémillon de Soleil, a sweet dessert wine. The Charles F. Shaw winery, situated on a fifty-acre vineyard called Domaine Elucia, produced its first Napa Valley Gamay in 1979, using traditional French techniques to achieve the style of a Beaujolais *cru*. The winery produced its first Chardonnay and Fumé Blanc in 1982, its first Gamay Nouveau in 1983. Ric Forman, the winemaker at Sterling Vineyards for the first ten years of its existence, joined Shaw in 1983; Foreman also has vineyards of his own on Howell Mountain.

The Freemark Abbey name, originally created in the 1930s,

was revived by a partnership in 1967. The winery specializes in Chardonnay and Cabernet Sauvignon, and also produces a wine labeled Cabernet Bosché, which comes from an eighteen-acre vineyard in Rutherford owned by John Bosché. In 1973 the winery made a very sweet Johannisberg Riesling from botrytised grapes that was labeled Edelwein. This special wine was produced again in 1976 and 1978, and in 1982 Freemark Abbey was able to make an even richer wine labeled Edelwein Gold. Round Hill Cellars, which markets a line of moderately priced wines, also uses the Rutherford Ranch label for Napa Valley Chardonnay, Cabernet Sauvignon, Sauvignon Blanc, and Zinfandel. Markham Vineyards, which produces a full range of varietal wines, is situated in an 1876 winery that was purchased in 1978 by Bruce Markham. St. Clement Vineyards, just across the road, was founded in 1975 by Dr. William Casey to produce Chardonnay, Sauvignon Blanc, and Cabernet Sauvignon. Markham and St. Clement have subsequently been sold to Japanese firms.

A number of wineries are situated on the slopes of Spring Mountain, the best known of which is Spring Mountain Vineyards, created by Michael Robbins in 1968. The winery makes Chardonnay, Cabernet Sauvignon, and Sauvignon Blanc from 150 acres of vineyards, as well as wines sold under the Falcon Crest label. (The property serves as the site of the fictional winery in the Falcon Crest television series.) John Williams, formerly the winemaker at Spring Mountain Vineyards, is a partner in Frog's Leap, which makes a limited amount of Sauvignon Blanc, Cabernet Sauvignon, and Chardonnay. On another part of Spring Mountain is Newton Vineyard, established by Peter Newton, one of the founders of Sterling Vineyards; the winery produces Cabernet Sauvignon, Merlot, and Sauvignon Blanc from its own hillside vineyards, and Chardonnay from grapes grown elsewhere in Napa.

Cain Cellars, founded in 1981 by Jerry and Joyce Cain on a 540-acre estate, produces primarily Cabernet Sauvignon and Merlot, as well as Chardonnay and Sauvignon Blanc. The Cains' interest in Bordeaux grape varieties led to Cain Five, a proprietary red wine blended from Cabernet Sauvignon, Cabernet Franc, Merlot, Malbec, and Petit Verdot. The Robert Keenan Winery, founded in 1977, produces Cabernet Sauvignon, Chardonnay, and Merlot, primarily from its forty-acre vineyard. Yverdon Vineyards, nearby, was established by the Aves family; Ritchie Creek

Vineyard produces limited quantities of Cabernet Sauvignon, Merlot, and Chardonnay.

Smith-Madrone Vineyards, high up on Spring Mountain, was established by Charles Smith and Stuart and Susan Smith, whose original twenty acres, planted in 1972, has doubled since. The Smith brothers, who made their first wines in 1977, produced Johannisberg Riesling, Chardonnay, Cabernet Sauvignon, and Pinot Noir from their own vineyards.

South of St. Helena, along the highway, is the Sutter Home Winery. Under the direction of Bob Trinchero, the winery, which once produced more than two dozen wines, now specializes almost exclusively in Zinfandel (a sweet white wine, Muscat Amabile, is also made). In 1968 Sutter Home began to make distinctive Zinfandels from Amador County grapes, and continues to produce that variety, with a California appellation; more recently it has achieved particular success with its appealing California White Zinfandel. The winery also produces occasional lots of Reserve Zinfandel and a sweet, fortified, portlike Dessert Zinfandel. Nearby is the V. Sattui winery, which incorporates a cheese shop, a gift boutique and picnic facilities. Raymond Vineyard, set back from the road, has an eighty-acre vineyard first planted in 1971. Raymond made its first wines in 1974, and produces primarily Chardonnay and Cabernet Sauvignon, as well as Fumé Blanc, Chenin Blanc, and Johannisberg Riesling.

The Flora Springs winery, whose owners have three hundred acres of vineyards in Napa, makes Chardonnay, Sauvignon Blanc, and Cabernet Sauvignon. The Whitehall Lane Winery, whose first wines were produced in 1980, specializes in Chardonnay, Sauvignon Blanc, and Cabernet Sauvignon. Franciscan Vineyards was acquired by the Peter Eckes firm of Germany in 1979. The winery owns more than four hundred acres of vineyards in Napa and in Sonoma's Alexander Valley from which it produces Chardonnay, Cabernet Sauvignon, Sauvignon Blanc, Merlot, and Johannisberg Riesling. The Alexander Valley wines are marketed under the Estancia label. At Rutherford Vintners, Bernard Skoda makes Cabernet Sauvignon, Johannisberg Riesling, and other varietal wines.

Grgich Hills Cellars was founded in 1977 by Mike Grgich and Austin Hills. Grgich, who achieved fame when he was the winemaker at Chateau Montelena, continues to produce fine wines from such varieties as Chardonnay, Sauvignon Blanc, Cabernet Sauvignon, and Johannisberg Riesling (the latter is sometimes made into a late-harvest wine), as well as

Zinfandel from Sonoma grapes. The Niebaum-Coppola Estate was established in 1978 by filmmaker Francis Ford Coppola, who purchased the original Inglenook Vineyard property that was once the home of Gustave Niebaum. The eighty-five-acre vineyard is planted primarily with Cabernet Sauvignon, plus Cabernet Franc and Merlot; the wine is labeled with the proprietary name Rubicon. Shown & Sons Vineyards concentrates on Cabernet Sauvignon and Chardonnay from its twenty-seven-acre vineyard. Sequoia Grove Vineyards, which focuses on Cabernet Sauvignon and Chardonnay made from its own twenty-four-acre vineyard and from selected Napa and Sonoma vineyards, was established in 1980 by the Allen family. Cakebread Cellars, created by Jack and Dolores Cakebread, produced its first wines in 1973. The winery makes approximately equal amounts of Chardonnay, Sauvignon Blanc, and Cabernet Sauvignon, part of it from a thirty-five-acre vineyard adjoining the winery planted in Sauvignon Blanc and Cabernet Sauvignon. Johnson Turnbull Vineyards produces a limited amount of estate-bottled Cabernet Sauvignon.

The Robert Pepi Winery was established in 1981 by a grape grower who has owned vineyards since 1966; most of its production is Sauvignon Blanc, the rest Cabernet Sauvignon, Chardonnay, and Sémillon. Across the highway is the DeMoor Winery, formerly Napa Cellars, acquired by a Belgian family in 1983; production is focused on Cabernet Sauvignon, Chardonnay, and Sauvignon Blanc. The Far Niente Winery, originally built in 1885, was completely renovated by proprietor Gil Nickel, and the adjoining hundred-acre vineyard was replanted as well; the winery produced its first Chardonnay in 1979, its first Cabernet Sauvignon in 1982. The Vichon Winery, founded in 1980, achieved immediate attention with the first wine it produced, an unusual blend of almost equal parts of Sauvignon Blanc and Sémillon labeled Chevrier Blanc. Chevrier is another name for Sémillon, and when new wine laws decreed that the name could only be used for a wine that contained at least 75 percent Sémillon, Vichon continued to make its blend under the proprietary name Chevrignon, along with two traditional varietal wines, Chardonnay and Cabernet Sauvignon. Vichon was acquired by the Robert Mondavi Winery in 1985.

High up in the Mayacamas Mountains, Robert and Elinor Travers produce limited quantities of intensely flavored Cabernet Sauvignon and Chardonnay at Mayacamas Vineyards, which they purchased in 1968. Their fifty-acre vineyard is planted with these two varieties and with a few acres of Sauvignon Blanc; they also make a small amount of Pinot Noir. The Mount Veeder Winery, whose twenty acres of hillside vineyards are planted primarily with Cabernet Sauvignon, is focusing its attention on that variety and Chardonnay.

The sparkling wines of Domaine Chandon, owned by Moët-Hennessy, are described elsewhere. The winery, located near Yountville, also houses a wine museum and an elegant restaurant that is very popular with visitors to the Napa Valley. Just north of Domaine Chandon is the sixty-five-acre vineyard owned jointly by Christian Moueix, who is associated with Château Pétrus, in the Pomerol district of Bordeaux, and the two daughters of the late John Daniel, who owned the Inglenook winery. The red wine from this vineyard, labeled Dominus, without a specific varietal designation, is made primarily from Cabernet Sauvignon, plus Cabernet Franc and Merlot; the first vintage was produced in 1983. Farther south, John and Janet Trefethen have planted more than six hundred acres of vineyards. About half of Trefethen's grapes are sold to other wineries, but Trefethen Vineyards has been producing wines since 1973, and now markets Chardonnay, White Riesling, Cabernet Sauvignon, and Pinot Noir, as well as a red and white proprietary wine labeled Eshcol. The Lakespring Winery, founded in 1980 by the Battat brothers, produces primarily Chardonnay and Sauvignon Blanc, plus Cabernet Sauvignon, Merlot, and Chenin Blanc.

Monticello Cellars was established by Jay Corley on two hundred acres to produce Chardonnay, Sauvignon Blanc, Gewürztraminer, and Cabernet Sauvignon; its first wines were made in 1980. In 1985 Corley acquired the Llords & Elwood firm. The St. Andrews Winery has been concentrating on Chardonnay since 1980. Closer to Napa is the Quail Ridge Winery, which produces primarily Chardonnay from both Napa and Sonoma grapes, as well as French Colombard and Cabernet Sauvignon.

In addition to the new vineyards that have been planted in the Carneros district, several wineries have been established there as well. The Carneros Creek Winery, established in 1972 by Francis Mahoney, was the first. He produces primarily Cabernet Sauvignon from Napa and Chardonnay from Carneros, as well as Pinot Noir from a twenty-acre vineyard near the winery, and occasional lots of Merlot. The Acacia Winery was founded in 1979 to produce Chardonnay and Pinot Noir from vineyards in the Carneros district. The winery bottles a range of widely acclaimed single-vineyard wines from its own Marina Vineyard and several others. Bouchaine Vineyards also emphasizes Pinot Noir and Chardonnay from Carneros; limited amounts of Cabernet Sauvignon were made in the early 1980s. Saintsbury, founded by David Graves and Richard Ward in 1981, is another Carneros winery specializing in Chardonnay and Pinot Noir; the latter is also made in a lighter version labeled Garnet. Hagafen Cellars produces several varietal wines, some from Carneros grapes, and all of them kosher.

Just east of Carneros, in Solano County, is the Green Valley-Solano viticultural area. Chateau de Leu, whose eighty-acre vineyard was first planted in 1954, produced its first wines in 1981; the winery concentrates on Chardonnay and Sauvignon Blanc.

SONOMA

Sonoma does not project as clear an image to consumers as does Napa. One reason is that the county encompasses several distinct districts, each with its own microclimate and its own appellation of origin. Another is that Sonoma has a particularly varied mix of producers that includes traditional wineries that are changing their marketing policies and winemaking techniques; large new wineries that have experienced growing pains; and dozens of small new wineries, many of them producing less than five thousand cases a year, whose first wines were released as recently as the early 1980s. Whereas Napa's fame is attributable to a number of long-established wineries whose reputations added prestige to that of the county, there are relatively few existing wineries in Sonoma whose identities go back more than twenty years; most of them did not sell much wine under their own labels until the 1960s, and much of what they did sell was in jugs with generic names. For example, as recently as 1970, Sebastiani still sold more wine in bulk to other wineries than it did under its own name; and Foppiano, founded in 1896, marketed its first Cabernet Sauvignon in 1972, its first Chardonnay in 1979.

The shift toward the production of fine wines can be seen in Sonoma, as in other California counties, by new plantings of better grape varieties. In 1965, there were about 10,000 acres under cultivation in Sonoma, two-thirds of them planted with Zinfandel, Carignane, Petite Sirah, and French Colombard. Such classic varieties as Cabernet Sauvignon, Merlot, Pinot Noir, Chardonnay, Sauvignon Blanc, and Johannisberg Riesling accounted for less than a thousand acres. Today there are more than thirty thousand acres of vineyards in Sonoma, and more than half consists of Cabernet Sauvignon, Chardonnay, Pinot Noir, and Sauvignon Blanc. Sonoma had long been a proven, if neglected, area for fine wines, but it wasn't until the early 1970s, when vineyard land in Napa became very expensive, that a number of new winemakers turned to Sonoma.

The extensive new vineyards created throughout Sonoma County present a special problem for the casual wine drinker because the geographical origin of Sonoma's wines cannot be grasped as easily as those of Napa. The well-known wineries that created the Napa Valley's reputation, and many of the newer ones as well, are concentrated along a fifteen-mile stretch from Oakville to Calistoga, and easily grouped on a map. In Sonoma County, however, there are two main wine regions, one in and around Sonoma itself, and the other near Healdsburg and Geyserville, almost fifty miles away. What's more, many Sonoma wineries do not feature the county appellation on their labels. Some large wineries that get grapes or wine from other counties must use California, North Coast, or Northern California, but even those wineries that are entitled to use the Sonoma County appellation often choose a more specific inner appellation such as Alexander Valley, Dry Creek Valley, Russian River Valley, or Sonoma Valley.

These districts within Sonoma County, and a few others, have now been defined as viticultural areas. Sonoma Valley, also known as the Valley of the Moon, is situated between the Mayacamas Mountains and the Sonoma Mountains and stretches for more than twenty miles from San Pablo Bay to north of Kenwood. This appellation, which encompasses more than six thousand acres of vineyards, also includes the Sonoma part of the Los Carneros district, the Bennett Valley, and Sonoma Mountain.

The Russian River Valley area includes the vineyards along that part of the river in the triangle formed by Healdsburg, Santa Rosa, and Guerneville. This extensive region encompasses two smaller viticultural areas, each with less than one thousand acres of vineyards: Chalk Hill, east of Windsor, and Sonoma County Green Valley (as it must be called to distinguish it from the Green Valley situated in Solano County,

east of Napa). Knights Valley is a small area northeast of the
Russian River Valley.

The Alexander Valley appellation encompasses about ten
thousand acres of vineyards located farther up the Russian
River Valley, along a fifteen-mile stretch that continues past
Geyserville and Cloverdale to the Mendocino County line.
West of the Alexander Valley is the Dry Creek Valley, a dozen
miles long, with about six thousand acres of vineyards.

The first vineyards north of San Francisco were established
near the town of Sonoma, which is only forty miles from San
Francisco and just fifteen miles due west of the city of Napa,
situated on the other side of the Mayacamas Mountains. Of
the wineries in this part of the county, known as Sonoma
Valley, Buena Vista has the longest history. Founded by
Agoston Haraszthy in 1857, it was revived in the 1940s by
the late Frank Bartholomew, who sold it in 1968. The new
owners, who expanded the vineyards and built a new winery,
then sold their interest in 1979 to Racke, a German wine and
spirits firm, which has continued Buena Vista's revitalization.
In 1984 Buena Vista acquired a thousand acres in the Carneros
district to supplement the 625 acres of vineyards it already
owned there, and is focusing on such classic varieties as
Cabernet Sauvignon, Chardonnay, and Pinot Noir. Buena Vista
introduced two proprietary wines — Spiceling, made from
Gewürztraminer and Johannisberg Riesling, and Pinot Jolie,
a light, fruity Pinot Noir — and has achieved success with
special lots of Cabernet Sauvignon, Pinot Noir, and Chardonnay labeled Private Reserve.

One of Sonoma's biggest wineries and one of the biggest
family-owned wineries in California is Sebastiani Vineyards.
Originally a supplier of bulk wines to other wineries, it has
achieved great success under its own name with a full range
of generic and varietal wines. Sebastiani was the first California
winery to market a Gamay Beaujolais Nouveau in the style
of France's Beaujolais Nouveau, and one of the first to make
a Pinot Noir Blanc, which is labeled Eye of the Swan. Since
the death of August Sebastiani in 1980, the firm has reduced
its range of wines and has focused on varietal wines from Sonoma Valley; inexpensive magnums of generic and varietal
wines are marketed under the August Sebastiani name. The
winery produces a number of single-vineyard Chardonnays,
a sparkling wine labeled Richard Cuneo, a Pinot Noir labeled
Black Beauty, less expensive wines labeled Vendange, and
special bottlings of such varieties as Cabernet Sauvignon,

Chardonnay, and Sauvignon Blanc with the designation Proprietor's Reserve.

There are several small wineries clustered around the town of Sonoma, including Hacienda, founded by Frank Bartholomew after he sold Buena Vista, and now under the direction of Crawford Cooley. The winery, part of whose production comes from its 110 acres of vineyards, markets several varietal wines, including a Chardonnay with the proprietary name Clair de Lune, Cabernet Sauvignon, Gewürztraminer, and Sauvignon Blanc. The Haywood Winery produces Chardonnay, as well as Cabernet Sauvignon, Zinfandel, and White Riesling from its ninety-acre vineyard. The Gundlach-Bundschu winery dates back to 1858, when the Rhinefarm vineyards were established. The winery was revived in 1973, and the property now includes nearly four hundred acres of vineyards which produce a full range of varietal wines, primarily Merlot, Cabernet Sauvignon, and Chardonnay.

Hanzell Vineyards, north of Sonoma, was created in the 1950s by James Zellerbach, who was determined to make Pinot Noir and Chardonnay wines equal to the best of Burgundy. He is generally credited with having introduced small French oak barrels to California, a practice that has been widely adopted throughout the state to give many red and white wines additional complexity. The winery, now owned by Barbara de Brye, continues to produce these two wines in limited quantities from thirty acres of vineyards, some of which are now planted in Cabernet Sauvignon. Carmenet was created by the owners of Chalone, in Monterey County. More than fifty acres of vineyards are planted with Cabernet Sauvignon and other red Bordeaux varieties. The winery also makes a Sauvignon Blanc, usually blended with Sémillon, from both Edna Valley and Sonoma County grapes.

The Glen Ellen Winery is owned by the Benziger family, who restored an old winery and replanted the property's vineyards, as well as establishing new vineyards in Carneros; they are concentrating on Chardonnay, Cabernet Sauvignon, and Sauvignon Blanc, and also produce moderately priced Cabernet Sauvignon and Chardonnay designated Proprietor's Reserve. The thirty acres of Laurel Glen Vineyard, situated on the slopes of Sonoma Mountain, were first planted with Cabernet Sauvignon and Cabernet Franc in 1968; the winery, which produced its first wines in 1981, markets only Cabernet Sauvignon. Grand Cru Vineyards was reestablished in 1970 at a winery that dates back to 1886. Most of the winery's production consists of Chenin Blanc, Gewürztraminer, and Sauvignon Blanc, plus Cabernet Sauvignon and Zinfandel; late-harvest Gewürztraminer from botrytised grapes is produced when conditions permit. Kistler Vineyards, whose first wines were made in 1979, produces primarily Chardonnay from Sonoma and Napa grapes, as well as limited amounts of Cabernet Sauvignon and Pinot Noir. Adler Fels, which is German for Eagle Rock, makes several vineyard-designated varietal wines.

Several wineries are situated near the town of Kenwood, among them Kenwood Vineyards, established in 1970. The winery produces a full range of varietal wines, as well as a Cabernet Sauvignon from the Jack London Vineyard, a Chardonnay from Beltane Ranch, and the Artist Series of Cabernet Sauvignons, whose labels are decorated with original art. St. Francis Vineyards produces Chardonnay, Gewürztraminer, Johannisberg Riesling, Merlot, and Pinot Noir from its hundred-acre vineyard, much of it planted in the early 1970's.

Chateau St. Jean has been producing highly acclaimed wines under the direction of winemaker Richard Arrowood since 1974. Its production is almost entirely white wines, and half of that is Chardonnay; other varieties include Fumé Blanc, Gewürztraminer, and Johannisberg Riesling. The winery bottles a number of single-vineyard wines every year — six different Chardonnays and four different Fumé Blancs is not unusual — and consumers have become familiar with such designations as Robert Young, Belle Terre, La Petite Etoile, and the winery's own seventy-seven-acre St. Jean Vineyards. Arrowood has achieved particular success with his late-harvest Johannisberg Rieslings, which are among the finest made in California and on a par with the best Beerenauslese and Trockenbeerenauslese wines of Germany. Chateau St. Jean also produces *méthode champenoise* sparkling wines at a separate facility in Graton. The winery was acquired by Suntory of Japan in 1984.

Matanzas Creek Vineyard, established in 1978 in the Bennett Valley, produces limited amounts of acclaimed Chardonnay, Merlot, and Sauvignon Blanc. Its original winemaker, Merry Edwards, left in 1984 to establish a winery called the Merry Vintners, which concentrates on Chardonnay. La Crema, situated east of Sonoma Valley, near Petaluma, focuses on Chardonnay and also makes an elegant Pinot Noir. Fisher

Vineyards, situated high in the Mayacamas Mountains north of the Sonoma Valley area, produces Cabernet Sauvignon and Chardonnay from its own vineyards.

A great many wineries are situated in the Russian River Valley area, northwest of Santa Rosa. Several are scattered around the town of Forestville, among them De Loach Vineyards, owned by a family that began as grape growers and continues to cultivate 150 acres; the winery's production consists primarily of White Zinfandel, Chardonnay, and Fumé Blanc, with lesser amounts of Zinfandel, Pinot Noir, and Cabernet Sauvignon. The Joseph Swan Vineyards produced its first wine, a Zinfandel, in 1969, and continues to make less than a thousand cases a year of that variety and Pinot Noir, Chardonnay, and Cabernet Sauvignon. Sonoma-Cutrer Vineyards encompasses five hundred acres of Chardonnay. Its widely praised estate-bottled Chardonnays — the only variety it produces — were first made in 1981 and include the single-vineyard designations Les Pierres and Cutrer Vineyard, and a third Chardonnay labeled Russian River Ranches. Mark West Vineyards was established by Joan and Bob Ellis, whose sixty-acre vineyard is planted with Chardonnay, Johannisberg Riesling, Pinot Noir, and Gewürztraminer; the winery also produces a sparkling wine and sweet, late-harvest wines. The Dehlinger Winery produces Chardonnay, Cabernet Sauvignon, Pinot Noir, and Zinfandel.

Iron Horse Vineyards, owned by Audrey and Barry Sterling and winemaker Forrest Tancer, produces estate-bottled wines from 110 acres of Chardonnay and Pinot Noir in Green Valley and thirty acres, in Alexander Valley, of Cabernet Sauvignon and Sauvignon Blanc. The winery, which occasionally uses the second label Tin Pony, also makes *méthode champenoise* sparkling wines, which account for about half of its total production. Domaine Laurier, whose vineyards are situated in Green Valley, concentrates on Chardonnay, Pinot Noir, Sauvignon Blanc, and Cabernet Sauvignon. Michael Topolos acquired Russian River Vineyards in 1978 and produces a full range of varietal wines labeled Topolos at Russian River Vineyards.

The F. Korbel Champagne Cellars, whose wines are described elsewhere, is located near Guerneville. The Davis Bynum Winery, which produces a full range of varietal wines, was founded in 1965 and moved to Sonoma in 1973. The Hop Kiln Winery, which gets its name from the converted hop kiln in which it is located, makes several varietal wines as well as a proprietary red, Marty Griffin's Big Red, and A Thousand Flowers, a proprietary white. The Belvedere Winery, founded by Peter Friedman, produces single-vineyard wines whose labels emphasize the name of the vineyard rather than that of the producer; among them are Chardonnay and Pinot Noir from both Winery Lake in Carneros and Bacigalupi in Sonoma, Cabernet Sauvignon and Merlot from Robert Young in the Alexander Valley, and Cabernet Sauvignon from York Creek in the Napa Valley. Belvedere also markets inexpensive varietal wines under the Discovery Series designation.

The original and impressive Sonoma Vineyards winery was built near Windsor in 1971 by winemaker Rodney Strong, who had previously established a successful direct-mail wine business under the label Tiburon Vintners and, later, Windsor Vineyards. The winery and its sixteen hundred acres of vineyards was acquired by Renfield Importers in 1984 and its name changed to Rodney Strong Vineyards. The firm produces a full line of vintage-dated varietal wines and a range of vineyard-designated wines including a Cabernet Sauvignon from Alexander's Crown and Chardonnays from Chalk Hill and River West. The Piper-Sonoma sparkling wines are produced in an adjacent facility that is now owned by the Piper-Heidsieck champagne firm of France.

The Louis J. Foppiano winery, established in 1896, shifted from bulk wines to bottled wines in the 1960s, and then from generic to varietal wines. The winery continues to make its popular Petite Sirah, as well as Cabernet Sauvignon, Sauvignon Blanc, and other varietal wines; less expensive generic and vintage-dated varietal wines are marketed under the Riverside Farm label. Hultgren & Samperton produces limited amounts of Chardonnay and Cabernet Sauvignon. At Mill Creek Vineyards, the Kreck family produces Chardonnay, Cabernet Sauvignon, Merlot, Sauvignon Blanc, and several other wines, including the proprietary Cabernet Blush, from its sixty acres of vineyards.

A number of wineries are located east of Highway 101, between Windsor and Healdsburg. Donna Maria Vineyards, whose 175 acres of vineyards are in the Chalk Hill area, established its winery in 1980 and concentrates on Chardonnay and Cabernet Sauvignon; the Chalk Hill Winery label is used for such wines as Chardonnay, Sauvignon Blanc, and Cabernet Sauvignon not made entirely from Donna Maria's own vineyards. Landmark Vineyards was established in 1974 by the

Mabry family, whose three vineyards are situated in the Sonoma Valley, Alexander Valley, and Russian River Valley; the winery concentrates on Chardonnay and Petit Blanc, a proprietary white wine made from Sauvignon Blanc, Chardonnay, and Chenin Blanc. The 250 acres of vineyards associated with the Balverne Winery were first planted in 1973 in the Chalk Hill area, and the wines — which include Chardonnay, Sauvignon Blanc, Cabernet Sauvignon, and Zinfandel — were introduced in the early 1980s.

The J. W. Morris Winery, which was created to produce port, was acquired in 1983 by Ken and Tricia Toth, owners of Black Mountain Vineyard. The winery produces Chardonnay, Cabernet Sauvignon, and Sauvignon Blanc, vintage-dated red and white wines labeled Private Reserve, and a range of ports. In addition, limited amounts of Chardonnay, Cabernet Sauvignon, and Zinfandel are marketed under the Black Mountain Vineyard label. Clos du Bois was founded by Frank Woods, who produced his first wines in 1974 from vineyards — which now amount to a thousand acres — planted ten years earlier in the Alexander and Dry Creek Valleys. Clos du Bois makes a full range of varietal wines from its own vineyards, as well as wines labeled with individual-vineyard designations, such as Marlstone, a Cabernet Sauvignon–Merlot blend, a Briarcrest Cabernet Sauvignon, and Chardonnays from Calcaire and Flintwood. Chardonnay, Cabernet Sauvignon, and generic red and white wines are produced from the same vineyards at a separate facility and sold under the River Oaks Vineyards label.

One of the best-known wineries in the Alexander Valley is Alexander Valley Vineyards, owned by the Wetzel family. The winery produces a full range of estate-bottled varietal wines from its 120-acre vineyard, which was first planted in 1964. Two-thirds of the acreage consists of Chardonnay and Cabernet Sauvignon; the rest includes Chenin Blanc, Johannisberg Riesling, Gewürztraminer, Pinot Noir, Zinfandel, and Merlot. Nearby, a number of varietal wines are produced by the Johnson family at Johnson's Alexander Valley Wines. The Field Stone Winery produces primarily Cabernet Sauvignon, Petite Sirah, and Sauvignon Blanc from its 140 acres of vineyards, as well as Johannisberg Riesling, Gewürztraminer, and rosés from both Petite Sirah and Cabernet Sauvignon, the latter labeled Spring-Cabernet. The Valfleur Winery, established in 1982, produces Chardonnay, Sauvignon Blanc, and

Cabernet Sauvignon from a 180-acre vineyard, known as Jimtown Ranch, planted in the mid-1970s.

The Jordan Winery, established by Tom Jordan in 1972 on a thirteen-hundred-acre estate, produced its first Cabernet Sauvignon in 1976, its first Chardonnay in 1979; the wines are made entirely from Jordan's own 250-acre vineyard in the Alexander Valley. The highly acclaimed Cabernet Sauvignon, not released until the fourth year after the harvest, is noted for its elegance and restrained style. Another Alexander Valley winery is that of Stephen Zellerbach, nephew of the man who founded Hanzell; whose seventy-acre vineyard is planted with Cabernet Sauvignon and Merlot. In addition to wines made from these two varieties, Zellerbach also produces an Alexander Valley Chardonnay from adjoining vineyards. Munro Lyeth introduced his first wines in 1985, a 1981 red and a 1983 white, each labeled simply Lyeth (pronounced *leeth*), without a varietal designation; the red is primarily Cabernet Sauvignon, the white is primarily Sauvignon Blanc with Sémillon.

The Simi Winery, which dates back to 1876, was revitalized in the 1970s and acquired by Moët-Hennessy in 1981. Under the direction of winemaker Zelma Long, the winery has achieved acclaim for its wines — about two-thirds of its production consists of Chardonnay and Cabernet Sauvignon, the rest of Sauvignon Blanc, Chenin Blanc, and a Rosé of Cabernet Sauvignon. Simi wines are made from Sonoma and Mendocino grapes, and in 1982 the firm began to plant vineyards that will eventually supply about half of its production.

Souverain Cellars, which overlooks the Alexander Valley, was acquired by Pillsbury in 1973, sold to the North Coast Grape Growers association, and is now under the same ownership as Beringer Vineyards. Souverain, one of the largest Sonoma wineries, produces a wide range of varietal wines. The Lytton Springs Winery has been producing intensely flavored Zinfandels from its Valley Vista vineyard, and other sites, since 1975.

Several wineries are situated in the Dry Creek Valley, the best-known of which is Dry Creek Vineyard, established by David S. Stare in 1972. The winery, whose eighty-acre vineyard is planted primarily with Sauvignon Blanc and Chardonnay, has achieved an excellent reputation for those two wines, which account for two-thirds of its production, as well as for its Cabernet Sauvignon, Zinfandel, Merlot, and Chenin Blanc; special lots bear the David S. Stare designation, and less expensive bottlings occasionally appear with the Idlewood name. Lambert Bridge produces estate-bottled Chardonnay, Cabernet Sauvignon, and Merlot from its 120-acre vineyard. Preston Vineyards' 125-acre vineyard is planted primarily with Sauvignon Blanc and Zinfandel, as well as Cabernet Sauvignon, Merlot, and Chenin Blanc; the winery produces both a rich Sauvignon Blanc and a second, lighter wine from the same variety labeled Cuvée de Fumé, made with some Chenin Blanc. The William Wheeler Winery, whose wines first appeared in the early 1980s, produces Cabernet Sauvignon and Zinfandel from its thirty-five-acre vineyard; it also makes Sauvignon Blanc and two Chardonnays, one from Sonoma, the other from Monterey County grapes. Fritz Cellars, too, is a relatively new winery with vineyards in thé Dry Creek Valley; Robert Stemmler, for many years a consultant to other wineries, now produces a limited amount of Pinot Noir, Chardonnay, and Cabernet Sauvignon under his own name. The Duxoup Wine Works makes a limited amount of Syrah, Napa Gamay, and Zinfandel. Bellerose Vineyard produces Cuvée Bellerose from its fifty-acre vineyard planted primarily with Cabernet Sauvignon.

The J. Pedroncelli Winery is another example of a long-established Sonoma winery that sold wines in bulk until the 1950s, when it began to bottle wines under its own name. The winery, which has 140 acres in the Dry Creek Valley, achieved particular success with its Zinfandel Rosé, and now produces a full line of moderately priced varietal wines, including Chardonnay and Cabernet Sauvignon, as well as generic wines labeled Sonoma Red and Sonoma White. The Geyser Peak Winery, whose history goes back to 1880, was modernized and considerably expanded in the 1970s by the Schlitz Brewing Company. In 1982 the winery was acquired by the Henry Trione family, who own nearly a thousand acres of vineyards in Sonoma. Geyser Peak markets a full range of varietal wines; selected lots labeled Trione; and a proprietary red called Reserve Alexandre, made primarily from Cabernet Sauvignon and Merlot.

Pat Paulsen Vineyards has thirty-four acres of Cabernet Sauvignon, Sauvignon Blanc, and Chardonnay planted on a five-hundred-acre ranch in the Alexander Valley; the winery also makes Gewürztraminer and a dry Muscat Canelli. The Bandiera Winery, founded in 1937, was revitalized by new owners in the early 1980s under the direction of wine-maker John B. Merritt. Bandiera produces a number of varietal wines with a North Coast appellation, as well as limited amounts of Cabernet Sauvignon, Sauvignon Blanc, and Chardonnay labeled Sage Creek Vineyards from two hundred acres in the Napa Valley; the John B. Merritt label is used for selected lots of Cabernet Sauvignon and Chardonnay from Sonoma.

MENDOCINO AND LAKE COUNTY

Mendocino

Mendocino County is north of Sonoma, and its principal city, Ukiah, is 120 miles from San Francisco. Vineyard acreage has doubled in the past fifteen years, and amounts to eleven thousand acres, but more than a third still consists of Carignane, French Colombard, and Zinfandel, an indication of the county's past role as a supplier of bulk wines. A number of viticultural areas have been defined in Mendocino, among them Anderson Valley, McDowell Valley, Potter Valley, and Cole Ranch, a sixty-acre vineyard owned by John Cole.

For many years the only winery associated with Mendocino was Parducci, which now concentrates on Chardonnay, Sauvignon Blanc, Chenin Blanc, and Cabernet Sauvignon, while continuing to produce French Colombard, Petite Sirah, and Mendocino Riesling. The winery, whose vineyards have been expanded to more than four hundred acres, occasionally marketed special lots of Chardonnay, Cabernet Sauvignon, Petite Sirah, Zinfandel, and Pinot Noir as Cellar Master's Selection; such wines are now labeled with a Reserve designation.

Fetzer Vineyards, a family-owned winery founded by the late Bernard Fetzer, first produced wines in 1968 from vineyards planted ten years earlier. Fetzer has achieved success with its Premium Red and Premium White jug wines, with a full range of varietal wines made primarily from Mendocino grapes, and with its Sundial Chardonnay and Valley Oaks Fumé; in addition, a moderately priced Cabernet Sauvignon and Zinfandel are made from Lake County grapes. The winery, which now owns more than seven hundred acres of vineyards, also markets several single-vineyard wines; selected lots designated Special Reserve and Barrel Select; and less expensive varietal wines under the Bel Arbors label. Fetzer winemaker Paul Dolan produces limited amounts of Chardonnay and Cabernet Sauvignon at his own Dolan Vineyard.

McDowell Valley Vineyards was founded by Richard and Karen Keehn, who concentrate on Cabernet Sauvignon, Chardonnay, Fumé Blanc, and Syrah from nearly four hundred acres of vineyards. The winery at Tyland Vineyards was built in 1978 by the Tijsseling family, who later built the larger Tijsseling Family Vineyards nearby to produce varietal and sparkling wines. The name Cresta Blanca, originally that of a winery created in 1882 in the Livermore Valley east of San Francisco, was bought by Guild in 1971 and is now used for a line of generic and varietal wines, some of which have been produced at a cooperative cellar in Mendocino. Other wineries situated in this part of Mendocino include the William Baccala Winery, the Braren Pauli Winery, Hidden Cellars, the Milano Winery, Olson Vineyards, the Parsons Creek Winery, and Whaler Vineyard.

A number of of wineries have been established in the Anderson Valley, east of Ukiah. Edmeades Vineyards, founded by Deron Edmeades in 1972, produces Chardonnay, Gewürztraminer, Cabernet Sauvignon, and Zinfandel as well as such proprietary wines as Rain Wine and Opal, a Pinot Noir Blanc. Navarro Vineyards has become known for its Gewürztraminer. Husch Vineyard, founded in 1971 and now owned by the Oswald family, was the first winery in Anderson Valley. Scharffenberger Cellars, best known for its *méthode champenoise* sparkling wine, also produces varietal wines labeled Eaglepoint. Other wineries include Greenwood Ridge Vineyards, Handley Cellars, Lazy Creek Vineyard, and Pepperwood Springs Vineyard.

Lake County

Lake County, east of Mendocino, had a flourishing wine business in the 1880s, with five thousand acres of vineyards and three dozen wineries. When Prohibition ended, there were no wineries left and almost no vineyards. New plantings occurred in the 1960s, and the Lake County appellation began appearing on labels of wines produced by wineries in neighboring counties from Lake County grapes. There are now three thousand acres of grapes in the county, primarily Cabernet Sauvignon and Sauvignon Blanc, and in 1977 Lower Lake

Winery became the first winery to produce wine in Lake County since Prohibition.

There are two viticultural areas in Lake County—Guenoc Valley and Clear Lake. The vineyards in the Guenoc Valley were planted by Orville and Bob Magoon, who founded the Guenoc Winery in 1981. The Magoons began planting 270 acres of vineyards in the early 1970s on a twenty-three-thousand-acre tract they had acquired some years before. The winery produces primarily Cabernet Sauvignon, Chardonnay, and Sauvignon Blanc as well as Chenin Blanc, Petite Sirah, and Zinfandel. Part of the estate and the house on it once belonged to actress Lily Langtry, and her picture adorns the Guenoc labels.

The Konocti Winery was established at the foot of Mount Konocti (pronounced con-*oc*-tie) in 1979 by an association of about two dozen Lake County grape growers. In 1983 John and George Parducci, who have a well-known winery in Mendocino, acquired an interest in Konocti Cellars, whose focus is now on Cabernet Sauvignon, Fumé Blanc, White Riesling, and Cabernet-Blanc. Kendall-Jackson Vineyards produces primarily white wines—Chardonnay, Johannisberg Riesling, and a proprietary Sauvignon Blanc labeled Chevrier du Lac—plus Cabernet Sauvignon and limited amounts of Zinfandel. Some of the wines produced by winemaker Jed Steele come from Kendall-Jackson's own vineyards, and bear the Clear Lake appellation; the winery also uses the Chateau du Lac label for certain wines. Channing Rudd Cellars is another new Lake County winery.

ALAMEDA, SANTA CLARA, AND THE SANTA CRUZ MOUNTAINS

Almost all of the vineyard acreage in Alameda County, southeast of San Francisco, is in the fifteen-mile-long Livermore Valley, whose best-known wineries are Wente Bros. and Concannon Vineyard. As a result of urbanization, the vineyards in this county were considerably reduced in the mid-1970s, to less than two thousand acres. Recent legislation, however, by which agricultural land is taxed at a lower rate than that devoted to real-estate development, had enabled existing vineyards to continue and has even permitted new plantings; there are now nearly three thousand acres in the county, most of them planted with white varieties.

Wente Bros. is a family-owned winery that dates back to 1883. The Wentes now own more than twenty-three hundred acres of vineyards, two-thirds of them in the Livermore Valley, the rest in the Arroyo Seco region of Monterey County. About 90 percent of the winery's production is of white wines, not only Chardonnay and Sauvignon Blanc, but also Grey Riesling, Pinot Blanc, Dry Sémillon, and Le Blanc de Blancs, made primarily from Chenin Blanc. The winery was the first to market Sauvignon Blanc as a varietal wine, in the late 1930s, and in 1969 Wente produced the first Spätlese type of wine from botrytised Johannisberg Riesling grapes grown in their Arroyo Seco vineyard. Wente introduced its first *méthode champenoise* sparkling wine in 1983 to celebrate its centennial.

Concannon Vineyard, just down the road from Wente Bros., was also established in the 1880s. Although the winery is best known for its white wines, it was among the first to market Petite Sirah as a varietal wine. Concannon wines have become more subtle and complex since the arrival, in 1981, of winemaker Sergio Traverso, who has concentrated on Sauvignon Blanc, Chardonnay, and Cabernet Sauvignon, while continuing to produce Petite Sirah. The winery's 180 acres of vineyards, used for Concannon's estate-bottled wines, are now planted almost entirely with Sauvignon Blanc, Sémillon, Cabernet Sauvignon, and Petite Sirah. The Chardonnay is made from grapes grown in Santa Clara and the Santa Maria Valley. A blend of Sauvignon Blanc and Sémillon called Assemblage was introduced in 1989.

Weibel is also in Alameda County, just south of Mission San Jose. The firm, known primarily for its extensive range of sparkling wines, also produces varietal table wines from vineyards established in Mendocino in the early 1970s. The Villa Armando Winery, whose production consists primarily of inexpensive jug wines, is located near the town of Pleasanton. A number of very small wineries are situated in the northern part of Alameda, near Berkeley and Emeryville; there are also a few wineries located across San Francisco Bay in Marin County. The latter include Woodbury Winery, which specializes in port; and Kalin Cellars, established by Terry Leighton, which produces small lots of Chardonnay, Pinot Noir, Sémillon, and other varieties from grapes purchased in several different regions.

Santa Clara now has only fourteen hundred acres or so of vineyards, and they are split up among several districts.

Although the Santa Clara appellation is not often seen on labels, the region is known to many wine-minded tourists because Almadén's home winery is located there. As urbanization has reduced the vineyards in Santa Clara, which amounted to more than eight thousand acres in the 1940s, Almadén expanded into San Benito and Monterey.

Almadén, which receives visitors at its winery in Los Gatos, traces its origins back to 1852, but it did not acquire its present name, which is Spanish for "the mine," until the late nineteenth century. Its present success really began in the 1940s, under the direction of Louis Benoist, and in 1956 Almadén created a large new vineyard near Paicines in San Benito County. The firm later planted vineyards at La Cienega in San Benito and in Monterey as well, for a total of nearly four thousand acres. Almadén introduced its popular Grenache Rosé in the 1940s, and markets a full line of generic and varietal table wines, as well as sparkling and dessert wines; special lots are labeled with the name of one of Almadén's founders, Charles Lefranc. The firm, which had been owned by National Distillers and Chemical Corporation since 1967, was sold to Heublein in 1987, and all the wines are now produced at facilities in Madera.

Paul Masson Vineyards also claims a founding date of 1852, but it was not until 1892 that Paul Masson, who came to America from Burgundy, gave the firm his name. Like Almadén, the firm dates its present success to the 1940s, when it was acquired by Joseph E. Seagram & Sons, who sold the firm to Vintners International in 1987, along with Taylor California Cellars, and the Taylor and Gold Seal wine companies in New York State. For many years Paul Masson's varietal table wines have been produced at the Pinnacles winery in Monterey County, where the firm planted extensive vineyards. In 1985, Paul Masson, whose Champagne Cellars in Saratoga were a popular tourist attraction, moved these facilities to Monterey. Besides a full line of table, sparkling, and dessert wines, Paul Masson also markets such proprietary wines as Emerald Dry and Rhine Castle, low-alcohol "light" wines, and an alcohol-free wine called St. Regis.

The history of Mirassou, located near San Jose, goes back to 1854, but it was only in the 1960s that the firm began to actively promote its own name rather than selling its wine in bulk to other wineries. Mirassou was one of the first to plant vineyards in Monterey, where it now has nine hundred acres, as well as two-hundred acres in Santa Clara, and both Santa

Clara and Monterey appellations appear on its labels. Mirassou produces a full range of varietal wines as well as such proprietary wines as Monterey Riesling and Petite Rosé; specially selected lots of certain varietals are marketed as Harvest Reserve. The firm also produces several styles of *méthode champenoise* sparkling wines.

The J. Lohr Winery (formerly Turgeon & Lohr), near San Jose, has nearly three hundred acres of vineyards in the Arroyo Seco region of Monterey; in 1984 the winery, which produces such varietal wines as Chardonnay, Pinot Blanc, Chenin Blanc, Cabernet Sauvignon, Monterey Gamay, Johannisberg Riesling, and Fumé Blanc, acquired additional acreage in the Napa Valley and more than two hundred acres near Clarksburg in the Delta region. The Pendleton Winery and the Page Mill Winery are also located in this part of Santa Clara.

A number of wineries, both old and new, are situated near the highway between Morgan Hill and Gilroy, and in the Hecker Pass district west of Gilroy. The best-known is the San Martin Winery, created as a cooperative at the beginning of the century and revitalized in the 1970s. The winery produces a full range of generic and varietal wines, some with a San Luis Obispo or Amador appellation. San Martin pioneered the production of semisweet, low-alcohol wines, which were marketed as "soft" wines. San Martin's Soft Johannisberg Riesling, Soft Chenin Blanc, and Soft Gamay Beaujolais contain only 8 or 9 percent alcohol and 2 to 4 percent residual sugar. Sarah's Vineyard, a winery established in 1978, specializes in Chardonnay. Other wineries in this area include Kirigin Cellars, Pedrizzetti, and Thomas Kruse.

Santa Cruz Mountains, which was defined as a viticultural area in 1982, includes vineyards in both Santa Clara and Santa Cruz counties. One of the best-known Santa Cruz Mountains wineries is Ridge Vineyards, known primarily for its intense and full-flavored red wines. The winery was founded in 1962, and winemaker Paul Draper joined Ridge in 1969. Ridge is generally credited with having changed the image of Zinfandel from a picnic wine to a big, long-lived red that can compete with many Cabernet Sauvignons. Ridge makes individual lots of wine, primarily Zinfandel and Cabernet Sauvignon, with some Petite Sirah, from grapes purchased in different winegrowing regions, and the exact origin of each wine is indicated on its label with such designations as York Creek and Howell Mountain from Napa, Geyserville from Sonoma, and Paso Robles from San Luis Obispo; Monte

Bello, the estate vineyard in the Santa Cruz Mountains, produces Ridge's most renowned Cabernet Sauvignon.

Martin Ray, who owned the Paul Masson winery for a few years, established his own vineyards on Mount Eden in the Santa Cruz Mountains in the early 1940s. Ray died in 1976, and the winery now concentrates on Chardonnay, Pinot Noir, Merlot, and Cabernet Sauvignon from selected sites in Napa and Sonoma. Mount Eden Vineyards produces Chardonnay, Cabernet Sauvignon, and Pinot Noir from some of the vineyards originally established by Martin Ray and from grapes purchased elsewhere; the latter are marketed with the MEV label. Congress Springs Vineyards is another winery situated in the Santa Clara part of the Santa Cruz Mountains.

Santa Cruz County has less than a hundred acres of vineyards, so almost all of the wineries situated there purchase grapes from regions as far apart as Mendocino and Santa Barbara. Many of the wineries situated in the Santa Cruz Mountains are small, producing three thousand cases or less, but a few have become more widely known. The David Bruce Winery, established in 1964, began by experimenting with a number of varieties vinified and aged in different ways. More recently, the winery, which has nearly twenty-five acres planted with Chardonnay and Pinot Noir, has concentrated on these two varieties plus Cabernet Sauvignon and Zinfandel, with Chardonnay from its own and other vineyards accounting for more than half its total production.

Roudon-Smith Vineyards, founded in 1972 by Bob Roudon and Jim Smith, focuses on Chardonnay, Cabernet Sauvignon, and Zinfandel from several regions. Felton-Empire Vineyards, situated on Felton-Empire Road, was originally known for different bottlings of Johannisberg Riesling, which still accounts for half its production. The winery, now under the direction of Leo McCloskey, also produces Chardonnay and a Pinot Noir labeled Tonneaux Français from vineyards situated in several counties. The Santa Cruz Mountain Vineyard, which was established by Ken Burnap in 1974 to concentrate on Pinot Noir, also produces Cabernet Sauvignon, Merlot, and Chardonnay.

Dick Smothers, the television comedian, purchased the Vine Hill estate in the Santa Cruz Mountains and achieved acclaim with the first wine marketed under his name, a 1977 Late Harvest Gewürztraminer. (Dick's brother, Tom, owns the Remick Ridge Ranch in Sonoma, planted primarily with Chardonnay and Sauvignon Blanc.) Bonny Doon Vineyard and Ahlgren Vineyards are also located in the Santa Cruz Mountains, as is the Obester Winery, situated farther north in San Mateo County. The Thomas Fogarty Winery, also in San Mateo, concentrates on Pinot Noir and Chardonnay.

MONTEREY, SAN LUIS OBISPO, AND SANTA BARBARA

Monterey

Much of the expansion that has occurred in the acreage of fine wine grapes has taken place south of San Francisco, in three counties often grouped together as the Central Coast—Monterey, San Luis Obispo, and Santa Barbara. As recently as 1969 there were less than two thousand acres of vines in Monterey; by 1975 thirty thousand acres had been planted, and there are now about thirty-three thousand acres. Wente Bros., Mirassou, and Paul Masson were the first major companies to create vineyards in Monterey, starting in the early 1960s. Almadén and a few small, new wineries followed; and a number of ranching companies, which sold their grapes to existing wineries, planted large vineyards as well. Most of the vineyards in Monterey County are situated in the Salinas Valley between the Santa Lucia Mountains on the west and the Gavilan Mountains on the east. The vineyards are cooled by ocean breezes, and water for irrigation is supplied by wells drilled into an underground river. The rows of vines were deliberately set out wide enough apart to facilitate mechanical harvesting, whereby the grape bunches are shaken loose from the vines by machine rather than being picked by hand. Since the vineyards were created in land that was never before planted with vines (the Salinas Valley is famous for vegetables, especially lettuce), it was assumed that the phylloxera louse would not be present in the soil. Most of the vines in Monterey are, therefore, planted on their own roots rather than being grafted onto phylloxera-resistant American rootstocks, as is the case elsewhere in California and throughout most of the world. (Unfortunately, phylloxera appeared in one vineyard in 1983.)

All of the principal varieties are planted in Monterey, but viticulturalists are still trying to determine which grapes are best suited to specific sites within this region. Monterey

CENTRAL CALIFORNIA

winemakers know that the region produces white wines with a particularly intense and cleanly defined varietal character, but an odd vegetal flavor marred some of the first Monterey red wines. The exceptionally cool growing season in the upper part of the region made it difficult for most red-wine varieties to mature properly, and recent experience suggests that the cooler upper Salinas Valley, nearest the ocean, may be more appropriate to white varieties, while Cabernet Sauvignon, Merlot, Petite Sirah, and Zinfandel can be successfully cultivated in the warmer, inland part of the valley—which extends northwest to southeast—and on hillside vineyards. More than two-thirds of the vineyards created in the early 1970s were made up of red varieties, but in recent years the acreage of Cabernet Sauvignon, Merlot, Petite Sirah, and Zinfandel planted in the cooler part of the valley has been to a large extent replaced by Charonnay, Pinot Blanc, Johannisberg Riesling, Chenin Blanc, and Gewürztraminer; as a result, about two-thirds of Monterey's vineyards now produce white grapes, and better site selection, combined with changes in grape-growing techniques, has reduced or eliminated the vegetal qualities in most Monterey wines.

A number of firms that own vineyards in Monterey, including Almadén, Paul Masson, Mirassou, Wente Bros., and J. Lohr, are discussed elsewhere. One of the best-known wineries in Monterey itself is the Monterey Vineyard, built in 1974 to the specifications of enologist Richard G. Peterson. The winery produces half-a-dozen white varietal wines, occasional small lots of such unusual dessert wines as Thanksgiving Harvest Johannisberg Riesling and Botrytis Sauvignon Blanc, and three moderately priced, vintage-dated wines labeled Classic Red, Classic Dry White, and Classic Rosé. The winery, which was purchased by the Coca-Cola Company in 1977, then acquired by the Seagram Wine Company in 1983, now shares a bottling facility in Gonzales with both Taylor California Cellars (whose successful line of generic and varietal wines was produced under the direction of Dr. Peterson until 1983) and Paul Masson.

The Jekel Vineyard was first planted in 1972 by Bill and Gus Jekel, who then built a winery in 1978. More than three hundred acres are now planted, primarily with Chardonnay and Johannisberg Riesling, as well as Pinot Blanc, Cabernet Sauvignon, and Pinot Noir. Ventana Vineyards was established as a winery in 1978 by Doug Meador, who had previously planted a three-hundred-acre vineyard. Smith & Hook, whose 225-acre vineyard is situated on a slope of the Santa Lucia Mountains, produces only one wine—Cabernet Sauvignon. The Morgan Winery, founded in 1982, produces Chardonnay and Sauvignon Blanc.

Durney Vineyard produces estate-bottled wines in the Carmel Valley, which has been defined as a viticultural area, from 140 acres. Half the acreage is devoted to Cabernet Sauvignon, most of the rest to Johannisberg Riesling, Chenin Blanc, and Chardonnay. Chateau Julien, also in the Carmel Valley, produced its first wines in 1983. The Monterey Peninsula Winery, founded in 1974, is best known for its range of Zinfandels; Cabernet Sauvignon, Chardonnay, and other wines are also made.

Chalone Vineyard, the oldest winery in Monterey, is situated on a benchland of the Gavilan Mountains, fifteen hundred feet above the valley floor. In 1969 the winery was revitalized by Richard Graff, who expanded its thirty acres to 125; half of that is Chardonnay, the rest Pinot Noir and Pinot Blanc, plus a small amount of Chenin Blanc. The winery, which has established the viticultural area Chalone for its vineyards, is known for its rich Chardonnay and Pinot Noir, produced in a Burgundian style. Chalone is co-owner, with Paragon Vineyard, of the Edna Valley Vineyard winery in San Luis Obispo, and also owns Carmenet Vineyard in Sonoma.

The vineyards in San Benito County, which adjoins Monterey, were first developed by Almadén, which has extensive acreage in both the Cienega Valley and Paicines viticultural areas. The Calera Wine Company, one of the very few wineries in San Benito, was established by Josh Jensen to concentrate on Pinot Noir. Jensen planted twenty-four acres of that variety in the mid-1970s on a particular limestone site in the Gavilan Mountains, and Pinot Noir from Calera's three plots are bottled separately as Reed, Selleck, and Jensen. Calera also produces rich Zinfandels from the Cienega Valley, and, from Santa Barbara vineyards, additional Pinot Noir and Chardonnay; the latter accounts for more than half the winery's production. Cygnet Cellars is also located in San Benito, as is Enz Vineyards, which has established Lime Kiln Valley as a viticultural area within Cienega Valley.

San Luis Obispo

The vineyard acreage in San Luis Obispo County has increased from just a few hundred in the late 1960s to more than six thousand. Most of the county's vineyards have been established in two regions that have become viticultural areas— Paso Robles, near the town of that name; and Edna Valley, south of the city of San Luis Obispo. The biggest firm in the Paso Robles area is Estrella River Winery, whose owners planted more than seven hundred acres in the 1970s. From these vineyards, and additional acreage purchased in 1984, Estrella River Winery produces a full range of estate-bottled varietal wines, including Muscat Canelli, Barbera, and French Syrah. The winery also markets a selection of less expensive, nonvintage varietal wines that are labeled simply Estrella. Hoffman Mountain Ranch, whose vineyards were established in the 1960s, came under new ownership in 1982, and the firm's name changed to HMR, Ltd., for Hidden Mountain Ranch; the winery produces Chardonnay, Cabernet Sauvignon, and Pinot Noir from its own vineyards, as well as Chenin Blanc and Sauvignon Blanc.

The York Mountain Winery, whose fifty acres of vineyards are in the York Mountain viticultural area, within the Paso Robles district, traces its origins back to 1882; best known for Zinfandel, it also produces Cabernet Sauvignon, Chardonnay, and Pinot Noir. Other wineries in the Paso Robles area include the Eberle Winery, which began to produce Cabernet Sauvignon and Chardonnay in 1984; the Caparone Winery, which makes primarily Cabernet Sauvignon and Merlot; and the Mastantuono Winery, best known for its range of Zinfandels. Creston Manor, situated east of San Luis Obispo, has 150 acres of vineyards on a five-hundred-acre estate. The winery, whose first wines were produced in 1982, concentrates on Sauvignon Blanc, Chardonnay, Cabernet Sauvignon, and Pinot Noir.

The Edna Valley has become known for its Chardonnay, Sauvignon Blanc, and Pinot Noir, and wineries as far away as Napa and Sonoma purchase grapes from this area. The Edna Valley Vineyard, whose first wines were produced in 1980, concentrates on Chardonnay and Pinot Noir; it is co-owned by Chalone and Paragon Vineyard, whose six hundred acres also supply grapes to Carmenet Vineyard, in Sonoma, and to other wineries. Corbett Canyon Vineyards, which was created as the Lawrence Winery, was acquired and renamed by Glenmore

Distilleries in 1984; the winery was acquired by the Wine Group in 1988. Corbett Canyon produces a full range of varietal wines, as well as generic and varietal wines labeled with the Coastal Classic designation. The firm also uses the Shadow Creek label for *méthode champenoise* sparkling wines. Chamisal Vineyard focuses on estate-bottled Chardonnay.

Santa Barbara

Santa Barbara County has more than nine thousand acres of vineyards, virtually all of them planted since 1970. Most of the acreage consists of white-wine grapes, primarily Chardonnay and Johannisberg Riesling, as well as Gewürztraminer, Chenin Blanc, Sauvignon Blanc, and other varieties. Most of the vineyards have been established in the Santa Maria Valley viticultural area, which extends for about fifteen miles east of the town of Santa Maria, and which straddles San Luis Obispo and Santa Barbara counties. Tepusquet Vineyards (pronounced *teh*-pus-kay) produces several wines from its more than fifteen hundred acres in the Santa Maria Valley, including Chardonnay and a proprietary blend of Cabernet Sauvignon and Merlot labeled Vineyard Reserve; it also sells grapes to a number of wineries throughout California, some of which use Tepusquet on their labels. The Los Vineros Winery was established in 1981 by eight Central Coast grape growers.

Most of the wineries in Santa Barbara are situated in the Santa Ynez Valley viticultural area, near the towns of Santa Ynez, Los Olivos, and Solvang. One of the best-known is the Firestone Vineyard, partly owned by Suntory of Japan, which began producing a range of varietal wines in 1975 from three hundred acres of vineyards. White Riesling, Chardonnay, and Rosé of Cabernet Sauvignon account for about two-thirds of the winery's production; other wines are Cabernet Sauvignon, Sauvignon Blanc, Gewürztraminer, Merlot, and Pinot Noir. Firestone's first winemaker, Tony Austin, established Austin Cellars in 1981, and produces mostly Pinot Noir and Sauvignon Blanc, plus limited amounts of Chardonnay and White Riesling.

The Zaca Mesa Winery produces primarily Chardonnay and Cabernet Sauvignon, as well as Sauvignon Blanc, Johannisberg Riesling, and Pinot Noir, most of it from 350 acres of vineyards situated in the Santa Ynez Valley and the Santa Maria Valley; special lots are bottled as American Reserve. The Santa Ynez Valley Winery produces mostly white wines in a converted dairy farm. The Brander Vineyard focuses on Sauvignon Blanc from its own vineyards. The Sanford Winery, established by Richard and Thekla Sanford, produced its first wines in 1981. The Sanfords, who have established their vineyard on a seven-hundred-acre estate, concentrate on Chardonnay, Pinot Noir, Sauvignon Blanc, Merlot, and an unusual rosé, labeled Vin Gris, made from Pinot Noir grapes. Sanford was originally a partner, with Michael Benedict, in Sanford & Benedict Vineyards, created in the 1970s to focus on Pinot Noir and Chardonnay. Other wineries in the Santa Ynez Valley include Ballard Canyon Cellars, J. Carey Cellars, and the Santa Barbara Winery.

There are vineyards and wineries south of Santa Barbara, near Los Angeles and San Diego. The best-known wine region in southern California is located near Temecula, about fifty miles north of San Diego, in an area also known as Rancho California; its most famous winery is Callaway Vineyard & Winery, established in the mid-1970s by Ely Callaway. The winery, whose first vineyards were planted in 1969, now concentrates almost exclusively on such white wines as Chardonnay, Sauvignon Blanc, Johannisberg Riesling, Chenin Blanc, and when weather conditions permit, an unusual botrytised Chenin Blanc labeled Sweet Nancy; in 1981 the Callaway winery was acquired by Hiram Walker & Sons. The Culbertson Champagne Cellars, situated a few miles west of Temecula, has achieved success with its Brut, Natural, and R.D. bottlings of *méthode champenoise* sparkling wines made primarily from Pinot Blanc and Chardonnay. San Pasqual Vineyards, northeast of San Diego, produces primarily white wines from grapes grown in the San Pasqual Valley viticultural area. The Ahern Winery, near Los Angeles, produces Chardonnay and other varietal wines.

AMADOR AND THE SIERRA FOOTHILLS

The wine region now referred to as the Sierra Foothills consists of vineyards on the western slope of the Sierra Nevada mountains in Amador, El Dorado, and Calaveras counties, about forty miles southeast of Sacramento. Vineyards and wineries were first established in this region, which is also called the Mother Lode, soon after the Gold Rush of 1849. By 1890 there were more than a hundred wineries there, but after Prohibition all but one, D'Agostini, had disappeared, and it was not until 1973 that new wineries were once again established. The impetus for the renaissance of the Sierra Foothills region was the discovery in the late 1960s that Amador vineyards, many of them planted before Prohibition, could produce particularly flavorful and intense Zinfandels. Sutter Home and Ridge were among the first wineries to produce Zinfandels from Amador grapes.

There are now about sixteen hundred acres of vineyards in Amador, most of them planted with Zinfandel, plus new plantings of Sauvignon Blanc and several other varieties. Acreage in El Dorado and Calaveras has increased in a dozen years from about seventy acres to more than six hundred, most of it in El Dorado. Many small, family-owned wineries were established in the late 1970s and early 1980s, and most of them focus on Zinfandel, as both a rich red and a *blanc de noirs*, as well as producing limited amounts of Sauvignon Blanc, Chardonnay, Cabernet Sauvignon, and other wines.

In Amador County, which contains the viticultural areas Fiddletown and Shenandoah Valley, both near the town of Plymouth, D'Agostini is the oldest winery in the region, and one of the oldest in California. Founded in 1856, it was acquired in 1911 by the D'Agostini family, who sold it to the Ozdiker family in 1984. Monteviña, established in 1973, is perhaps the best-known Amador winery; it produces a full range of varietal wines from 175 acres of vineyards. Baldinelli Vineyards, which has sixty acres planted, focuses on Zinfandel, made as a red, white, and rosé, and on Cabernet Sauvignon. Shenandoah Vineyards, founded in 1977, has become known for its Zinfandel, as has Story Vineyard. Other Amador wineries include the Amador Foothill Winery and the Argonaut Winery.

The Boeger Winery was the first established in El Dorado County, north of Amador; it produces several varietal wines and a proprietary wine labeled Hangtown Red; Hangtown was the original name of nearby Placerville. Other El Dorado wineries include the Fitzpatrick Winery, Granite Springs, Madrona Vineyards, Sierra Vista, and the Gerwer Winery (previously called Stoney Creek Vineyards). The best-known winery in Calaveras County, south of Amador, is Stevenot Winery, founded by Barden Stevenot in 1974; the winery produces primarily Zinfandel and Zinfandel Blanc, as well as Chardonnay, Sauvignon Blanc, Chenin Blanc, and Cabernet Sauvignon.

THE SAN JOAQUIN VALLEY

The San Joaquin Valley, also known as the Central Valley, extends for more than two hundred miles from Stockton down to Bakersfield. More than 80 percent of California's wine grapes come from this region, and if the table and raisin grapes used for wine are included, the Central Valley (plus the vineyards around Lodi, twelve miles north of Stockton) accounts for more than 90 percent of the wine made in the state. There are a number of gigantic wineries situated in the valley; some produce wines that are shipped in bulk to other wineries throughout the state, some bottle their own wines and market them under a variety of names.

E & J Gallo, located in Modesto, is the biggest wine firm in the world, and accounts for more than one out of every four bottles of wine sold in this country. The company, founded in 1933 by Ernest and Julio Gallo, markets a complete range of generic and varietal table wines, dessert wines, sparkling wines, and such flavored wines—known as special natural wines—as Thunderbird, Tyrolia, and Boone's Farm. Gallo's most popular table wines are Hearty Burgundy and Chablis Blanc, and Gallo also markets a range of moderately priced varietal wines, selected lots of Chardonnay and Cabernet Sauvignon, the Carlo Rossi jug wines, such proprietary wines as Paisano and Polo Brindisi, and André sparkling wines, which account for more than a third of all the sparkling wines produced in California. Although Gallo crushes a substantial quantity of Central Valley grapes at several wineries—the enormous Modesto facility, which includes a glass factory, is used only for blending, aging, and bottling—the firm also buys as much as a third of the grapes grown in Sonoma, and a significant share of the Napa and Central Coast crop.

United Vintners, which the Heublein company sold back to the Allied Grape Growers cooperative in 1983, produces the Italian Swiss Colony wines, and also owns such popular brands as Petri, Lejon, G&D, Jacques Bonet, and Annie Green Springs.

Guild, another major California producer, is a cooperative association of a thousand grape growers. Guild wines are bottled at Lodi, and the firm markets such brands as Winemasters' Guild, Cribari, Roma, Tavola, and Cresta Blanca. Other Central Valley wineries include Franzia Brothers, East-Side (whose brands include Oak Ridge and Royal Host),

Delicato Vineyards, JFJ Bronco, Giumarra, Gibson, La Mont (which owns the Guasti and Ambassador labels), and the Sierra Wine Company (which acquired the Perelli-Minetti name).

In addition to these large wineries, there are a number of smaller firms located in the Central Valley. At Papagni Vineyards, near Madera, Angelo Papagini produces a number of estate-bottled varietal wines, including Chardonnay, Chenin Blanc, Late Harvest Zinfandel, Alicante Bouschet, and a sweet Muscat wine labeled Moscato d'Angelo. Ficklin and Andrew Quady, discussed elsewhere, produce port. Farther north, in Lodi, the Turner Winery produces a range of wines from nearly six hundred acres of vineyards in Lake County.

Extensive new vineyards have been planted in the Clarksburg region of the Sacramento Delta, just south of Sacramento. A number of North Coast wineries purchase Chenin Blanc and other grapes from this district, which contains the Clarksburg and Merrit Island viticultural areas; the best-known wineries are R & J Cook and Bogle Vineyards.

OTHER WINES OF
THE UNITED STATES

NEW YORK STATE

New York State, which ranks a distant second to California in wine production, accounts for about 7 percent of all the wine consumed in this country. Nearly one-third of that is made up of sparkling wines, dessert wines such as port and Cream Sherry, and wine coolers, which are prepackaged mixtures of wine, carbonated water, and citrus flavors. And many of the table wines consist of simple, fairly sweet red, white, and pink wines with the pronounced aroma and distinctive taste that many people associate with fresh grapes, grape juice, and jelly. Nevertheless, New York State is very much an area in transition: two-thirds of the more than eighty wineries in the state were created since 1976; new wine regions have been established and traditional ones expanded; and there has been a significant increase in the number of fine wines — particularly whites — produced there.

The story of the rapidly evolving New York wine scene has as much to do with the kinds of grapes grown in the state as it does with the appearance of dozens of new wineries. New York is unusual in that its wines are made from native grapes, French-American hybrids, and European vinifera varieties, and it's not uncommon for a winery to make wines from all three types of grapes.

Grape vines had to be specially introduced into California, but the earliest settlers in the eastern United States found a number of native grapes already growing wild all along the Atlantic Coast. Encouraged by this profusion of vines, a few colonists imported cuttings of European *Vitis vinifera* varieties during the seventeenth and eighteenth centuries and tried to establish new vineyards on the East Coast. Invariably, these vines died, and we now know that this was a result of phylloxera, fungus, and very cold winter temperatures to which *vinifera* vines were not resistant. In the early nineteenth century, successful experiments were carried out with existing native varieties, notably Catawba, and native American wines began to be produced commercially in several Eastern states. These native grapes, made up for the most part of *Vitis labrusca*, impart a pungent aroma and flavor to the wines made from them, and their taste often seems strange to those who are used to European or California wines. This pronounced grapy character is most clearly demonstrated by the Concord grape—used primarily for juice—which accounts for about two-thirds of the grape crop in New York State. Actually, only half the total crop is crushed to make wine— the equivalent of about fifteen million cases a year—but most of that still consists of such *labrusca* varieties as Concord, Catawba, Delaware, Niagara, Dutchess, Elvira, and Ives. The *labrusca* varieties that dominate the eastern vineyards are cultivated in only a few other places—such as Washington, Canada, and Brazil—and the unique wines they produce should be approached with this in mind.

A wine labeled New York State may contain up to 25 percent wines from outside the state. This permits New York wineries to diminish the intense *labrusca* taste of many of their wines by blending in neutral California wines. If a wine contains more than 25 percent wine produced outside the state, it must be labeled American. Because *labrusca* grape varieties are typically low in sugar and high in acid, a wine's volume may legally be increased by as much as a third by the addition of sugar and water. The sugar increases the wine's eventual alcohol content, the water dilutes its acidity.

Like California wines, many New York State wines are marketed with generic place-names of European origin, such as Sauterne, Rhine Wine, Chablis, and Burgundy. Because *labrusca* grapes are used to make most of these wines, they bear no resemblance to wines from those French and German districts or to California generic wines, which are made from *vinifera* grapes. Nevertheless, people who enjoy the distinct flavor of certain table grapes find these wines very pleasing indeed, and their wide distribution in this country attests to their popularity. Some wineries also produce varietal wines from native grapes, which are labeled with such names as Pink Catawba, Rosé of Isabella, Delaware, and Dutchess.

In recent years there has been a significant increase in the acreage of French-American hybrids in New York State vineyards. These are crossings that combine the hardiness of the American vines, specifically their resistance to disease and extremes of cold, with the more delicate flavor of the *vinifera* grape. Hybrids are named after the individuals who developed them and carry the serial number of the original seedling, such as Baco 1, Seibel 5279, and Seyve-Villard 5276. Most of these hybrids were developed in France at the end of the nineteenth century, and over the years they have acquired names that are more attractive than the original combinations of name and number. The most popular hybrids (and the names by which they are commonly known) are, among the red varieties, Baco 1 (Baco Noir), Seibel 10878 (Chelois), Seibel 13053 (Cascade), Seibel 5898 (Rougeon), Seibel 7053 (Chancellor), Seibel 9549 (De Chaunac), Kuhlman 194-2 (Leon Millot), and Kuhlman 188-2 (Maréchal Foch). The best-known white varieties include Seibel 5279 (Aurora), Seyve-Villard 5276 (Seyval Blanc), Ravat 6 (Ravat Blanc), Ravat 51 (Vignoles), and Vidal 256 (Vidal Blanc). French-American hybrids account for 20 to 25 percent of the wines produced in New York States; Aurora, De Chaunac, and Baco Noir are the most extensively planted. The wines, in which the *labrusca* flavor is considerably diminished or entirely absent, are sometimes blended with *labrusca* wines to reduce the latter's grapy taste. Many hybrids are also bottled on their own as varietal wines, especially the crisp Seyval Blanc.

The wines produced from the more than one thousand acres of *vinifera* grapes now planted in several different regions are the most dramatic development in the recent history of New York State viticulture. They are the result of the pioneering work done by Dr. Konstantin Frank, who had successfully cultivated *vinifera* in his native Russia before emigrating to this country. Frank first began grafting European vines on native American rootstocks in the early 1950s for the late Charles Fournier of Gold Seal, and later went on to establish his own company—Vinifera Wine Cellars—to produce and market such *vinifera* varieties as Johannisberg Riesling,

Chardonnay, Gewürztraminer, Pinot Noir, and Gamay. Gold Seal continued to expand its acreage of *vinifera* varieties, primarily Chardonnay and Johannisberg Riesling, and now has more than a hundred acres planted. Although *vinifera* accounts for only 3 or 4 percent of New York State's vineyards, and for the equivalent of less than 150,000 cases of wine a year, more than thirty wineries now produce Chardonnay, Johannisberg Riesling, and other *vinifera*-based varietal wines.

The Finger Lakes district, which has been established as a viticultural area, is the biggest wine-producing region outside of California. Although it has only a third of New York's forty-two thousand acres of vineyards, the Finger Lakes produce about 80 percent of the state's wine. The region, situated three hundred miles northwest of New York City, gets its name from several elongated lakes that resemble an imprint made by the outspread fingers of a giant hand. The region is subject to great extremes of temperature, but the lakes exert a moderating influence on the microclimate of the vineyards situated along their sloping shores. Vines were first planted in this district in 1829 in a clergyman's garden in Hammondsport, at the southern tip of Lake Keuka. The first commercial winery was established in 1860, and by the end of the nineteenth century, four major Finger Lakes firms—Taylor, Great Western, Gold Seal, and Widmer's—had been established. Each markets a somewhat different range of wines.

The Taylor Wine Co., located in Hammondsport, is known for its sparkling and dessert wines, and for such proprietary table wines as the Lake Country line and the sweeter, low-alcohol Lake Country Soft wines similar to the popular Italian Lambruscos. (The Taylor California Cellars selection of moderately priced generic and varietal wines, introduced in the late 1970s, is produced and bottled in California.) Great Western is the brand name of the Pleasant Valley Wine Company, which was acquired by Taylor in 1961. Great Western markets a range of sparkling wines and such varietal wines as Aurora, Baco Noir, Seyval Blanc, Rosé of Isabella, and Dutchess, as well as limited amounts of Johannisberg Riesling, Vidal Blanc, and Ravat. Gold Seal, which was the first to plant *vinifera* varieties in the Finger Lakes, continues to make limited amounts of Chardonnay and Johannisberg Riesling. The Charles Fournier name is used for certain table wines and for a *blanc de blancs* sparkling wine. The firm, whose best-selling wines include Catawba Pink, Red, and

White, also produces sparkling wines under the Henri Marchant label. Gold Seal was purchased by Joseph E. Seagram & Sons in 1979; in 1983 Seagrams acquired Taylor and Great Western as well, and has since closed the Gold Seal winery and consolidated production for the three brands at Taylor.

Widmer's Wine Cellars is located in Naples, at the southern tip of Lake Canandaigua. In addition to a range of generic wines, Widmer's markets several popular proprietary wines, including Lake Niagara, a sweet white wine, and Lake Roselle. The winery also produces such varietal wines as Cayuga White, Seyval Blanc, Vidal Blanc, and Maréchal Foch, as well as limited amounts of Johannisberg Riesling and Chardonnay. Widmer's is also known for its barrel-aged sherries, which are stored outdoors on the winery's roof.

The Canandaigua Wine Company, founded in 1945 but a relative newcomer to the Finger Lakes, is now situated at the northern end of that lake. Canandaigua, one of the biggest wine producers in the country, has been very successful with such brands as Richard's Wild Irish Rose, Virginia Dare, J. Roget sparkling wines, and Sun Country wine cooler.

The Bully Hill winery, near Hammondsport, was established in 1970 by Walter S. Taylor, whose grandfather founded the Taylor Wine Company. The firm specializes in wines made from French-American hybrids.

In 1976 new legislation changed the face of winemaking in New York State. The Farm Winery Bill gave special consideration to wineries producing fewer than fifty thousand gallons a year. Annual fees were greatly reduced, but, more important, farm wineries—unlike the large, established firms that rely on national distribution to market their wines—were permitted to sell as much of their production as they wanted to directly to the public. By liberalizing the regulations governing wine sales, the bill, and subsequent amendments, encouraged grape growers to make wines from their own grapes, and enabled wine enthusiasts to start their own wineries. More than fifty wineries have been established since 1976, most of them specializing in varietal wines made from *vinifera* grapes and French-American hybrids.

Some of the new Finger Lakes wineries are Casa Larga, Chateau Esperanza, Finger Lakes Wine Cellars, Glenora Wine Cellars, Heron Hill Winery, McGregor Vineyard, Plane's Cayuga Vineyards, Wagner Vineyards, Hermann J. Wiemer Vineyard, and Wickham Vineyards. Most of these wineries are situated along the shores of Keuka, Seneca, and Cayuga lakes.

The Lake Erie district, recognized as a distinct viticultural area, parallels the southern shore of Lake Erie, in the western part of New York State. The region contains nearly two-thirds of the state's vineyard acreage, but over 90 percent of that is planted with Concord grapes, which are used for juice. French-American hybrids and *vinifera* varieties are also planted, and several wineries produce wines from these grapes, as well as from native varieties. Johnson Estate wines were first marketed in the 1960s; wineries established more recently include Merritt Estate and Woodbury Vineyards, which has planted more than one hundred acres of *vinifera* varieties, primarily Chardonnay.

The Hudson River region, the oldest wine-producing district in New York State, and the first to be recognized as a viticultural area, has witnessed a renewed interest in winemaking in recent years and now contains nearly twenty wineries. The best-known is Benmarl, located near Marlboro, seventy-five miles from New York City. Owner Mark Miller, a pioneer in New York viticulture, began replanting the estate in the 1950s and now has 110 acres of vineyards, almost all French-American hybrids, plus a few acres of *vinifera*. Benmarl's first wines were produced in 1971, and its principal labels are now Marlboro Village and Benmarl Estate, with occasional lots of Seyval Blanc and Chardonnay. William Wetmore planted Cascade Mountain Vineyard in 1972, and in 1977 Ben Feder established Clinton Vineyard, whose seventeen acres produce a widely acclaimed Seyval Blanc and a limited amount of Seyval Natural, *méthode champenoise* sparkling wine. Eaton Vineyards produces Seyval Blanc; North Salem Vineyard makes Seyval Blanc and Maréchal Foch; West Park Vineyards concentrates on Chardonnay; and Walker Valley Vineyards produces a limited amount of varietal wines from French-American hybrids and *vinifera*.

The Brotherhood Winery, the Royal Kedem Winery, and the Hudson Valley Wine Co., all in the Hudson River region, are popular tourist attractions. High Tor Vineyards, only thirty miles from New York City, was originally established in the 1940s, and recently reopened under new ownership.

The newest wine region in New York State and the only one devoted exclusively to *vinifera* is on eastern Long Island. Alex and Louisa Hargrave established their vineyard in 1973 in Cutchogue, on the North Fork of Long Island, on the site of an old potato farm. The forty-five-acre Hargrave Vineyard is planted with Chardonnay, Sauvignon Blanc, Cabernet Sauvignon, and Pinot Noir. There are now more than seven hundred acres of vineyards on Long Island, and several new wineries, among them Lenz Vineyards and Pindar Vineyards, not far from the Hargrave Vineyard; and on Long Island's South Fork, the Bridgehampton Winery, which concentrates on Chardonnay and Johannisberg Riesling.

New York State is also an important producer of kosher wines, made primarily from Concord grapes by three major companies: the Monarch Wine Company, in Brooklyn, New York (which uses the Manischewitz label); the Royal Kedem Winery, in the Hudson River region; and the Mogen David Wine Corporation, in the Lake Erie district.

WASHINGTON AND OREGON

Until recently, many consumers assumed that the vineyards of Washington and Oregon, which are often grouped together under the geographical designation Pacific Northwest, were simply an extension of those in California. An increasing number of wine drinkers realize that the climatic conditions of these two states (most of whose vineyards are actually quite a distance from the Pacific Ocean) are not only quite different from those of California, but different from each other as well. The Cascade Range divides Washington and Oregon from north to south: almost all of Washington's vineyards are east of the Cascades, in a warm region with an average annual rainfall of less than ten inches; most of those in Oregon are west of the Cascades, in a cool area where more than forty inches of rain a year is not uncommon. As result, winemakers in the two states do not focus their efforts on the same grape varieties, and they produce wines whose styles are different as well. The emergence of Washington, Oregon, and, more recently, Idaho as producers of fine wines is dramatic: in 1960 not a single winery was making *vinifera* wines; today there are more than ninety.

Washington

Wines had been produced in Washington in the nineteenth century, but the current era of winemaking can be traced back to 1962, when Dr. Lloyd Woodburne and a few friends formed Associated Vintners and planted five acres of vineyards. They produced their first commercial wine in 1967, the same year that the winery which was to become Chateau Ste. Michelle made its first commercial wine as well. Although the first wineries were located near Seattle, so that they and their wines would be more accessible to the state's consumers, almost all the Washington vineyards are situated two hundred miles southeast of that city, in the Yakima Valley and the adjoining Columbia River Basin. This area, protected from the Pacific rains by the Cascades, is a semiarid desert that has been transformed by extensive irrigation; it is now one of the nation's principal agricultural regions and is becoming known for its wines as well. About twelve thousand acres of classic European varieties are cultivated in Washington, which makes that state second only to California as a source of *vinifera* wines. (In addition, more than twenty thousand acres are planted with Concord grapes, most of which are used for juice and jelly.) Johannisberg Riesling is the most widely planted variety in Washington; others are Chardonnay, Sauvignon Blanc, Sémillon, Gewürztraminer, Chenin Blanc, and Muscat Canelli among whites; red-wine grapes include Cabernet Sauvignon, Merlot, and some Pinot Noir. There are more hours of sunlight and heat per day east of the Cascades than in California, but the cold desert nights enable the grapes to retain their natural acidity. As a result of these special growing conditions, the ripe grapes are high in acid as well as sugar, which gives the white wines, in particular, a crisp, lively taste. The region east of the Cascade Range has now been defined as the Columbia Valley viticultural area; the smaller Yakima Valley viticultural area is contained within the Columbia Valley.

More than eighty wineries have been established in Washington, most of them since 1980. Chateau Ste. Michelle, which owns about three thousand acres of vineyards, is by far the state's biggest wine firm, producing a full range of varietal wines, primarily Johannisberg Riesling, Chenin Blanc, Sémillon, and Cabernet Sauvignon, as well as *méthode champenoise* sparkling wines, at its three wineries. The one at Woodinville, about fifteen miles northeast of Seattle, is a popular tourist attraction, although the major facility is at Paterson, near the Columbia River. Associated Vintners, which changed its name to the Columbia Winery in 1984, produces a range of varietal wines, including a number of single-vineyard bottlings, under the direction of winemaker David Lake. Other Washington wineries include Arbor Crest, Hinzerling Vineyards, F. W. Langguth (which also uses the Saddle Mountain Winery label), Paul Thomas Wines, Preston Wine Cellars, Quail Run Vintners, and Snoqualmie Winery, established by Joel Klein, formerly the winemaker at Chateau Ste. Michelle. Mont Elise Vineyards and Salishan Vineyards are situated in the southwest part of the state. Several wineries have also been established in the Walla Walla Valley, in the southeastern part of the state, and in Spokane.

Oregon

The history of winemaking in Oregon goes back to the 1820s, but Prohibition put an end to commercial wine production in the state. The current revival of interest in winemaking began as recently as 1961, when Richard Sommer created Hillcrest Vineyard near Roseburg in the Umpqua Valley, 180 miles south of Portland. A few other wineries have since been established nearby, but most of Oregon's wineries are situated in the Willamette Valley (pronounced will-*am*-et), within a forty-mile radius south and west of Portland.

In 1966 David Lett planted the first *vinifera* grapes cultivated in the Willamette Valley since Prohibition, at what is now the thirty-acre Eyrie Vineyards. Like many other wine pioneers in Oregon, he had a particular interest in Pinot Noir and came north from California in search of a cooler microclimate that would be favorable to lighter, more elegant wines than California was then producing. Dick Erath planted vines not far from the Eyrie Vineyards in 1968, and later joined Cal Knudsen to set up the Knudsen Erath Winery, which has 110 acres of vineyards, in the town of Dundee, William Blosser and his wife, Susan Sokol, founded the Sokol Blosser Winery, also in Dundee, and produced their first wines in 1977, as did Joe and Pat Campbell at Elk Cove Vineyards. William and Virginia Fuller began planting the eighty-acre Tualatin Vineyards in 1973. There are now more than sixty wineries in Oregon, and about four thousand acres planted, including more than four hundred acres of new vineyards east of the Cascade Mountains, along the Columbia River.

Western Oregon's cool growing season favors such varieties as Pinot Noir, Chardonnay, and White Riesling (as Johannisberg Riesling is labeled in Oregon), and these three varieties account for most of the total acreage. Other varieties planted include Gewürztraminer and such unusual ones as Pinot Gris, Müller-Thurgau, and Muscat Ottonel. Three varieties widely planted in California and Washington, but less frequently seen in Oregon, are Cabernet Sauvignon, Merlot, and Sauvignon Blanc. A number of Oregon winemakers buy grapes from Washington, however, either to make wines until their own acreage begins to bear fruit, or to supplement their production in years when their own crop has been reduced by poor weather. As a result, some Oregon wineries produce Chardonnay, Pinot Noir, and White Riesling from their own grapes, and Cabernet Sauvignon, Merlot, Sauvignon Blanc, and Sémillon from Washington grapes. The origin of the grapes must be clearly stated on the label, as Oregon has particularly strict labeling requirements. If a wine is labeled with the name of a specific variety, at least 90 percent of the wine must be made from that grape. (The California minimum, which conforms to the federal requirement, is 75 percent.) The sole exception is Cabernet Sauvignon, which may be blended with up to 25 percent of such complementary varieties as Merlot and Cabernet Franc. Generic names, such as Chablis and Burgundy, are not permitted in Oregon, with the result that wineries market their blended wines with proprietary names such as Solstice Blanc, Oregon Harvest, and Bouquet Blanc.

Most Oregon wineries are fairly small, and produce less than five thousand cases a year. The three biggest wineries are Tualatin, Sokol Blosser, and Knudsen Erath, each of which produces twenty-five thousand cases or more. Oregon wineries in addition to the ones already mentioned include Adelsheim Vineyard, Amity Vineyards, Chateau Benoit Winery, Forgeron Vineyard, Henry Winery, Ponzi Vineyards, Shafer Vineyard Cellars, and the Oak Knoll Winery, which is famous for its fruit and berry wines as well as its Pinot Noir.

Idaho

Idaho's first major post-Prohibition winery was Ste. Chapelle Vineyards, which is situated between Boise and the Oregon border to the west. The six hundred acres of vineyards near the winery—which is modeled after the chapel on the Ile de la Cité, in Paris, from which Ste. Chapelle Vineyards derives its name—are planted at an elevation of about twenty-five hundred feet above the Snake River. The first Ste. Chapelle wines were produced in 1976 under the direction of winemaker Bill Broich, and the winery has achieved particular acclaim for its Chardonnay and Johannisberg Riesling. The winery, which produces more than 150,000 cases a year, also markets several other varietal wines, including Chenin Blanc, Gewürztraminer, and Pinot Noir, as well as Cabernet Sauvignon from Washington grapes, and a Charmat-process sparkling wine made from Johannisberg Riesling. Additional acreage has been planted in Idaho, and several new wineries have been created.

OTHER STATES

Wine is now made in forty states, and a great many new wineries have been created throughout the country in the past few years: of the more than eleven hundred wineries in the United States, about five hundred are outside California. About a third of these are in New York, Washington, and Oregon, but more than three hundred wineries have now been established in other states. Most of them make wines from *labrusca* and French-American hybrids, but about one hundred wineries now produce at least some of their wines from *vinifera* grapes.

Almost all of the three hundred-odd wineries situated outside California, New York, Washington, and Oregon produce limited amounts of wine that they sell locally—in fact, they account for less than 3 percent of the wine produced in this country—but a few have come to the attention of a wider audience. One of the smallest firms was also one of the most important in the recent history of American wines: Boordy Vineyard, established by Philip Wagner near Baltimore, Maryland. Wagner's pioneering work with French-American hybrids, which he first planted in the 1930s, is considered the major factor in the increased use of these varietals in other eastern vineyards.

Ohio was one of the earliest sources of American wines, and once made more than California, but its production today is considerably less than that of New York State. Catawba and Concord are the most extensively planted varieties. Meier's Wine Cellars, the leading producer, continues to market a range of wine from native grapes, but cultivates hybrids and *vinifera* varieties as well. In the Ozark plateau region of Arkansas, Wiederkehr Wine Cellars makes wine from *labrusca* and from such *vinifera* varieties as Johannisberg Riesling, Chardonnay, and Cabernet Sauvignon.

More than one thousand acres of vineyards have been planted in Virginia, most of them with *vinifera* varieties, and nearly thirty wineries have been established, including Meredyth Vineyards, Piedmont Vineyards, Shenandoah Vineyards, Oakencroft Vineyard, Rapidan River Vineyards, and the Barboursville Winery. Pennsylvania now has more than forty wineries, among them Allegro Vineyards, the Chaddsford Winery, Penn-Shore Vineyards, and the Presque Isle Wine Cellars. Wine production began in Texas in the mid-1970s, and more than a dozen wineries now make wine, mostly *vinifera*, from about three thousand acres of vineyards; producers include Chateau Montgolfier Vineyards, the Pheasant Ridge Winery, the Llano Estacado Winery, and the Fall Creek Vineyards. Ste. Genevieve Vineyards, in association with the University of Texas and the Cordier firm of Bordeaux, produced its first wines in 1984 from one thousand acres planted with such varieties as Chenin Blanc, Sauvignon blanc, Chardonnay, French Colombard, and Cabernet Sauvignon.

Some of the wineries around the country that have established more than a local reputation include Byrd Vineyards and Montbray Wine Cellars in Maryland; the Haight Vineyard in Connecticut; Sakonnet Vineyards in Rhode Island; Chicama Vineyards and the Commonwealth Winery in Massachusetts; Tewksbury Wine Cellars in New Jersey; the Markko Vineyard in Ohio; Tabor Hill and Fenn Valley Vineyards in Michigan; the Alexis Bailly Vineyard in Minnesota; and Chateau Elan in Georgia.

THE WINES OF
SOUTH AMERICA

CHILE

Although Chile is not the biggest wine-producing country in
South America, its wines, especially the reds, have traditionally been considered to be the best of that continent. Chile
extends for about three thousand miles along the west coast of
South America, in a thin strip rarely more than a hundred
miles wide, between the Pacific Ocean and the Andes Mountains. The country has a wide variety of terrains and climates,
and the best grape-growing area of table wines is in the
central valley of Chile, north and south of Santiago. Wines
were first brought to Chile by Spanish missionaries in the
sixteenth century, but winemaking did not really get started
on a commercial basis until the mid-nineteenth century. At
that time French wine experts, many of them from Bordeaux,
were brought over to Chile, as were a number of French
grape varieties. To this day, there are extensive plantings of
the classic Bordeaux vines, such as Cabernet Sauvignon,
Merlot, Cabernet Franc, Malbec, Sauvignon Blanc, and
Sémillon.

Most Chilean table wine is sold in barrels or in large jugs,
and comparatively little is marketed in the familiar bottle
sizes used in other countries. Exports, limited in the past, are
being encouraged under government supervision. There has

been an increase in the sales of Chilean wines here, and an improvement in the quality of the wines now available. Some wines are marketed with generic names, such as Burgundy and Rhine Wine, others with such varietal names as Cabernet Sauvignon, Pinot Noir, Riesling, and Sauvignon Blanc. There is actually very little Pinot Noir and Riesling planted in Chile: wines labeled Burgundy and Pinot Noir are made primarily from Cabernet Sauvignon, those labeled Rhine Wine and Riesling are usually made from Sémillon and Sauvignon Blanc. A limited amount of other varieties, including Chardonnay, Chenin Blanc, and Gewürztraminer, have recently been planted. Among the firms whose wines are distributed here are Concha y Toro, Viña Undurraga, Monte Cañeten, and Miguel Torres.

ARGENTINA

Argentina makes more wine than any other country in the Western Hemisphere, and is one of the five biggest producers in the world. Most of this consists of ordinary wine that is consumed within the country: the per capita consumption in Argentina is about a hundred bottles a year. In recent years, however, a number of Argentine producers have begun to export their wines to this country. Some are labeled with generic names, and many with such varietal names as Malbec (by far the most widely planted of the better varieties), Cabernet Sauvignon, Chardonnay, and Chenin Blanc. Sylvaner is often marketed as Riesling, Chenin Blanc as Pinot Blanc. Argentine wines suffered in the past from old-fashioned winemaking methods and excessive aging in wood, which often resulted in faded reds and oxidized whites. In an effort to increase their exports, a number of wineries have adopted modern vinification techniques and are now producing more attractive wines. Some of the firms that export to this country are Bianchi, Navarro Correas, Norton, Toso, and Trapiche. Andean Vineyards is a brand name created for the export market; the wines are produced by Peñaflor, the largest winery in Argentina.

The wines produced in Brazil, made primarily from *Vitis labrusca* and French-American hybrid grape varieties, are rarely seen here. In recent years, a number of American and European wine companies have invested in Brazil, and new vineyards have been planted with *Vitis vinifera* grapes.

VARIOUS WINES

AUSTRALIA

There are interesting parallels to be drawn between wine production in Australia and in the United States. Commercial winemaking began at about the same time in both countries—the 1830s—and developed in several different regions rather than in a single area. Fortified wines were made in far greater quantities than table wines, and only in the past two decades has each country reversed that trend. As recently as the early 1960s, sherry- and port-type wines accounted for two-thirds of Australia's total wine production. Today, table wines account for three-quarters of that country's wines. Per capita consumption has nearly doubled in ten years and, in fact, is more than twice that in the United States.

James Busby, a Scottish-born educator and French-trained winemaker, is often referred to as the father of the Australian wine industry, and his role seems to have been quite similar to that of Agoston Haraszthy in California. Busby brought over a great many European vine cuttings in 1831, distributed them to a number of growers in the Hunter Valley, north of Sydney, and also contributed a treatise on viticulture to aid new winemakers. Vineyards were rapidly established in different parts of Australia, and there are now about 170,000 acres producing the equivalent of fifty million cases of wine;

more than half of that is marketed as table wine; the rest is distilled or transformed into fortified wines.

About two-thirds of Australia's vineyards are planted with white-wine grapes, but much of that consists of Sultana, or Thompson Seedless, Muscat Gordo Blanco, and Palomino—most of the wine from these grapes is distilled. The principal wine grapes include Sémillon and Rhine Riesling. Chardonnay, virtually unknown in Australia in the early 1970s, is now widely planted, as is Muscat Blanc, Traminer, and Sauvignon Blanc. Among red grapes, Grenache and Mataro are used primarily to make fortified wines. The most widely cultivated red-wine grape is Shiraz, the Syrah of the northern Rhône, also known in Australia as Hermitage. Cabernet Sauvignon has also become widely cultivated in recent years, and there are relatively new plantings of Merlot and Pinot Noir as well.

As in the United States, there is widespread use of such generic names as Burgundy, Claret, Chablis, Sauternes, Hock, and Moselle; and Riesling, which may be used for any mild white wine. Most firms also use proprietary names, and some are among Australia's best-selling wines, including Ben Ean Moselle, Jacob's Creek, and Long Flat Red. About two-thirds of wine sales in Australia consists of inexpensive bag-in-the-box wines. These wines are packaged in a box lined with inert plastic or other materials that are meant to be impermeable to air and thus prevent spoilage as the wine is depleted. The boxes, which may contain two to five liters for home consumption, or ten to twenty liters for use in bars and restaurants, are broached by inserting a spigot into the container.

An increasing number of Australian wines are labeled with a combination of a varietal name and the district of origin, but consumers unfamiliar with Australian nomenclature may find some labels puzzling. For example, just as the Syrah may be called Shiraz or Hermitage, so a Sémillon produced in the Hunter Valley may be marketed as Hunter Riesling, and a wine labeled Clare Riesling is likely to be made from Crouchen. Furthermore, it is traditional to blend such varieties as Shiraz and Cabernet Sauvignon, or Chardonnay and Sémillon, and such wines are so labeled. Also, it is common practice for a winery to blend wines from two regions that may be hundreds of miles apart; thus, one firm's Cabernet Sauvignon may be made from grapes grown in two districts, while another firm's Cabernet-Shiraz is made from Cabernet grown in one region, Shiraz in another.

There are more than five hundred wineries in Australia,

and as in the United States, many of them were established in the late 1960s and early 1970s. The country's wine-producing districts extend along a boomerang-shaped, four-thousand-mile crescent from Stanthorpe in Queensland to Perth in Western Australia, and include traditional regions that were established in the nineteenth century and new areas that have been producing wines for less than a decade. Australian wines are not widely available in the United States, but here is a listing of the better-known regions and a few of their wineries. Most of Australia's biggest wine firms—Penfolds, Lindemans, Orlando, Seppelts, McWilliams, Hardys, Smith's Yalumba—have wineries in several different regions.

The principal wine-producing states of Australia (and their capital cities) are New South Wales (Sydney), Victoria (Melbourne), South Australia (Adelaide), and Western Australia (Perth). Probably the most famous wine region in New South Wales is the Hunter Valley, situated about one hundred miles north of Sydney; some of its best-known wineries include Rosemount Estate, Wyndham Estate, Tyrrell's, Arrowfield, Lake's Folly, Hungerford Hill, Saxonvale, and Rothbury Estate.

Mudgee, a small area west of Sydney, is the home of such wineries as Botobolar, Huntington Estate, and Montrose. Cowra and Rooty Hill are other small districts in New South Wales, whose most extensive wine region is the Murrumbidgee Irrigation Area, known as the MIA. McWilliams has pioneered the production of table wines in this area, which has been a traditional source of fortified wines and, in recent years, of fine late-harvest wines as well.

There are wine regions situated throughout the state of Victoria, some of whose labels as quite well-known, including Seppelts Great Western sparkling wines, Chateau Tahbilk, Taltarni, and the range of wines produced by Brown Bros. in Milawa, 150 miles northeast of Melbourne. The Corowa-Rutherglen region is on the border of Victoria and New South Wales; two other districts are the Yarra Valley and Sunrasia.

South Australia's best-known region is the Barossa Valley, situated about thirty-five miles northeast of Adelaide. A number of Australia's largest firms have their principal wineries there, as do Leo Buring, Wolf Blass and the Barossa Valley Cooperative, now owned by Penfolds, whose wines are marketed as Kaiser Stuhl. Farther north is the Clare-Watervale region, where Quelltaler and Tim Knappstein's Enterprise Wines are situated. The Adelaide Hills, just outside the city, was the original home of Penfold's Grange Hermitage, one of

Australia's most acclaimed red wines; the Petaluma winery, originally established in the Riverina district of New South Wales, is now situated near Adelaide. McLaren Vale, twenty-five miles south of Adelaide, is the center of the Southern Vales region. Coonawarra, about 260 miles southeast of Adelaide, is a long-established region whose name often appears on labels; Redman, Mildara, and Wynn's have wineries there.

Perth, in Western Australia, is twelve hundred miles west of Adelaide which is, in turn, seven hundred miles west of Sydney. The Swan Valley, not far from Perth, is one of Western Australia's oldest wine regions. Newer ones include the Margaret River district, about 150 miles south of Perth, where Leeuwin Estate, Moss Wood, Cullen's Willyabrup, and Vasse Felix are situated; and the Frankland-Mount Barker region, about two hundred miles southeast of Perth.

An interesting feature of the Australian wine scene is the importance given to the wine competitions held in the major cities on a regular basis. Almost all of the wineries compete—as many as two thousand wines may be entered—and the prizes confer considerable prestige on those who make them. It has even been said that some large Australian wineries employ two winemakers—one to make wines for the public, the other to make the wines that are entered in competition.

The vineyards of New Zealand have increased in the past twenty-five years from less than one thousand acres to more than four thousand. Müller-Thurgau (also called Riesling-Sylvaner) is the most widely planted variety; other whites include Gewürztraminer, Rhine Riesling, Chardonnay, Sauvignon Blanc, and Chenin Blanc. Red-wine varieties include Cabernet Sauvignon, the Pinotage of South Africa, Gamay, and Pinot Noir. Some of New Zealand's better-known producers are Cooks, Corbans, McWilliams, and Montana Wines.

SOUTH AFRICA

Vines are first planted in South Africa by Dutch settlers in the middle of the seventeenth century, but only recently have modern winemaking techniques and plantings of new varieties begun to transform the country's wine scene. Best known for its well-made fortified wines in the style of sherry and port, South Africa is now gaining a reputation for its range of table and sparkling wines as well.

Generic names, such as Chablis and Burgundy, are not widely used in South Africa, whose wines are most often labeled with proprietary names—such as Lieberstein, Autumn Harvest, Fonternelle, and Bouquet Fleur—or the name of the grape variety used. Steen, which is the Chenin Blanc, is the most widely planted white-wine grape; Cinsault is the principal red-wine grape. Pinotage, a cross of Pinot Noir and Cinsault (which is known there as Hermitage), is a popular red variety that is indigenous to South Africa. Cabernet Sauvignon is widely planted, and is considered to produce the country's finest reds. There are, in addition, new plantings of such classic varieties as Chardonnay, Sauvignon Blanc, Merlot, Cabernet Franc, and Rhine Riesling (what is called Riesling in South Africa is thought to be the Crouchen of France). Appellations of origin were established in 1973; the best-known are Paarl and Stellenbosch.

Although South Africa produces the equivalent of a hundred million cases of wine in some years, much of that is distilled into brandy. The Cooperative Wine Growers' Association, known as K.W.V., controls all wine production, and, in fact, most of the country's wines are made by cooperative cellars. South Africa's biggest wine firm is the Stellenbosch Farmers' Winery, whose labels include Zonnebloem Cabernet Sauvignon and Oude Libertas Dry Steen; one of its properties is the Nederburg estate, site of an annual wine auction. Other wine estates include Groot Constantia, Meerlust, and Twee Jongegezellen.

ISRAEL

Although the wine production of Israel is relatively small by world standards (about one-third that of Switzerland, for example), Israeli wines are widely distributed in this country. Most of them are mellow red and white table wines and sherry- and port-type fortified wines, but many drier wines are now being marketed as well. Vines were growing in Palestine over three thousand years ago, but the modern wine industry of that country dates from the 1880s, when Baron Edmond de Rothschild sponsored the creation of new vineyards. Carignan, Grenache, and Alicante are the principal varieties cultivated, but in recent years there have been new plantings of Cabernet Sauvignon, Sauvignon Blanc, and Sémillon as well. A cooperative society formed in the early years of this century now accounts for about three-quarters of Israeli wine production, and for almost all of its exports to this country, under the brand name Carmel.

More than two hundred acres were planted in the Golan Heights in the 1970s, and a winery was established in 1983. The Sauvignon Blanc and Cabernet Sauvignon produced there are marketed as varietal wines under the name Yarden.

ALGERIA

Not long ago, Algeria was a relatively important producer of wines; today, its production is about a third of what it was in the 1950s. Algeria is a Muslim country, and Muslims are not permitted to consume alcoholic beverages, so Algeria is in the paradoxical situation of maintaining an industry whose product cannot be marketed within its own borders. Robust Algerian wines, almost all of them red, were traditionally shipped to France to add color, body, and alcohol to the lighter *vin ordinaire* produced in the Midi region. After Algeria obtained its independence from France in 1962, shipments to France decreased, and when the Common Market was established, French wine firms realized that it was economically more advantageous to import blending wines from Italy than from Algeria. In recent years the biggest customer for Algerian wines has been Russia.

At one time, a dozen Algerian wines were entitled to the French V.D.Q.S. appellation. More recently, Algeria set up its own appellation laws for seven of these wines: Medea, Dahra, Coteaux de Mascara, Coteaux du Zaccar, Coteaux de Tlemcen, Monts du Tessala, and Aïn Bessem-Bouïra. Their labels bear the phrase *Appellation d'Origine Garantie*, and some of them, such as Dahra and Medea, are shipped here.

LEBANON

Lebanon has achieved a place on the world's wine map because of a single wine, Château Musar, a long-lived red made primarily from Cabernet Sauvignon and Cinsault. The winery, located fifteen miles north of Beirut, was established in the 1930s by Gaston Hochar; since 1959 it has been under the direction of his son, Serge, who studied enology in Bordeaux.

The vineyards that produce Château Musar are in the Bekaa Valley, forty miles south of Beirut; its 320 acres are planted with Cabernet Sauvignon and Cinsault, as well as small amounts of Merlot, Syrah, and Pinot Noir. About a third of the wine from these vineyards is sold as Château Musar, which contains 50 to 75 percent Cabernet Sauvignon. The rest of the crop is sold as Cuvée Musar, a lighter wine that contains more Cinsault than Cabernet Sauvignon. Because of the wars that have been fought in and around Beirut in recent years, certain vintages have been harvested under dangerous conditions, and, in fact, the 1984 crop could not be picked at all.

CHAMPAGNE AND
SPARKLING WINES

It has been said that you can have too much champagne, but you can never have enough. The most festive of wines, champagne adds gaiety and distinction to any occasion at which it is served. Unfortunately, most of us drink champagne only at crowded receptions, where we enjoy its convivial effect without the chance to appreciate its quality. It's a pity that most people consider champagne so special that they reserve it for infrequent celebrations. Although fine champagne is never cheap, it is no more expensive than a good bottle of Bordeaux, Burgundy, or California Chardonnay; and the appearance of a bottle of champagne at any gathering is greeted with pleasure and enthusiasm.

Because almost all champagne is marketed with the name of the producer, rather than that of an individual vineyard, it is not a difficult wine to buy. It's a wine, nevertheless, that is made in a fairly exacting way, and a visitor to any of the famous champagne houses in Reims, Epernay, or Ay invariably leaves with the impression that champagne is not expensive considering the number of complex steps necessary to produce it.

There are a great many sparkling wines produced in France and throughout the world (these will be discussed separately), but true champagne is made only within the delimited Champagne region situated about ninety miles east of Paris. Although wine has been made there for more than fifteen hundred years, until the late seventeenth century that wine was still, not sparkling, and pale red in color. In the second half of the seventeenth century, members of the French and English courts developed a preference for light, sparkling wines, and producers in the Champagne region began to transform their wine into the product we know today. They had noted that the wines of Champagne often developed a sparkle in the spring following the vintage. In effect, not all of the natural grape sugar had been transformed into alcohol at the time of the vintage, because early winters tended to stop fermentation before it ran its course. When warmer weather returned in the spring, the remaining traces of sugar began to referment, and the wines in barrel took on a natural effervescence. Dom Pérignon, a Benedictine monk who was the cellar master at the Abbey of Hautvillers, is credited with having invented champagne, but what he may have done was to help devise a better way of creating and retaining its natural sparkle. He also seems to have realized that a more harmonious sparkling wine was obtained if the grapes from various Champagne vineyards were blended together. He thus established the concept of a *cuvée*, or blend, which has enabled the champagne shippers (who now blend wines, not grapes) to maintain a consistent style year after year. It is this fact that makes champagne unusual among fine wines, for unlike the best Bordeaux and Burgundies, which owe their distinction to the soil and exposure of a specific vineyard and to the characteristics of a particular vintage, champagne is a wine blended from different grape varieties, different vineyards, and, for the most part, different vintages. It is in blending that champagne achieves its quality and personality. One confirmation of this is the number of champagne firms in existence, each producing a slightly different champagne by blending available wines in different proportions.

The Champagne vineyards are divided into three principal districts: the Valley of the Marne, the Mountain of Reims, and the Côte des Blancs. About three-quarters of the Champagne region's sixty-two thousand acres are planted in black grapes, Pinot Noir and Pinot Meunier; Pinot Noir is, of course, the variety used to make the great red Burgundies. The white Chardonnay grape makes up the rest of the plantings, and is predominant in the Côtes des Blancs. Although Chardonnay vineyards account for only one-quarter of the total acreage, this variety produces more tons per acre than do the other two, so that about one-third of the wines are made from this grape.

The shipping houses market about two-thirds of the region's wines, but they own less than 15 percent of the vineyards; most of the vineyards are in the hands of thousands of small proprietors. At vintage time, those farmers who are not members of the more than 125 cooperative cellars in Champagne, or who are not among those who estate-bottle the wine made from their own grapes, sell their grapes to the shippers—who cannot rely on their own acreage alone to maintain their stocks of wine—at a price per kilo that is negotiated each year just before the harvest. The established price of the grapes is then multiplied by the official rating of the soil from which each particular load comes. There are a dozen villages whose vineyards are rated at 100 percent quality, including Ay, Cramant, Bouzy, Sillery, and Avize. Others are rated on a sliding scale that goes down to 77 percent. About one-third of the wines produced in Champagne come from soil rated 90 percent or higher.

Because most of the grapes harvested are Pinot Noir and Pinot Meunier, and because the color of red wines comes from pigments on the inside of the skin that dissolve in fermenting must, it is essential that the red grapes be pressed and separated from their skins as quickly as possible. For this reason the shipping houses maintain presses at strategic locations throughout the vineyards, so that the journey from vine to press is kept to a minimum. It is to these press houses that the growers take their grapes, which are then loaded in lots of four thousand kilos, or nearly nine thousand pounds. The presses are wide and flat, rather than high, so that the grapes can be spread out and the juice can run out of the presses quickly. Two or three fast pressings produce the equivalent of ten barrels, each holding 205 liters, about fifty gallons. This is known as the *vin de cuvée*, or first pressing (although actually more than one pressing is needed to produce this much wine). Further pressing produces three more barrels of wine, called *tailles*, and this too can be made into champagne, although this wine is worth much less. Sometimes a fourteenth barrel is squeezed out, known as the *rebêche*, but this cannot be made into champagne. The thirteenth barrel, incidentally, may be worth only 60 percent as much as a *vin de cuvée*, and there are some shippers who seek out the *tailles* to make a less expensive champagne. If these shippers further specify that the *tailles* may come from vineyards rated at, say, 80 or 85 percent, there can be quite a difference in quality between what they market and the wines of the leading champagne houses.

The pressed juice is transferred from the fields to the cellars of the shippers or the cooperatives, and there the fermentation begins that will transform it into a still, dry white wine.

In January or February the tasting of the new wine begins, so that a *cuvée* may be made up for bottling. Each of the top shipping houses has, as always, obtained grapes from throughout Champagne to give itself flexibility in making up its usual blend. Tasting the new wines may take four or five weeks, and might take the following form. First the wines of each pressing are tasted and compared to other lots from the same district. Then the wines of different districts within Champagne are compared, and their respective qualities noted. One village may produce wine known for its bouquet, another for its body, a third for its delicacy and finesse, and so on. Each shipper also decides on the proportion of Pinot Noir, Pinot Meunier, and Chardonnay wines to be used. Some shippers may use 40 or 50 percent of Chardonnay for elegance, others prefer a richer wine with more Pinot Noir in the blend. The proportion will vary to some extent from year to year, and is likely be different for a firm's vintage and nonvintage wines.

Finally, wines kept back from previous vintages, called reserve wines, are tasted to determine in what proportion they should be used. Remember that nonvintage champagne (and this accounts for more than 80 percent of the total) is made up of wines of more than one harvest. Certain years may produce rather thin wines, others rich wines that lack elegance. The characteristics and flaws of each vintage can be adjusted by the use of reserve wines, which may account for 15 to 30 percent of a *cuvée*. This complicated and delicate blending process, in which a dozen to fifty different lots of wine may eventually be combined, is the key to determining and maintaining a house style, upon which the reputation of each firm rests.

When a shipper considers that a particular vintage is especially successful, he will make—in addition to his nonvintage blend—a *cuvée* predominantly from grapes harvested that year, and the bottles will display the vintage year on their labels. Shippers do not always agree on the quality of the wines produced in any given vintage, and the years in which vintage champagne is produced will vary from one shipper to another. Paradoxically, a vintage champagne made entirely from the wines of a single harvest may not be typical of a shipper's traditional style, since the *cuvée* is not balanced by the use of reserve wines. The laws governing the production of vintage champagne do not prohibit the use of reserve wines, however, and in practice a certain amount of reserve wine is almost always used even in vintage champagne, so that the wine displays both the personality of the vintage and the style of the shipper.

Once the sample *cuvée* has been made up, the wines are blended accordingly and bottled, usually between March and May of the year following the harvest. A little bit of sugar syrup—*liqueur de tirage*—is added to the wine, along with yeast, to provide the elements necessary for a second fermentation. The bottle is then firmly stoppered with a temporary cork—most firms now use a crown cork similar to that previously used for soft drinks—and is placed on its side. Fermentation will now transform the sugar into alcohol and carbon dioxide gas, and because the bubbles are imprisoned in the bottle, they combine with the wine. The artificially induced second fermentation in individual bottles, which is the essence of the *méthode champenoise*, takes two or three months.

It was 150 years after Dom Pérignon first conducted his experiments that the key step of bottle fermentation began to be adequately controlled. (For that matter, it was not until several years after Dom Pérignon's death that producers in the Champagne region were first permitted to ship their wines in stoppered flasks, rather than wooden casks.) A French chemist devised away to measure any residual sugar left in the still wine after blending, as well as a method for calculating how much additional sugar had to be added to the wine to produce the desired amount of gas pressure in the bottle. Until then, making champagne was a fairly hazardous undertaking, as the pressure resulting from a second fermentation could not be controlled, and the bottles of the day were not uniform. It was not unusual for half the contents of a cellar to be destroyed by a series of bottle explosions. Today such breakage has been reduced to less than 1 percent, but champagne production is so immense—a large crop can yield more than 200 million bottles—that several hundred thousand bottles a year are still lost in this way.

After the second fermentation, the bottles, now filled with

sparkling wine, are piled up and left to mature. The extraordinary underground cellars of Champagne are carved out of the chalky subsoil of the region, and enable the champagne producers to maintain their enormous stocks—which in recent years have varied from 400 to 700 million bottles—at a constant low temperature. The bottles are said to be resting *sur lie*, that is, on the lees, the dead yeast cells thrown off as a by-product of fermentation. The interaction between the sparkling wine and the lees, known as autolysis, adds complexity and character to the bouquet and taste of the wine: long aging *sur lie* is an important factor in the quality of fine champagne. A nonvintage champagne must be aged *sur lie* for a minimum of one year. A vintage-dated champagne cannot be sold until three years after the harvest, which means it may age *sur lie* less than three years. In practice, most major firms age their wines *sur lie* well beyond the legal minimums.

Although the lees add to the flavor of champagne, the presence of this cloudy deposit makes the bottle unsalable to today's consumers. A series of complicated steps, first introduced in the eighteenth century, now takes place; its sole purpose is to rid each bottle of its deposit without losing the imprisoned bubbles. The bottles are put into *pupitres*, known in this country as riddling racks, A-shaped wooden boards with holes in which each bottle can be separately manipulated. A highly skilled *rémueur* now takes each bottle, which is at a slight downward slant, and gives it a little twist to dislodge the sediment, at the same time tipping the bottle over slightly to lower the corked end. This delicate process goes on every day for several weeks, and ends with each bottle standing upside down—*sur pointe*—with all of its sediment lying against the cork. Today, a number of champagne firms have installed labor-saving riddling bins that each hold five hundred bottles or more. The bins can be manipulated, little by little, the way individual bottles are—imagine a cube on its side being gradually turned and raised until it rests on one of its corners—and each load of bottles ends up *sur pointe* in less than two weeks. The latest versions of these bins are fully automated and can be programmed by a computer.

The bottles are now ready for the *dégorgement*, or disgorging process. Still upside down, they are put on a conveyor and their necks dipped in a cold brine solution, which freezes the sediment to the temporary cork. The cork is then popped off, the pellet of sediment is disgorged, and the familiar champagne cork is inserted under great pressure.

Just before this cork is inserted, however, some sugar syrup is added to each bottle, along with as much champagne as is needed to replace whatever was lost when the sediment was expelled. This *liqueur d'expédition*, also referred to as the dosage, is what determines the relative dryness of a champagne. The driest of all champagne is Brut, which receives the least amount of dosage—it contains no more than 1.5 percent sugar, usually less. Extra Dry or Extra Sec, the next-driest style, may contain 1.2 to 2 percent of sugar. Dry or Sec is somewhat sweeter and, in fact, not really dry; and Demi-Sec, with 3 to 5 percent of sugar, is the sweetest champagne that most firms market. A few shippers occasionally market a champagne with no dosage at all, but such bottles are rare.

Some champagne shippers claim that many Americans like to see the word Brut on the label, but actually prefer the taste of Extra Dry, and that may be true. Fashions change, of course; during most of the nineteenth century the prevailing taste was for very sweet wines. It was only in the 1870s that dry champagnes established their present popularity, although certain markets—South America and Scandinavia, for example—still demand fairly sweet champagnes. Because the relative sweetness of champagne is determined only when the final cork is inserted, it is not difficult for any shipper to make up a champagne that will conform to his customers' demands.

One aspect of a Brut champagne that deserves mention is that the less sweetening is added, the better the wine has to be, as its quality cannot be masked. Also, a Brut does not taste at its best when served at the end of a meal, with dessert. The richness and sweetness of most desserts make the dry, delicate wine taste somewhat thin and sharp by contrast.

It's worth noting that the bottle-fermentation method described is used only for bottles, magnums (which hold two bottles), and usually, but not always, for half-bottles. Other sizes are produced by decanting bottles of Champagne into six-ounce splits and into larger sizes such as the jeroboam (four bottles), rehoboam (six bottles), and methuselah (eight bottles). Obviously, splits have the greatest chance of going flat, and are in any case poor value, ounce for ounce, compared to a half-bottle or bottle.

In addition to marketing nonvintage Brut, vintage Brut, and

Extra Dry champagnes, a number of firms have also created luxury champagnes that are two or three times the price of a nonvintage Brut. Moët & Chandon's Dom Pérignon is perhaps the most famous of these deluxe champagnes, which are known as *cuvées speciales*; others include Taittinger Comtes de Champagne, Louis Roederer Cristal, Krug Grande Cuvée, Bollinger R.D., Dom Ruinart Blanc de Blancs, Piper-Heidsieck Rare, Veuve Clicquot La Grande Dame, Mumm René Lalou, Laurent Perrier Grand Siècle, and Perrier-Jouët Fleur de Champagne (known as Belle Epoque in France). The *cuvées* for these champagnes are prepared with particular care, the wines are usually aged longer on the lees, and most of them are marketed in distinctive, specially designed bottles.

Some champagnes are labeled Blanc de Blancs, which indicates that the wine has been made entirely from white Chardonnay grapes. A Blanc de Blancs tends to be lighter and more delicate, and there are many who prize its particular elegance. Note that this phrase has a very specific meaning in Champagne, where most of the vineyards are planted with black grapes. But when the phrase is used on white-wine labels from other districts or other countries, it usually has no meaning, because white wines are made from white grapes as a matter of course. A champagne labeled Blanc de Noirs has been made entirely from black grapes without the use of Chardonnay in the *cuvée*.

Many firms now market a rosé champagne, almost always made by adding a small amount of red wine to the *cuvée*, just enough to give the blend the desired pink color. The wine is not easy to make, because after the bottle fermentation takes place, the color may fade or turn brown. Although pink champagne has a frivolous reputation, perhaps because of the many cheap versions made elsewhere, the best examples combine elegance with body and flavor.

Some shippers market a *crémant*, which is a wine that does not have the full sparkle of a champagne, but rather a more delicate *pétillance*. *Crémant* should not be confused with Cramant, which is a village in the Côte des Blancs whose wines are occasionally marketed under its own name.

A quantity of nonsparkling wine is also produced in the Champagne district from the same vineyards and the same grapes as champagne. Of course, all champagne begins as a still wine, but these go to market as such. Until 1974, the still wines of the Champagne region were labeled *Vin Nature de la Champagne*. They were almost never exported and were difficult to find even in France. The still wines were in short supply because for many years virtually all of the Champagne crop was transformed into sparkling wines to meet the increasing worldwide demand. Also, shippers were reluctant to export a nonsparkling wine that had the word Champagne on its label, for it might confuse many consumers. In the past twenty-five years, however, new plantings have more than doubled the size of the Champagne vineyards, and production increased accordingly. In 1974, the name of the still wines of champagne was changed to Coteaux Champenois, and what was then an excess of production was bottled as nonsparkling wine. For a few years both production and sales of Coteaux Champenois—a light-bodied and relatively acid white wine—increased substantially, and examples from a number of different shippers were available both in France and in this country. Then, as a result of a series of very small crops, coupled with increased sales of champagne, shippers once again transformed all their wines into champagne, and nonsparkling wines from this region have become less readily available. (There is also some still red wine produced in Champagne, the best-known of which comes from the village of Bouzy.)

Here is an alphabetical list of champagne firms whose wines can be found in the United States. There are, of course, other shippers doing business here, but the firms listed below account for almost all the champagne sales in this country. In fact, two of them—Moët & Chandon and Mumm—ship about half of all the bottles sold here.

Ayala	Krug
Besserat de Bellefon	Lanson
Billecart-Salmon	Laurent Perrier
Bollinger	Moët & Chandon
Charbaut	Mumm
Veuve Clicquot-Ponsardin	Perrier-Jouët
De Venoge	Piper-Heidsieck
Deutz & Geldermann	Pol Roger
Gosset	Pommery & Greno
Heidsieck Monopole	Louis Roederer
Charles Heidsieck	Ruinart
Henriot	Taittinger

OTHER SPARKLING WINES

Although the Champagne region of France produces, by general accord, sparkling wines with the greatest style, complexity, and finesse, a number of other sparkling wines are made in France and, of course, throughout the world. Many of them are produced by the bulk process of tank fermentation, called *cuve close* in France, and also known as the Charmat process, after the Frenchman who first developed the technique about eighty years ago. The second fermentation of the base wine takes place in large sealed tanks rather than in individual bottles. The resulting sparkling wine is then drawn off under pressure and bottled. This method is obviously much quicker and cheaper than bottle fermentation: using the Charmat process, tanks of still wine can be transformed into bottles of sparkling wine in two weeks or less.

Another technique, called the transfer process, is often used—except in Champagne—to lower the cost of bottle-fermented sparkling wines. After the second fermentation has taken place and the wines have aged for some months, the bottles of sparkling wine are emptied, under pressure, into tanks, where the appropriate dosage is added. The wines are then filtered and rebottled. The transfer process is obviously cheaper than having to disgorge each bottle separately, and its use accounts for the fact that the labels of many sparkling wines—especially in the United States—carry the phrase "individually fermented in the bottle" while others, made by the *méthode champenoise*, are labeled "individually fermented in this bottle."

In France, all sparkling wines not produced in Champagne have always been called *mousseux*, no matter how they are made. There are *mousseux* produced along the Loire, notably in Saumur, Vouvray, Touraine, and Anjou, primarily from Chenin Blanc; many are made by the *méthode champenoise*. Familiar labels include Bouvet, Gratien & Meyer, Ackerman-Laurance, Blanc Foussy, Monmousseau, Veuve Amiot, and Langlois-Château. A great deal of *mousseux* is produced in Burgundy, both red and white; Kriter, owned by Patriarche, is the best-known brand. Because of the word *mousseux* may be used both for bottle-fermented sparkling wines and for less distinguished ones, new appellations were created in 1975 for certain *méthode champenoise* wines from *Appellation Contrôlée* regions. Crémant de Loire, Crémant de Bourgogne, and

Crémant d'Alsace are names that can now be used for sparkling wines from these regions if they conform to certain regulations concerning the grape varieties used, minimum aging *sur lie*, and other aspects that affect quality. Other French sparkling wines that are only occasionally seen here include Saint-Péray, a dry *mousseux* from the Rhône made primarily from the Marsanne grape; Clairette de Die, also from the Rhône, which may be a dry wine made entirely from the Clairette grape, or a semisweet wine that contains a substantial proportion of Muscat; and the slightly sweet Blanquette de Limoux, produced near Carcassonne. Sparkling wine is also made in the village of Seyssel in the Haute-Savoie, in the Jura, and in Bordeaux.

The sparkling wines of Italy—dry and sweet, white and red—are labeled *spumante*. The most famous is Asti Spumante, produced in northern Italy around the village of Asti. Made from the distinctive and aromatic Muscat grape, Asti Spumante has a unique, intense bouquet reminiscent of ripe grapes and a sweet pronounced taste that many people find delicious with fruit and dessert. Asti Spumante is relatively low in alcohol—under 9 percent—and contains between 7.5 and 9 percent sugar. Virtually all of it is made by the Charmat process, called *autoclave* in Italy. Well-known producers of Asti Spumante include Gancia, Martini & Rossi, and Cinzano.

Italians are among the leading consumers of French champagne (in fact, for several years in the 1970s, Italy was the Champagne region's most important export market), so it is not surprising that a number of bone-dry *méthode champenoise* sparkling wines are made by the Italians themselves. The best of these, which come from the regions of Trentino, Alto Adige, Franciacorta, and the Oltrepò Pavese, are made from such varieties as Chardonnay, Pinot Bianco, Pinot Nero, and Pinot Grigio. Leading producers, most of whom make limited quantities, include Ferrari, Equipe 5, Contratto, Carpenè Malvolti, Antinori, Frescobaldi, Fontanafredda, Cinzano, Calissano, Gancia, Riccadonna, Berlucchi, Ca' del Bosco, and Venegazzù. Sparkling wines from these producers and others that are made by the traditional champagne method are labeled *metodo champenois*. Many attractive Brut *spumanti* are also made by the Charmat process.

The Prosecco grape, planted near the village of Conegliano and Valdobbi in the Veneto region, is used to make dry and semidry sparkling wines. A number of well-known red and white still wines are, on occasion, transformed into sparkling wines. These include Soave, Verdicchio, and Frascati among whites, and such reds as Freisa and Nebbiolo.

Sekt is the generic name for German sparkling wines, which are produced in tremendous quantities. Historically, the thin, acid German wines of poor years were used as the base for Sekt, but demand has become so great that most of the still white wine transformed into Sekt is now imported from neighboring countries, primarily Italy and France. Today, more sparkling wine is made in Germany than in Champagne, although almost all Sekt is produced by the Charmat process. Sekt can be an agreeable wine, and is characterized by a fruity taste and, more often than not, a slight sweetness. Henkell Extra Dry is the best-known brand in this country; others include Deinhard Imperial and Fürst von Metternich, the latter made by the *méthode champenoise*.

The sparkling wines of Spain—dry, well made, and moderately priced—have become increasingly popular in the United States in recent years. Almost all of Spain's *espumosos* are produced in or near San Sadurní de Noya, about twenty-five miles west of Barcelona, in the Penedès region. Most of the firms situated there use the traditional *méthode champenoise*, and such wines may be labeled *cava*. The principal grape varieties used are Xarello, Macabeo, and Parellada. It was in San Sadurní de Noya that automatic riddling machines, call *girosols* in Spain, were first used on a commercial basis. Some of major firms (and their proprietary brands) are Codorníu (Brut Clasico, Blanc de Blancs), Freixenet (Cordon Negro, Carta Nevada), Castellblanch (Brut Zero), and Segura Viudas. Other brands include Conde de Caralt and Paul Cheneau. In 1984, Castellblanch, Segura Viudas, and Conde de Caralt were acquired by Freixenet.

Despite the fame of champagne and the increasing popularity of other imported sparkling wines, about three-quarters of all the sparkling wines sold in this country are made here, primarily in California. To the dismay of the French, the word "champagne" may legally be used on the labels of American sparkling wines as long as it is preceded by an indication of its origin: California, New York State, American. Most American sparkling wines are made by the Charmat, or bulk, process, and this fact must appear on the label. (Actually, one such wine—André, produced by Gallo—accounts for more than a third of all the sparkling wines produced in California.) There are, in addition, many producers who bottle-ferment their wines and then disgorge them by the transfer process. Well-known producers are Almadén, the Christian Brothers, Paul Masson, and Weibel.

Two well-established California wineries that specialize in *méthode champenoise* wines are Korbel, which produced its first sparkling wines in 1882, and now markets, in addition to its Brut and bone-dry Natural, a Blanc de Blancs and Blanc de Noirs; and Hanns Kornell, established in 1952, which offers several styles, including the very dry Sehr Trocken.

In recent years, there has been a dramatic increase in the number of California wineries producing fine sparkling wines. Not only do these firms employ the *méthode champenoise*, followed by extended aging on the lees, but, just as important, they are using the classic Chardonnay and Pinot Noir grapes of Champagne, rather than such grapes as Chenin Blanc and French Colombard, which produce agreeable but neutral and undistinguished sparkling wines. Schramsberg, a small Napa Valley winery created by Jack Davies in 1965, was the first to specialize in sparkling wines made from Pinot Noir and Chardonnay grapes. Among its wines are Blanc de Blancs, Blanc de Noirs, Cuvée de Pinot, and a semidry Crémant.

In 1973, the French firm Moët-Hennessy bought land in the Napa Valley and soon after began construction of a sparkling wine facility, Domaine Chandon. They do not use the word "champagne" to describe their wines; first released in 1977, they are labeled Chandon Napa Valley Brut and Blanc de Noirs, the latter made entirely from Pinot Noir grapes. More recently, another champagne firm, Piper-Heidsieck, joined with Renfield Imports to produce sparkling wines in Sonoma County that are labeled Piper-Sonoma. The first Piper-Sonoma wines—Brut, Blanc de Noirs, and Tête de Cuvée—were produced in 1980 under the direction of Rodney Strong. Other French firms have begun to produce *méthode champenoise* wines in California: Mumm, in the Napa Valley; Louis Roederer, in Mendocino's Anderson Valley; and Deutz & Geldermann, in the Arroyo Grande district between San Luis Obispo and Santa Maria. Freixenet, a leading Spanish firm, has established vineyards and a winery in Sonoma; its first sparkling wine, labeled Gloria Ferrer, was released in 1984.

California wineries known primarily for their table wines that also produce *méthode champenoise* wines include Chateau St. Jean, Mirassou, Sebastiani, and Wente Bros. Other California firms that are producing limited amounts of *méthode champenoise* wines include S. Anderson, Culbertson, Robert Hunter, Iron Horse, and Scharffenberger Cellars.

Until the mid-1960s, New York State produced more sparkling wine than did California. Although New York State champagne now accounts for only 10 percent or so of all sales, it is still very popular throughout the country. The native grapes, notably Delaware and Catawba, that give New York State table wines a special grapy taste have traditionally produced a very agreeable sparkling wine with a flavor of its own. Today, many of these distinctive sparkling wines display less of the taste of native grapes than in the past, and, in fact, some producers are using a substantial proportion of French-American hybrids. The major brands of New York State champagne are Taylor, Great Western, and Gold Seal. The white and pink sparkling wines produced in America are usually called champagne, and the red wines are labeled Sparkling Burgundy. Cold Duck, theoretically a blend of champagne and Sparkling Burgundy, is a pink sparkling wine that was quite popular for a time.

Champagne and sparkling wines should be opened with some care. There are few sounds that fill us with as much pleasant anticipation as the loud pop of a champagne cork, but this is usually accompanied by a wasteful explosion of foam and wine, so it's worth noting the simplest and most effective means of opening a bottle. Ideally, you should put a napkin or handkerchief between your hand and the bottle, partly to avoid warming the wine with the heat of your palm, but also as a safety measure, in case a bottle should ever crack. Then remove the foil and loosen the wiring. Try to hold the bottle so that your thumb keeps the cork in place as you twist the wiring with your other hand. In any case, make sure the bottle is not pointed toward you or anyone else, because once the wire is loosened, the cork may explode out. Then hold the cork firmly in one hand and twist the bottle away from the cork with the other. The cork should come out easily, but if it doesn't, try to work it loose without shaking the bottle excessively. The bottle should be at a 45-degree angle, so that a larger surface of wine is exposed to the atmosphere as the cork comes out, which reduces the pressure in the narrow neck of the bottle. This procedure may be a bit too deliberate for celebrating a sports victory in a locker room, but you'll find it easy enough to manage in your home.

The so-called champagne glasses often used at receptions—

wide, shallow, sherbet-type—are in fact the worst of all. Their flat, wide bottoms dissipate the bubbles very quickly, and they are awkward to drink from. Either a tulip-shaped glass tapering to a point where the bowl joins the stem or a traditional flute in the shape of an elongated V is a better glass. If the bubbles rise from a single point, they will last longer and present a more attractive appearance.

FORTIFIED WINES

Fortified wines are those to which a certain amount of brandy has been added to bring the total alcoholic content up to 17 to 21 percent. Wine producers in this country refer to all such wines—whether they are dry or sweet—as dessert wines. Sherry and port are the most famous examples of fortified wines, and Madeira, Marsala, and Málaga are also fairly well known. Vermouth is a fortified wine that has also been flavored with a variety of herbs and spices, and traditional aperitif wines are made in a similar way.

It is common to divide fortified wines into two classes—the dry wines, which are usually served before meals, and the sweet ones, which traditionally make their appearance after dinner. In practice, however, this division has too many exceptions. Many people enjoy a sweet sherry before a meal, the French often drink a sweet port before sitting down to dinner, and both sweet and dry vermouth are often served along with cocktails.

SHERRY

Sherry is perhaps the most versatile of all wines: it can be bone-dry, mellow, or richly sweet; it can be served before or after a meal, or at almost any time of day. Its name derives

261

from the town of Jerez de la Frontera, in the southwest corner of Spain. Until the thirteenth century this part of Spain was under Moorish domination and Jerez was situated along the frontier (*frontera*) between the Moors and the Christians.

Jerez, which is the center of the sherry trade, forms a triangle with the towns of Puerto de Santa María and Sanlúcar de Barrameda, and within this triangle are found the best grape-growing districts for the making of sherry. The best soil, *albariza*, is made up of white chalk, and that district is planted entirely with the Palomino grape. A certain amount of Pedro Ximénez is also planted, and P.X., as it is called, is vinified in a special way to make very sweet wines used in the final blending of some sherries.

Sherry, virtually unique among the world's wines, is made in a rather special way. The juice is fermented into a completely dry wine, with no residual sugar, and is then stored in butts, or barrels, in the *bodegas*—high-ceilinged warehouses—of the various firms. Whereas almost everywhere else barrels of new wine are filled to the top, so that air cannot get to the wine and spoil it, in Jerez the butts are not completely filled, and oxidation is actually encouraged. In the weeks following the vintage, each of the thousands of butts of new wine in a particular cellar develops somewhat differently. Even wines from the same vineyard, stored in adjoining butts, may not evolve into identical wines. In some, a white film of yeast cells, called *flor*, or flower, forms on the surface of the wine, and these are classified as Finos. Others develop very little *flor*, or none, and are classified as Olorosos. Finos and Olorosos are the two basic categories of sherry, which is, in effect, a deliberately oxidized wine. The fuller-bodied and less delicate Olorosos are fortified with brandy to 18 percent, and will be used primarily to make sweet Cream Sherries. Finos are fortified to only 15.5 percent, so that the *flor*, which gives these wines their individuality, will not be destroyed. In time, Finos are classified once again: some remain Finos; others, slightly richer and fuller, become Amontillados.

Although it is true that two butts of sherry from the same vineyard may turn out somewhat differently, their evolution is not quite as mysterious and unpredictable as it is sometimes made out to be. The shippers know, for example, that certain vineyards traditionally produce Finos, others Olorosos; that wines from severely pruned vines are likely to turn into Finos; and that younger vines will probably produce Olorosos. After all, if a particular shipper sells mostly Fino, he cannot just put new wine into barrels and hope for the best. His experience enables him to produce Finos, just as a shipper who specializes in Cream Sherry is able to make wines that will develop into Olorosos.

As Finos and Olorosos continue to age, the exact style of each butt of wine is determined, and it is earmarked to become part of a particular *solera* within the firm's *bodegas*. It is the *solera* system of blending and aging, unique to sherry, that is at the heart of the production of this wine. A *solera* can be visualized as several tiers of barrels, all containing wines similar in style, with the oldest wines at the bottom. When some of the wine from each barrel in the bottom row is drawn off to be blended, bottled, and shipped, the loss is made up with wines from the second tier, which contains the next-oldest wines. These, in turn, are replaced with wines from the third tier, and so on. At each level, the older wine already in the barrel is said to "educate" the younger wine that is added. Although the entire collection of barrels is usually referred to as a *solera*, technically speaking, it is the barrels containing the oldest wines that are the *solera;* each tier that feeds the *solera* is called a *criadera*, or nursery; and the youngest *criadera* is replenished from an *añada*, a wine only one or two years old. Because the amount of wine withdrawn from a *solera* is limited to, say, no more than a third of a barrel at one time, the *solera* system enables the shipping firms of Jerez to maintain a continuity of style for each of their sherries, year after year. In practice, a *solera* system is more varied and complex than this simple visualization. A Fino *solera* may consist of four tiers, or scales; an Oloroso of seven or eight. Sometimes, the youngest *criadera* in an Oloroso *solera* may be replenished not by a young *añada*, but by the oldest wine in another *solera*, so that the wine that is bottled may have passed through twelve or fourteen scales. Since each scale in a *solera* may consist of two or three hundred barrels, they are not actually piled one on top of another, and may even be scattered throughout several cellars.

The amount of wine drawn off from a *solera* differs depending on the style of wine. One-third of a Fino *solera* may be drawn off four times a year, whereas in an Oloroso *solera* only a quarter may be withdrawn twice a year. Also, to make up a particular sherry, a shipper will often combine wines from several *soleras*, so that the final blend consists of wines of slightly different styles. Since sherry is produced by a system of fractional blending that includes a number of successive vintages, and wines from many vineyards, sherry is never vintage-dated, nor is it identified by the name of an individual vineyard.

Although sherries are classified as Finos and Olorosos, they are marketed in four main categories. A Manzanilla is a Fino that has been matured in the seacoast village of Sanlúcar de Barrameda, fifteen miles from Jerez. This bone-dry wine acquires a distinctive tang, sometimes attributed to the salt air, but more likely the result of higher humidity, which produces a richer *flor*. Curiously enough, if a Manzanilla is shipped back in barrel to Jerez, it gradually loses its special taste. A Fino is a dry sherry, but many shippers do not emphasize this word on their labels, preferring instead to feature such proprietary brand names as La Ina or Tio Pepe. A good Fino, delicate and complex, is a difficult wine to make, and some cheap examples are not even dry. An Amontillado is usually described as nuttier than a Fino, and since Amontillados are often Finos with more barrel age, they tend to be fuller-bodied. The most obvious difference between the two, however, is that the Amontillados shipped here are distinctively sweeter than Finos. It is possible to find a dry Amontillado in Spain, where the best of them are very much admired, but the popular brands available here are all somewhat sweet, even those labeled as dry. As with Finos, the word Amontillado does not always appear on the labels of these wines. The fourth category of sherry is Cream Sherry, which is almost always made from Olorosos. Although an Oloroso is completely dry as it ages in its *solera*, its bigger body and fuller flavor lends itself to transformation into a Cream Sherry by the addition of specially made sweet wines during the final stages of blending. The sweetness of a Cream Sherry varies from shipper to shipper, but most contain 7 to 10 percent sugar. Amoroso is still used occasionally on a label to indicate a golden sherry that is between an Amontillado and a Cream Sherry in color and sweetness. Brown Sherry, rarely seen in this country, is even darker and sweeter than a Cream Sherry.

Dry sherries taste best chilled, and it's better to put a bottle of Fino in the refrigerator than to serve it with ice cubes, which dilute its delicate flavor. An open bottle of sherry lasts longer than a table wine because of its higher alcoholic content. Nevertheless, most sherry shippers agree that once opened, a good Fino will begin to lose its character within a week or two.

When buying sherry, it is the name of the shipper that is important rather than that of a village or vineyard. Furthermore, many sherry shippers have individualized certain of their wines by the use of proprietary brand names, some of which are better known than the names of the firms that produce them. Some sherry houses (and their leading brand names) are Croft (Original), Pedro Domecq (La Ina), Duff Gordon (Club Dry), Gonzales Byass (Tio Pepe), Harveys (Bristol Cream), Sandeman (Character, Armada Cream), and Williams & Humbert (Dry Sack).

About one hundred miles northeast of Jerez is the Montilla-Moriles district, whose wines are labeled simply as Montilla. The name Amontillado is derived from Montilla, and these wines are similar in style to sherry. They are made primarily from the Pedro Ximénez grape, which in this region is fermented out until the wines are dry. Montilla has a natural alcohol content of about 16 percent, so Finos may be bottled and shipped without being fortified with brandy.

Wines labeled Sherry are also made in the United States, primarily in California and New York State; in fact, considerably more sherry is made in this country than in Spain. However, most American sherries are made by baking neutral white wines to age them artificially, which is a technique used in Madeira, not in Jerez. Consequently, the drier sherries are often less successful than the Cream Sherries, whose baked taste can be more easily masked by sweetening. A number of American wineries age at least some of their sherries in small barrels, but the traditional *solera* system of blending is not practiced here. Many wineries now use a submerged *flor* process: *flor* yeast is mixed with dry white base wines, the mixture is put into large pressurized tanks in which oxygen circulates, and after one to four weeks, the wine is drawn off the yeast and aged in barrels. There is a difference, however, between wines exposed to *flor* for a short time and those that react with *flor* for many years. Furthermore, many California *flor* wines are later blended with baked wines before bottling. Although sherries produced in the United States generally lack the distinctive nutty quality and complexity of taste typical of Spanish sherry, many of them are soundly made and the best of them are a good value.

PORT

Port is a sweet, red, fortified wine made along a delimited section of the Duoro River in northern Portugal. (White port has also been made for a hundred years, but most of it is used for blending.) Port takes its name from the town of Oporto, at the mouth of the Douro, although the offices and warehouses of the famous port shippers are located across the river in Villa Nova de Gaia. Port has long been popular in Great Britain and was, in fact, specifically developed for the British market, but it has been slow to catch on in this country. Perhaps the image of cheap American port has discouraged consumers from discovering how good authentic port can be, or it may be that our drinking habits don't lend themselves to the appreciation of a sweet red wine that is usually served after a meal.

In 1968, in an effort to distinguish true port from imitations produced in this country, the Portuguese government took the unusual step of declaring that port shipped from Portugal to the United States must be labeled Porto. Although wines bottled in Portugal now carry the phrase Vinho do Porto, many shippers continue to feature Port, rather than Porto, on their labels. In addition, the decree does not apply to wines shipped in bulk to England and bottled there for sale in this country. Despite the ruling, the wine continues to be called port by both shippers and consumers alike.

The red wines of the Douro were known as unexceptional table wines until the early eighteenth century, when political considerations made it cheaper for the English to import wines from Portugal than from France. As more Portuguese wines were exported to England, some shippers began to add brandy to the wines to fortify them for the long voyage, and port as we now know it gradually evolved. Today port continues to be popular in England, but surprisingly enough, France now imports three times as much of this wine as does England. The French drink port before the meal, as an aperitif.

Port is produced along the upper Douro River on steeply terraced vineyards planted with more than a dozen different grape varieties. Today, grapes are crushed by mechanical means, but as recently as twenty-five years ago all the grapes used for port were crushed by foot in large cement troughs, and some firms still use this old-fashioned treading for selected lots of grapes. The purpose of treading is not to squeeze juice from the grapes, which can be done more effectively with a press, but to extract as much color and tannin as possible from the skins in the relatively short time that they are in contact with the fermenting juice. As the grapes are crushed, fermentation begins, converting the sugar in the juice into alcohol. At a certain point, brandy is mixed with the incompletely fermented wine. This sudden dose of alcohol stops the fermentation completely, and the resulting fortified wine contains 5 or 6 percent unfermented grape sugar and about 20 percent alcohol. White port is made in the same way and mostly used for blending with reds, although some is fermented out until it is dry and marketed as an aperitif wine. In the spring, following the vintage, the new wine is transported from *quintas*, or vineyard estates, along the Douro to shippers' cellars, called lodges, in Vila Nova de Gaia. There the wine is aged in wooden casks, called pipes. A pipe of port, the traditional measure in that region, holds the equivalent of a little more than seven hundred bottles.

Young port is a deep red-purple wine, quite fruity and grapy, which has not yet absorbed the brandy with which it was mixed. It is not a harsh or unpleasant wine—its sweetness masks its tannin and alcoholic content—but it is not fine or complex, and has yet to develop its character. Almost all port is wood port, that is, aged for several years in cask before being bottled. (The exception is Vintage Port, which will be discussed further on.) The two basic styles of wood port are Ruby and Tawny. Ruby Port is darker in color, more fruity and vigorous in style. Tawny Port is lighter in color, as its name suggests, generally older, softer, more delicate, and often more complex. This distinction is blurred by the fact that the only requirement of wood ports is that they be aged about three years before being shipped. It takes six or seven years for a young port to develop into a Tawny, and fine Tawnies are aged considerably longer. Aging wines is expensive, of course, and consequently many Tawnies on the market are simply Rubies to which a certain amount of white port has been added to lighten the color and soften the taste. It is by no means unusual for a shipper to market a Ruby and Tawny that are both three years old, the principal difference being that the Tawny contains as much as a third of white port in the final blend. It is a mistake, therefore, to assume that an inexpensive Tawny is necessarily older than a Ruby, even though it is lighter in color. As a matter of fact, the Ruby may well be a more interesting and typical wine, since it retains the distinctive character and body of port, compared to the somewhat diluted and bland taste of a Tawny that contains a lot of white port. An authentic ten- or twenty-year old Tawny, however, can be a very fine example of port, and some connoisseurs even prefer it to Vintage Port. Ruby and Tawny Ports are ready to drink when they are bottled, and do not improve with bottle age.

Although wood ports account for virtually all of the six or seven million cases of port produced annually, the most famous and glamorous wine of the region is undoubtedly Vintage Port. It is a wine made entirely from the grapes of a single harvest and bottled after about two years in wood, so that it matures in bottle rather than in cask. A shipper "declares" a vintage only when he thinks the quality of the wine exceptional enough to warrant it, and this usually occurs only three or four times in a decade. The decision is not made until the second spring after the vintage, in case the second of two consecutive vintages turns out better than the first, and every shipper decides for himself whether or not to declare a vintage. For example, more than thirty shippers made a Vintage Port in 1960, only seven in 1962, about thirty in 1963, twenty-odd in 1966, only five in 1967, about forty in 1970, only five in 1972, nearly thirty in 1975, and about twenty in 1977 and 1980; a number of firms declared the 1982 vintage, others preferred to bottle their 1983s. Even in a year when a shipper declares a vintage, only a very small part of his production, perhaps 5 percent, is set aside to be bottled as Vintage Port. The rest is needed to maintain the quality and style of his wood ports. The total amount of Vintage Port produced in a given year rarely exceeds 200,000 cases, and even in an abundant vintage, few firms are likely to bottle more than twelve or fifteen thousand cases each.

Vintage Port is unquestionably one of the finest wines made, and since it is bottled only in good vintages—unlike, for example, red Bordeaux—it is perhaps the most dependable of all fine wines. Wine ages in bottle much more slowly than in wood, however, and since the wines begin as exceptionally tannic and intense examples of port, most shippers suggest that a Vintage Port needs a minimum of ten or fifteen years to be drinkable. Since Vintage Port throws a heavy deposit as it ages, careful decanting is a necessity. Vintage Port was traditionally bottled in England, because that is where almost all of it is drunk. Since 1974 all Vintage Port must be bottled in Portugal; the 1975s, for example, are all Portuguese bottled. Despite the demands that Vintage Port makes on the patience of its admirers, there has been a resurgence of interest in this wine in the past few years, and a wide selection of recent vintages is now available in many shops in this country.

In addition to Vintage Port, there are two other styles of port on whose labels the word "vintage" may appear. Late Bottled Vintage Ports, known as LBV, are, like Vintage Ports, produced from wines of a single vintage but are bottled only after four to six years in wood. (The year of bottling appears on the label.) Some shippers use the wines of a generally declared vintage year; most use intermediate years. They are meant to combine the character of a Vintage Port with additional barrel age and are, in a manner of speaking, specially selected aged Rubies. A shipper's LBV will be a richer and more intense wine than his Ruby, but more evolved than a Vintage Port of about the same age. They can be drunk when they are bottled, although some shippers say they will continue to improve in bottle for three or four years.

There are also a few bottles to be found labeled Port of the Vintage rather than Vintage Port. These wines have nothing whatever to do with Vintage Port, but are simply old Tawnies from a specific year, often refreshed with younger wines and bottled after many years in wood. (The date of bottling must now appear on the label.) These wines are almost always overpriced, and often misleadingly advertised as if they were Vintage Ports.

Crusted Port is a blend of two or more vintages bottled before the wine has matured. It throws a crust, or deposit, as it ages in bottle, hence its name. Crusted Port has pretty much been replaced by Late Bottled Vintage Port.

Some port shippers whose wines are found in this country (and their best-known proprietary brands) are Cálem, Cockburn (Special Reserve), Croft (Distinction), Delaforce (His Eminence's Choice), Dow (Boardroom), Fonseca (Bin 27), Graham, Harveys (Gold Cap, Directors' Bin), Hoopers, Niepoort, Robertson (Dry Humour), Sandeman (Founders Reserve), Smith Woodehouse, Taylor Fladgate, and Warre (Warrior, Nimrod). Most of these firms also ship Vintage Ports, as do Ferreira, Gould Campbell, Offley Forrester (labeled Offley Boa Vista), Quarles Harris, Rebello Valente, and Quinta do Noval, among others.

California Ports are produced by a great many wineries and vary widely in quality. Most of them are full, fruity, mellow wines that nevertheless lack the subtlety and complexity of the wines from the Douro. There are, however, a few small California wineries that specialize in Port. Ficklin Vineyard, near Madera, has been producing Port from traditional Douro varieties since 1948. Andrew Quady, whose winery is in Madera, has been making limited quantities of vintage-dated Port from Amador County Zinfandel grapes since 1975. The Woodbury Winery in San Rafael, north of San Francisco, whose first vintage-dated Port was made in 1977, uses such varieties as Petite Sirah, Cabernet Sauvignon, Zinfandel, and Pinot Noir. J. W. Morris, in Sonoma County, continues to make vintage-dated and Founders Port along with a number of varietal table wines. Port made in New York State tends to retain more of the native *labrusca* flavor than does New York State Sherry.

MADEIRA

Madeira is a small Portuguese island off the coast of North Africa whose distinctive fortified wines range from fairly dry to very sweet. In colonial times, Madeira was probably the most popular wine in America, and was specially imported by connoisseurs in Boston, New York, and Charleston. Only a small quantity is imported today. The vineyards of Madeira were devastated by two plagues in the second half of the nineteenth century, first the fungus oïdium, then phylloxera, and its production has never regained its former size.

As is the case with port, the fermentation of Madeira was traditionally stopped by the addition of brandy at a point determined by just how sweet the finished wine was meant to be. Although this technique is still occasionally used, most Madeira is now fermented out until it is dry, just like sherry. In the past the fortified wines were then put in rooms called *estufas*, or ovens, and the wines slowly baked for several months. Today, large concrete vats heated by internal pipes are used to bake the wines. The wine must be baked for a minimum of ninety days at a temperature no higher than 122°F. This concentrated aging process is meant to approximate the beneficial effects of a long sea voyage, as it was discovered in the eighteenth century that the voyages to which all cargo was subjected seemed to improve the wines of Madeira.

Madeira has a special pungent taste that comes from the volcanic soil in which the vines are planted, a relatively high acidity, and a distinctive cooked or burned taste that it acquires in the *estufas*. At the time of bottling each lot of wine is sweetened to produce the appropriate style of wine. Sercial is the driest of all Madeiras, Verdelho the next driest; Malmsey is the sweetest, and Bual, or Boal, is medium-sweet. Although these four names are those of specific grape varieties once cultivated on the island, the wines are no longer from the grape with which each is labeled. In fact, only Bual and Sercial are still cultivated in more than token amounts; a variety called Tinta Negra Mole accounts for about 80 percent of Madeira production today. The grape names are now used simply to indicate the relative style and sweetness of each wine. Some shippers also market their wines with proprietary brand names such as Island Dry, Saint John, Duke of Clarence, and Viva. Rainwater Madeira, typically pale in color, is a generic name for a medium-sweet wine. Madeira is among the longest-lived of all wines, and it is still possible to find fifty- or one-hundred-year-old single-vintage Madeiras (as opposed to vintage-dated *solera* wines, which are actually blended from many vintages): good examples are by no means faded, and offer a remarkable tasting experience.

One of the principal shippers on the island is the Madeira Wine Company, which produces and markets such brands as Blandy's, Cossart Gordon, Leacock, and Rutherford & Miles. Other shippers include Barbeito, Borges, Henriques & Henriques, and Justino Henriques.

Marsala is a fortified wine made in Sicily. As is the case with sherry, the wine is completely fermented until it is dry, then later fortified and sweetened. Even dry Marsala is not completely dry. Most firms market not only a sweet Marsala, but specially flavored Marsalas as well, using egg yolks, almonds, oranges, and so forth.

The city of Málaga, situated along the southern coast of Spain, gives its name to a sweet, fortified wine made primarily from Muscatel and Pedro Ximénez grapes. Málaga is rarely encountered here.

VERMOUTH AND APERITIFS

Vermouth, both sweet and dry, is most often used in mixed drinks, but it is also popular as an aperitif, and is usually served with ice and a twist of lemon peel. Vermouth has a wine base, and is fortified, sweetened, and flavored with various herbs, spices, and, increasingly, flavor extracts, according to each firm's secret recipe. Traditionally, Italian vermouth is red and sweet, while French vermouth is pale and dry, but both types are made in each country, and two-thirds of the vermouth consumed here is made in this country. The French town of Chambéry, near the Swiss-Italian border, has given its name to a distinctive pale and dry vermouth.

Anything that is drunk before a meal—sherry, vermouth, white wine, champagne, or even a cocktail—could properly be described as an aperitif, but the term "aperitif wine" usually refers to certain proprietary brands, such as Dubonnet, St. Raphaël, Byrrh, and Lillet. They can be red or white and some are made primarily from *mistelle*; must whose fermentation has been arrested by the addition of alcohol, thus retaining a high proportion of grape sugar. Most aperitifs have a more pronounced and distinctive flavor than vermouth because they are meant to be drunk by themselves, with ice and perhaps a splash of soda water. Quinine or an equivalent flavoring agent is a traditional ingredient that contributes a slightly bitter aftertaste to temper the sweetness of the aperitif.

Pineau des Charentes is an unusual aperitif produced in the Cognac region of France. It is a blend of sweet, unfermented grape juice and young cognac, and is bottled with about 17 percent alcohol.

COGNAC AND
OTHER BRANDIES

Although this book is primarily concerned with wine, a meal at which good wines are served often ends with a glass of brandy, which is, almost always, distilled from wine. The word is derived from *brandewijn*, a Dutch word for burned (distilled) wine. Wherever grapes are grown and fermented into wine, brandy of some kind is also made. The most famous and most highly regarded of all brandies is cognac, which is distilled from wine produced in a specifically delimited area in southwest France, about sixty miles north of Bordeaux. All cognac is brandy, but there is only one brandy that can be called cognac.

It was in the early seventeenth century that the white wines produced in the valley of the Charente River were first distilled to make a *vin brûlé*, presumably to provide an alcoholic beverage for export markets that would be less bulky to ship than wine. The city of Cognac, which lies on the bank of the Charente, gave its name to this brandy in the eighteenth century, and only as recently as a hundred years ago did the various cognac producers first begin to bottle and label their brandy in their own cellars, thus establishing the brand names by which almost all cognac is marketed today.

We have seen how important soil is to the quality and characteristics of various wines, and this is equally true for the wines used to make cognac. There are six clearly defined districts whose wines are permitted to be distilled into cognac. The two most important inner districts are called Grande Champagne and Petite Champagne, but these names bear no relation to the sparkling wines of Champagne. *Champagne* in French means open fields, a distinction made even clearer by the name of the four other districts, three of which refer to *bois*, or woods: Borderies, Fins Bois, Bons Bois, and Bois Ordinaires. These legally delimited areas were established when it was discovered that the wines from each district, when distilled, produced cognacs with marked differences in quality. The very best cognacs come from Grande Champagne and Petite Champagne, which now account for about 40 percent of the total production of cognac.

A cognac labeled Grande Champagne or Grande Fine Champagne has been distilled entirely from wines made from grapes grown in the Grande Champagne district, and this is the highest appellation possible. More familiar is Fine Champagne Cognac, which indicates that the brandy comes from both Grande and Petite Champagne, with at least 50 percent from Grande Champagne. Because of the importance attached to these appellations, some cognacs are labeled Fine Cognac or Grande Fine Cognac, phrases as meaningless as they are misleading.

There are three grape varieties used to make Charente wines, but it is the Saint-Emilion (also known as the Ugni Blanc, and unrelated to the Bordeaux wine district) that has almost totally replaced the Folle Blanche and the Colombard. The white wine of the Charente is thin and sour, usually 7 to 10 percent alcohol, and unattractive to drink. Oddly enough, the wine produced in Grande Champagne from its predominantly chalky soil tastes even worse than the rest, and yet it produces the finest cognac. There are no quantity limits per acre to the wines produced in the Charente, but the growers must vinify their wines carefully, because any off-taste or defect in the wine will show up even more strongly in the distilled brandy. Much of the annual wine crop is sold directly to big distilling houses that are owned by or under contract to the biggest cognac shippers, but thousands of small growers also distill their own cognac, to be sold later to the shippers.

Once the wine has been made, distillation takes place in old-fashioned pot stills, which resemble giant copper kettles, and proceeds for several months on a twenty-four-hour schedule. Cognac is unusual in that it is doubly distilled. The first distillation produces a liquid of about 60 proof (or 30 percent alcohol), called *brouillis*. This is redistilled to make the raw cognac, known as the *bonne chauffe*, which comes out of the still at 140 proof. It takes about ten barrels of wine to make a barrel of cognac. Distillation is deliberately slow, so that the characteristics of the wine are imparted to the brandy. The congeners, or flavoring elements, retained during distillation give cognac its particular character, whereas a fast, high-proof distillation would result in a relatively flavorless alcohol.

The new cognac, which is colorless, is then aged in oak barrels. These barrels were traditionally made of Limousin oak, but the forest of Limousin can no longer supply all the needs of the cognac shippers. Today, about half the barrels in the cellars of Cognac are made of Tronçais oak, from a forest about two hundred miles away. It is the interaction between oak and brandy, as well as the continual oxidation that takes place through the porous wood, that gives cognac its superb and distinctive flavor. The basic elements are present in embryonic form in the new cognac, but it is barrel-aging (during which the brandy also picks up color and tannin from the oak) that refines a harsh distillate into an inimitable beverage. Cognac, like all brandies, ages only as long as it remains in wood, and undergoes no further development once it is bottled. It is not the vintage that matters, as with wine, but the number of years spent in wood.

Aging is expensive, however, not only because the nearly one million barrels of cognac lying in the warehouses of the big shippers and in small cellars throughout the countryside represent an enormous capital outlay, but also because cognac evaporates as it ages, at the rate of about 2 percent a year (the equivalent of nearly twenty million bottles at 80 proof.) This explains not only why fine cognac is expensive, but also why most cognacs on the market are considerably younger than consumers imagine.

The finest cognacs will continue to improve in barrel for about forty years, after which there is a danger that they will dry out and take on a woody or stalky flavor. Very old cognacs are therefore stored in glass demijohns or in old barrels that will not alter the brandy's flavor. Cognacs from lesser districts, on the other hand, will mature and mellow for only a few years, at which time they are already quite pleasant. They can naturally be improved by being combined with older cognacs from other districts, and it is at this point that the blender's skill comes into play. Apart from cognacs that may have been distilled especially for them, all the cognac houses constantly buy young cognacs from the thousands of grower-distillers in the region. Tremendous stocks of different cognacs of various ages must be maintained by the shippers in order to make up their respective house styles on a continuous basis.

As cognac ages, its alcoholic content diminishes slowly, but it is obviously not possible to age every cognac until it arrives at a marketable strength—usually 80 proof—and the shippers must therefore add distilled or deionized water to their final blends to achieve the desired proof.

Note that color is irrelevant as an indication of the age or quality of a cognac: a cognac aged in new wood for only two or three years may be darker than one aged in old wood for ten, and it's common practice at most firms to adjust the color with caramel to ensure continuity from one shipment to the next.

There are a number of markings—stars, initials, and phrases—that traditionally appear on cognac labels, and some of these are more meaningful than others. Most of the cognacs marketed here fall into two basic categories—those labeled Three Star, Five Star, VS, or VSP, and those labeled VSOP (Very Superior Old Pale). The number of stars on a bottle of cognac is completely meaningless, except to place the brandy in the youngest age category. By French law a cognac must be aged at least eighteen months, but our federal laws stipulate that all brandy must be at least two years old. Because stars have no legal meaning, and because so many other brandies have now adopted the star system that originated in Cognac, many shippers dropped this designation from their labels and introduced proprietary brand names such as Régal, Célébration, and Gold-Leaf. Today, most shippers have replaced stars and proprietary names with the initials VS or VSP, but neither of these designations has any particular significance with respect to the age of the cognac.

VSOP, however, does have a special meaning: any cognac so labeled must be at least four years old. Clearly, the increasing use of the initials VS and VSP is an attempt not only to get away from the meaningless star system, but also to blur the distinction between younger cognacs, which account for perhaps 80 percent of sales, and the VSOPs. Fantastic claims to the contrary, it's safe to say that virtually all VSOPs consist primarily of four- or five-year-old cognacs, with very small amounts of older reserves added to the blend to enrich it.

A cognac labeled Napoléon—the next higher step in quality— must be at least six years old, as must one labeled Extra or XO. Six years is the maximum age that is officially controlled by the Cognac Bureau (it was five until 1978). Consequently, the actual age of older cognacs is determined by each shipper— one firm's Napoléon may be only six years old, another's fifteen years or more; the same applies to Extra or XO. Some shippers market their oldest cognacs with these designations, others use such proprietary names as Cordon Bleu, Triomphe, Très Vénérable, and Paradis. Anyone who has occasion to compare some of the more expensive cognacs—at a well-stocked bar, for example—will discover not only that they are noticeably older and finer than the VSOPs, but that each shipper has developed an individual style that brandy connoisseurs can distinguish and appreciate.

Finally, a word about Napoléon cognacs that supposedly date from the days of the emperor. Even if you came across an authentic bottle dated, say, 1812, you would have no way of knowing how long the brandy had spent in wood. If the cognac had been bottled in 1813, it would simply be a one-year-old cognac, for once in bottle brandies no longer improve. As it happens, bottles of 1811 Napoléon Cognac regularly show up at London auctions. Some experts believe that they were bottled at the turn of the century, and they have the heavy, somewhat caramelized taste that was preferred eighty years ago. No one really believes that they have anything to do with 1811 or with Napoléon.

Cognac is most often served in special brandy glasses, which are available in a variety of sizes. It is traditional to cup the bowl with your palm, so that the applied warmth releases the brandy's bouquet. For this reason very small and very big glasses are less comfortable than those with a bowl whose size is somewhere between that of a tangerine and an apple. Good cognac is noted for its complex and refined bouquet, and in fact brandy glasses are also known as snifters. A professional cognac taster actually relies more on his nose than on his palate when buying young cognacs or making a final blend, and if you pause a moment to inhale cognac before tasting it, you'll be surprised at how much this will tell you about its style and quality.

The best-known cognac firms, listed alphabetically, are:

Bisquit	Hine
Camus	Martell
Courvoisier	Monnet
Delamain	Otard
Denis-Mounié	Polignac
Gaston de Lagrange	Rémy Martin
Hennessy	Salignac

Cognac may be the most famous of all brandies, but there are quite a few others that serve admirably to round out a meal. After cognac, the best-known of all French brandies is Armagnac, which is somewhat richer and fuller in taste than cognac. If it lacks the finesse and distinction of cognac at its very best, Armagnac nevertheless offers good value for those who enjoy its more direct taste: Armagnac of a given age is likely to be less expensive than a cognac of equal age.

Armagnac is produced in the region of Gascony, in a delimited area situated within a triangle formed by Bordeaux, Toulouse, and Biarritz. First made in the fifteenth century, it predates cognac by nearly two hundred years. But unlike the Cognac region, which is about 120 miles to the north, the Armagnac region is a relatively inaccessible place, which is one reason that its brandy is still unfamiliar to many consumers. Almost all of the fifty thousand acres of vineyards whose wines can be distilled into Armagnac are situated in the two districts of Bas-Armagnac and Tenarèze. The former is considered the best source of fine brandies, and its name sometimes appears on a label. A third district, Haut-Armagnac, is less well thought of, but virtually no Armagnac is currently produced there.

A number of grape varieties, including Ugni Blanc, Folle Blanche, Colombard, and Baco 22A, a French-American hybrid, are planted in the Armagnac region. As in Cognac, the wine is thin, acid, and low in alcohol. The traditional difference between the two brandies has been in the way each is distilled. In Armagnac, wine is transformed into brandy by a continuous still—the wine goes in at one end, the colorless brandy trickles out at the other at 104 to 112 proof. (Cognac is twice-distilled and emerges at 140 proof.) The higher the proof, the fewer flavoring elements, known as congeners, are found in the distillate. That's why Armagnac has more flavor than cognac, which is, in turn, characterized by more finesse.

Not so many years ago, many small farmers in this region

had barrels of old Armagnac aging in their cellars or behind the barn. These farmers were able to produce brandy, despite their lack of facilities, because it was the custom for portable stills to be carried throughout the region from November through the following April, transforming wine into Armagnac. These portable stills, which resemble small locomotives, are less frequently seen today, and about a quarter of the region's production now comes from cooperative cellars.

To accommodate certain Common Market requirements, new regulations were introduced in 1972 that permit Armagnac producers to distill as high as 144 proof. Those regulations also permit the use of the traditional cognac pot still to produce Armagnac, and a few firms, notably Janneau and Samalens, now use both the continuous still and the pot still. The advantage of the pot still is that it produces a lighter and more refined brandy that matures more quickly in wood and is therefore useful for less expensive blends of younger Armagnacs.

Armagnac is aged in barrels made of the local Monlezun oak and, increasingly, in Limousin and Tronçais oak as well. Like cognac, Armagnac shipped to this country must be aged a minimum of two years. Those labeled VO, VSOP, or Réserve must be aged no less than four years; and five years in oak is the minimum for Armagnacs labeled Napoléon, Extra, Hors d'Age, or Vieille Réserve.

Armagnac producers have one important advantage over Cognac producers—they are permitted to market vintage-dated brandies. This privilege has often been abused in the past, and it's a rare restaurant in France that does not have a bottle of "1893" Armagnac for sale. Nevertheless, authentic examples of vintage-dated Armagnacs do exist, and are worth seeking out.

Many Armagnacs are marketed in the distinctive, flat-sided *basquaise* bottle. Well-known names include Marquis de Caussade, Marquis de Montesquiou, Samalens, Janneau, Sempé, Larressingle, Clès des Ducs, de Montal, and Loubère.

A brandy that provokes strong feelings pro and con is marc (pronounced *mar*), which is also produced in Italy as grappa. Marc itself, called pomace in America, is the residue of skins, pits, and stalks from which wine has been pressed out. Water is added to the marc, which still contains enough sugar so that fermentation takes place, and the low-alcohol result is then distilled to produce a very pungent and distinctive brandy. The best-known marc is Marc de Bourgogne, although the brandy is also produced in Champagne, the Rhône Valley, and Alsace, where an unusual Marc de Gewürztraminer is made. Marc, which has a strawlike bouquet and somewhat leathery taste, is occasionally made from pressings of an individual vineyard and so labeled, such as Marc de Chambertin. By comparison, the grappa of Italy is colorless and is not usually aged in wood. Consequently, it is likely to be more pungent and less mellow than the best French marc.

Brandies from France, labeled simply French Brandy, are widely available here, but they are the cheapest and least interesting group of all. All French brandy is purchased by the shippers from the French government, which distills a certain amount of cheap wine each year. Despite this anonymity of origin, many French brandy labels bear such designations as Napoléon, VSOP, Ten Star, and Grande Réserve, none of which has any legal meaning at all. In fact, all of the leading brands available here are shipped in bulk and bottled in this country.

Spanish brandies, noted for their fullness rather than their finesse, are sweet compared to the brandies of France, and this mellowness must certainly contribute to their popularity here. Spanish brandies are distilled throughout that country from a number of different, and inexpensive, wines, and many of them are then blended and bottled in Jerez because a number of sherry firms are major brandy producers as well. Fundador of Pedro Domecq is the best-known brand.

Asbach Uralt is the best-seller here among German imports; it is a dry, delicate, and attractive brandy in the French style.

The United States produces two-thirds of the brandy consumed in this country, and virtually all of it comes from California. California brandies are very slightly sweetened, but they also have a distinctive, spicy, wood-fruit flavor that gives them a complexity of taste lacking in brandies that are merely sweet. California brandy is made primarily from raisin and table grapes, and the wines are distilled at 160 to 170 proof, producing a brandy that is relatively light, clean, and fairly neutral and does not require much aging. California brandies are inexpensive, and many of them are appealing, but they are often marketed as an alternative to whiskey and other traditional spirits in mixed drinks and highballs, rather than as a brandy to be drunk from a snifter. The Christian Brothers and the E&J label of Gallo are the leading brands. RMS Vineyards is a joint venture created in the Napa Valley by the Rémy Martin Cognac firm and Schramsberg Vineyards to produce a California brandy distilled in the traditional cognac pot still, known as the *alambic charentais*; it is labeled California Alambic Brandy.

There are also a few well-known brandies that are made from fruits other than grapes. The most unusual, often the most expensive, and to some palates the finest of all brandies are those distilled from wild fruits in Alsace, Switzerland, and the Black Forest of Germany. *Kirsch* (wild cherry), *framboise* (wild raspberry), *mirabelle* (yellow plum), *quetsch* (purple plum), and *poire* (pear) are the best known, and because they are colorless, they are known generically as *alcools blancs*, or white alcohols. Actually, all distillates are colorless when they come from the still, but most are aged in wood and are pale brown when bottled. (Vodka and gin are obvious exceptions.)

The *alcools blancs* are made in a special way. In the case of pears, cherries, and plums, clean, ripe fruit is crushed and allowed to ferment. The mash, called *marmalade*, is then distilled. Berries have too little sugar to ferment easily, so they are macerated for a month in high-proof alcohol distilled from wine, and that alcohol is then redistilled. Whatever process is used, the result is a colorless distillate that concentrates the essence of the fruit. A great deal of fruit is needed to produce a bottle of brandy—25 to 35 pounds of Williams pears for a bottle of *poire*, up to 30 pounds of raspberries for a bottle of *framboise*—which is one reason these brandies are so expensive.

Although the labels of most fruit brandies sold here state that the brandy "is a finished product when it leaves the still and does not require mellowing in oak to perfect its quality," the fact is that many fruit brandies are aged for two or three years, sometimes even longer. The aging takes place in glass demijohns or, increasingly, in glass-lined tanks so that the brandies do not acquire any color. The bouquet developes finesse through subtle oxidation without taking on color. It is the delicate and fragrant bouquet of these white alcohols, each reminiscent of the original fruit in its ripe and undistilled state, that makes the best of these brandies so remarkable and so different from grape brandies.

Fruit brandies are distilled at about 140 proof and sold at about 90 proof: for all their haunting bouquet they are by no means bland. These *alcools blancs*, which are completely dry, bear no relation to various fruit-flavored brandies, such as blackberry brandy or apricot brandy, which are made in an entirely different way, appropriately colored, and quite sweet.

Another famous fruit brandy is Calvados, made from apples in France's Normandy region. The name dates back, indirectly, to 1588 and the Spanish Armada, one of whose ships, El Calvador, ran aground on the Normandy coast. An area along the coast became known by a corruption of that name, Calvados, and in the nineteenth century the name also began to be used for the apple brandy that had been distilled in the Normandy region since the sixteenth century.

The apple harvest takes place in the last three months of the year. The appellation laws recognize over a hundred varieties of apples as acceptable for Calvados, although about a dozen— none of them eating apples—account for most of the total harvested. The apples are grated, crushed, and pressed; the resulting juice is then left to ferment for at least a month. Cider for distillation usually contains about 5 or 6 percent alcohol—it is dry, high in acid, cloudy, and disagreeable to drink. The fermented cider is then distilled and emerges colorless from the still at 140 proof (70 percent alcohol).

There are two methods of distillation permitted in the eleven Normandy districts that produce Calvados. In ten of them, the brandy is produced in a continuous still and is usually labeled simply *Appellation Réglementée*, without the name of the specific district from which it comes, such as Contentin, l'Avranchin, Domfrontais, Pays de la Risle, and so on. Calvados from the Pays d'Auge district, a delimited area south of Deauville and Honfleur, between Rouen and Caen, is twice distilled in a traditional pot still similar to that used in the Cognac region. It is the only Calvados district entitled to *Appellation Contrôlée* status, and Appellation Pays d'Auge Contrôlée will always appear on the label.

Calvados from the Pays d'Auge—which accounts for only 25 percent of all Calvados, but for most of what is shipped to the United States—is considered the finest apple brandy, partly because of the way it is distilled, partly because of the soil and the particular mix of apples grown there. A well-made Calvados from outside the Pays d'Auge district may be more appley when young, and quite appealing, but a Pays d'Auge, even when young, already displays more richness and depth. As the brandies age in cask, the Pays d'Auge will acquire more complexity and length of flavor than one from outside the district, which will almost always remain relatively simple.

As is the case for cognac and Armagnac, there are minimum age requirements for Calvados, and these are reflected in the rather extensive list of letters and phrases that may appear on labels. Any Calvados shipped here must be aged at least two years in barrel; those labeled Vieux or Réserve must be aged a minimum of three years; VO or Vieille Réserve, four years; VSOP, five years; and Extra, Napoléon, Hors d'Age, and Age Inconnu, six years. In practice some firms use one or more of these designations for their different bottlings, others use none, preferring such undefined terms as *fine, grand fine*, Prestige and so on.

Leading Calvados producers whose brandy can be found here are Boulard and Busnel; other labels include those of Bizouard, Ducs de Normandie, La Pommeraie, Montgommery, and Père Magloire.

THE ENJOYMENT
OF WINE

STARTING A CELLAR

In the English translation of a French guide to wine, the 1945 Bordeaux vintage is described as "exceptionally great . . . full and round . . . wines to lay down with." Not all of us are prepared to look after our wines quite so conscientiously, but anyone who enjoys wine recognizes the advantages of setting aside at least some storage space in an apartment or a house.

Among the reasons for maintaining a cellar, even if it consists of only half a dozen bottles, are that you needn't make a trip to the store whenever you want a glass of wine, and you are spared the awkwardness of running out of wine halfway through a meal with guests. Then there's the chance to save money: if you have storage space you can take advantage of wine sales, and you can also benefit from the discount offered by most stores when you buy a full case of twelve bottles. If you have a larger collection you can easily arrange an interesting comparison when friends stop by—two different California Zinfandels, the wines of two adjoining vineyards in Bordeaux, or two vintages from the same producer. Also, fine red wines that have thrown a deposit may need a few days' rest if they have been badly shaken up. If such bottles are already resting in your cellar, you'll be sure of getting the most they have to offer. Finally, don't underestimate the real pleasure of being able to choose a wine from your own collection—red, white, or rosé—that suits your dinner and your mood.

The wine cellar itself can be as simple as a whiskey carton turned on its side, and the guides to maintaining a store of wines are simple and logical. The first rule, of course, is to lay a wine bottle on its side, so that the cork is kept moist and expanded, preventing air from entering the bottle. Ideally, wines should be kept at a constant cool temperature, away from daylight and vibrations. To keep wines in a home or apartment, you should remember that evenness of temperature is at least as important as the temperature itself, within limitations, because constant fluctuations of heat and cold will hasten a wine's evolution and eventual decline. Therefore, keep wines away from boiler rooms, steam pipes, or kitchen ovens. Don't store wines in a place where they will be subject to a lot of knocking about, such as the closet where the brooms and vacuum cleaner are kept. And keep wines away from direct exposure to sunlight, which seems to decompose them in a short time (whether in your house or in a retailer's window). If the temperature of your storage area stays much above 70°, you should limit yourself to no more than a year's supply of wines or, in the case of sturdy reds, two years. With these general rules in mind, you should be able to figure out a good place to store a few bottles.

If you intend to put aside good bottles for more than two years, your storage space must be temperature-controlled and maintained at a steady 55° to 60°. An air-cooled closet, an air-conditioned basement or storage room, a prefabricated walk-in cellar, or, in some cities, public warehousing are some possibilities. Another is to purchase one of the refrigerated units that function as a self-contained cellar. These wine vaults, which can accommodate anywhere from a few dozen up to several hundred bottles, are fairly expensive, but they are useful to store the finest bottles in a collection—those you expect to keep for several years. If the initial cost of an ideal cellar seems expensive, you may be able to get two or three wine-minded friends to share the expenses and the space.

Wine racks are available from most department stores and, in many states, from liquor stores. Many of these racks are designed to be stacked, and those are the ones you should look for, so that you can expand the capacity of your cellar. Never store fine red wines in racks in which the bottles lie at a downward angle, neck lowest. The cork will be kept moistened, but any sediment present in such wines will slide toward the cork and may adhere to it. You will thus drink cloudy wine from your first glass. It's also a good idea to store wine bottles with their labels facing up. This makes it easier to locate any bottle without having to twist it around, and, in the case of red wines with sediment, you'll know that the deposit always lies along the side opposite the label.

As you determine the wines you like most, you will want to increase the size of your collection. Before buying a substantial amount of wine, however, you should adopt a buying strategy that conforms to the way you actually consume wine. This means noting, for example, the ratio of fine wines to moderately priced ones; whether you serve more red or white wine; whether you usually serve a wine before dinner; and whether you tend to have larger dinner parties, at which many bottles of one or two wines are served, or small wine dinners, at which one bottle each of several wines are compared.

There are sound reasons for buying wines to be consumed in the future. Certain wines, such as red Bordeaux and Vintage Port, are usually least expensive when they first appear on the market, and then gradually increase in price. Other wines, such as Burgundies, the best of California, and a number of fine Italian wines, are often produced in such limited quantities that they disappear from retail shelves within a few months or a year. Those who purchase such wines early will have the satisfaction of knowing that their cellars include bottles that have become much more expensive or that are virtually unobtainable.

A certain amount is written about wine as a financial investment. To begin with, only long-lived wines with established reputations are appropriate for this purpose, which limits your purchases to the finest red wines in the best vintages. Such wines will almost certainly increase in value over the years, but whether that appreciation will be greater than what can be achieved by investing your capital in other ways is not certain. Furthermore, it's illegal for a consumer to resell wine without the necessary licenses, which most people find complicated and impractical to obtain. And even if you can find a retailer willing to buy your wines, you will not get the current market price, since he must allow for his profit margin. The best way to resell your wines is at one of the wine auctions that now take place in this country on a regular basis. Unless you are prepared to follow the wine market carefully, however, it may be wiser to think of your wine purchases as an investment in future pleasure, rather than as a way of making a profit.

Buying and drinking wine is easy. The one onerous task connected with a varied collection of wines is to maintain an inventory. Even a collection of only twenty randomly chosen bottles almost always includes four or five that are past their prime. A cellar full of wine will invariably include quite a few that should be drunk up, and without an inventory they are likely to be forgotten for months at a time. Also, if you keep a record of your wines, you are less likely to overlook special bottles when the appropriate occasion arises; you'll be able to match specific bottles with the guests who'll enjoy them most; and you can more easily plan a wine evening at which a number of carefully chosen bottles will be served.

An inventory can be kept in a notebook, on cards, or even on a home computer. The simplest method is to ask for legible invoices whenever you buy wines, make photocopies of the invoices so they are all on a standard page size, and keep the sheets together as a "cellar book" in which you can make appropriate comments in the margins as you consume the wines.

SERVING WINES

Serving wine—or more specifically, drinking wine—is certainly not very complicated and can be briefly summarized: chill white wines and rosés; serve red wines at cool room temperature; use large, stemmed glasses that are slightly curved in at the top, and fill them only halfway. This covers the subject in a general way and gets you started as a wine drinker. There is so much conversation and snobbism about the proper way to drink wines, however, that it might be useful to describe the various steps in serving a wine. What follows is not meant to discourage anyone by its attention to detail, but rather to suggest, for reference, the most logical way to get a wine from the cellar into your glass. The degree of special effort to be made will depend on the wine and the occasion: a sandwich doesn't require special presentation, nor is an elaborately prepared dish shown to best advantage on paper plates.

Temperature

Red wines are supposed to be served at room temperature, which is to say, not at the cooler temperature of the ideal cellar. Because few of us have real cellars, the bottle has presumably been lying in a closet or in a rack along the wall, so the wine is already at room temperature. Remember that the concept of serving wines at room temperature originated before the day of central heating. Actually, red wines often taste dull, flat, and alcoholic if served too warm, much above 70°, say, no matter what the temperature of the room is. In the summer, it's advisable to cool down a light red wine (Beaujolais, California Burgundy, Valpolicella) by putting it in the refrigerator for an hour or so. This will give the wine an agreeable freshness and actually seems to improve its flavor. A complex red wine, however, should never be chilled: the wine will be numbed and the puckerish taste of tannin will become more pronounced.

Since almost all whites and rosés are less complex than most reds, their basic appeal has more to do with their refreshing qualities than with nuances of taste and texture. Such wines are more enjoyable and thirst-quenching when properly chilled, just as water, juice, and soft drinks are considered more appealing served cold or cool than at room temperature. Two or three hours in the refrigerator will do the job. If you want to chill a bottle of white wine or rosé on short notice, or need a second bottle to serve with a dinner in progress, empty one or two ice trays into a tall pot, fill it with water, and put in the bottle. It should be cool in fifteen or twenty minutes. The trouble with most wine coolers and ice buckets is that they are too shallow and chill only half the bottle. Chilling a wine in ice and water is actually quicker than putting the bottle in the freezer; and if you forget about a bottle in the freezer, it may be frozen by the time you remember to take it out. The colder a wine is, the harder it is to taste, and some people use the trick of overchilling a poor bottle of white wine to mask its defects. For the same reason, a fine bottle of white wine should not be chilled too much, or you will deaden the qualities for which you have paid.

Corkscrews

A corkscrew is really the only piece of equipment that a wine drinker needs, and as it will last for years, it pays to

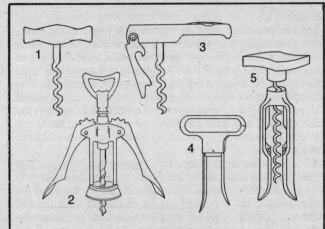

CORKSCREWS

A good corkscrew should have a bore at least two inches long with smooth edges, so that it can completely penetrate a long cork without crumbling it. The bore should also be in the form of a real coil, rather than having an awllike solid core: a corkscrew must be able to grip an old cork, not drill a hole in it. The simplest corkscrew (1) may require some awkward tugging; a corkscrew with leverage (such as 2) is more convenient. This model is popular, easy to use, and usually effective, but note that it does not have a true coil, nor is the bore long enough to penetrate long corks. The folding corkscrew (3), which usually has a long bore in the form of a true coil, is favored by waiters because it can be carried in a pocket, has a knife with which to cut the capsule, and has good leverage. The two prongs of this popular corkpuller (4) are inserted between the cork and the neck of the bottle, and the cork is then twisted out. The very effective Screwpull (5) has a long bore in the form of a true coil that is coated with an antifriction substance for easy insertion. As the handle is twisted continuously in one direction, the cork climbs the bore without having to be pulled out.

look for a good one. In the first place, the screw part, called the bore, should be at least two inches long. Because good wines are long-lived, they are bottled with long, strong corks, and a poor corkscrew will often break the cork of an expensive bottle of wine. Second, the bore should be in the form of a true coil, not a wiggly line. A coil will get a real grip even on an old cork, whereas a wiggly line will just bore a hole in it. Finally, get a corkscrew that gives you leverage. A simple T-shaped corkscrew, even with an excellent bore, requires too much tugging, and you will find yourself gripping the bottle between your feet or your knees, which can lead to messy accidents.

To open a bottle of wine, first remove the lead foil that covers the cork and part of the neck. Because lead foil may impart an unpleasant taste, cut it off well below the lip of the bottle, so that the wine will not be in contact with the foil when it is poured. Wipe off the top of the cork and insert the corkscrew into the center of the cork. Remember to pull the cork gently, because if you give it a sharp tug, the vacuum that is momentarily created between the wine and the rising cork may cause some wine to splash out of the bottle.

If you break the cork—and this occasionally happens even with a bottle of sound wine—reinsert the corkscrew at an angle to get a grip on the remaining piece. If the cork crumbles, you can simply strain the wine into another container, or directly into wine glasses, through a clean tea strainer.

Incidentally, you should never wrap a wine bottle in a napkin: it's considered bad manners not to let your guests see what is being poured into their glasses. If you're worried that a few drops of wine may spill onto the tablecloth, you can tie a small napkin around the neck of the bottle.

Breathing

Most wine drinkers believe that a red wine should be uncorked half an hour or an hour before it is to be served because this exposure to air, called breathing, will develop the wine's bouquet and soften the tannic harshness of a young wine. A number of enologists have tested this theory and feel that the surface of wine exposed to air in the neck of the bottle is too small to have any effect on the taste of the wine, even after several hours. It seems reasonable to assume that if exposure to air is beneficial to a red wine, a more effective way of letting a wine breathe would be either to pour it into a carafe or to pour it into large glasses fifteen or twenty minutes before starting to drink it. Many people assume that letting a wine breathe is synonymous with uncorking it, but there are obviously more efficient ways to achieve whatever improvements aeration may accomplish.

As to the concept of letting wines breathe, there are a number of professional wine people who believe that unnecessary exposure to air actually diminishes the quality of a wine. Older wines, which are often fragile, will fade in the decanter; younger wines will lose some of their intensity and definition without achieving any improvement in bouquet or flavor. Occasionally you may come across a wine, either red or white, that has an off-odor, and this may be dissipated by swirling the wine in your glass for a few minutes. Also, wines that have experienced several years of bottle age may require a few minutes in the glass for their bouquet and flavor to show themselves. Extended exposure to air, however, may well be an error. One exception to the view that wines should simply be opened and poured is in the case of older red wines that have thrown a deposit. Such wines should always be decanted (as described below) so that the sediment does not spoil one's enjoyment of the wine, but the decanting should take place just before the wine is to be served, which is usually not the same thing as decanting before the start of the meal.

The observation that wines are not improved by being allowed to breathe is a controversial one, but it's one that you can easily test for yourself. Next time you plan to serve two bottles of the same red wine, whether it be a young, vigorous one or an older, mature one, simply decant one bottle an hour ahead of time, and then compare a glass of that wine with one from a bottle that has just been opened. After a few experiments of your own, you can decide whether or not you prefer the taste of wines that have been allowed to breathe.

Decanting

Decanting red wines may seem complicated or affected, but it's very simple and very useful. The sediment that red wines develop after ten years or so, although harmless, is also distracting when it appears in the last two or three glasses that are poured. Decanting a wine, which simply involves transferring it from its original bottle to another container, permits you to serve a wine that is completely brilliant and unclouded to the very end, and at the sacrifice of only an ounce or two of wine. First, you must stand the bottle up for an hour or two to allow all the sediment to fall to the bottom. Your decanter can be any clean container, whether it's a crystal wine decanter, an inexpensive carafe, or a glass pitcher. Hold the decanter firmly (remember, it will soon contain a full bottle of wine) and transfer the wine slowly in one continuous motion—otherwise the sediment will wash back and forth. Traditionally, the shoulder of the wine bottle is held over a candle, so that you can see when sediment begins to approach the neck of the bottle and can stop pouring at that moment. Because we now have electricity and because the heat of a candle is not going to do an old wine any good, you may find it easier to use a flashlight standing on end.

If you are worried about decanting an expensive bottle of wine, decant the very next wine you drink, whatever it is, just to get the hang of it. Decanting is really the only way to get your money's worth out of older wines, when you can afford them. A decanter of wine on a dining table is also a most attractive and appropriate sight and enhances the enjoyment of wine. If you're concerned that a good wine will go unnoticed because it's unlabeled, you should know that it's customary to put the empty bottle alongside the decanter, so that your guests will know what they're drinking.

There is one other point about decanting, which may seem finicky, but remember, you've got an old, expensive bottle, and you want to get the most out of it. Because these bottles don't come our way very often, the decanter may be musty or have an off-odor from whatever was in it last. Therefore, you might first pour a few drops of wine into the decanter, swirl, and pour it out. This will not only remove any odor that may be in the decanter, but will give the decanter the bouquet of the wine that's about to go into it.

Wineglasses

Wineglasses have been discussed earlier, in the chapter on tasting, but to summarize: use a stemmed, clear glass with a bowl that is slightly tapered at the top to retain the wine's bouquet, and with a capacity of at least eight ounces. Small glasses seem stingy and don't permit a wine to be swirled to release its bouquet. Glasses with tall stems and colored bowls are sometimes recommended for German wines, but they only

1   2   3   4

WINEGLASSES

The ten-ounce all-purpose wineglass (1) can be used for all table wines, as well as for sherry and port, if need be. It should be filled only about halfway, so that the wine can be swirled to release its bouquet. The first glass is in the traditional Bordeaux shape; the second all-purpose glass (2) is in the traditional Burgundy shape. The classic champagne glass (3) displays bubbles more attractively and releases them more slowly than does the familiar wide-bottomed saucer-shaped glass. The traditional brandy glass (4) may vary in total capacity from about six to twelve ounces: a much smaller or much bigger glass is difficult to cup in one's hand, as is done to release the brandy's bouquet.

hide the delicate golden colors of a fine Moselle or Rhine wine. These glasses originated when winemaking techniques had not been perfected, and a bottled wine was apt to turn cloudy. Colored bowls hid this defect.

Almost every major wine region has its traditional glass, just as it has its traditional bottle, but it is completely unnecessary to have different glasses to serve and enjoy wine properly. When two or more wines are served at a meal, it does dress up the table to use differently shaped glasses, but even here an all-purpose wineglass is perfectly acceptable. If you do use glasses of two different sizes, the smaller one is traditionally used for white wines, the larger for reds. If you serve two reds, the better wine should be poured into the bigger glass.

Leftover Wine

As a general rule, expensive red wines will not keep a second day, and you had better plan to drink them when opened. Their flavor tends to become somewhat dulled and indistinct, at best, and may taste rather sharp and vinegary at worst. Almost all white wines can usually be kept in the refrigerator for several days and are only slightly the worse for wear. Inexpensive red and white wines, especially those from California, will keep much better, perhaps because they are less complex to begin with. It doesn't hurt to keep even red wines, once opened, in the refrigerator, just as you would milk or any other perishable product.

The most useful point to remember about leftover wine is to cork it up as soon as possible. It is excessive exposure to air that spoils a wine, and it doesn't help a half-empty bottle to be left open an extra hour or two.

When you put the cork back into a bottle for any reason, remember not to put the top, which is usually dirty, in contact with the wine. If the bottom of the cork has expanded, once pulled, and cannot be easily replaced, the simplest solution is to slice a quarter inch off the top and then reverse it.

If you do find yourself with leftover wine that has lost some of its flavor but is still drinkable, there are several ways it can be used. You can use red wine to make *sangría*, a cold wine punch, by adding sugar or sugar syrup (which disguises the tartness of leftover or inexpensive wine), a couple of slices of lemon and orange, and ice cubes. When you pour out the *sangría*, add a splash of club soda to give it zest. You

can use white wine to make a spritzer by adding club soda—
it's a refreshing aperitif. And finally you can make your own
wine vinegar. Although wine that's been left out for a while
will be attacked by the vinegar bacteria and will soon taste
sour, it will not actually turn to vinegar by itself. You must
add a quantity of good vinegar to the leftover wine to start the
process properly.

The amount of wine needed for a dinner will naturally vary
depending on the occasion, the menu, and the extent to which
each of your guests enjoys wines. Even assuming that we are
talking about people who normally drink wine with their
meals, the amount of wine you should serve seems to increase
in an almost geometrical proportion to the number of people
present. Two people having a light supper may be happy to
share a half-bottle. Four people can easily drink two bottles,
and six people at a big dinner might comsume four bottles
without any signs of overindulgence, especially if more than
one kind of wine is served. The simplest approach is to have
on hand—unopened—an extra bottle or two of whichever
wine you're serving.

WINE AND FOOD

The question of which wine to serve with which food is one
that seems to intimidate many people. Some respond by
following charts that dictate the right wine for every dish.
Others democratically maintain that any wine goes with any
dish if it pleases you, an attitude that is perfectly acceptable if
everyone shares your taste. The best approach to this subject
is one that combines an experimental attitude with some understanding of the elements that create harmony between a dish
and its accompanying wine.

The three basic tastes found in wine are acid, bitter, and
sweet—with this in mind, it's easier to understand how the
interaction between food and wine can diminish a wine or
enhance it. To take a common example, the vinegar in a
salad dressing will alter a wine's taste by suppressing its
acidity. This is, the intense acidity of vinegar makes it impossible to taste the less intense acid that is actually present in a
wine, and makes the wine taste flabby. When you realize why
the wine's taste is altered, you can see that substituting lemon
juice for vinegar does not solve the problem. The simplest

solution is not to drink wine while eating salad (which is why serving salad and cheese together is unwise if you plan to serve an interesting wine as well), but if the main course is a salad or a dish that features a vinegar-based sauce, then you should choose a wine with high acidity, such as a Sancerre, or a pungent California Sauvignon Blanc.

An example of the way a dish can enhance a wine occurs whenever meat, poultry, or cheese accompanies a young, tannic red wine. Just as the protein in milk combines with, and diminishes, the tannin present in strong tea, so the protein in many foods diminishes the tannic harshness of, say, a young red Bordeaux or California Cabernet Sauvignon, and makes the wine taste softer and more attractive than if it were drunk without food.

Different foods alter the taste and texture of wine in different ways. Anything oily, such as mayonnaise, will emphasize a wine's acidity; a rich cream sauce is likely to rob a wine of some its body and may make a light-bodied wine taste thin, as will fatty dishes, such as pâté; egg yolks, which appear in such popular brunch dishes as eggs Benedict, will dull the taste of any wine; dry wines drunk with sweetened sauces—as in *canard à l'orange*, for example—will taste thin and sharp; and foods prepared with mustard or peppercorns will overwhelm delicate wines. Chocolate tends to overwhelm wine, even the sweet white wines that sometimes accompany chocolate desserts. Spicy foods also overwhelm wine, and beer is a more appropriate accompaniment for curries and highly seasoned Chinese dishes. Generally speaking, red wines do not taste right with fish. The oiliness of most fish seems to give red wines a somewhat bitter and unpleasant taste, and the refreshing quality of a chilled white wine is much more enjoyable. It must be added, however, that a number of restaurateurs and gastronomes in France consider a light-bodied, chilled red wine such as Beaujolais to be a suitable accompaniment to many fish dishes.

Perhaps the most practical rule to follow in choosing wines is, the richer the dish, the richer the wine. Just as there are differences in weight between skim milk and cream, and in texture between, say, poached fish and steak, so there are similar, if less obvious, differences between wines. Whether a wine is light and delicate or rich, robust, and chewy is an important consideration when trying to match it with a specific dish, as is its intensity of taste.

Very often, when choosing a wine to accompany a particular dish, the primary consideration is not the basic ingredient, but how it's prepared. Pasta, chicken, and veal, for example, can be prepared in ways so varied that the most appropriate wine can range from a light, crisp white to a robust red. A plan rack of lamb will show off a subdued, mature red; lamb Provençal, with tomatoes and garlic, is best accompanied by a younger, more vigorous red, just as the balanced Bordeaux or mature Cabernet that accompanies a grilled steak might be replaced by a flavorful Zinfandel if the meat is served with a peppercorn sauce.

Choosing wines to accompany specific dishes or meals means, therefore, focusing on a wine's taste, weight, and texture, rather than its place of origin. In any case, it's always more fun to experiment, guided by your own common sense, than to stick to a few safe but unimaginative rules.

The Sequence of Wine

So far we have been matching a dish with a wine, but for more elaborate dinners you may want to serve more than one wine. There is certainly nothing unusual or particularly fancy about serving two or three wines with a meal, and it can be more fun than serving two or three bottles of the same wine, especially when you have several enthusiastic wine drinkers at the dinner table. There are some traditional guidelines concerning the service of more than one wine: white before red, dry before sweet, young before old.

White before red simply conforms to the normal sequence of food, assuming you are having a light appetizer, or shellfish, or even a cooked fish dish, before a main dish of meat. Also, because red wines are usually richer and more complex than white wines, serving a dry white wine second would diminish its qualities by comparison. Dry before sweet is traditional because sweet foods dull our taste buds (and our appetite) for the more delicate foods to follow (which is why dessert is served last). This rule supersedes the previous one in that a sweet white wine such as Sauternes or a German Auslese is usually served at the end of the meal, and therefore after the red wine.

Young before old is a traditional rule in most wine regions, and indicates that similar wines are usually served in order of increasing age and interest, to avoid an anticlimax. For example, if you are serving two red Bordeaux or two California Cabernet Sauvignons, the older one, presumably more mature and distinguished, will be preceded and, so to speak, introduced by the younger wine. If you are not serving different vintages of the same or similar wines, however, you may find it more appropriate to serve the best wine of the evening with the main course. You can then continue with a completely different wine that need not be older and finer, but that should be interesting enough to follow the previous bottle.

Champagne is often suggested as the one wine (along with rosé, I suppose) that can be served throughout a meal. Although this is a generous gesture and will be greeted with enthusiasm, champagne does not complement all foods, especially full-flavored meats, and its taste may pall at the end of an evening. One alternative is to serve champagne as an aperitif before the meal. Another is to serve it with dessert, but in that case choose an Extra Dry rather than the drier Brut.

Cheese and wine are traditional partners, although a cheese course is not as common here as in Europe. Even restaurants of the highest caliber, for example, will rarely present a cheese tray that is adequate. At a dinner party, a cheese course, which precedes the dessert, gives the host or hostess the opportunity of serving a fine old wine. Although cheese is considered an ideal accompaniment to wine, many cheeses actually overwhelm mature and subtle wines. If you decide to bring out a good bottle at this point, select the cheeses carefully so that they enhance the flavor of a delicate wine. If you prefer rich, creamy cheeses, tangy goat cheeses, or strongly flavored blue cheeses, it may be best to choose a younger and more vigorous wine.

Sweet white wines such as Sauternes, Barsac, and German Auslese are not often served these days, but if they are, they usually accompany dessert. Actually, the sweetness of most desserts diminishes the richness and concentration of flavor that characterizes the best sweet white wines, thereby depriving you of the qualities that make these wines so distinctive. German winemakers, for example, prefer to serve Auslese and Beerenauslese wines by themselves, without food, and in Bordeaux most vineyard proprietors in Sauternes and Barsac prefer not to serve their wines with rich desserts. You might consider serving Sauternes, German Auslese wines, and late harvest Johannisberg Rieslings from California as an alternative to dessert, or perhaps with nothing richer than plain cake or ripe fruit. Because sweet wines are not consumed in large quantities, it's not inappropriate to open just a half-bottle for three or four people at the end of a meal.

Calories and Wine

A myth about wine that is of particular interest to diet-conscious consumers is that white wines have fewer calories than reds. This misconception may stem from the fact that most white wines are light, refreshing, and easy to drink, whereas many reds are sturdy, fuller-flavored, and have a tannic astringency that makes them, for some people, less appealing. Actually, the caloric content of a red or white wine is based on two of its components—alcohol and, if there is any, sugar. Each percent of alcohol in wine accounts for 41 calories per standard 75-centiliter (25.4 ounce) bottle. Thus a bottle of dry wine with 12 percent alcohol contains about 500 calories. (Certain extracts found in all wines contribute another 30 to 45 calories a bottle.) The caloric difference between one dry wine and another depends on its alcohol, not its color—a delicate red Gamay with 11 percent alcohol would have about 120 calories less per bottle than a rich white Chardonnay with 14 percent alcohol. As a matter of fact, the white wines from a given region usually have slightly more alcohol than the reds. Thus a comparison of red and white Bordeaux, Valpolicella and Soave, or Napa Valley Cabernet Sauvignon and Chardonnay would reveal that, based on alcohol content, the white wine in each pair is likely to have slightly more calories than the red.

It would be a mistake, however, to try to calculate the exact caloric content of a wine from the alcohol percentage listed on its label. Federal law permits a producer to put any figure under 14 percent on the label of a table wine, and many use the same phrase, such as "12 percent by volume," for all their wines. On a California label, the figure is allowed to vary by 1.5 percent either way as long as the actual alcohol content does not exceed 14 percent. (If it does, the label must show this.)

But even if the alcohol content is accurately stated, it's not the only element that contributes calories; the other is sugar. One percent of sugar adds about 29 calories to a bottle of wine, so a German Liebfraumilch or a California Chenin Blanc with 2.5 percent of sugar would each have about 73 calories a bottle from sugar alone. And since there are many more white wines that are semisweet than reds, the extra calories contributed by sugar are more often to be found in whites than in reds. In fairness, however, it must be added that a number of appealing, semidry whites are comparatively low in alcohol—10 or 11 percent is not uncommon.

What all this means is that a five-ounce serving of wine— whether a simple jug wine, a fine Bordeaux, a delicate Moselle, or a vintage-dated champagne—probably contains between 100 and 110 calories. (Dessert wines, of course, are significantly higher in calories. A fine Sauternes contains about 160 calories per five-ounce glass, Vintage Port, about 200, and Cream Sherry, 220 or more.)

Cooking with Wine

There is a product called Cooking Wine sold in food stores that are not licensed to sell wine. It contains an excessive amount of salt to render it unpalatable as a beverage, which, of course, makes it unattractive as an ingredient in a prepared dish. The term "cooking wine" is more often used to describe a cheap wine that can be used in recipes, but it's a mistake to imagine that you can cook with a wine that you wouldn't want to drink. Most of the alcohol in wine will evaporate during cooking, and what's left is its flavor. It's not necessary to use an expensive bottle of Chambertin to make a *boeuf bourguignon* or a *coq au vin*, but if you try to economize by using a poor wine, all of its defects will be concentrated in the sauce.

Furthermore, it is actually uneconomical to buy cheap wine for cooking. Say that an elaborate lobster dish calls for a spoonful or two of sherry to heighten its flavor. A cook who runs out to buy a bottle of cheap sherry will diminish the taste of an expensive and time-consuming dish with a quarter's worth of wine. What's more, because the wine is a poor example of its type, it may not be enjoyable to drink, so the spoonful of wine has, in fact, cost the full price of the bottle.

WINE IN RESTAURANTS

One of the pleasures of dining out in Europe is the opportunity to drink wines inexpensively and without fuss. Winemaking is so widespread in Europe, and particularly in France and Italy, that a bistro or inn almost anywhere will feature local wines, often served in carafes, and no more expensive than a bowl of soup or a dessert. Unfortunately, wine drinking in American restaurants is neither so easy nor so cheap. All too often restaurant lists are both unimaginative and expensive, and the service of wine ranges from the indifferent to the pretentious. Ideally, the service of wine should be both correct and unobtrusive, but the sad fact is that many waiters know less about wine than all but the least knowledgeable of their customers.

Most of the elements of service that apply in the home are equally valid in restaurants. There are some aspects of wine service, however, that are more relevant to restaurants, and these are reviewed here briefly. If you plan to have wine, ask for the wine list while you are looking at the menu; otherwise you may be subjected to a long wait between the time you order your meal and the moment when a wine list is finally put into your hands. Once you've ordered a wine, make sure that it is brought to the table and uncorked as soon as possible, to avoid the possibility of a forgetful waiter opening the bottle long after he has served the dish that the wine was meant to accompany. Getting wine brought to the table in time is particularly important if you plan to have a bottle of wine with the first course, which is often prepared ahead of time and brought to your table minutes after you've ordered it.

White wine should be chilled, of course, but not too cold. If a wine is placed in an ice bucket at the beginning of a meal, and then served with the main course, it may be well be overchilled and have lost almost all its taste. Don't hesitate to take the bottle out of the cooler and stand it on the table. Also, note that many restaurants use ice buckets that are not deep enough for a bottle of wine, especially German or Alsatian wines. The easiest solution is to turn the bottle upside down for a moment before the first glass is poured: this may look odd, but the alternative is to drink the first two or three glasses of white wine at room temperature.

Red wines are sometimes served in wine baskets, but they are actually pointless as used in most restaurants. An older red wine lying on its side in the cellar will have thrown a deposit. Because it is not possible in a restaurant to stand the wine up for a couple of hours to let the sediment fall to the bottom of the bottle, the alternative is to move the bottle, carefully, always on its side, from its bin to a wine basket, and then bring it to the table without disturbing the sediment. Ideally, the wine should be decanted at this point, or at any rate poured very carefully into large wineglasses. What actually happens four times out of five is that the waiter grabs the bottle any which way and carries it carelessly to the service station. There he puts the bottle into a waiting basket and brings it to the table. To make the farce complete, some waiters insert a corkscrew by rotating the bottle in its basket. If you order a young red wine without sediment, as most people do in a restaurant, there's no reason at all to use a basket.

When you've ordered a wine, the waiter or captain should always show you the bottle before he opens it to make sure the wine is exactly the one you ordered, and of the vintage specified on the wine list (or at any rate, one acceptable to you). If it's a better-than-average wine that you've ordered, especially an older one, be sure that there is no more than the usual space between cork and wine: older wines sometimes develop too great an air space, and this may in turn affect the wine adversely. If you note too much ullage, as this is called, draw it to the waiter's attention to let him know that you'll be on your guard against an oxidized wine.

After opening the bottle, the waiter may show you the cork, or even hand it to you: the cork should be sound and the wet end should smell of wine, not of cork. You can give the cork a squeeze and a sniff if you want, but the wine in the glass is what's really important. The waiter will then pour some wine into the glass of whoever chose it, so that he or she can determine whether or not it is defective in any way. If you happen to be eating your first course when the red wine is poured, don't try to judge the wine against smoked salmon, tomato salad, creamed herring, vichyssoise, or whatever may be in your mouth. Take a piece of bread first, or else tell the waiter that you'll taste the wine a little later, at your convenience. If a wine is corky (that is, contaminated by a faulty cork and with a distinctly moldy bouquet and taste) or spoiled (an oxidized white, a vinegary red), it should naturally be sent back. Some restaurants will do this more gracefully than others. Even the most accommodating restauranteurs will privately complain, however, that much of the wine that is sent back is perfectly sound—either the customer was trying to show off, or he had made an uninformed choice and mistakenly expected the wine to have a different taste. Remember that the reason you taste a wine in a restaurant is not to evaluate its quality, but simply to determine whether or not there is anything wrong with the bottle in front of you.

Wineglasses in restaurants are often too small, and those ubiquitous three- and four-ounce glasses are inappropriate not only because they don't permit a good wine to be swirled and sniffed, but also because using a small glass seems such a stingy way of drinking wine. The simplest solution is to ask for empty water goblets and fill them only a third. You can expect six to eight glasses of wine from a bottle, depending on how generously the waiter pours. It's a pity to run out of wine halfway through a meal, and if a second bottle seems too much, an extra half-bottle might be the answer.

Choosing a wine can be complicated by an assortment of dinner choices in a party of four or more. Rosé is one solution, but certainly not the best one, especially if fine food is being served. It's easy enough to order a half-bottle each of red and white. Another possiblity is to order a bottle of white and a half-bottle of red. Everybody gets a glass of white wine with his or her first course, then those having fish as a main dish continue with white wine, those having meat go on to the red.

These general observation aside, the most important question is, Which wine to order? This will naturally depend on the kind of restaurant you're in, the food you plan to eat, and the variety and prices of the wines offered. Today, many people simply order a glass of the red or white bar wine. This is likely to be an acceptable but neutral jug wine from California, Italy, or France. Since many restaurants now charge as much for a five-ounce glass of wine as for a cocktail, you may end up paying a rather high price for thirty or forty cents' worth of wine. If wine is available by the carafe, it's usually a better value, especially if the restaurant uses liter carafes, which hold thirty-three ounces. An increasing number of restaurants now offer carafe wines, including relatively expensive establishments. Many restaurateurs have discovered that even knowledgeable customers don't always want to take the time to pore over a wine list.

An increasing number of restaurants now offer a choice of wines by the glass, and many have installed a Cruvinet or similar machine. A Cruvinet replaces the wine drawn out of a bottle with inert gas, thus preventing the wine left in the bottle from oxidizing. This device permits a restaurateur to offer fine red and white wines by the glass without having to worry that the remaining wine will spoil before the bottle is depleted.

There are now a great many restaurateurs around the country

who take a particular pride in their wine lists, and a selection of a hundred or more wines is no longer an unusual as it was only a few years ago. Unfortunately, the majority of wine lists are still inadequate. Far too many neglect to indicate the producer or shipper of a wine, or the vintage. This gives the restaurateur some flexibility in replacing a wine if his supplier runs out, but it also makes it difficult for his patrons to make an intelligent choice. If you walked into a retail store you'd be surprised to see shelves marked Beaujolais, Nuits-Saint-Georges, or Chianti on which were standing bottles wrapped in paper bags. Yet a restaurateur who doesn't list the producer is asking you to make the same blind choice, and at much higher prices. One solution is to pick out two or three potentially interesting wines and ask the waiter to bring the bottles to your table. After you examine the labels, you can select one and send the others back.

As for vintages, they always matter, if only to indicate the age and relative freshness of the many popular wines meant to be consumed young. And when you turn to the pages listing wines at twenty dollars or more, vintages naturally matter a great deal with respect to both quality and value.

Fortunately, many restaurateurs do list producer and vintage and are also committed to reprinting or rewriting their wine lists at frequent intervals. Others, with smaller budgets, have adopted the sensible policy of using well-designed typewritten or computer-generated lists that are easy to read, contain the relevant information about each wine, and are easily updated. These lists are a welcome change from the cumbersome leather-bound books that, as often as not, offer a limited choice.

When looking over a list, remember that the least expensive wine is often a poor value, since its price is based not on its cost but on what the restaurateur feels is the minimum he or she should charge for a bottle of wine. For example, in most Italian restaurants, the least expensive wines are Soave and Valpolicella. If you visited a dozen restaurants, you'd find that although most of them are offering the same two or three popular and similarly priced brands, the wines might be listed at anywhere from eight to fifteen dollars. Obviously, the price of the wine has more to do with the decor of the restaurant and the price of the food than with the actual cost of the wine. Usually, if you spend another dollar or two, you are likely to get a wine whose price more accurately reflects its value.

Just as it is usually a bad idea to order the least expensive wines, so should you avoid the most expensive wines, whatever your budget. Even if, for example, fine red Bordeaux châteaux are listed, they are likely to be of recent vintages and therefore too young to drink. It's a waste to pay what is inevitably a great deal of money for glamorous wines that are not yet showing the qualities for which they are famous. As for ordering expensive, mature red wines, if they are listed, remember that they are likely to contain sediment, so you must make sure that the waiter or captain is knowledgeable about old wines and is prepared to decant the wine carefully for you.

Looking through a wine list can often be a frustrating experience, and there are times when you find yourself not so much making a choice as resigning yourself to ordering the least objectionable wine. Nevertheless, varied and fairly priced wine lists are not as uncommon as they were, and there are a growing number of restaurants throughout the country that are even better known for their wine cellars than for their kitchens.

VINTAGES

For some reason, many people who are relatively unfamiliar with wines are nevertheless unduly concerned about vintages. Some pontificate about what they imagine to be the best vintage years, others simply become uneasy about whether or not a particular wine represents a good year. It seems to me that a wine's vintage is almost always the last fact to consider when deciding what to drink with dinner: the primary consideration should be the kind of wine that you would like. Often enough, its vintage will turn out to be of little importance. After all, more than three-quarters of all the wine produced in the world is meant to be consumed within a year of the harvest, and a great deal of what we drink is at its best within two years. Since the chief attribute of many wines is their freshness, the vintage date is often more useful as an indication of the wine's age than of its quality.

The importance given to vintages is of relatively recent origin. For centuries new wines were poured into goblets directly from the barrel. If bottles were used as an intermediate step, they were loosely stoppered up with oil-soaked rags or a wooden peg. In the eighteenth century, when an effective cork made of bark first became generally available, it was discovered that port improved with a certain amount of bottle age. In consequence, the port bottle evolved during the eighteenth century from a squat shape to the kind of bottle that we see today. What emerged was the binnable bottle—a bottle that could be stored on its side, thus keeping the cork wet and expanded, and preventing air from entering the bottle and spoiling the wine. It is possible that the first Bordeaux to be bottled and stored away was Lafite 1797, and a few bottles are still displayed today at the château. The effects of bottle age became so greatly admired that in the second half of the nineteenth century red Bordeaux was vinified in such a way as to retain its qualities for forty or fifty years, and these wines were rarely drunk before they were fifteen or twenty years old.

The concept of a vintage year or a vintage wine is often misunderstood. A vintage, or harvest, occurs every year in all of the world's vineyards. Consequently, every year is a vintage year, although some are better than others. Now, in the case of port and champagne, it is traditional to blend together the wines of several years. When an exceptionally good growing season results in better-than-average wines, however, the producers may decide to bottle part of that crop without blending in wine from other years, and the resulting wine bears on its label the year in which the grapes were harvested. In all other wine-producing regions, however, the words "vintage year" or "vintage wine" have no special meaning.

There are a number of factors that make one vintage better than another in a particular region, but the most important is the amount of sunshine and heat between the flowering of the vines in June and the harvest in late September or early October. (In the southern hemisphere the seasons are reversed, of course, and the harvest takes place in March.) As grapes ripen in the sun, their natural acidity decreases and their sugar content increases. Ideally, the vintage takes place when the sugar/acid balance is in correct proportion. The wine will consequently have enough alcohol (from the sugar in the grapes) to be stable, and enough acidity to be healthy and lively. Cold and rainy summers result in immature grapes that produce less alcohol, more acidity, and less coloring matter in the skins for red wines. The wines are therefore weak, tart, and pale. In general, there are more good vintages for white wines than for reds—within a given district—because white wine grapes normally ripen earlier and do not require as long a growing season as do red grapes, and they make fine wine at lower levels of sugar. In addition, color is not as important to the appearance of white wines, extra acidity does less harm to their taste, and they do not need the depth of flavor that is expected of red wines.

The quantity produced in a vintage may be affected by poor weather during the flowering, which will diminish the crop, or by brief summer hailstorms, which can destroy part of a vineyard's production in minutes. A sudden frost in the spring may kill the new growth on the vines and can drastically reduce the crop in a wine region overnight. Many growers in northerly vineyards are now using modern frost-control devices to protect their vines during cold spells, but frost is still a danger.

Although it is axiomatic that a wine cannot be judged before it is made, it is not uncommon for a vintage to be publicized as excellent—by the wine trade and by the press—before the grapes have even been picked. Unfortunately, even an excellent growing season that gives every promise of producing fine wines can be marred by bad luck. Rain just before a harvest can swell the grapes and dilute the intensity of the wine, and continued rain can transform ripe grapes into rotten ones. Rain during the vintage means that the pickers are harvesting water along with grapes, which may result in weak wines lacking in flavor. Although the personality of a vintage can be determined once the wines have finished fermenting, many winemakers and professional tasters prefer to reserve judgment until the following spring, when the wines have become more clearly defined. This suggests that the first impression of a vintage, even a good one, may not be completely accurate, but by the time knowledgeable wine people have determined the character of an overpublicized vintage, consumers may have already heard and read too much about it for their impression to be corrected, much less reversed.

Any discussion of vintage years must take into account two basic factors: How accurate is the vintage date on the label? How useful is it?

The first question is basic, because if vintage dates are inaccurate, than it's obviously a mistake to attach too much significance to them. California wines must be made 95 percent from grapes harvested in the year shown on the label. German wines can be blended with up to 15 percent of wines from a vintage other than the one shown. French wines must come entirely from the vintage indicated, but since vintage years are not part of the *Appellation Contrôlée* laws, but another set of laws, it is possible that the labels of some blended wines are not as accurate as those of single-vineyard wines. In many other countries, vintage years are not taken seriously except for the finest wines, and even then it is not unusual for wines that undergo long barrel aging to be refreshed with younger wine.

Even when vintage dates are accurate, how useful is the information? Although many consumers have at least some acquaintance with the best recent vintages in Bordeaux, Burgundy, and perhaps along the Rhine and Moselle, what do most of us know about good and bad vintages for Barolo, Valpolicella, or Chianti; for Rioja; for Hungarian Tokay, Austrian Gumpoldskirchner, or Yugoslavian Cabernet; or for the wines of Chile, Argentina, Australia, or South Africa (where their harvest takes place in our spring)? For that matter, what are the best recent years for Napa Cabernet Sauvignon, Sonoma Zinfandel, and Monterey Chardonnay?

There are, however, many wines whose vintages are both accurate and important. These include most of the world's fine wines, and as a general rule, the more you pay for a bottle, the more important its vintage becomes. Most fine wines are made in regions where hot and sunny summers cannot be taken for granted, and where wide variations exist from one year to the next. Furthermore, in such regions as Bordeaux and Burgundy and along the Rhine and Moselle, the finest and most expensive wines come from individual vineyard sites whose proprietors are not even permitted to blend together wines from neighboring vineyards or villages to offset some of the deficiencies of a lesser year. The best varietal wines of California too, display greater variations from one year to another than many people imagine. Although the weather in California is more consistent than in Burgundy or along the Rhine, there are nevertheless differences between, say, Napa and Monterey, which are nearly two hundred miles apart. Furthermore, if a number of different grape varieties are planted side by side, the same growing season is unlikely to be equally successful for each of them.

The problem with evaluating vintages of fine wines is that knowing just a little is usually not enough, and as these wines are often expensive, mistakes can be more costly than for most other wines. Consumers generally seem to be most familiar with the best years for red Bordeaux, and the reputation of those vintages inevitably has an effect on many people's perception of vintage years in other regions. Actually, the best vintages in Bordeaux are not even the same for fine red wines and for the sweet white wines of Sauternes. Vintages for red Bordeaux and red Burgundy do not match, nor do those for red and white Burgundy. Bordeaux and Burgundy vintages do not necessarily have any relevance to the best years in the Rhône Valley or along the Loire, and of course, French vintages do not correspond with those of Germany or Italy. The best years for Vintage Port bear no relation to those for most other European wines, and European vintages are quite different from those for the best California varietals, produced six thousand miles away.

Vintage charts, with their numerical rating system, can be useful as a rough guide to recent years for the best-known wines. The system is too summary, however, to indicate much more than the comparative overall reputation of those vintages. The basic flaw in vintage charts, most of which are prepared by shippers and importers, is that they are so often self-serving, especially for recent vintages that are still currently available. Good years are rated as excellent, poor years are rarely rated as less than acceptable. It is often pointed out that not all the wines of a top-rated year are equally good, and conversely, that certain vineyards may have produced decent (and less expensive) wines in a year rated only fair. While variations naturally exist between the wines of one producer and another within a vintage, the main characteristic of poor years—those in which wines are made from unripe or even partially rotted grapes—is that they are unsound and cannot last. Even if there are a few bargains to be found, they are unlikely to maintain what little quality they possess for very long. Although vintage charts may be faulted for perpetuating the public's tendency to focus only on the best vintages, it is nevertheless true that, among fine wines, it is the best wines of the best vintages that are the most dependable and the longest-lived, and that will eventually provide the greatest pleasure.

On the other hand, an unfortunate result of the attention given even to indisputably fine vintages is that the public, anxious to buy these wines as soon as they appear, consumes the best wines of each vintage long before their prime. The wave of anticipation that accompanies a publicized vintage carries in its wake the disappointment that must inevitably occur when a good red wine is drunk too young. A fine Bordeaux or California Cabernet Sauvignon will demonstrate its quality only with the passage of years, when it has fully matured. If you drink such a wine soon after it has been bottled, you can perceive only in rough outline the particular qualities that have made it sought-after and expensive. Of all the comparative tastings that can be arranged, few are more instructive or surprising than to compare fine red wine from the same vineyard or the same winery in two good vintages that span at least three or four years. You will understand, as you taste the more mature wine, why certain wines are so highly acclaimed, and you will also realize, as you taste the younger wine, that to drink expensive red wines too young is pretty much a waste of money.

The success of a vintage is one element in a wine's quality and appeal, its ability to age is another. While it's true that all wines change during their life in the bottle, not all wines change for the better. The consideration of a vintage takes on a different dimension for wines whose virtues are charm, lightness, and fruit than for wines characterized by tannin, depth of flavor, and a slowly developing bouquet. On most vintage charts a great year is great forever, but every wine has a life cycle of its own, based on the combination of soil, grape, and climate that produced it, as well as on grape-growing and winemaking techniques that may differ from one producer to another. Some wines are at their best when they are bottled, remain good for a year or two, and then decline rapidly. Others reach maturity only after a few years in bottle, maintain their excellence for several years, and then very gradually decline. Age alone is no guarantee of quality, nor is a good vintage, in itself, a guarantee that the wine will be enjoyable today.

Finally, an observation about nonvintage wines, those on whose labels the year of the harvest does not appear. The trouble with such wines is not that they are blended from wines of more than one year, but that it is difficult for the consumer to determine just how old a particular bottle is. As most nonvintage wines are inexpensive (except for port and champagne) and meant to be drunk without any bottle age, not knowing how long such wines have been around means that you will sometimes come across faded and disappointing examples.

PRONUNCIATION GUIDE

Abboccato	ah-bo-*kah*-toe
Alella	ah-*lay*-l'yah
Aligoté	ah-lee-go-tay
Aloxe-Corton	ah-lox cor-tawn
Alto Adige	*ahl*-toe *ah*-dee-d'jay
Amabile	ah-*mah*-bee-lay
Amarone	ah-ma-*roe*-neh
Amontillado	ah-mon-tee-*yah*-doe
Anjou	ahn-joo
Auslese	*ow*-slay-zuh
Auxey-Duresses	oak-say duh-ress
Baco	bah-coe
Barbaresco	bar-bah-*ress*-coe
Barbera	bar-*bear*-ah
Bardolino	bar-doe-*lee*-no
Barolo	bar-*oh*-loe
Barsac	bar-sack
Batârd-Montrachet	bah-tar mon-rah-shay
Beaujolais	bo-jo-lay
Beaune	bone
Beerenauslese	*beer*-en-*ow*-slay-zuh
Bereich	buh-*rye'k*
Bernkastel	bearn-castle

Blanc de Blancs	blahn duh blahn
Blanc Fumé	blahn foo-may
Bocksbeutel	box-boyt'l
Bodega	bo-*day*-gah
Bonnes Mares	bon mar
Bordeaux	bore-doe
Bourgogne	boor-*gon*-yuh
Brouilly	brew-yee
Brunello di Montalcino	brew-*nell*-oh dee mon-tahl-*chee*-noe
Brut	brute
Bual	boo-ahl
Cabernet	ca-bear-nay
Calvados	cahl-vah-dohss
Carruades	cah-roo-ahd
Cassis	cah-seece
Cave	cahv
Chablis	shah-blee
Chai	shay
Chambertin	sham-bear-tan
Chambolle-Musigny	shahm-bol moo-seen-yee
Chardonnay	shahr-doe-nay
Chassagne-Montrachet	shah-sahnyuh mon-rah-shay
Chasselas	shass-lah
Château	shah-toe
Châteauneuf-du-Pape	shah-toe-nuff-doo-pahp
Chénas	shay-nahss
Chenin Blanc	shay-nan blahn
Chiroubles	shee-roobl
Climat	clee-mah
Clos de Bèze	cloh duh behz
Clos Vougeot	cloh voo-joh
Colheita	cul-*yay*-tah
Consorzio	con-*sorts*-ee-oh
Corbières	cor-b'yair
Corton	cor-tawn
Cosecha	co-*say*-chah
Côte de Beaune	coat duh bone
Côte Chalonnaise	coat shah-lo-nayz
Côte de Nuits	coat duh nwee
Côte d'Or	coat dor
Coteaux Champenois	coat-toe shahm-pen-wah
Côtes du Rhône	coat doo rone

Côte Rotie	coat ro-tee
Crémant	creh-mahn
Cru	crew
Cru Classé	crew clah-say
Cuvaison	coo-vay-zohn
Cuvée	coo-vay
Dão	down
Dolcetto	dole-*chet*-toe
Douro	doo-roe
Echézeaux	eh-shay-zoh
Edelfäule	ay-del-foil
Einzellage	*ein*-tsuh-lah-guh
Egri Bikavér	egg-ree bee-ka-vair
Entre-Deux-Mers	ahn'tr-duh-mair
Erzeugerabfüllung	*air*-tsoy-guh-*ahb*-foo-lung
Estufa	esh-*too*-fah
Fendant	fahn-dahn
Fiaschi	fee-ahss-kee
Fino	*fee*-no
Fixin	fix-ahn
Fleurie	fluh-ree
Framboise	frahm-bwahz
Frascati	frahss-*ca*-tee
Freisa	fray-zah
Frizzante	free-*zahn*-tay
Friuli	free-*ooh*-lee
Gamay	gam-may
Gattinara	gah-tee-*nah*-rah
Gevrey-Chambertin	jev-ray shahm-bear-tan
Gewürztraminer	guh-*vurts*-trah-*mee*-ner
Gigondas	jee-gon-dahss
Grands-Echézeaux	grahnz eh-shay-zoh
Graves	grahv
Grenache	greh-nahsh
Grignolino	gree-n'yohl-*ee*-no
Grosslage	*gross*-lah-guh
Gumpoldskirchen	goom-poles-*kir*-ken
Haut	oh
Hermitage	air-mee-tahj

Heurige	*hoi*-ree-guh
Hospices de Beaune	oh-speece duh bone
Jerez	hair-reth
Johannisberg	yoh-*hah*-niss-bairg
Juliénas	jool-yeh-nahss
Kirsch	keersh
Labrusca	la-*broos*-ca
Lacryma Christi	*la*-cree-mah *kriss*-tee
Mâcon	mah-kohn
Maderisé	mah-dair-ree-zay
Malmsey	*mahlm*-zee
Manzanilla	man-zah-*nee*-ya
Marc	mar
Margaux	mahr-goe
Médoc	meh-dock
Merlot	mehr-loe
Meursault	muhr-soe
Mise en bouteilles	meez ahn boo-tay
Montilla	mon-*tee*-yah
Montrachet	mon-rah-shay
Morey-Saint-Denis	moh-ray san-deh-nee
Moulin-à-Vent	mooh-lahn-ah-vahn
Mousseux	moo-suh
Müller-Thurgau	*moo*-lair-*toor*-gahw
Muscadet	muhss-ka-day
Musigny	moo-see-nyee
Nahe	nah
Nebbiolo	neh-b'*yoh*-low
Neuchâtel	nuh-shah-tell
Nierstein	neer-shtine
Nuits-Saint-Georges	nwee-san-jawrj
Oechsle	*uhk*-sluh
Oloroso	oh-lo-*ro*-so
Oltrèpò Pavese	ohl-treh-*poe* pah-*veh*-seh
Orvieto	ohr-vee-*ay*-toe
Pauillac	paw-yack
Pays	pay-yee

Pétillant	pet-tee-yahn
Petit	puh-tee
Phylloxera	fil-*lox*-uh-rah
Piesport	*peez*-port
Pinot Grigio	pee-noe *gree*-d'joh
Pinot Noir	pee-noe nwhar
Poire	pwahr
Pomerol	pom-uh-rohl
Pommard	poh-mar
Pouilly-Fuissé	poo-yee fwee-say
Pouilly-Fumé	poo-yee foo-may
Pourriture noble	poo-ree-toor nohbl
Premier Cru	preh-m'yay crew
Puligny-Montrachet	poo-lee-n'yee mon-rah-shay
Puttonyos	puh-tohn-yosh
Qualitätswein mit Prädikat	kvah-lee-*tayts*-vine mitt *pray*-dee-kaht
Quincy	kan-see
Quinta	*keen*-tah
Recioto	ray-*t' shot*-oh
Retsina	ret-*see*-nah
Rheingau	rine-gow
Rheinhessen	rine-hessen
Rheinpfalz	rine-faltz
Richebourg	reesh-boor
Riesling	*reece*-ling
Rioja	ree-*oh*-ha
Rosé	roh-zay
Ruwer	*roo*-vuh
Saar	sahr
Sancerre	sahn-sair
Sangiovese	san-joh-*vay*-zeh
Sauternes	saw-tairn
Sauvignon Blanc	saw-vee-n'yohn blahn
Scheurebe	*shoy*-reh-buh
Secco	say-co
Sekt	sekt
Sémillon	seh-mee-yohn
Soave	so-*ah*-vay
Solera	so-*lair*-ah
Sommelier	so-mel-yay

Spätlese	shpaht-lay-zuh
Spumante	spoo-mahn-tay
Sylvaner	sil-*vah*-ner
Tafelwein	*tah*-fell-vine
Tastevin	taht-van
Tavel	tah-vell
Terroir	tehr-wahr
Tête de cuvée	teht duh koo-vay
Tonneau	tun-oh
Traminer	trah-*mee*-ner
Trentino	tren-*tee*-no
Trockenbeerenauslese	*trok*-en-*beer*-en-*ow*-slay-zuh
Valdepeñas	val-day-*pain*-yass
Valpolicella	val-poh-lee-*t'chell*-ah
Valtellina	vahl-teh-*lee*-nah
Vaud	voh
Veltliner	velt-*lee*-nuh
Verdelho	vehr-*dell*-yoh
Verdicchio	vehr-*dee*-kee-oh
Vinho Verde	*veen*-yoh *vair*-day
Vinifera	vin-*if*-uh-rah
Vosne-Romanée	vohn ro-mah-nay
Wachau	*vah*-kow
Wehlen	*vay*-len
Yquem	ee-kem

INDEX

By the year 2000, 2 out of 3 Americans could be illiterate.

It's true.

Today, 75 million adults...about one American in three, can't read adequately. And by the year 2000, U.S. News & World Report envisions an America with a literacy rate of only 30%.

Before that America comes to be, you can stop it...by joining the fight against illiteracy today.

Call the Coalition for Literacy at toll-free **1-800-228-8813** and volunteer.

Volunteer Against Illiteracy. The only degree you need is a degree of caring.